China's Quest for Innovation

The transition from a catching-up style economy to an innovation-driven economy poses a major challenge for China. This book examines the major issues at stake, outlines developments in crucial business fields and industries, and discusses the roles of top-down politics and bottom-up entrepreneurship. It focuses in particular on the institutional foundations of innovation, arguing that successful innovation relies on the favourable interplay of business, politics, and society, and that comprehensive institutional and organizational changes will be required in China in order for innovation to succeed. Overall, the book assesses how far China will be able to depart from the Western paradigm of successful innovation regimes and create its own innovation system with Chinese characteristics.

Shuanping Dai is Junior Professor at the Institute for East Asian Studies and Mercator School of Management at the University of Duisburg-Essen, Germany.

Markus Taube is Professor of East Asian Economic Studies/China in the Mercator School of Management at the University of Duisburg-Essen, Director of the IN-EAST School of Advanced Studies at the University of Duisburg-Essen and Co-Director of the Confucius Institute Metropolis Ruhr, Germany.

Routledge Contemporary China Series

Re-engineering Affordable Care Policy in China
Is Marketization a Solution?
Peter Nan-shong Lee

The Land Question in China
Agrarian Capitalism, Industrious Revolution, and East Asian Development
Shaohua Zhan

Radio and Social Transformation in China
Wei Lei

Internet Video Culture in China
YouTube, Youku, and the Space in Between
Marc L. Moskowitz

Securitization of the Umbrella Movement in Hong Kong
The Rise of a Patriotocratic System
Cora Y.T. Hui

Non-Governmental Orphan Relief in China
Law, Policy and Practice
Anna High

Living in the Shadows of China's HIV/AIDS Epidemics
Sex, Drugs and Bad Blood
Shelley Torcetti

China's Quest for Innovation
Institutions and Ecosystems
Edited by Shuanping Dai and Markus Taube

For more information about this series, please visit: www.routledge.com/Routledge-Contemporary-China-Series/book-series/SE0768

China's Quest for Innovation

Institutions and Ecosystems

Edited by Shuanping Dai and Markus Taube

Routledge
Taylor & Francis Group
LONDON AND NEW YORK

First published 2020
by Routledge
2 Park Square, Milton Park, Abingdon, Oxon OX14 4RN

and by Routledge
605 Third Avenue, New York, NY 10017

First issued in paperback 2021

Routledge is an imprint of the Taylor & Francis Group, an informa business

British Library Cataloguing-in-Publication Data
A catalogue record for this book is available from the British Library

Library of Congress Cataloging-in-Publication Data
A catalog record for this book has been requested

ISBN 13: 978-1-03-208619-4 (pbk)
ISBN 13: 978-1-138-49714-6 (hbk)

Typeset in Bembo
by Apex CoVantage, LLC

Contents

List of figures vii
List of tables ix
List of contributors x

Institutional foundations of China's quest for innovation: introduction 1
SHUANPING DAI, MARKUS TAUBE

1 **Innovation depends: Between sustainable change and destructive over-turbulence; On the complex "deep structure" of innovation** 10
WOLFRAM ELSNER

2 **Technology, social beliefs, and national system of innovation policies: reflections on China's innovation policies after 2006** 50
SHUANPING DAI, ALEKSANDRA DAVYDOVA, YANG LIU

3 **China's research and development sector: progress and outlook** 71
YANRUI WU

4 **Technological capabilities in China: patterns of specialization toward a knowledge-intensive economy** 90
ICIAR DOMINGUEZ LACASA, MAHMOOD SHUBBAK

5 **Economic transition and innovation development in China from an evolutionary economics perspective** 106
JUTTA GÜNTHER AND JULIA SINNIG

6 **Architecture-based innovation strategies in the development of China's passenger vehicle sector** 126
MARCUS CONLÉ

7 **Moral capital and organizational legitimacy: evidence from the private sector in China** 149
JUN LI

8 **The interdependency of innovation obstacles in Chinese manufacturing firms** 169
JUN HOU

9 **Innovation in the digital age: an opportunity for China's catching up** 195
YONGMIN WU AND YUSHAN JI

10 **Realizing stretch goals via exploratory bricolage: the case of Chinese entrepreneurial firms** 216
SHIHAO ZHOU, PETER PING LI, AND MONSOL ZHENGYIN YANG

11 **Open innovation ecosystem and traditional industrial cluster upgrading: a case study on the special cable industry cluster in Gaogou Town, Anhui Province** 235
GANG LIU AND JIE LIU

12 **An "Iron Triangle" in Northeastern China: revisit the new Northeast phenomenon and its innovation ecosystem** 259
DONGLIN SONG, CHANGCHENG YAO AND XIN FAN

Index 284

Figures

1.1 Network structures with right-skewed (power-law) centrality-degree distributions of agents (scale-free networks) 20
1.2 A right-skewed (power-law) distribution of centrality degrees, as compared to a normal distribution (based on random network and process) 21
1.3 Mobility and social capital 36
2.1 The conception of China's NIS in 2006 60
3.1 R&D intensity in China, 2000–2018 72
3.2 Granted invention patents, 2006–2017 73
3.3 Five components of embodied R&D in selected years 74
3.4 Domestic networks in 2000 vs. 2010 75
3.5 High-tech product exports by ownership, 2016 78
3.6 Allocation of fund during 2006–2013 80
3.7 Distribution of Chinese OFDI in 2017 82
3.8 R&D intensity and GDP per capita in selected economies, 2008 83
3.9 R&D intensity in Chinese regions, 2017 85
3.10 Shares of patent applications, 2017 86
4.1 Behind-frontier patent intensity (priority patents per capita) 1980–2015 in China and in selected countries 97
4.2 Frontier patent intensity (transnational patents per capita) 1980–2015 in China and selected countries 97
4.3 Classification of technological sectors in countries 2003–2012 101
5.1 Annual GDP of China 1978 to 2016 in constant bn. 2010 US$ 114
5.2 Annual inflow of foreign direct investment to China 1978 to 2016 (current million US$) 116
5.3 Top ten sectors according to the number of FDI projects 2015 118
5.4 R&D expenditure (as % of GDP) in China 1996 to 2015 119
5.5 Patent applications in China 1985 to 2015 121
6.1 Types of innovation according to their disruptive effects 129
6.2 The two dimensions of design and manufacturing tasks 133
8.1 Positive complementarity versus negative complementarity 172
9.1 Internet population in China (billion) 203

9.2 The scale of China's digital economy (RMB trillion) 204
9.3 Retail e-commerce sales share in China, the US, and worldwide, 2015–2020 (% of total) 205
9.4 The smile and wave curves 207
10.1 The overall pattern of exploratory bricolage 221
11.1 Innovation network diagram of the Gaogou cluster 243
11.2 The centrality of the nodes in the Gaogou cluster 243
11.3 Information sources of market demand in the Gaogou cluster 245
11.4 Cooperative relationships for new product development in the Gaogou cluster 246
11.5 Testing institutes in innovation network in the Gaogou cluster 247
11.6 Cooperative relationships for human capital training in the Gaogou cluster 248
11.7 Motivation and upgrade mechanism of endogenous traditional industry clusters 251
12.1 China regional innovation capacity evaluation (2016) 261
12.2 Evaluation of comprehensive scientific and technological progress in China (2016) 264
12.3 High-tech industries full-time equivalent of R&D per capita in the Northeast (man-year) (2006–2016) 265
12.4 High-tech industries R&D internal expenditure in the Northeast (hundred million Yuan) (2006–2016) 265
12.5 High-tech industries new product sales in the Northeast (hundred million Yuan) (2006–2016) 266
12.6 High-tech industries effective patents in the Northeast (piece) (2006–2016) 267
12.7 Industrial full-time equivalent of R&D personnel in the Northeast (man-year) (2006–2016) 268
12.8 Industrial R&D internal expenditure in the Northeast (hundred million Yuan) (2006–2016) 268
12.9 Industrial new product sales in the Northeast (hundred million Yuan) (2006–2016) 269
12.10 Industrial effective patents in the Northeast (piece) (2006–2016) 269
12.11 Government deficit changes in the Northeast China (hundred million Yuan) (2006–2016) 271
12.12 Higher research institutes of the Northeast full-time equivalent of R&D personnel (man-year) (2006–2016) 272
12.13 Higher research institutes of the Northeast R&D internal expenditure (hundred million Yuan) (2006–2016) 272
12.14 The Iron Triangle Model 274

Tables

2.1 Sector and Scientific Focuses in China's S&T since 2006 56
3.1 R&D Spending shares (%) by ownership, 2017 76
3.2 R&D Spending by the top ten industrial sectors in 2017 77
4.1 Priority filings in 35 technology fields and five technological sectors 1983–2012 94
4.2 Shifting sectors of RTA (five technological sectors) in China and other emerging economies 1983–89/2003–12 99
4.3 Opportunity areas (35 technological fields) for countries 2003–2012 102
7.1 Correlation matric 159
7.2 Logistic regression results: dependent variable =YES (working capital primarily relying on bank loans) 161
7.3 Logistic regression results: dependent variable =YES (business development capital primarily relying on bank loans) 162
8.1 Variables definition and summary (mean and SD) 176
8.2 R&D and innovation output status of all and across each group (mean values) 179
8.3 Obstacles across R&D and innovativeness (mean values and percentages) 180
8.4 Tobit estimation results: Full sample, size and technology levels 182
8.5 Complementarity test results 185
8.6 Marginal effects, calculated with mean values of each obstacle 186
8.7 Sequence of eliminating obstacles with respect to the marginal gains to innovation 186
10.1 Summary of three cases 229
11.1 Basic information of survey samples of the Gaogou cluster 241
11.2 The structural indicators of the innovation network of the Gaogou cluster 244
12.1 Patent of colleges and universities in China (2016) Unit: 10,000 pieces 273

Contributors

Marcus Conlé is a postdoctoral research fellow at Jacobs University in Bremen and an associate researcher at the GIGA German Institute of Global and Area Studies in Hamburg. Before joining Jacobs, he was a research fellow at the IN-EAST School of Advanced Studies, University of Duisburg-Essen. He received a graduate degree in modern China studies and economics from the University of Cologne and a doctor's degree in business administration from the Mercator School of Management, University of Duisburg-Essen. His research interests include the structure and evolution of Chinese industries and innovation service sectors.

Shuanping Dai is Junior Professor at the Institute for East Asian Studies, and Mercator School of Management at the University of Duisburg-Essen, Germany, and is Adjunct Researcher at the Research Center for China's Public Sector Economy, Jilin University, and Visiting Professor at the Nankai University. He finished his doctoral study at the University of Bremen in 2013, and received both master's and bachelor's degrees at Jilin University in 2008 and 2006 respectively. His research mainly focuses on the issues of understanding social-economic emerging properties from social interactions and human behavior perspectives. He is the author of the book "*Networks of Institutions*" (Routledge, 2015) and many journal articles.

Aleksandra Davydova is a Ph.D. student at the IN-EAST School of Advanced Studies at the University of Duisburg-Essen, Germany. Her research interests lie in Chinese firms' mergers and acquisitions, and innovation.

Iciar Dominguez Lacasa is Professor for Economics at the Technical University of Applied Sciences Wildau and a research fellow at the Fraunhofer Center for International Management and Knowledge Economy IMW. Her research interests focus especially on the nexus of technology and institutional change. She also develops and implements sets of empirical indicators for tracing processes of technical change and institutional evolution.

Wolfram Elsner was Professor of Economics at University of Bremen, Germany (retired 2016). After having received his Ph.D. and "venia legendi" ("Habilitation," 1985), he worked as head of a regional economic development agency, head of the Planning Division of the Ministry of Economic Affairs of the State of Bremen, and the Bremen State Government's economic research institute, 1986 to 1995. He served as President of the *European Association for Evolutionary Political Economy (EAEPE)*, 2012–2014 and 2014–2016. He has affiliations at the University of Missouri in Kansas City, USA, and Jilin University, Changchun, PR China. He also has served on the boards of several journals; on different committees of several heterodox economic associations; edited and coedited a number of books and book series; published in numerous journals; was Managing Editor of the *Forum for Social Economics*, 2012–2019; and is Editor-in-Chief of the *Review of Evolutionary Political Economy* (*REPE*, Springer).

Xin Fan is an associate professor at the School of Economics in the Jilin University, China and a Postdoc Researcher in the Renmin University of China. He obtained his Ph.D. in political economy from Jilin University. His research interests mainly cover regional economies and capital markets.

Jutta Günther studied economics and social sciences at universities in Oldenburg, Osnabrück, and Albany, New York. She graduated from her doctoral studies in 2002 at the University of Osnabrück's chair of economic theory. From 2002 to 2014, she was employed as an economist at the Halle Institute for Economic Research (IWH) where she served as Head of Department (2008–2013) and member of the executive board (2011–2013). In the year 2014, she successfully finished her habilitation (German postdoctorate degree) at the Faculty of Economics at the Friedrich Schiller University in Jena. In April 2014, she was appointed as Professor of Economics at the University of Bremen. Her research interests include innovation processes, structural change, and economic transition.

Jun Hou is Senior Lecturer in Economics at the University of Lincoln, UK. Dr. Hou was previously a research officer (postdoc) at the Department of International Development (QEH), University of Oxford. He engaged in several EC– and ESRC–funded projects, focusing on MNEs, FDI, innovation, and development issues in developing countries. Dr. Hou also worked in several international organizations including the Overseas Development Institute, London (ODI) and The United Nations Environment Program (UNEP).

Yushan Ji is Professor of Economics at Jilin University, China. He is one of the pioneer scholars in internet economy studies since the 1990s in China and has published extensive works in the field, for example, *An Introduction to Network Economics* (1999) and *Knowledge Economics* (2001). He serves as Head of the Research Center for Knowledge Economy. He was visiting professor at the Kwansei Gakuin University (1987), Wakayama University (2000), etc.

Jun Li is Senior Lecturer in Entrepreneurship and Innovation at Essex Business School, University of Essex, UK. He previously held posts at the Chinese

Academy of Sciences and was the President of the Chinese Economic Association (UK/Europe) in 2012–2013. He currently also serves as Editor of the *Journal of Entrepreneurship in Emerging Economies*. He teaches and researches in the areas of entrepreneurship and policies, innovation management, and Chinese entrepreneurship. Among his previous publications are *China's Economic Dynamics: A Beijing Consensus in the Making?* (2014, Routledge) and *Incentives for Innovation in China* (2015, Routledge).

Peter Ping Li is Li Dak Sum Chair Professor of International Business at the University of Nottingham at Ningbo, China; Research Director, the Greater China Region of US–based Center for Creative Leadership (CCL), and Professor of Chinese Business Studies at Copenhagen Business School, Denmark. His primary research focus is on building geocentric (West-meeting-East) theories from cultural and historical perspectives. He is regarded as the global thought leader in the two fastest growing areas: (1) indigenous management research, and (2) emerging multinational firms. He has published over 100 journal articles, 20 book chapters, and six books. He serves on the editorial boards of ten business journals. He is the founding Editor-in-Chief of *Journal of Trust Research* as well as Senior Editor of *Management and Organization Review* and former Senior Editor of *Asia Pacific Journal of Management*.

Gang Liu is Professor at the School of Economics, Nankai University, China. He is currently the director of the Economic Research Institute in the same University. His main research interests are modern enterprise theory, innovation economy, and innovation policy. He currently serves as the chief economist of the research institute of China's new generation of artificial intelligence development strategy and works on the innovation-driven mechanism of the artificial intelligence industry in China.

Jie Liu is a doctoral student at the Economic Research Institute of in the Nankai University, China. Her primary research interest is the industrial innovation ecosystem. Now she focuses on the research of the innovation ecosystem of China's artificial intelligence technology industry.

Yang Liu is a Ph.D. student at the IN-EAST School of Advanced Studies at the University of Duisburg-Essen, Germany. Her research interests lie in entrepreneurship theory and poverty reduction.

Mahmood Shubbak is Postdoctoral Researcher at the University of Duisburg-Essen. His research interests are related to innovation systems and technology upgrading in the cutting-edge fields of renewable energy, climate change, and artificial intelligence. He obtained his Ph.D. in economics at the University of Bremen (Germany). He holds master's degrees in automation engineering from Bremen University, and communication technology management from Cardiff Metropolitan University (UK). In his recent research, he studied the innovation, economic, and environmental aspects of the Chinese solar photovoltaic industry over time, geographical space and institutional frameworks. In 2018, he won Herbert-Simon Prize in Nice (France).

Julia Sinnig obtained her B.Sc. and M.Sc. degrees in business economics at the Universities in Cologne, Bremen, and Barcelona. She recently completed her Ph.D. at the University of Bremen, where she now works as a postdoctoral researcher. Her research interests lie in the area of brand management, consumer behavior, especially in the age of social media, and international marketing.

Donglin Song serves as the professor at the School of Economics in the Jilin University, China. His research interests cover the theoretical study of the socialist market economy and capital markets. He worked in Jilin University's Finance and Economics (China) as the president and was engaged in several national philosophy and social science funded projects, mainly focusing on the economic transformation of the Northeast Old Industrial Base.

Markus Taube holds the Chair for East Asian Economic Studies /China and is the Director of the IN-EAST School of Advanced Studies at the University of Duisburg-Essen. He holds Visiting Professor positions at Jilin University (Changchun), Nankai University (Tianjin), Wuhan University and Huazhong University of Science and Technology (both Wuhan). Taube started his academic career studying sinology and economics at the universities of Trier, Bochum, and Wuhan (PR China). Before joining the University of Duisburg-Essen, he worked at the ifo Institute for Economic Research, Munich.

Yanrui Wu is an economics professor specializing in development economics, the Chinese economy, energy and environment, and applied econometrics. His research interests include the Asian economies (particularly China, India, and Indonesia), innovation economics, productivity analysis, and resource and environmental economics. He has published extensively in these fields. He is the author of several books including *Productive Performance in Chinese Enterprises* (Macmillan, 1996), *China's Economic Growth* (Routledge, 2004), *Productivity, Efficiency and Economic Growth in China* (Palgrave Macmillan, 2008) and *Understanding Economic Growth in China and India* (World Scientific Publishing, 2012).

Yongmin Wu is Associate Professor in the School of Management, Jilin University, China. He received his bachelor's degree in Economics at Northeast Normal University, and master's degree and Ph.D. in economics at Jilin University. He researches in the areas of the theory of innovation economics and financial development, especially concerning the issues of technological innovation and financial development in China. His research interests include evolutionary economics, financial history, internet finance, and supply chain finance.

Monsol Zhengyin Yang is a third-year Ph.D. student at the Business School of University of Nottingham, Ningbo, China. His research interests range from invisible-touch integration of Chinese firms' reverse M&A to Chinese traditional philosophies and modern management. He earned an MBA degree from Southwest University in 2013 and a bachelor's degree in English from Nankai University in 2008. He had four years' working experience in consulting for Chaordic Projectification Management and spent another four years in international business and as an assistant to the general manager who took charge of the construction of an industrial park in Thailand.

Changcheng Yao is a Ph.D. candidate in School of Economics at the Jilin University, China. He obtained his M.Sc. degree in international finance from ESC-RENNE business school (France) in May 2015. Before that, he studied at Nanjing Agricultural University (China), majoring in Business Management. His graduation paper focused on regional development and innovation. His research orientation now includes regional economy and innovation ecosystems.

Shihao Zhou is an assistant professor in the Department of E-Commerce, School of Business at the Nanjing University, China. He received his Ph.D. in management from Virginia Tech. His research interests focus on digital innovation, corporate R&D, and information technology strategy. He has published in the *Journal of Management Information Systems*, *International Journal of Human Resource Management*, and *Journal of Knowledge Management* and presented his research at the annual meetings of the Academy of Management and the Strategic Management Society.

Institutional foundations of China's quest for innovation

Introduction

Shuanping Dai, Markus Taube

In recent years, innovation research has clearly shown that innovation-driven economic development relies on a broad foundation of benign cultural, social, political, and economic framework conditions (Ahmed, 1998; Metcalfe, 2001; Nelson, 2002; Happer, 2018). Institutions based in a multitude of regimes for human interaction and coordination must incentivize innovation-creating behavior as well as the acceptance and diffusion of these very innovations in society. Institutions, i.e., a set of rules for joint action and co-existence, may reduce uncertainties of others' behaviors for innovation activities by providing contextual information and behavioral constraints. There exists no "one-fits-all" institutional setup outlining the preconditions for successful innovation-driven development. Cultural idiosyncrasies, variations in the availability and costs of specific resources and competencies, specific goals of ruling elites, etc. all lead to specific manifestations and combinations of institutions that in their totality promote innovation in varying intensity and on different social and technological trajectories (Edquist and Johnson, 1997).

Post-Maoist China provides a highly interesting case study for the evolution of a national innovation regime in a rapidly changing institutional environment and the specific roles various organizations and ecosystems play in this very process. When Deng Xiaoping initiated China's reform and global opening reform, he enforced a radical break with the ideological and institutional foundations of the Maoist era and set out to develop a new socio-economic system for China. In this context, the institutional environment supporting, directing or hindering the generation and adoption of innovative ideas, technologies, and products also evolved in twists and turns. Ideas imported from abroad and their assimilation into the Chinese socio-economic environment played a crucial role for innovation in general. China's highly successful catching-up growth and development trajectory is based on this very phenomenon. But, after three decades of highly successful catching-up economic development based on the emulation of foreign institutions, business models, and technologies, this mode of development has reached its limits. The Chinese economy has now reached a stage where it needs to foster more endogenous innovation in order to evade (relative) stagnation in what has become known as the "middle-income trap" (Asian Development Bank, 2012). Today, China's further socio-economic development relies predominantly on its own innovative capabilities. This requires substantial alterations not only in the structural setup and incentive systems governing the Chinese economy, but also in the fabric and underlying norms and values structuring society as well as the self-understanding of the political elite and its organization of political processes.

The beginnings of a targeted and consistent approach to the top-down creation of a new comprehensive innovation system in China's increasingly marketized socio-economy date back to the first years of the twenty-first century. The "National Guidelines for the Medium- and Long-Term Plan for Science and Technology Development (2006–2020)" (State Council, 2005) and the "Decision on Implementing the Outline of the Scientific and Technological Plan and Enhancing Independent Innovation Capacity" (State Council, 2006) constitute historic milestones in the evolution of China's modern innovation system. With these documents, China's political leadership set out to establish an effective comprehensive framework for endogenous innovation and reduce the country's dependence on foreign innovation trajectories. As a matter of fact, these initiatives have eventually been quite successful. Taking some standard innovation indicators like research and development (R&D) expenditure, research infrastructures, patent applications, scientific publications, etc. as a measure, China has established a high-capacity innovation system featuring noteworthy output. While this does not transform China into the world's leading innovation hub yet, and commentators debate the true quality of patents granted, there is no question that today China has become a major force in the global drive for innovation. China's telecommunications firms like Huawei, Xiaomi, etc.; its e-mobility champions BYD, NIO, et al.; and firms in many other sectors have already become globally recognized as high-performing innovation-driving global players.

With the Chinese business sector already responding to the policy call for more endogenous innovation in all sectors and segments of the economy, the pressure to enact complementary changes in China's social fabric is mounting. As new technologies transform analog living environments into digital spaces, and artificial intelligence revolutionizes both industry as well as the services sector, people are forced to adjust their lifestyles, social interaction patterns, consumer behavior and professional careers. As a consequence, shared beliefs, norms, and values shift toward new equilibria. But, while China's business sector is showcasing its entrepreneurial dynamism and agility, China's socio-political system is characterized by significant inertia. The Chinese Communist Party and Chinese government are obviously fully committed to reforming China's state-capitalist economy and establishing an innovation-friendly institutional setup, but they have no intention whatsoever to significantly change the political system of the country and put their claim to power to the test of democracy. The question arises in how far these two regimes, i.e., a dynamic innovation-driven socio-economic regime and a static one-party political regime, can co-exist over a longer period of time. The Hayekian postulate, according to which only free (democratic and market-based) societies can feature dynamic and innovation-driven development (Hayek, 1960), instantly comes to one's mind as a "belief" of Western institutionalism and German "Ordnungspolitik." This postulate and its framework conditions certainly need to be reflected upon in the modern Chinese context.

But China constitutes a puzzle to the paradigms of today's complexity economics as well. Novelty emerges in the market process whenever organizations like firms realize and promote individual knowledge as a collective understanding and activity (Metcalfe, 2010). The development of national economies, understood as intricate knowledge and labor systems, depends on how emerging novelty created in individual minds is embedded into enterprise activities. China's efforts in advancing knowledge and innovation seems to contradict the propositions of these complexity views on innovative development. Such contradictions invite us to further probe China's idiosyncratic political-economic mix and, in particular, its innovation and industry policies.

The Chinese approach to establishing an innovation-driven economy destined to be the leading innovator in the world is highly idiosyncratic and deviates significantly from established paradigms and theoretic dogma. This volume brings together prominent scholars from Europe and China to probe into these issues and gain new insights into the Chinese puzzle. Together, they explore the institutional dynamics of China's emerging innovation economy: the rise of new institutional regimes, their friction with existing (old) ordering structures, and the differential capacity of institutional arrangements to facilitate, accommodate, and regulate innovative behavior in various sectors and governance environments.

Outline of this book

This book comprises 12 analytical chapters. In the first contribution following this introduction, **Wolfram Elsner** starts off with a theory-oriented discussion of the institutional preconditions for the rise of an innovation-driven economy (Chapter 1). Elsner's approach is deeply rooted in complexity sciences and the literature on complex adaptive economic systems. These suggest that innovation may be anything between a flexible, smooth, improving, and sustainable change on the one hand, and highly idiosyncratic and turbulent motions perceived as over-complex on the other. Mostly, this triggers conservative and restrictive ("anti-innovative") Polanyian countermotions from agents who tend to be cognitively overburdened. Basing his argument on this proposition, the author considers innovation proper as a new technique, including related behavior, solving a clearly defined common or collective problem. The contribution applies the Veblenian or philosophically "pragmatist" criterion of "instrumental" vs. "ceremonial" behavior through emergent social institutions to analyze typical problem constellations at hand. It focuses on the conditions of, first, the size of the relevant interaction arena and the coevolving institutional platform (and its carrier group) and, second, of the basic network structure. This chapter considers conditions required for sustainable systemic innovation proper, in an understanding of individuals' problem-solving future-oriented behavior. In the opinion of the authors, the elimination of mass poverty, social and health insurance, improving education, wages, work conditions, and workers' rights, "Hukou," a good infrastructural and regulatory framework, and a qualified, strong state agency have made China a country capable of implementing an appropriate complexity-innovation policy in the frame of its new development and industrial policies, which even includes fostering mass entrepreneurship.

In the following Chapter 2, **Shuanping Dai**, **Aleksandra Davydova**, and **Yang Liu** start the empirical investigation of China's evolving innovation system with a review of China's innovation policies after the inauguration of the 2006 national innovation agenda. Looking back at two five-year–plan periods, the authors understand China to have gradually established a comprehensive national system of innovation that is continuously refined – with a view to achieving open, shared, and entrepreneurship-based innovation. From an analytical perspective, they suggest that a comprehensive framework for innovation policies should cover those that: (1) focus on specific areas of science and technology, (2) provide ancillary facilities and resources for innovation activities, and (3) help innovators to have several common tags for policies of the first two types, as well as coordinate and generate common beliefs on innovative actions. Taking this set of policies as a reference system, the authors argue that China's recent innovation policies have focused strongly on the first two categories but neglected the third. Based on this assessment, the authors outline a potential development trajectory for an integrated national system of innovation policies in China.

Following in their tracks, **Yanrui Wu** puts the spotlight on China's R&D sector in Chapter 3. This chapter presents a critical review of China's R&D policy and the role of key players in the sector. The author shows that in recent years, China has become a leading investor in R&D. He argues that, if the current growth momentum is maintained, the country is on track to transform itself from the world's manufacturing powerhouse to a technological superpower. He shows that, due to its extensive investment activities, China has already become the world's leading R&D investor (in value terms) and has the largest pool of researchers. Looking at the sources of investment, the state has stepped back in the second row. The business sector, including private businesses, has today become the leading player in the country's R&D activities. State-owned enterprises are still major investors in R&D, but lack dramatically in terms of output performance and efficiency. In terms of the sectoral distribution of R&D, the author highlights the important role of high technology. About 50% of Chinese R&D investment has gone into the high-technology sectors, for example: pharmaceuticals; medical equipment; computer, electronic, and communication equipment; and aerospace.

Iciar Dominguez Lacasa and **Mahmood Shubbak** take a deeper look at the high technology bias of China's R&D activities in Chapter 4. They study the evolution of technological capabilities in China since 1980 using patent indicators. They find that, compared with other emerging economies, China has been able to accumulate a considerable stock of technological capabilities over the past decades. Despite its latecomer position, China has reached impressive levels of patenting activity at the technological frontier and behind. China was mainly specialized in the chemistry sector Chemistry and, more specifically, in the fields of Biotechnology, Pharmaceuticals, Chemical Food and Microstructural and Nanotechnology. However, in their assessment, China has not adjusted its specialization and technological sectors in a proper way. Until 2012 it was neither able to enter into new technological sectors nor was the country accumulating significant capabilities in the most dynamic technological sectors such as Electrical Engineering and Other fields" (including fields such as Games, Consumer Goods and Civil Engineering). This rather conservative approach, however, seems to have been overcome in recent years when future-oriented technologies have come to be the focus of government policies and corporate strategies.

In Chapter 5, **Jutta Günther** and **Julia Sinnig** examine China's innovation development from an evolutionary perspective. Evolutionary theory looks at the economy as an ever-changing system with no static features but different degrees of dynamism. Intertemporal path dependencies play a crucial role. As such, the transition from imitation to innovation cannot easily be explained using existing (new) growth theory if at all. The authors argue that a powerful state with ever-changing regulations (as in China) causes much uncertainty for actors in private business. New procedures or products (innovations) are therefore eventually found through processes of trial and error and not on the basis of straightforward cost-benefit considerations. They further reason that the adaptation of new business strategies through learning and change is another crucial element of evolutionary theory that fits the real-world situation in China much better than an optimization strategy. In light of evolutionary thinking, foreign investors, for example, do not only enter the Chinese market because of (transaction) cost calculations, but also in order to accumulate knowledge and to benefit from a network of cross-border relationships.

Giving the discussion a slightly different twist, **Marcus Conlé** investigates China's innovation strategy from an architecture-innovation perspective in Chapter 6. By examining the links between architectural innovation, institutional and organizational setup, and domestic corporate performance in the relevant industries, the author explores the distinctive features of China's pattern of architectural innovation, showing how the prevalent domestic conditions enable firms to source product components and mix and match them in unparalleled ways. Through an in-depth analysis of China's passenger vehicle industry, Conlé comes to the conclusion that in China a distinct pattern of architectural innovation has emerged. This pattern rests on the interplay of three factors. First, modularization has taken hold as the dominant cognitive frame in many industrial sectors, including the focal passenger vehicle sector. Second, the domestic development of a comprehensive population of supplier firms, including local branches of virtually all major transnational leaders and a wide range of domestic firms, accompanied by very high localization rates and high levels of competition have rendered it easy to shop domestically for all product-related parts and components. Third, the effective feasibility of using existing car models as reference designs has introduced a system of de facto standards that enable industry-wide component sharing.

In a transition economy like China, legitimacy building is of especially great importance for private enterprises. In Chapter 7, **Jun Li** asks the question of whether moral capital helps private enterprises build organizational legitimacy. And, in a second step, he drives the analysis further by asking whether moral capital has a complementary effect to political capital in assisting private enterprises to build organizational legitimacy. The study employs private enterprises' charitable donations as a measure of moral capital and access to bank loans by private enterprises as an indicator of organizational legitimacy. Based on logistic regression analysis, the author finds that moral capital has a positive effect on organizational legitimacy with some evidence also suggesting that moral capital may be a substitute for political capital in building organizational legitimacy. Research in this chapter implies that private enterprises in China will perform well in innovation if they are able to leverage political capital and moral capital to establish legitimacy and win support from stakeholders.

Chapter 8, written by **Jun Hou,** examines the obstacles that block innovation or cause innovation failures. In his study, the author employs data in Chinese manufacturing firms from 25 major cities. He directs the spotlight at the complementarity between the obstacles and their corresponding policy responses as such complementary obstacles usually present adverse outcomes for innovation activities. This chapter investigates four types of obstacles firms face – in finance, skilled labor, informal competition, and tax– and finds out that complementarity exists between labor-force and tax-related obstacles in the innovation function, with additional obstacles exerting no further negative effect if existing obstacles are already preventing a firm from becoming a product innovator. Findings also confirm that complementary or substitutive relationships between obstacles are less frequent for firms in high-tech sectors or for firms with a larger number of employees. Firms in high-tech industries or firms featuring significant economies of scale are comparatively more resource abundant, due to skilled labor or accumulated experience. They are less likely to encounter obstacles during the course of innovation, as well as interactions between obstacles. Hence, the author concludes policy instruments should be designed to eliminate obstacles altogether rather than removing them individually.

Yongmin Wu and **Yushan Ji** concern themselves with the issue of technological catch-up in Chapter 9. They reason that technological catch-up is not a linear process. Furthermore, they claim that it would be unrealistic for developing countries to adopt strategies for rapid technological development in order to replace incumbent economies and corporate oligopolies as technology leaders on an already established mature technological trajectory. Developing economies and their firms must rather wait for "windows of opportunities" in which they can establish new technology trajectories and position themselves as leading protagonists. In order to be ready once such a window of opportunity opens, developing economies should implement mission-oriented policies. In their assessment, China is well prepared to realize the full potential of such windows of opportunities and may already be in the middle of exploring such a field. In their understanding, the current emerging technological revolutions in digitalization and artificial intelligence open windows of opportunity that China is well equipped to leverage in its quest for technology catch-up and global technology leadership.

In Chapter 10, **Shihao Zhou**, **Peter Ping Li,** and **Monsol Zhengyin Yang** take a different perspective on this issue. They focus on Chinese firms operating under non-optimal conditons and with deficient resources, but attaining significant business success. Combining theoretical analysis with case-study research, the authors put an emphasis on the "how questions," i.e., how have they done that and what are the core mechanisms and processes leading to success? The team of authors examines the three cases of Yuanjia Village, ZBOM Cabinets Co., and Huawei. In their conclusion, they identify *exploratory bricolage* as the key to the success of these firms. *Exploratory bricolage* has put these firms into a position to explore novel solutions by converting or transforming ordinary resources and/or seemingly valueless non-resources at hand into radical outcomes fit to attain a stretch goal.

Gang Liu and **Jie Liu** take a closer look at a typical Chinese innovation ecosystem in Chapter 11. The authors focus on the Gaogou cluster constituted of 268 enterprises specializing in the production of cables. Concentrating on low-end products of minor technological complexity, the enterprises in this cluster faced the threat of being crowded out of the market by more competitive imports. In response to this threat, the cluster enterprises neither tried to absorb technologies from their foreign competitors nor link up with another large domestic enterprise; instead, they set out to upgrade their products and technological capacities by setting up "learning" networks and venturing to introduce and apply innovative resources economically accessible to them. Portraying an open innovation ecosystem created by 14 sampled enterprises and one research institute, the authors identify three major success factors of industrial upgrading: (i) establishment of an open industrial innovation ecosystem, (ii) creation of R&D departments in enterprises no matter how small, and (iii) access to external innovation resources. In addition, the authors note the crucial role of an active (positive) response by local government to the demands of these enterprises for access to specific input and supplies as well as the establishment of cooperative patterns. Based on the insights derived from their case study, the authors argue that local governments intending to promote industrial upgrading in their constituencies should actively develop innovative enterprises within the cluster as well as establish new R&D organizations to absorb, introduce, and integrate creative resources in the local cluster.

In contrast to the active and constructive support from local government in establishing an innovation ecosystem described in the preceding chapter, **Donglin Song**, **Changcheng Yao,** and **Xin Fan** introduce an "Iron Triangle" model to demonstrate the economic failure in Northeast China in Chapter 12. China's three Northeastern provinces – Liaoning, Jilin, and Heilongjiang – command outstanding science and education resources and rank, in terms of knowledge competitiveness and technological facilities, in the leading group in China. Nevertheless, their economic and innovation performance is disappointing. The authors argue that local institutional mechanisms, industrial structure, and specific microeconomic actors are operating in an interdependent setting which results in overall blockage. The institutional setup of China's Northeast has a long tradition of powerful governments combined with weak markets, where government agents interfere in the market mechanism and play a decisive role in resource allocation. The negative effect of these structures is aggravated by the state-directed industrial layout in the region, which differs markedly from the more market-oriented industry-structure development in other parts of China. The region's large state-owned enterprises, however, have become habituated to these structures and exert little pressure to shift the local ecosystem toward more dynamic and efficient structures.

In its entirety, this volume brings together theoretical and empirical papers that highlight the links between institutional structures, production systems, and industrial policies in China's evolving innovation regime. It provides deep insights into some of the most critical issues and initiatives that will decide the success of China's quest for an innovation-driven economy.

Acknowledgments

We are thankful to the participants of the launching workshop "*To be an innovative China: risk, institutions and paths*" of this edited volume. The workshop was co-organized by the IN-EAST School of Advanced Studies and the Research School "Risk & East Asia" (GRK, 1613), both located at the University of Duisburg-Essen, Germany, and held in this very city on January 21, 2016. We wish to extend our gratitude to Philipp Böing, Marcus Conlé, Torsten Heinrich, Antonia Hmaidi, Zhe Sun, Shixu Zeng, and our anonymous reviewers for their constructive comments and suggestions to individual chapters. We also thank Mengjie Tang for her excellent assistance in preparing this publication. Finally, we are very grateful to the German Federal Ministry of Education and Research (BMBF) for its financial support.

References

Ahmed, Pervaiz K. (1998) "Culture and Climate for Innovation." *European Journal of Innovation Management* 1(1): 30–43.

Asian Development Bank (2012) *Growing beyond the Low-Cost Advantage: How the People's Republic of China can Avoid the Middle-Income Trap*, Manila: Asian Development Bank. Available at http://hdl.handle.net/11540/867 (accessed April 27, 2019).

Edquist, C. and B. Johnson (1997) "Institutions and Organizations in Systems of Innovation." C. Edquist (ed.), *Systems of Innovation: Technologies, Institutions and Organizations*, London and New York: Routledge.

Happer, D. (2018) "Innovation and Institutions from the Bottom Up: An Introduction." *Journal of Institutional Economics* 14(6): 975–1001.

Hayek, Friedrich (1960) *The Constitution of Liberty*, Chicago: University of Chicago Press.

Metcalfe, J. S. (2001) "Institutions and Progress." *Industrial and Corporate Change* 10(3): 561–586.

Metcalfe, J. S. (2010) "Complexity and Emergence in Economics: The Road from Smith to Hayek (via Marshall and Schumpeter)." *History of Economic Ideas* 18(2): 45–75.

Nelson, R. R. (2002) "Technology, Institutions, and Innovation Systems." *Research Policy* 31(2): 265–272.

State Council (2005) *National Guideline for the Medium- and Long-Term Plan for Science and Technology Development (2006–2020)*, State Council of the People's Republic of China.

State Council (2006) *Decision on Implementing the Outline of the Scientific and Technological Plan and Enhancing the Independent Innovation Capacity*, State Council of the People's Republic of China.

1 Innovation depends

Between sustainable change and destructive over-turbulence; on the complex "deep structure" of innovation

Wolfram Elsner[1]

1 Introduction

In this chapter, we will revisit and rectify the dominant everyday understanding of "innovation." This too often appears too simplistic and naïve, in everyday rhetoric, consciousness, and policies, and sometimes even in academic conceptualizations. It too often appears to be reduced to some quasi-automatic, and predominantly technical, change rather than highly dependent and *idiosyncratic*, as well as interdependent *technical and behavioral* change coevolving. Similarly, it is too often considered to be just some fundamentally "positive," always "*improving*" things *per se*, providing some welfare-enhancing excess of Schumpeterian *creation* over Schumpeterian *destruction*, while, in fact, it should be judged as a *complex*, and thus *volatile*, process proper, one of the cores of a complex adaptive economic system (economic CAS) and its evolutionary dynamic. As such, it is to be *embedded* in, and considered against, the broad socio-economic and societal, common and collective real-world problems that it solves – or does NOT solve, either by being completely *blocked* and not occurring at all, or by being flawed, degenerated, perverted, *counterproductive*, and even straightly *evaded* or counteracted by agents, under inappropriate conditions.

Particularly, *neoclassical* and *neoliberal* economics and politics, which have been imposed for four decades now, have struggled hard to make people believe that any "change" in a "*market economy*," generated by its deregulated, autonomous "supply side" working, is an "innovation" *per se*, thus a "good thing," a "progress" and an "opportunity," the ideology of "technological optimism" (as Tainter et al., 2018, p. 66ff., coin it somewhat friendly). But as we will argue, the usual neoliberal nexus of "market" deregulation, privatization, financialization, upward redistribution, and austerity policy, particularly stressing labor-market and innovation "flexibilities," usually has, in face of the reality of economic CAS, *counterproductive* effects on agents', and thus the entire system's, longer-run flexibility and innovation capacity (e.g., Vega-Redondo, 2013; Kleinknecht et al., 2016; Cetrulo et al., 2018; Dosi et al., 2018).[2]

In that sense, innovation appears as a *black box* in its overall use, even mostly in economics. That is, it lacks a criterion to distinguish counterproductive change – e.g., a dynamic perceived by agents as *over-turbulent*, *overly complex*, and *cognitively overstressing*, or some misled and futile "change" under fundamental uncertainty and opacity of agents – from some welfare-enhancing innovation proper (for a recent example, see, e.g., the international call for papers *The Dark Side of Innovation*, with more recent references on that; see Coad et al., 2018).

Insights from complexity sciences and economic CAS, in fact, suggest that "innovation" may be anything between properly flexible, smooth, improving, and sustainable change on the one hand and a highly idiosyncratic, turbulent, often exclusive and even destructive motion on the other, perceived as overly complex and then often triggering conservative ("anti-innovative") *Polanyian countermotions* by cognitively overstrained agents (notably by both humans and firm organizations) (from the recent broader wave of critical innovation literature, e.g., Swann, 2015; Antonelli, 2017a, 2017b; Godin and Vinck, 2017; Grant and Moses, 2017; Kingston, 2017; Lueders et al., 2017; Ruth and Goessling-Reisemann, 2018; von Schomberg and Hankins, 2018; Tainter et al., 2018).

Therefore, innovation is not sufficiently considered in mainstream thought to be *highly dependent* on configurations of factors, if it really is to serve broad, inclusive socio-economic problem-solving and betterment. Rather, it is often simply considered easily feasible, readily "*manageable*," and improving anytime under any "market" working. And this situation obviously has to do with the dominating, overly simplistic general economic comprehension, theorizing, and modeling.

In fact, we will argue, innovation is highly idiosyncratic *vis-à-vis* such (interdependent) factors as:

1 *incentive* and *interdependence* structures,
2 perceived levels of *complexity* and *turbulence*,
3 relative *informational* endowment and *cognitive* capacities, in particular the degrees of boundedness of rationality, as related to too little or too abundant information,
4 initial *interaction arena* or *group sizes* and *emerging-network sizes*,
5 initial and emerging *network structures* ("initial networks" – IN – and emergent cooperation platforms, or "emergent networks" – EN),[3]
6 interaction histories and experience made and related future *expectations* (culturally acquired time and *planning horizons*),
7 degrees of disembedding (uprooting) *mobility*, and
8 initial and emergent *institutions* of coordination and cooperation.[4]

In the following, therefore, we will strive to show that *innovation proper* should be conceived of as a *broad, inclusive, common and collective*, and evolutionary *problem-solving* process, depending on myriads of individual everyday actions and their ongoing interactions – i.e., an understanding of a basic *culture* of innovation that is required and needs to have emerged. "Innovation proper" thus is considered a new *technical-behavioral complex* which solves defined common or collective problems. A broader and less simplistic innovation perspective then is interaction-based, boundedly rational, systemic, and related to learned, emergent institutions – rather than based on hyperrational and isolated individual agents, coordinated by a "perfect market" – and procedural, evolutionary, and "open" – rather than "closed" toward a unique, optimal equilibrium.

So "innovation" is to be properly explained as embedded in a modern *complexity* economics (CE) framework, where critical factors of a *"deep" structure* of CAS (interaction, network, institutional structure) come to the fore. In dealing with real-world economies and their continuing idiosyncratic change as CAS, the theoretical challenge then is the identification of the *self-organization* mechanisms constituting their emergent dynamics and emergent structures, and particularly those mechanisms that exist in real capitalist economies. In terms of dynamics, they make that CAS may undergo sudden turbulent and even destructive changes as well as some lasting stasis and even some petrifaction in so-called fixed points or (transient) attractor areas, often to be conceived as a lock-in or a hysteresis in an inferior state.[5] On the other hand, proper political structuration, regulation, embedding, and management of CAS and their dynamics may entail a largely smooth, both *properly stable* and *properly flexible*, and sustainable innovative change. In all, therefore, it should have become apparent that innovation economics (IE) is one of *the* fields proper of CE, as related to CAS and their idiosyncratic dynamics.

We will further derive some typical policy implications of CE and complex IE, indicating that a new policy paradigm is to be suggested in order to deal with real-world innovation as CAS. And we will apply such insights to sketch a "*complex innovation policy*."

Finally, we will take a look at *China*, considering some of its conditions, its comprehensive, "embedded" development and innovation policies, and its experience made with "market" processes. We will apply our complex innovation-policy considerations in an effort to further improve China's broad innovation policy approach while reducing social costs. However, this chapter will remain the most general one in this volume, i.e., specialized least on China.

This chapter will proceed as follows: Section 2 very briefly discusses the simplistic approach to economics and its flawed policy orientations. Section 3 will briefly display CE and CAS and some of their policy implications. Section 4 will consider some selected recent critical innovation literature and argue that it all points to innovation, IE, and innovation policy having to adopt a complexity perspective. Section 5 will delve exemplarily into some real-world "self-organization" mechanisms, namely in deregulated neoliberal capitalist systems, which may explain the problematic course of many innovations as indicated in section 4. Section 6 will provide a very simple (but not simplistic) formal illustration of an evolutionary process of emergent problem solving through the institutionalization of *innovative cooperative behavior*. Section 7 will briefly refer to China's development process, while section 8 will conclude.

2 The simplistic neoclassical/neoliberal economic orthodoxy: the ideal "market economy" and its sterile innovation and policy conceptions

Idealization and simplification: the unique "market"-equilibrium

The neoclassical and mostly neoliberal economic mainstream, or orthodoxy, reflects both an old religious and early bourgeois-philosophical ideal of an autonomous, decentralized, spontaneous, stable, self-equilibrating, and "optimizing" mechanism. This has been called at times a "creator," an "invisible hand," and an ideal "market" or "market economy." The invisible hand once was invoked by the Scottish Enlightenment and early classical economists as a political parole of the day against feudalism, also reflecting the early bourgeois historical optimism of the eighteenth century. The invisible hand was supposed to be a mechanism working "behind our backs" to generate the best outcome for "the greatest number" and suggested the existence of *only positive unintended consequences* of (selfish) individual behavior.

A hundred years later, the neoclassical *general equilibrium theory* (GET) allegedly tried to reflect and formalize this, suggesting that all may just follow their hyperrational, individualist (i.e., short-run maximizing) interests in isolated ways, to generate the highest utility for the largest number. This was done through a set of axioms and assumptions that allows a very particular mathematical formalization, using a *representative agent* with its particular maximization under (budget, cost, technological etc.) restrictions (the Lagrange algorithm) and the restriction of the universe of real complex systems to an artificial price-quantity space of partial markets interrelated (and coordinated) with each other by a price vector. In this way, the *possible state space* of an economy was purposefully *restricted* so that the basic orthodox "market" model and a particular mathematics could be applied and would necessarily generate an identifiable unique, pre-determined equilibrium.

The representative agent's ideal timeless (constrained) maximization, in fact, could never be a fruitful microfoundation, as it *assumes away* anything that constitutes a real-world socio-economy: the manifold forms of (mostly repeated) direct interactions among many and potentially diverse individual agents, their real struggles for some *coordination* and *cooperation* under fundamental uncertainty, and the potentially diverse dynamic, emergent structuration among them (emergent institutions and network structures), rather than a simple static summing up of "optimal" quantities. *Complex aggregates*, in fact, usually behave (both empirically and in synthetic settings) fundamentally different from individual agents and their just statically summed-up supply or demand quantities. The representative agent, thus, proved to be "the fiction by which macroeconomists can justify equilibrium analysis and provide pseudo microfoundations" (Kirman, 1992, p. 125; also, e.g., Elsner, 2017; Jayasinghe, 2017).

This approach also has little to do with individualism, as its proclaimed ideal liberalism proved to analytically require a gray *uniformism* (i.e., the representative agent, with even identical homothetic utility functions formally required). Furthermore, the equilibrium could only be justified, as an "optimal," unique, and stable GE through the construction of a Walrasian auctioneer, which again turned out to be the complete contradiction of any true individualism, as it needs to restrict behavioral options to an exchange at equilibrium prices only, which the auctioneer had to determine first, in the famous (timeless) tâtonnement prior to any exchange – in fact, the *most authoritarian and centralist* instance implied in the historical "proof" and message of the neoclassical GET. In this way, high theoretical and methodological cost, in terms of non-realism and extreme reductionism, incurred in order to maintain the economic mainstream's historical message of the "market economy" as the climax and end of human history.

Modeling and simulating a more realistic decentralized "market" economy as a multi-agent process with local interaction, with exchange also possible at "false" prices, and without a central authority may lead to some "equilibrium" as well, which will, however, be anything but unique and "optimal" (e.g., Albin and Foley, 1992). No wonder, too, that also macroeconomists, who have performed *computation* runs of neoclassical macro models based on those "microfoundations," found that they cannot explain the many intricate real-world macro phenomena (e.g., Jayasinghe, 2017, pp. 70–72).

Note that *Adam Smith* was already more enlightened in all this. His fundamental social work on the emergence of basic social institutions, the *Theory of Moral Sentiments*, basic to his applied political-economic *Wealth of Nations*, demonstrated that there can be no reasonably working, decentralized spontaneous economic mechanism without an interactively learned basic informal *institutional embedding* (i.e., some learned culture of cooperation) (e.g., Elsner, 1989). Untamed selfishness would generate giant social dilemmas, and only some institutionally moderated, socially learned "*prudence*" (Smith) could render a decentralized, liberal system workable and sustainable. So while a "market" could be anything from the most fatal human nightmare to some reasonably helpful instrumental mechanism, unless defined by its specific institutional embedding, it also needs to be formally *regulated* by the state in order to render it a reasonably working device, as Smith stressed throughout his WN.

Presumptions and critiques, and the exhaustion of the GE research program

In the neoclassical birth period and again later, in the Samuelsonian mathematization period of the 1940s, economic orthodoxy particularly tried to draw parallels to the formalism and reputation of physics, and in flawed ways (e.g., Georgescu-Roegen, 1975; Mirowski, 1989). In particular, the socio-economy was not a closed system with energy conservation, or in a stable equilibrium, like a gas in a closed container with no change in pressure or heat. Both cases were attempts to grant to economics the authority, reputation, legitimacy, and (alleged) determinacy of mechanical physics, to achieve the ideal of a "*social physics*" and the related political and general public *rhetorical* and *ideological* dominance that could be exerted that way in the rivalry with different "heterodoxies" in the probably most contested scientific discipline of economics (e.g., Milonakis, 2017; O'Boyle and McDonough, 2017; Payson, 2017).

Its related heroic assumptions have long been well known and cannot be discussed here. Among the long-standing and well-known *"heterodox" critiques* ranked are the evolutionary-institutional theory of the ubiquity of *institutionalized and habituated behavior* (Veblen, 1899); the ubiquity of externalities and of increasing returns to scale (Sraffa, 1926; Young, 1928); the impossibility of a static aggregation into general supply and demand functions and their identical (stable) reproduction without considering income *distribution*, as demand and supply structures always change with prices (and thus income distribution) in the economic circuit (Sraffa, 1926); the necessity to recognize *historical time, process*, and *sequentiality*, with statistical non-stationarities, idiosyncratic mood shifts, and ubiquitous systemic structural breaks (Keynes, 1936); the nonexistence in reality of complete and well-defined preference orderings; and the impossibility for humans to compute infinite-dimensional optimization problems in vanishing time, *incomplete information*, and *bounded rationality* (Simon, 1955; Sen, 1974); and many more.

In particular, the boundaries of the neoclassical research program were demonstrated "from inside" through the famous proofs in the early 1970s of the *nonexistence of a unique equilibrium* in all but extremely special cases (the "SMD" proofs: Sonnenschein, 1973; Mantel, 1976; Debreu, 1974). So, while the proof of an existence of a GE in an n-dimensional differential-equation system (n partial markets) by Arrow and Debreu (1954) had fanned the initial attractiveness of the research program, the proof of its *uniqueness* failed; there exist infinitely many linearly dependent functions, and the aggregate (excess) demand function, as derivable from the usual lean and simple axioms of "individual rationality," has only very general properties and not necessarily the form that is required for a GE ("GMD"). Thus, there may exist infinitely many equilibria, many of which may be meaningless (with negative prices or quantities). The lean, minimalist characterization of the "perfect" individual agent does not provide enough "structure" for a unique equilibrium to be inferable. These proofs implied in fact the exhaustion of the neoclassical research program and its historical message (e.g., again, Mirowski, 1989).

Nowadays, therefore, the neoclassical research program, custom-made for an ideal "market economy" as a global benchmark, is rejected by modern system (or complexity) sciences. Nevertheless, economic orthodoxy still pretends the existence of a sound theoretical basis (somewhere "in the background") for the claim of the relative optimality, welfare maximization, and self-equilibrating property of a "market economy" taught to hundreds of thousands of economics and business students only through the model of a *partial market*, and thus continues to be the authoritative provider of the everyday rhetoric and ideology in media and politics.

Policy implications: "T-i-n-a" and "ever more of the same" in face of market degeneration and failure

Consequently, orthodoxy usually postulates a unique policy: "T-i-n-a – There is no alternative," since "There is no such thing as a society" (M. Thatcher) to the neoliberal minimalist welfare state, to deregulation cum privatization, social austerity, redistribution to the top ranks, and subsequent financialization, reinforcing, after the major financial crashes and bail-outs, increasingly restrictive and authoritarian government (e.g., Rasmus, 2016; Kingston, 2017).

But its very theoretical and methodological basis is incapable of identifying the dynamics and trajectories from any real ("non-ideal" or "second-best") state of the economy toward their alleged "first best" state. Already, the famous *theory of the second-best* (Lipsey and Lancaster, 1956) showed, within the frame of the neoclassical logic, that there is no linear, monotonic way of improvement from any real "second-best" when there are obstacles to attain the "first best" by just removing or linearly improving on any one of them. In fact, the systemic state could become even worse, and even more "ideal" conditions may have to be hurt to achieve improvement – an indication that the system is non-linear and complex. In all, the mainstream has no proper dynamical analytics for proper trajectories – and thus also no adaptive policy conception for improvement under real-world conditions.

What we can observe, however, are considerable negative impacts of the "ideal" policy measures, of decades of "T-i-n-a": a quick and accelerating self-degeneration, particularly of deregulated markets, into highly *centralized power* systems (see, e.g., the famous network analysis of ownership, interlocking, and mutual control of the 43,000 largest firms through a group of only around 40 mega-entities; Battiston et al., 2011). Under these conditions, a dominance of financialized rent-seeking and redistribution to the top tends to *displace* real production and *real innovation* (e.g., Battiston et al., 2015; Kingston, 2017).

But the common reaction of the mainstream to manifold systemic flaws, socio-economic failure, and repeated major crises is "ever more of the same," displaying again its simplistic and linear system conception. The latter then paradoxically generates a persistent state *planning for the market* and an increasing *ad-hocery of interventions*, massive bail-outs of the most powerful, systemically relevant, and *too-big-to-fails* during crises, at the expense of the taxpayer (e.g., Rasmus, 2016).

And, in fact, the visible hand of the state, namely in the field of research, technology, and innovation, has always created the "markets" through organizing and financing basic research, innovation, and the demand for them; carrying and socializing the largest and most basic early risks – altogether nowadays known as the conceptions of the *developmental or entrepreneurial state* (in the tradition of the early developmental economist Friedrich List: List, 1841; see, e.g., Chang, 2002; Mazzucato, 2013, 2016).

Innovation in particular: exogenous, erratic, and "residual"

In fact, technological change or innovation could, in that simplistic frame, always only be conceived of as "exogenous" and erratic. "Exogenous shocks" then only cause comparative statics from one equilibrium (path) to another. And empirical-statistical *growth models* based on neoclassical microfoundations, from Solow-Swan to even P. Romer's "Endogenous Growth Theory," always had to resort to statistical residuals in "explaining" innovation, be they called "total factor productivity" or "human capital" or just "ideas" (e.g., Payson, 2017, pp. 295–318).

So we will have to set the conceptual and theoretical basics right for a proper understanding of the ever-changing real economy and, at its core, of coevolving technical and behavioral innovation and corresponding innovation policy.

3 Economic complexity in a nutshell

Real-world economic systems: cognitive capacities, arena size, emergent institutions, and network structures

"Markets," in reality, are *networks*. Ideal, perfect "markets," and the largely deregulated ones in reality (i.e., designed, created, shaped, and regulated after the simplistic ideal), might be considered complete networks (if not dimensionless "point markets" or Walrasian-auctioneer systems, i.e., star networks). However, a complete network, in reality, would quickly generate a high complexity, at least in terms of the number of relations (r), with a growing number of agents (n): $r(n) = n(n-1)/2$, an exponential increase of potential interactions/relations.

In addition, if agents have to deal with real-world problems, such as coordination or social-dilemma (SD) problems, they always have several options to behave in an ongoing process in a population, such as, for instance, striving to exploit others or to share information with them. That is, there usually are more or less intricate problems involved, particularly in ideal, decentralized complete networks, such as collective-good problems.[6] Then, in fact, a minimum of four potential relations (as between each two players in a normal-form game) exist, and complexity tends to further increase. With, say, eight agents, the number of potential relations would increase, according to $r(n) = \left[n(n-1)/2\right]4$, to 112 potential relations. And the mere increase of the number of relations may, in an evolutionary process in a population, be complemented by a realization of a diversity of agents (namely their strategies): diverse agents might emerge, thus a higher complexity.

Particularly, with more real-world interdependence structures such as coordination, anti-coordination, or dilemma problems of different variants (stag hunt, chicken, and many more) and with different levels of (numerical) fierceness, ubiquitously existing and repeatedly "played" in a population, many different kinds of agents may emerge in an evolutionary process with strategy search and repeated differential replication. Many and potentially heterogeneous agents, in fact, represent the core of systemic complexity.

In a real-world perspective, anthropological, cognition/brain, and behavioral research need to be considered. They all tell us that human agents have definite *limits of cognitive and computational capacity*, and, compared to the potential information always generated in a CAS, always have to act under radical uncertainty (as distinct from calculable risk), i.e., bounded rationality, and, particularly when meeting strangers, they act under some initial radical strategic uncertainty.

This then corresponds with the cognitive process of building and maintaining relations, namely the *relative probabilities of meeting neighbors, acquaintances or strangers*. It has to do with the *size of relevant neighborhoods, interaction arenas or groups*, modulated by the (emotional) *intensity of the interaction* according to family, kin, band, clan, residential or social neighborhood, professional network, larger community, ethnic group, entire nations or the global arena.

Anthropological research informs us that stable migrating and settling bands of hunters and gatherers had the size order of 35–40 agents, and larger clans (with, on average, less intensive relations and less frequent interactions between any two members) displayed the size order of 150 members. This was cognitively reflected in the phase of early human development, when social-emotional capacities, face recognition etc. developed together with the (biologically relatively late) development of the neocortex part of the human brain (e.g., Dunbar, 1993, 2008). Genetic, cognitive, neuro, and brain sciences have confirmed this *social-brain thesis*, and the relevant maximum *group sizes* that humans can cognitively accommodate (around 40) at relatively high interaction-intensity levels (e.g., Marlowe, 2005). In this size order they can generate sufficiently high expectations of cooperation, or what we will call a sufficiently high "*general trust*" for effective cooperation to sustain. A general trust is embodied as a cooperation expectation vis-à-vis a *stranger* even in an expected *one-shot* interaction.[7]

In contrast, subject to constellations of other factors beyond group size (emotional intensity and density of interaction, intensity of mobility, fierceness of incentive structures, group network structure and others), over-complexity and over-turbulence may easily be perceived, with potential disadvantageous consequences for the system.

In both basic possibilities agents' cognitive *capacities* have a bearing on their subjective *willingness* to remain open to change, i.e., their attitude and proclivity to *be innovative* in a broad sense. So *arena sizes*, in which interactions take place, their initial or emerged *network structures*, and the related cognitive conditions, including experienced *expectations* to meet a cooperator next interaction (again, see section 6 for detail), will thus be themes from CE for the analysis of the innovation potential of an economy and a corresponding innovation policy.

What then do agents really do in face of ubiquitous possibilities of perceived over-complexity and over-turbulence? In fact, they will strive to reduce (over-) complexity, adapt it to their cognitive capacity, restrict arena and group sizes, select partners as far as possible (some "*preferential attachment*" or "selective mixing"), try to *extend (prolong) interactions* with those partners, with whom they perform successfully and who they have learned to trust, and to attenuate direct factors of turbulence, such as high in- and out-*mobility* in their peer groups. In fact, they strive to establish *stable patterns* in their relations, not only according to family and kin, but also to spatial/social neighborhood etc.

For instance, in the pursuit of avoiding over-turbulence, people often invent, develop, and carry out Polanyian *counter movements* against deregulated and globalized (highly anonymous) "market" environments (Polanyi, 1944). And even the largest "global (firm) players" strive to reduce perceived over-turbulence and partially exclude the mechanisms of the "market." Their most sensitive research, technology, and production divisions will be locally *clustered* and *networked* with other firms' divisions, and manifold forms of frequent and stable cooperative interaction will be established, as known since A. Marshall's agglomeration studies (Marshall, 1890/1920). This is why we talk about "*meso*" sizes, "regionalization," "globalization," clusters, and the like.

In all, we are dealing here with institutionalizations of relational and network patterns. But as soon as agents cluster, some hierarchization and centralizations emerge, in turn triggering further preferential attachments, thus (often cumulatively) differentiating centrality, hierarchy, power, and related central network functions such as, e.g., "gatekeepers," "bridge builders" etc. Many real-world ENs (or platforms of institutionalized behavior) then display particular *distributions of centrality degrees* of agents (or nodes generally), which then typically are *right-skewed* (long-tail distributions) and particularly so-called power-law distributions. The latter represent so-called scale-free networks that have similar distributions (and the distribution graph has similar slopes) at all scales. The left part of Figure 1.1 (a and b) shows a quite simple synthetic example at its right hand (a) as compared to a random network on its left (b); the right part of the figure (c) shows an empirical network example, also illustrating the property of scale-free networks with its obvious clustering around different more or less central hubs.

In fact, many relevant processes and *self-organization mechanisms* in the dynamics of CAS lead to right-skewed statistical distributions of centrality degrees with heavy (long, fat) tails, rather than representing random process, which then would entail normal distributions, as were assumed in stochastic versions of neoclassical (financial "market") models. Long-tail distributions were empirically found for income and wealth (Pareto, 1897), firm sizes (Gibrat's Law), city sizes (Zipf's Law), asset prices and returns (e.g., Mandelbrot and Hudson, 2006), price changes, or financial-speculation sector agents' centralities (e.g., Lux and Marchesi, 1999), further appearances of words in languages, citations in citation networks, and many others in both natural and social systems.

Under mechanisms that generate such distributions, major sudden system motions, such as economic and financial *crises*, will occur with higher probabilities than under random process and normal distributions, the now famous *black-swan* phenomena (e.g., Taleb, 2007), "improbable" under presumed Gaussian normal distributions, for which such relevant areas of the resulting graph hardly exist. And the "tail" makes a considerable difference; the system-relevant agents, the "too-big-to-fails" or *tail risks* are located there, on the far right of the distributions, with multiple size orders of power and centrality than the average.

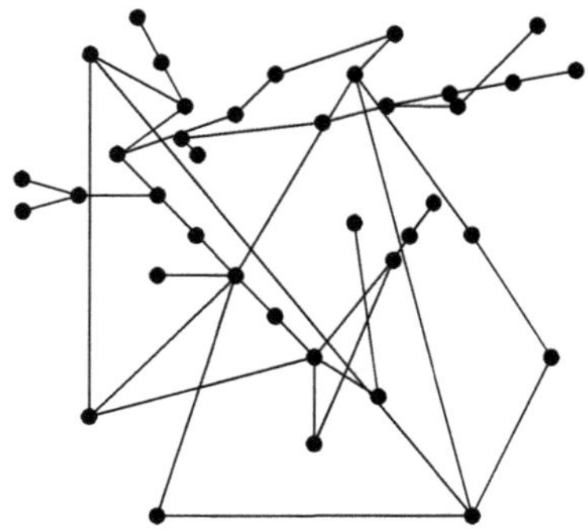

(a) random network

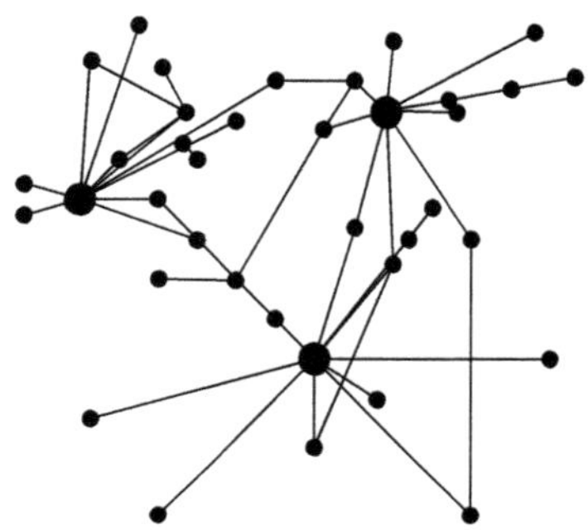

(b) scale-free network

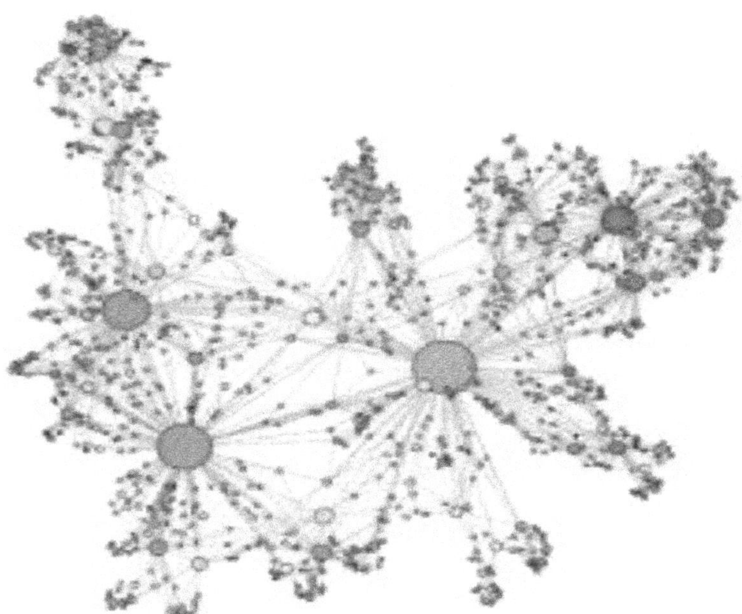

(c) An example of scale-free network

Figure 1.1 Network structures with right-skewed (power-law) centrality-degree distributions of agents (scale-free networks)

Source: a, b: author's own; c: Bianconi and Rahmede, 2015, p. 3

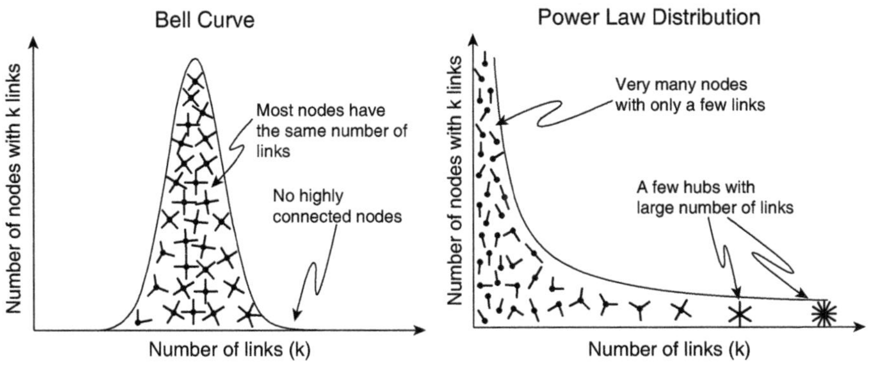

Figure 1.2 A right-skewed (power-law) distribution of centrality degrees, as compared to a normal distribution (based on random network and process)

Source: Barabási, 2002, p. 71

Figure 1.2 illustrates a "normal" centrality distribution as compared to a long-tail (particularly power-law) distribution.

Theorizing CAS: self-organization mechanisms and over- and under-innovation

In a CE perspective, socio-economies are CAS, consisting of *many* and (potentially) *heterogeneous* components, in micro-based systems usually individual agents. These usually have different behavioral/strategic options and are directly interacting (often repeatedly) with each other in a manifoldly structured population (an *IN*; spatially, behaviorally structured). They usually do so in different, more-or-less intricate *problem* (decision, incentive) *structures* (SDs/PDs, coordination/stag hunt/battle-of-the-sexes, chicken/anti-coordination or dis-coordination games), on different potential *network topologies* with (social or spatial) neighborhoods as well as in long-distance interactions (e.g., among gatekeepers). All of them usually are endogenously changing in a process. Agents then face (initial) fundamental (strategic) uncertainty between each two of them. Agents then react and adapt to each other, to the average performance of their neighborhoods, to their peer groups, to local or global conditions of the system (depending on their information), through search, learning, imitation, experimentation etc. They do this in real *historical time* and sequentially (action-reaction chains) and in *non-trivial* and systematic ways (e.g., imitating, herding, anticipating) depending on different social organization mechanisms. A *non-linear* aggregation results from that, often with destabilizing (disequilibrating) cumulative *positive feedback* loops. This is equivalent with *path-dependent* and *non-ergodic* historical development. Generally, a wide variety of dynamics will result: first, high *idiosyncrasies* with bifurcations and sometimes so-called deterministic chaos where short-term prediction will no longer be possible (the famous prototype of such dynamics is the "logistics map," May, 1976); second, high *rigidities* (fixed points/attractors), which are usually transitory. A number of other emergent system properties will emerge, such as certain persistent structures – which then cannot be traced back to the properties of the individual agents (which is the very definition of emergence), indicating particular "self-organization" mechanisms, which are mechanisms of just systematic interaction (so not necessarily something "good" or problem-solving). Usually CAS generate multiple (and transient) equilibria (e.g., Kauffman, 1993). Structures and properties emerge "from the bottom up" at meso (subsystem) and macro (system) levels (e.g., Epstein and Axtell, 1996), but also will exert subsequent *reconstitutive downward effects* (e.g., Hodgson, 2002) onto individual behaviors (both restricting and empowering). In all, this results in a multilevel system, micro – meso – macro, with the levels interacting.

Both dynamic properties and emergent structures of CAS thus stem from self-organization mechanisms, which form the *theoretical-analytical* research program proper of CE (e.g., Kauffman, 1993; Epstein and Axtell, 1996).

Self-organized systems often return to some relatively stable path again after having gone through some highly volatile phase or "crisis" (so-called phase transitions at so-called tipping points, into so-called "deterministic chaos"). They then display some "meta-attractor," or "*self-organized criticality*" (Bak et al., 1987), increasing, from lower levels of complexity, their complexity "in some order" again, approaching the next highly volatile phase (e.g., repeated capitalist and particularly financial-sector crises). Note that the dynamic properties of CAS themselves usually also display a right-skewed distribution of the sizes of those repeated critical motions, be it such different systems as sand-pile or snow avalanches, earthquakes, or financial sector crises. This indicates that some identical self-organization mechanisms may be working even after repeated crises and at different system scales.

Given the different *adverse self-organization* mechanisms often dominating in decentralized spontaneous capitalist "market" economies, we need to consider badly adapted socio-economic systems indeed, which may well run into *repeated crises*. Thus we need to consider inner conditions, self-organization mechanisms, of socio-economic CAS that may render them subject to repeated crisis and manifold other malperformance, including non-resilience and, last but not least, *over- and under-innovation*.

In particular, Heinrich (2016, 2018b) has considered evolutionary systems and processes under the criterion of optimal "forgetting," or *information loss* vs. *information retention*. Under combinations of *insufficient vs. excessive diversity* generation (i.e., too little or too much innovation) and insufficient vs. excessive selection pressure of a system, only certain areas of combinations of levels of diversity generation and selection pressure will entail proper rates of information loss or retention, and thus system resilience. Outside these areas, systems will be subject to non-resilience, insufficient adaptability, or even elimination of the entire population.

Socio-economic CAS in particular are developing today under ubiquitous (1) microelectronic digitization and (2) network effects. They may, Heinrich (2018b) argues, under condition (1) generate a *volatile innovation* with close-to-zero marginal costs, the system thus easily being subject to *too high rates of change* (too high diversity generation or *over-turbulent innovation*), a subsequent *lack of stability* and a potential error catastrophe (carrying too much information along). Under condition (2), the system may generate cumulatively dominating standards, homogenization, monopolization/oligopolization tendencies, and related (technological) lock-in[8] and thus become, through *insufficient diversity/innovation*, subject to excessive loss of information, some petrifaction, and a subsequent potential crisis and non-resilience, too. In both cases they may eventually collapse, or face repeated major crises ("chaotic" phases). The two cases together may render the system *insufficiently innovative* over repeated cycles of crises, when change rates overall become too volatile between high turbulence and lock-in (also, e.g., Bloom et al., 2005; Vega-Redondo, 2013).

Note that systems which are either permanently too complex or permanently not complex enough may thus not be sustainable, so systems should always be institutionally structured, regulated, and politically managed to remain "*at the edge/onset of chaos*" (as coined by, e.g., S. Kauffman, D. Farmer).

As an example, consider the financial-speculation sector with its repeated major crises. Product and behavioral standardization, imitation, and herd behavior under uncertainty, cumulative centrality, size, and power concentration, and fat-tailed centrality distribution will entail insufficient diversity generation (too little information variance), while fierce rivalry and a race for profit may lead to excessive selection pressure (too little stability or too fast information loss). Both processes are in interaction, which in total may entail repeated phase transitions into disorder, chaos, and crisis (e.g., Lux and Marchesi, 1999; Mandelbrot and Hudson, 2006).

Note that a typical self-organization mechanism in physical and economic network analysis has been coined by physicists as *the-rich-get-richer* or a preferential attachment mechanism (Barabási and Albert, 1999). The more relations or power an entity has, the more it tends to get, thus, some positive feedback cumulative mechanism will be reflected in skewed distribution structures with its crisis-prone implications.

No "optimality" nor absolute and stable "fitness" under changing social ecologies

In a population that forms a CAS, a continuously changing social ecology (strategy composition of the population) renders it impossible that a certain behavioral strategy can be persistently "optimal" or "fit." In a complex evolutionary process, there is mostly *no sufficient structural stability* to provide sufficient time for some selection mechanism to operate in any "meliorating" way. Rather, there is continuous endogenous change of the social ecology, through ubiquitous behavioral adaptation, diversification, experimentation, and search, which usually outrun any "meliorating" selection mechanism. Rather, there will result a "*rugged and moving fitness surface*" with usually no clear-cut direction in systems that are insufficiently institutionally embedded, politically regulated and managed.

In particular, with dynamic populations, i.e., when the population share of a particular strategy develops non-linearly in dependence on its previous share, initial "fitness" advantages may cumulate. This may reflect a continuing "the-rich-get-richer" mechanism or first-mover advantage. Then a *survival of the first or "fattest"* may become a dominant pattern. Alternatively, an initial advantage may get exhausted through its very success, and may shrink, and a *survival of all* (with usually very different population shares) may realize (e.g., Nowak, 2006; for persistent multi-standard situations in network-industries, e.g., Heinrich, 2013).

Some basic policy implications

In response to the 2000ff. dotcom crisis and 2008ff. financial crisis, there occurred an upsurge in the elaboration of policy implications regarding CE (e.g., Mandelbrot and Hudson, 2006; Taleb, 2007; Salzano and Colander, 2007; OECD, 2009, 2017; Geyer and Rihani, 2010; Chen, 2010; Room, 2011; Beinhocker, 2012; Fontana, 2012; Colander and Kupers, 2014; Geyer and Cairney, 2015). Some exemplary policy orientations elaborated in this literature include the following:

Socio-biologist D.S. Wilson (2016) demonstrated that all complex systems are somehow (self-)regulated and that the idea of a maximal deregulation would be downright absurd. Rather, elaborating the *right kind of regulation* and a "wise managing of evolutionary process" would be the issue at stake (also, e.g., Clement and Puranam, 2018).

Some complexity economists elaborated the orientation toward a *control* of the processes behind *right-skewed* (long-tail or heavy-tail, and often power-law) *centrality distributions*, namely avoiding too many, too big, and too long-lasting power and centrality positions, i.e., the big financial and industrial corporations, which are the "tail risks," and their property rights often cumulatively favored in the "market" and by the governments (e.g., Gallegati et al., 2007; Güth et al., 2013).

Further, "complexity policy" orientations have been elaborated with a focus on generally *dampening the volatility and idiosyncrasy* of CAS, stabilizing the system by reducing financial leverages, cumulative mechanisms in general (such as imitation and herding behavior), and related positive feedback loops (e.g., Radzicki, 1990; Room, 2011). In particular, problem-solving *institutionalization* may be promoted as stabilizing "institutional control variables" (Room, 2011) and even *complexity-harnessing* devices (e.g., Page, 2012; Bednar et al., 2015; Clement and Puranam, 2018), preferably by shaping framework conditions to publicly support learning of informal institutionalization of cooperation among the private agents.

In general, the *higher complexity of the political control system* over the controlled target system, i.e., its higher capacity to assume a large variety of system states, together with the computational capacities required for such a qualified future state agency, have become major issues (see already Ashby, 1956; more recently: Velupillai, 2005, 2007; also, e.g., Clement and Puranam, 2018).

And implications for conceptualizing innovation

In socio-economic CAS, innovation can never be anything exogenous to the system; it is always *endogenous* to the complex system and part of its development, thus coevolving together with the sectoral, distributional, institutional, and macro-aggregates structures. It also is always broadly understood as both technical and behavioral change coevolving, given the microeconomic problem structures (interdependence/decision structures) and the self-organization mechanisms at work.

The character and the particularities of innovations depend on the structure, dynamics, and state of the system and may range from completely *blocked innovations* to different forms of welfare-enhancing but also of kinky, perverted, and degenerated ones, and to otherwise *negative unintended forms and effects* of innovations (e.g., Kingston, 2017; Lueders et al., 2017; Grant and Moses, 2017; von Schomberg and Hankins, 2018). Whether intended welfare-improving innovations do come about or are blocked, get locked-in or appear degenerated in other ways, will depend on, as already indicated, the *size* of INs and ENs of a relevant population, e.g., whether they are too large to generate sufficient general expectations, in any interaction, to meet a cooperative interaction partner (again) next interaction;[9] further, on the structure of IN/EN, e.g., whether they are highly concentrated and centralized, hierarchical, and fat-tail distributed in centrality degree and power, or more evenly distributed. "Good" innovation will also depend on the kind and severity (intricacy) of the problem situation that agents face in their everyday interactions, e.g., whether they usually face fierce SD problems with high incentives to hyperrational maximization, resulting in cultures of *short-termism* and *the-winner-takes-it-all* (e.g., Jennings, 2005; Aspara et al., 2014; Pogach, 2018). Related degrees of (perceived) complexity and turbulence in the relevant repeated decision situations, arenas, groups, population, or network also count, e.g., whether there is a high disembedding *mobility* and turnover among agents, each then frequently meeting complete strangers, or a dense and lasting interaction generating acquaintances, who then have relatively high longer-run incentives to develop cooperation. Innovation is dependent on the degree of learned and habituated *institutions* of cooperation and of the establishment of their carrier groups and EN platforms, on the related average *futurity* orientation, or long-termism of expectations, decisions, and actions, or the planning horizon, with its related possible longer-run calculations and rationality. The self-organization mechanisms predominant in a population count as well: for example, whether agents mostly orientate toward the most central agents and preferentially attach to them, imitate them, herd, follow short- or long-term incentives, etc. Innovation will also depend on the degree in which a system tends to become locked-in in certain established technological standards and then follow an "old," "outmoded," "degenerated," and "petrified" institution (e.g., David, 1985; Elsner, 2012; Heinrich and Schwardt, 2013), or, more general, the frequency and duration in which a system moves into, and remains in, a technologically and institutionally conditioned attractor, and whether this attractor is superior or inferior to what is aspired by private and/or policy agents. Finally, innovation also depends on the degree in which the system (by itself, or through some superior, better-informed, and dominating regulating policy) is able to generate mechanisms for proper *combinations of stability and smooth change, standardization/institutionalization and diversification, lock-in and break-out*, in order to prevent a process where some stability degenerates into petrified lock-in, preventing, for instance, that the rich get ever richer, the powerful ever more powerful, the central ever more central.

Thus, making welfare-enhancing innovation feasible from an old, locked-in technological and behavioral standard requires to *break up* certain factor constellations, as indicated, and certain cumulative feedback loops that had moved the system into such inferior attractor. This is to trigger diversity and *seed parallel standards*, without destroying the required coordinating technical and behavioral standard, to set new incentives and regulations, through a qualified, well-informed, and high-capacity *state* and its particular collective rationality. This is a delicate process, and a delicate policy fine-tuning is required to change standards and to *disruptively* innovate in order to seed new standards and institutions without generating too high social costs, and it may be feasible only within some particular time window (e.g., Heinrich, 2013, 2018a).

With all this, it becomes obvious that innovation in reality is highly *contingent*, as the CAS itself, and may easily become the contrary of its alleged "welfare-enhancing" connotation – unless embedded in a carefully shaped and regulated set of conditions and policies. We will provide a first corroboration and illustration of this interim result by briefly referring to some related conclusions, as stated in some of the most recent complexity-innovation literature.

4 Innovation as a prime field of complexity economics

Under conditions of a relatively high complexity and turbulence, and relatively little institutional and regulatory stabilization of deregulated capitalist "market" systems, and of their often adverse self-organization mechanisms, as indicated (see more below), it would come with no surprise that we increasingly may encounter innovation that is idiosyncratic in intensity, form, and effect, and that unintended and "wicked" aspects of innovation become more blatant while institutions, rather than coordinating in problem-solving ways, often quickly ossify under ubiquitous uneven power structures (right-skewed centrality distributions) and under incentives to hyperrational, short-run maximization. A general status quo orientation, conservativism, and individual, social, and political regression, averse to broad problem-solving innovation, consistent with Polanyian counter movements, then may spread (e.g., Vega-Redondo, 2013; Kleinknecht et al., 2016), as can often be observed in the neoliberal and financialized "market" economies nowadays.

Some brief examples from the recent innovation-complexity literature include:

- Perceived over-complexity and over-turbulence often render socio-economic CAS counterproductive, generating *individual and systemic rigidities* through adverse cognitive conditions and low general trust, entailing *reduced innovation* or flawed or pseudo innovation, often with considerable social costs (e.g., Bloom et al., 2005; Vega-Redondo, 2013; Kleinknecht et al., 2016; Grant and Moses, 2017; Lueders et al., 2017; Sautua, 2017) while sufficient stability would provide conditions of realistic self-confidence and thus future investments of agents (e.g., Dessi and Zhao, 2017).
- *Financialization*, then, through its often asymmetric information and thus dominant incentives to short-run *redistribution*, defection and exploitation, profit reaping, and rent-seeking enforces *myopia* and a winner-takes-all culture, reduces social commitment, and may *displace* behavioral and technological *innovation* (e.g., Garcia-Vega and Huergo, 2017; Kingston, 2017; Lueders et al., 2017).
- Competition, then, may become an overly fierce, counterproductive, destructive, and power-related *oligopolistic rivalry* which may *decrease innovation* in favor of power and monopolization strategies (e.g., Boudreau et al., 2008).
- Large, *monopolized firms* (the "tail risks" mentioned) in particular may utilize innovative activities as a tool for predation and redistribution, rather than socio-economic development and welfare enhancement ("*predatory innovation*," Schrepel, 2017), while "inequality (asymmetric information in that case – WE) causes economic collapse" (Goerner, 2017) or long-run slack and stagnation, the usual late-Schumpeter (*Schumpeter Mark II*) scenario.
- Schumpeter's earlier (Schumpeter Mark I) usually positive connotation of *creative destruction*, conceived of under still more competitive conditions, then may fundamentally change its character, and exclusive, protected, hidden-away, and thus asymmetric information, further austerity policy, monopolistic market restriction, and other forms of *destruction* in the context of innovation and change may easily *outpace creation*, again becoming a scenario consistent with the late Schumpeter (e.g., Komlos, 2016; Swann, 2015; Godin and Vinck, 2017; Langley and Tulloch, 2017).

A few general and more concluding quotes from the complexity-innovation literature may further underpin such a perspective:

- C. Christensen, *The Innovator's Dilemma* (1997), already identified constellations, where some over-turbulence may be mirrored by increasing *disruptive innovation*, and "disruptive technologies... (would make) ... best-managed companies ... susceptible to failure."

- Kauffman et al. (2013), in a constitutional, paradigmatic article for the journal *Complexity*, argued in favor of reconceptualizing technological innovation to take place under an "*evolutionary ecology*" with no welfare enhancement guaranteed.
- Fontana (2013), in an article on *complexity and innovation*, carved out the "intertwining of innovation economics and complexity economics."
- C. Antonelli, *Evolutionary Complexity of Endogenous Innovation* (2017a), also reconceptualized innovation in a CE perspective, specifying that "access conditions to knowledge. . . (are) shaped by the system, in which firms operate. . . (which) can knock firms further out-of-equilibrium . . . a path-dependent loop of interactions between the system properties and the individual actions." (also Antonelli, 2017b).
- C. Herrmann-Pillath, in a series of papers on a future all-encompassing *Technosphere Science* (e.g., 2018), specified "the technosphere (to be) an open, non-linear and non-equilibrium system."
- Mulgan (2017), in an outline for some future *cognitive economics*, reflected on innovation as a complex group process, arguing that "(the) traits generally associated with innovation. . ., which were once thought to be the preserve of a small minority, may also be the ones needed in much higher proportions in groups seeking to be collectively intelligent."

In all, there is considerable reflection in the recent literature that innovation is, and should be conceptualized and analyzed as, a genuinely endogenous, uncertain, procedural and path-dependent, non-linear and non-ergodic, systemic and network-based, non-"equilibrium" and non-"optimal" phenomenon, idiosyncratically dependent on institutions and regulations in order to release its welfare-enhancing potential and increase the dynamic resilience of its larger system and the innovation process. In this sense we contend that innovation, IE, and innovation policy are all complex dynamical phenomena par excellence, prime fields of real-world complexity and CE (e.g., Lueders et al., 2017; Ruth and Goessling-Reisemann, 2018; von Schomberg and Hankins, 2018).

To further substantiate the perspective, we need to take a closer look at the "self-organization mechanisms" working in the "deep structure," or the *real microfoundations*, of real-world capitalist "market" economies. We can do this only in a brief and exemplary way, but it would be here, where the theoretical core of both CE and IE is, its theoretical "proof of the pudding."

5 The theoretical research program: "self-organization mechanisms" in deregulated capitalist market economies

In economic theory, well-elaborated components of *adverse technology-related* self-organization-mechanisms do exist, such as scale economies in production and network-externalities in the use of network technologies. With their implications of coordination being required through immanent tendencies toward technological standardization and monopolization, they might support the proposition of relevant agents pushing innovation (at least for some time), but also of the system getting locked in quite quickly, in the case that some homogeneous oligopolization (or even a strict monopolization) takes hold (*technological lock-in*; Arthur, 1989). In the second case, sooner or later, *inferior technologies* then may easily prevail.

Break out, then, will not be easy to initiate and may require costly major turbulence (a phase transition/bifurcation or a phase of deterministic chaos or "catastrophe"), i.e., some crisis, in which a *new and superior technological standard* would become feasible as a new systemic attractor (e.g., Heinrich, 2013, 2018a). Note that coexisting and rivaling network technologies with their respective rivaling standards, in reality, require considerable minimum installed bases to usually allow only for very few global corporate players and thus narrow oligopolistic structures. Among the costs of break-out from a "petrified" (locked-in) technological path are potentially phases of fierce oligopolistic *standard wars* with lack of coordination or cooperation.

Known *adverse behavior-related* self-organization-mechanisms, particularly in deregulated capitalist market economies, have likewise been notorious in (critical) economics:

- Under complex dynamics, fundamental (strategic) *uncertainty* and *opacity* usually dominate and thus, bounded rationality, with often only local information, allowing only for local rather than absolute improvement or "maximization."
- At the same time, ubiquitous social-dilemma structures, with their dominant incentives in favor of short-run hyperrationality, may foster a culture of short-termism and winner-takes-all, which again will entail an inferior situation with insufficient innovation or non-innovation. And the fiercer the quantitative dilemma structure, the stronger the tendency toward short-termism.
- Likewise, opacity and myopia may easily trigger cumulative positive feedback of different kinds, such as emulation of those who were more successful, or herding, which is a complex convergent imitation process, with usually multiple potential equilibria. This relates to *first-mover advantages*, as first movers tend to get imitated.
- Parallel to technological lock-in, *institutions* have an inherent tendency toward an overly long use because of the high *sunk fixed costs* of their intricate interactive learning and establishment in ubiquitous repeated SDs.[10] Institutions then may easily become empty shells, increasingly detached from the problem structure they "instrumentally" solved for some time, while the problem structure changed in the meantime. The reason for people to cling to the same behavioral form, collectively applying the same institutionalized behavior as often as possible, then may change from "problem-solving" to "saving decision costs" (e.g., Elsner, 2012).

- If connected to hierarchies, some superiors may profit more than others from the original instrumental win-win, and, through this, even a new SD may emerge, without people realizing it at first. Then, the motivation to stick to the old institution may change from "instrumental" to "*ceremonial*," i.e., upholding differential status and power while the inferiors in the earlier "winning team" still may have a motivation of receiving identity from the same old formal behavioral rule, identifying with the original institutionally cooperating and winning group (e.g., Elsner, 2012; Heinrich and Schwardt, 2013). Institutions then tend to become "sclerotic," under conditions of power-based network structures in the population, with a fat-tailed centrality distribution, and will lose their initial problem-solving function, the famous *institutional lock-in* (David, 1985).

In fact, human agents in complex systems may strive to *reduce* uncertainty, perceived (over-)*complexity* and (over-)turbulence of their decision situation, be it by learning stable instrumental institutions to improve their outcomes in the longer-run or be it by trying to establish a practice of improving at the expense of others, i.e., exploitation and redistribution, the myopic behavior, striving for differential status and power, the ceremonially motivated institutional behavior. In this case, an emerged and initially instrumental institution may degenerate through an *unequal distribution* of its initial collective cooperation benefits, which in turn could lead to the emergence of a strong *individualist culture*. Thus, self-organization mechanisms as reflected by institutionalization may also cause behavioral change entailing *social costs* rather than collective problem-solving, including welfare-enhancing behavioral innovation (again, Elsner, 2012).

At the system level, thus, there may emerge forms of either some stability plus continuing and sustainable change, based on institutionalized instrumental behavior, including value-creating innovation, or some ceremonial institutional petrifaction, rigidities, and lock-ins. And this was already a core part of the microfoundations of the original evolutionary-institutional economics (OIE) of Thorstein Veblen (1899). The particular social interaction (self-organization) mechanisms in what he considered historically received "predatory" societies, namely "invidious distinction" from those in one's own social layer, exemplified in "conspicuous consumption," and striving to emulate those at higher societal layers, a ubiquitous struggle between herding and anti-herding, for relative social positioning, will entail fashion waves, a "trickle-down" of the values and behaviors of the top social strata throughout society to the lowest social tiers, paradoxically reducing social mobility and, thus, the potential for broad innovation, tending to make society behaviorally uniform, reducing diversity and eventually systemic resilience. Such socio-economies tend to generate little and only narrow innovation maximum for short-run profit, rather than benefitting the societal and ecological commons. This has been repeatedly confirmed empirically in broad international surveys (e.g., OECD, 2011; Corak, 2013).

In all, different social self-organization mechanisms, from appropriate to adverse and from instrumental to ceremonial, would be statistically reflected by different distributional centrality structures, representing different topologies (network structures and types), different types and quantitative strengths of interdependence (incentive, decision, interaction) structures, and different resulting system dynamics (reflected in stationarities/non-stationarities of long time series) including institutionalizations (e.g., Acemoglu et al., 2017; Schlossberger, 2017), entailing very *different innovation forms and performances*.

6 The example of the "evolution of cooperation": behavioral innovation, social institutions, and policy

The approach in a nutshell

For a simple formal illustration of our argument, we just refer to one of the earliest models, agent-based formalizations, and computational simulations of emergent institutionalization of cooperation, the so-called "evolution-of-cooperation" approach, a simple PD-supergame (SG) "single-shot" solution, in an evolutionary game theory (EGT) framework, which established a whole strand of evolutionary-institutional research over the last three decades (e.g., Axelrod, 1984/2006; Lindgren, 1989; Watts, 1999; Kendall et al., 2007) and, while models have proceeded considerably, still provides very crucial insights today. Its archetype starts from a PD normal form:

$$\begin{matrix} a, a & d, b \\ b, d & c, c \end{matrix}$$
given $b > a > c > d$.

For a population in an evolutionary process, in the EGT frame (with a differential replication of population shares of strategies at least implied), a particular condition of a non-invadability of the strategy of institutionalized conditional cooperation (i.e., the well-known simple "tit-for-tat" – *TFT*) by defectors (i.e., the always defecting – the *ALL-D* strategy) is that incumbent cooperators should at least play better against each other in repeated games (SG) than defectors against incumbent cooperators:

$$P_{TFT/TFT} >!\ P_{ALL\text{-}D/TFT}.$$

The superiority (in the sense of non-invadability) of such contingent cooperation (a cooperative but responsive strategy, i.e., a "trigger strategy") then is given by the capitalized current values of relative future SG-payoffs (the limit values of the sums of two infinite geometric series):

$$a/(1-\delta) >!\ b - c + c/(1-\delta)$$
or
$$\delta >!\ (b-a)/(b-c).$$

This solution had established a class of models determining conditions for *behavioral institutionalization*, i.e., an *emergent instrumental cooperation*, the superiority of instrumental cooperation to solve ubiquitous SD. Behavioral cooperation would then be the superior, more successful, and thus evolutionarily stable strategy (ESS). Cooperative behavior then is also considered *innovative behavior* as compared to the short-run individualist hyperrational benchmark behavior of *All-D*.

Note, first, that obviously, this solution can only be realized non-hyperrationally, as a learned and *habituated* behavioral institution (a social rule with the endogenous sanction, the thread of retaliation by a cooperative trigger strategy, in order to prevent short-run maximization).[11] With hyperrational behavior, the solution could never come about, as agents would play a series of one-shot games, always defecting, and never learning, developing and culturally acquiring a longer-run perspective and related *longer-run rationality* and calculation. Hyperrationality thus must be replaced by a *rule-based behavior*, justified through the longer-run perspective, rationality, and calculation as indicated. Longer-run oriented agents, then, will be "rational fools" (Sen, 1977), i.e., fools in the strictly neoclassical sense.

Note, second, that the reverse question of invadability of an incumbent defective population by invading *TFT*-cooperators, a more demanding question than the preceding original Axelrodian one, is formally not symmetric to that approach, since *TFT*, according to the preceding EGT-criterion would not be an ESS, as *TFT*-cooperators against *All-D*s always lose in the first interaction and then perform as bad as the *ALL-D* players, so will lose in total. They can only play better than incumbent defectors through generating relevant *minimal critical masses* of their own kind, which is equivalent with making themselves meet their kind often enough in order to fare better overall. This more general condition (with k the number of cooperators in a population of n), then, is the general population approach:

$$(k/n)\left[a/(1-\delta)\right]+\left[(n-k)/n\right]\left[c/(1-\delta)+d-c\right]>!$$
$$(k/n)\left[c/(1-\delta)+b-c\right]+\left[(n-k)/n\right]\left[c/(1-\delta)\right].$$

Conditional cooperators will be more successful overall, then, if they (1) are sufficiently many (a sufficiently large k or k/n) and/or (2) playing relatively successful with each other (a relatively large a and a relatively low c and b), while defectors against each other are relatively unsuccessful anyway (through the PD structure $a > c$), and/or (3) are able to play relatively longer, i.e., with relatively higher probability in each interaction to meet each other again rather than meet with defectors. In this way they generate a larger δ for themselves, as far as possible, while defectors play with a very low δ anyway; they just don't care and play in a one-shot perspective anyway.

Third, agency capacities required for such *behavioral innovation* toward cooperation in an evolutionary population process, where agents interact repeatedly and strive to change from short-run rationality (defection) to longer-run, Pareto-superior cooperation, *improving themselves and the entire socio-economy* above the individualistic hyperrational benchmark, as logically derived and modeled in full-fledged formalizations of a sequential evolutionary process with replication, are among others:

- innovative agents need to be *non–risk-averse*, as they easily may be exploited, at least once;
- similarly, they need to be *non-envious*, as the *All-D*–exploiter (even if she is exploited only once and switched over to joint cooperation thereafter) would have fared better at the end of the day;
- furthermore, they have to have some *memory* of their earlier interactions (a logical requirement of cooperative SG-strategies; e.g., one period memory in the simplest case of a cooperative strategy, *TFT*);
- and, in a well-mixed population with random encounters, they should be able to particularly increase their knowledge about other agents beyond just their own interactions, through some *monitoring* of others' interactions, through building own reputation and using *reputation* chains through others; and
- have some capacity of *partner selection* (preferential attachment) and of *extending* the length of *successful* relations and reducing the length of unsuccessful ones, as far as possible.

To develop such capacities, they would be *motivated* by:

- evading the *repeated frustration* from the negative unintended consequences of hyperrational one-shot behavior (always aspiring the maximum, but commonly ending up in the second worst situation, the common defective one-shot Nash equilibrium); and/or
- aspiring *economic improvement* (a Pareto superiority as illustrated in the normal form) by, for example, "*idle curiosity*" (Veblen) to find out, what could be gained by *innovating* one's behavior from defection to cooperation; and/or
- expressing some "*instinct of workmanship*" (Veblen), finding some benefit or pleasure in creating something (new) cooperatively.

Most crucially, the solution depends on an *innovator's culturally acquired longer-run perspective*, or "futurity" (Commons, 1934; further, e.g., Jennings, 2005; Masiliunas, 2017), represented formally by the discount factor, i.e., the (experienced and expected) probability of "meeting (again)" next interaction either

- the *same* interaction partner as before or
- a "*knowing*" partner, informed through a reputation chain or
- a general *cooperator* occurring with average probability as experienced in many interactions throughout the population.

Such futurity needs to relate to the strength (fierceness) of the incentive structure, as the preceding formal inequality illustrates.

In a substantial consideration, the typical (behavioral) innovator is not only risk-friendly and non-envious, as said, but also will follow her long-run perspective, independent, at first, of what the others do. So she will start friendly and cooperative, but will not be a masochist and will therefore properly retaliate should she experience attempts of others to exploit her. But she also is forgiving, no longer punishing the other one should he switch to longer-run rationality as well. This is exactly what Adam Smith had developed as *prudent* behavior or what Axelrod derived from his computer tournaments as evolutionary successful. In other words, "good" innovators need to be *not just technological* inventors/innovators but *behaviorally smart.*

Systemically then, for instance, with *increasing futurity*, i.e., an increasing average expectation "to meet (again)" as, e.g., in a *decreasing relevant-population size* (a smaller interaction arena, neighborhood, relevant group, locality, firm cluster etc.), or with less enforced disembedding/uprooting *mobility*, thus less perceived turbulence and more "meeting (again)," or put differently, with stronger general trust, a higher general expectation to meet a cooperator next interaction, and subsequent disposition toward cooperation, in all: with more favorable cognitive conditions, SDs will be easier solved in an evolutionary population process, and cooperation as the innovative behavior will thrive and expand in the population and take it over as the dominant culture.

Behavioral innovation and corresponding institutionalization of cooperation, thus, will have to coevolve with technological innovation and will often even (have to) come prior to it, as it lays the foundations for agents to be *cognitively able* (and then perhaps *emotionally willing*) to generate or adopt technological innovations (e.g., Elsner, 2012).

Implications for policy, governance, and management of innovation

The recognition of interdependence, of the *interdependence structures* (the kind of the "games") and their quantitative fierceness (e.g., a strong or weak SD), therefore, need to be trained among agents. "Recognized interdependence" has in fact been an old evolutionary-institutional issue (e.g., Bush, 1999). The more directly the relation between own action and others' reactions can be (cognitively) perceived, the better; which, again, is also a question of the *size* of the relevant arena or group.

Also, the awareness and the weight of *futurity* are to be increased and developed as a culture, e.g., by supporting a culture of longer-run rationality (vs. myopia/short-termism), namely in connection with the prevailing incentive structures, namely the adverse incentive to make extra profits in the very short run through pure redistribution at the expense and through exploitation of others.

Further, memory, monitoring, and reputation chains as well as transparency of interaction histories have to be supported, in this way strengthening expectations "to meet (again)" and futurity.[12] Partly based on those factors, agents need to expect *reciprocation*, positive as negative, particularly general retaliation (*punishment*) in case of own exploitative defection. That practically would require considerable transparency and some general discourse.

As Axelrod had already developed, all this can be achieved by drawing agents into *sequential cooperative projects* (at all levels) always overlapping in time, in this way promoting opportunities of reciprocation in the future. In the same vein, policies need to address and shape neighborhood structures, clustering, and networking, increasing relative interaction frequencies and in his way improving expectations of mutual cooperation.

Also, as said, *incentive structures* need to be improved, and perhaps even the *game type* as such (from more to less intricate decision problems); in the case of SDs, this may imply rewarding cooperation, punishing defection, and reducing "winner-takes-all" one-shot incentives – which must not necessarily imply massive subsidies, let alone pecuniary ones, and must not necessarily dissolve the PD structure as such. But the SD structure may be transformed into a *less intricate coordination problem* structure through a general solving of SD-SGs between each two agents (e.g., Elsner, 2012).

With all this, of course, any sclerotization through (over-)opportunism and (over-)conformism need to be avoided. As an important example, network structures may be very helpful here: proximity and interaction frequency in neighborhoods need to be balanced with refreshment of ideas through *long-distance relations*. In sum, well-shaped *small-world network* structures will have to be cared for (see the following).

The agents involved themselves, or a neutral "network manager," or the public-policy agent proper could be the carriers of corresponding (self-) *governance*, *management* or *policy* measures. And all this is about shaping relevant framework conditions in order to trigger problem-solving adaptive interaction processes of the private. We have called such "complexity policy" a *framework policy* approach or an *institutional policy*, as it aims at shaping those critical factors that tend to structure the interaction processes of the private toward instrumental institutionalizations. We also have called this new policy perspective *double-interactive*, as the policy system interacts adaptively (having to be the more complex control system) with the target CAS, i.e., the interaction system of the privates, which then is forced to adapt properly (e.g., Elsner, 2017).

The public-policy agent would also have to care for the levels of perceived complexity of the individual decision structures and the turbulence of the system processes, and develop strategies to generate an *innovative culture* with sufficient *time horizons*, but also *time* for the interactive learning and habituation processes, for stabilizing mutual expectations, building reputation, trustworthiness, and trust, establishing longer-run relations and corresponding behavioral capacities ("social capital"). As shown previously with a number of references, too much "flexibility" (turbulence), including too fierce rivalry ("competition"), may paradoxically generate rigidities of individuals and the system and deteriorate innovation capacities throughout.

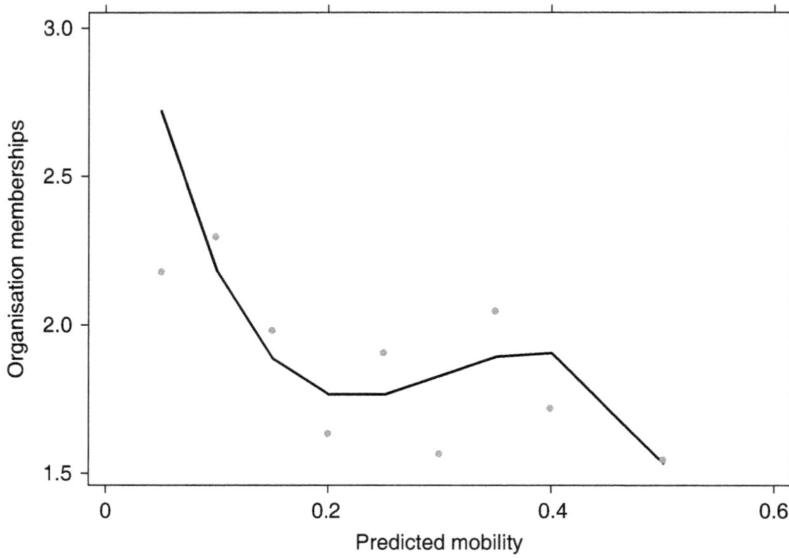

Figure 1.3 Mobility and social capital

Source: The decline of social capital (indicated by organizational membership) as depending on increasing (professionally conditioned) spatial mobility in the US – an empirical illustration (Glaeser et al., 2002, p. F451)

As an example, enforced uprooting and disembedding *spatial mobility* is to be reduced to improve the cognitive and "expectational" conditions, as has been increasingly addressed in a world of growing volatility, turbulence, and enforced mobility, including increasing refugee and poverty migrations of all kinds nowadays (e.g., Solari and Gambarotto, 2014; Glaeser et al., 2002; Battiston et al., 2015). This obviously is in stark contrast to the conventional wisdom of the superiority of an always productivity-increasing and welfare-enhancing mobility. As an empirical illustration, see Figure 1.3 for the example of (enforced, and in this case only professionally conditioned and only within-border) mobility and social-capital deterioration.

Finally, and interdependent with the factors mentioned, the *structures* of initial interaction *arenas* (i.e., IN) as well as of emerging cooperation platforms (EN) have to be a focus of public policy ("shaping the connective geometry," Room, 2011; also, e.g., Ormerod, 2012). This firstly includes size. Relevant arenas and emerging groups will have to be shaped toward proper *meso* sizes for interaction, learning, and institutionalization processes to be properly experienced and to be adapted over time in order to meet the cognitive conditions and make favorable expectational structures emerge. Second, the system's *modularity* (Simon, 1962) needs to be developed. Functionally *overlapping* and *hierarchically layered* networks ("multiplex" networks), related to the spatial, social, production-wise, and otherwise functional reaches of the "goods" and services at stake, public and private, need to come into the focus of a future complexity policy (e.g., Loasby, 2012; Ormerod, 2012; Helbing, 2013; Gilles et al., 2015; Biggs et al., 2015).

Third, *network structures* need to be shaped, both for entire nations/populations and groups/subpopulations. Effective, problem-solving network structures need to display conditions for clustering and neighborhood properties in order to make feasible or facilitate the emergence of instrumental institutions, and thus fast, comprehensive, and inclusive innovation processes. But this should go together with selected long-distance relations among such local clusters, which in sum then should generate effective *small-world* networks (with a high cluster coefficient for effective coordination/cooperation and a low overall diameter/average path length) for a *fast innovation* diffusion.

But note that the gatekeeper positions that connect local clusters may exactly be those "tail risks" in the right-skewed centrality and power distributions as mentioned, which therefore may need to be exchanged among several agents in due time frames.

Before we conclude with a compact view on complex innovation, IE, and innovation policy, we will briefly consider, what we can learn from the Chinese experience so far, and how the Chinese experience might be further informed and qualified through a CE perspective on innovation and innovation policy.

7 Considering conditions of the comprehensive innovation process in China

As a somehow "*mixed economy*" and through its long cultural history of learning, change, and innovation, as well as cohesion and cooperation, China today has both considerable informal and formal institutions of cooperation and networking, plus strong regulations of its socio-economy. It thus has developed a considerably high collective and *public-action capacity*, particularly compared to the neoliberal countries that have been degraded in most of their public-investment and public-action capacities that would have been needed for proactive policies and a broader and innovative development. Indeed, in China, those capacities seem to be mainly used for a comprehensive and continuously updated national development strategy and a wide range of instrumental institutions of cooperation and collective problem-solving. It thus has also an impressive capability to invest in *infrastructures* of high complexity and to activate unexpected and unprecedented levels of *innovation* (technological, structural, behavioral) in most relevant areas – not the least through encouraging entrepreneurship in the broadest sense.

In this process, China is largely making use of decentralized, spontaneous mechanisms, among them "*markets*," however well-embedded, and many kinds of *networks* more generally, often left unregulated for some time before the government starts regulating a particular new field, then forcing that "market," sector or field to adapt – surprisingly similar with how it was meant to be in the original ideas of the "market economy," such as in Adam Smith's *WN*. With this particular approach to an *agile industrial and innovation* policy,[13]

China also has entailed, and deliberately condoned, considerable levels of technological and general socio-economic progress and catch up in a global dimension.

China is one of the few countries in the world that may seriously be considered a substantially mixed economy in the sense that although it undertakes considerable instrumental use of spontaneous, decentralized price-based mechanisms ("markets") to develop its productive forces, this private-sector mechanism is strongly *regulated* by the central government (on the mixed economy in China, e.g., Chen et al., 2000; Robins, 2010).[14] With this particular mix, namely its strong *instrumental utilization of the "market"* (e.g., Herrmann-Pillath, 2017) in a clear understanding of the long-run broad development goals, China has leapfrogged two centuries and caught up from a less developed country to a middle-income country within four decades (e.g., Lin, 2017). It has realized projects in all areas (ecology, society, production, technology, industrial change, mega-city government, construction, infrastructure, etc.) of size orders and levels of complexity that have become infeasible even for leading neoliberal capitalist countries. As examples, one might pick the technological, organizational, and societal developments in areas from *photovoltaic* to *e-mobility* to *quantum computation*, from bullet trains to the *Great Green Wall*, fighting desertification in its western areas, a project considered by the UN unique in global terms, requiring high levels of combination of scientific knowledge and agent coordination over long periods. Not least, and concurrent to that, Chinese firms have become global leaders in most relevant innovation areas (e.g., McKelvey and Jin, 2018).

China has also clearly become what nowadays is called, in innovation and broader development policies, an *entrepreneurial state* (Mazzucato, 2013, 2016, see previous), as entrepreneurial spirit and business start-ups are fostered and financially supported and turn out to be particularly successful in the general regulatory, socio-economic, and systemic frame, where entrepreneurs are not only really and effectively supported but act in an environment with an apparently quite appropriate incentive structure and speed of change and little existential uncertainty (e.g., Fu, 2017), in which the latter predominates in neoliberal "entrepreneurial" states that in fact have little public funding to give to SMEs and start-ups and consider an entrepreneur-friendly climate just as deregulation.

In this way, a whole number of critical issues in complex innovation, development, and catching-up processes, such as potentially *destabilizing* effects of just deregulated *open platforms*, unregulated networks effects generating the highly skewed distributions of the power to innovate (e.g., Pairolero, 2018), proper risk reduction, appropriate incentive structures (neither too much nor too little inciting), proper *information flow*, or the famous issue of an appropriate multitude and diversity of often only weakly defined *property forms* in China (e.g., Cao and Gong, 2017), can all be kept within limits, controlled, managed, and apparently turned into a viable, effective, and sustainable working for individuals and the entire socio-economy.

This, in turn, allows for making broad innovation processes work for *inclusive growth*, as often postulated by heterodox and complexity socio-economists who have advocated innovation under a partnership culture, proper *social protection*, *decent work conditions*, and a *regulatory framework* (e.g., Pyke, 2018). This is what China seems to be able to develop while neoliberal financialized capitalism no longer can.

However, the phase of dominant deregulation in China since the late 1970s also entailed a considerable increase of complexity and turbulence, perceived by many as over-complexity and over-turbulence. The unprecedented dynamics, growth, and manifold structural (sectoral, spatial, institutional) change that was triggered in the country was captured, for instance, by the fact that up to approximately 290 million *migrant workers* left their rural villages in the less developed West of the country for the booming Eastern and South-Eastern coastal areas.

The liberal impetus of just "letting go" in that phase combined with the then still quite inflexible institution of the *Hukou* residential registration system, which in fact subsequently dismantled migrant workers from their kin, communities, villages, and towns, and *guanxi* networks – all existentially important for traditional Chinese. Together with the then still largely lacking public health and old-age insurance this caused considerable societal *uprooting*.

One of the macro-social indicators of a widely perceived over-complexity, over-turbulence and stress was a decrease of the level of *general trust* that occurred in China particularly in the 1990s and early 2000.[15] This indicated considerable *social costs* in the interaction "deep structure" of the highly dynamic process that had deliberately been triggered since the late 1970s.

As a high general-trust level is closely correlated with high economic performance, the societal absorption capacity of structural change, and particularly the subjective capacities and willingness to *innovate* (e.g., Elsner and Heinrich, 2009), the entire development of a country may be easily negatively affected in the longer-run by such deep-structure imbalances. China would not have been able to afford just to continue a policy of deregulation and "letting go" with 290 million people directly affected and probably many more family members indirectly.

While not being completely avoidable under given circumstances and while many of the problems and relevant factors have already been addressed in the last decade or so, such experience still raises the question of an improved and better-informed change and innovation policy. This should be complexity-related and thus further qualify the public agent to generate broader innovation cultures and more *inclusive innovation* processes in the future while further *limiting social costs*.

With the now fast *development of the rural Chinese West* and the return of many migrants to their home areas, the *reform of Hukou*, and the fast introduction of general health and pension insurances, the situation has measurably improved and the general trust levels recovered somewhat in the last WVS wave (Dai and Elsner, 2015).

Such recovery of general trust has not just accidentally occurred with the general push of China's economic, societal, ecological, and innovation developments in recent years but must be due to a change to the better of critical conditions of myriad microeconomic interactions. Therefore, the case provides us with a deeper understanding and illustration of the interrelations and mutual impacts of economic and social factors and processes in a complex system. So the policy orientations derived in the preceding do apply in order to avoid "unexpected" social costs of a change too fierce and to better balance factors and conditions for societally most effective innovation processes in the future.

8 Conclusion: toward a better understanding of innovation processes and a qualification of innovation policies

In this chapter, we strived to demonstrate that, as we have to assume the perspective of all modern sciences, namely systemic complexity, the whole idea, conception, causalities, processes, and policies of innovation become much broader, i.e., simultaneously behavioral and technological, genuinely endogenous to the myriad of microeconomic "deep" interaction processes of the system, and less obviously just "good," creating, improving, and enhancing, but more contingent, idiosyncratic, and open.

But from CE and the complexity sciences, we also derived some better-informed innovation-policy orientations, in a systemic, institutional, and "double-interactive" complexity policy (again, e.g., Elsner, 2017), targeting no less than the most basic mechanisms of socio-economies. Such policy will largely be a framework-policy approach, shaping relevant arena sizes and network structures; interaction conditions and institutionalization processes; regulating critical factors; framing cognitive, informational, and "expectational" conditions; and influencing critical factors toward the better, sometimes heavily and lastingly intervening, sometimes only briefly "nudging," as depending on the status and heading of the system.

Such innovation policy must be based on a *superior complexity of the policy system* itself, which then must be able assume more states than the target system while in fact reducing the target system's state space. It must further be based on the state's deeper knowledge and permanent *anticipatory analysis* of the socio-economic target system and its structures and dynamics ("initial," "emerging," and "aimed at"). Qualified government and state action, thus, has to use big data, big computation, modeling, simulations, and algorithms to shape interaction conditions in order to make private agents interactively adapt their behaviors and generate instrumental institutions of cooperation, toward system attractors that are considered superior (for the time being). We have called this "double-interactive" in the sense that it neatly interacts with the interaction systems of the privates, sets its necessary regulations and shapes its favorable conditions, and then relies on adaptive interactions of the private.

It is obvious that this requires a *"strong" and qualified state*, the action capacity of which does not mainly depend on its legal capacity or its monopoly of police, military or court power. Its strength will also depend on a neat analysis of mass behavioral data, permanent *computation*, and prediction of the system. While point predictions have always been the big myth, and failure, of the neoclassical and neoliberal orthodoxy, the perspective will have to switch toward prophylactic stabilization of change processes despite increasing complexity and order while avoiding conformism, petrifaction, and lock-in. This would include a *sufficient pace of change*, avoiding perceived over-turbulence and the system's phase transitions into "deterministic chaos." And the state will have to head for permanent learning and adaptation itself, always being alert to massively and lastingly intervene. Such policy will have to generate no less than the broadest and most *inclusive innovative capacities* of the socio-economic agents. Such policy then will foster broad behavioral *capacities and willingness to innovate*.

Such institutionally oriented complexity-innovation policies have to deploy complexes of measures simultaneously at micro, meso, and macro levels. It will balance *local cultures of change and innovation* with fast *interregional diffusion of knowledge*. Such policy, in the last instance, will balance two permanent trade-offs, between:

- the *change dimension* of the system, i.e., the kind and velocity of systemic dynamics, change, and innovation, ideally an adequate problem-solving/instrumental "*flexibility*," contrasting and avoiding chaotic dynamics and a perceived over-turbulence; and
- the *stability dimension*, diagonal to the change dimension, i.e., the kind and durability of a problem-solving stability under increasing order and complexity, contrasting and avoiding all kinds of "ceremonial" rigidity, institutional petrifactions, or lock-in.

With this, we hope to have provided some deeper understanding of the complexity and contingency of innovation, innovation economics, and innovation policies.

Given the already existing degree of public-action capacity in China, the foundation of its innovation and change policies on a thorough understanding and deliberate shaping of its socio-economic CAS on the awareness of the manifold dynamics, potential evasions, negative unintended consequences, and potential social costs of over-turbulence, could further qualify its long-run development objectives. If, in the foreseeable future, there will be any country in the world able to perform the preceding two-dimensional balancing, a "squaring of the circle," while properly adapting and innovating for socio-economic and ecological improvement, then, as it currently appears, this will be China. The reader will learn a lot more in this volume about one of the largest experiments in human history, setting new pathways of innovation and human development.

Notes

1 I am grateful to the editors of this volume for a number of most helpful comments on an earlier version, which improved the chapter considerably. However, all remaining shortcomings are my responsibility.

2 Note that we do not generally argue against "the market." We consider "markets" decentralized, spontaneous, evolutionary mechanisms, where prices may play some role, working on different possible network topologies and on different interdependence structures (different coordination and dilemma problems). As such, however, they may be anything, good or extremely bad, unless specifically defined in terms of the informal institutions that have emerged in the evolutionary process, and of the formal political/legal institutions/regulations embedding them. Under proper institutional arrangements and political regulations, they may indeed work as devices for some betterment of human conditions. Everything else would be just abstract neoclassical "market" rhetoric and neoliberal "market" ideology. Unless we speak of such a well-defined real-world market, we therefore use this very delicate and ideologically fraught term with quotation marks. Surprisingly enough, we will argue that the well-regulated and embedded market mechanism in China seems to work most effectively for national development.

3 Note that our consideration here is methodological: in a formal complex modeling and computational simulation, we would have to define initial sizes and structures, but usually also would reach conclusions about which sizes and kinds of structures, be it network topologies or learned social institutions, may emerge in the evolutionary process (e.g., Elsner, 2017).

4 We will explain below the difference between a simpler initial "common" coordination problem and a more intricate and demanding initial "collective" dilemma problem, and their emergent solutions, a coordinating social rule and a cooperation-providing social institution.

5 We should stress that systemic "lock-ins" usually have their microeconomic correspondence in some gained agents' coordination or cooperation, also to be considered a technical/behavioral standardization. Note that "lock-in," in the original simple modeling (e.g., Arthur, 1989), just had the neutral (rather than negative), and purely technical, connotation of a cumulative process leading the system into a (stable) fixed point (attractor), where it cannot break out from by itself. While microeconomic coordination/cooperation is an achievement with some systemic stabilization effect, this by no means determines that such stabilization takes place at some superior (nor inferior) attractor.

6 Note that we use the following terminology (see also note 4): a coordination problem is modeled as a coordination game, where the solution is realized coordination, which in turn is just a common problem as it requires just parallel behavior, and coordination is in everyone's immediate short-run (hyper-rational) interest; so the tool for solution (coordination) is just a learned social rule, which is difficult enough. A collective-good or social-dilemma problem is more intricate, as defection is in everybody's hyper-rational interest. The solution thus requires a learned and habituated sacrifice of the short-run maximum in favor of the longer-run Pareto-superior solution (and potential new Nash equilibrium). This situation is considered a collective problem, and the solution is called cooperation. Cooperation thus is coordination plus a sacrifice. The latter can be realized among "rational" agents only through a credible threat of a sanctioning through some cooperative but responsive (trigger) strategy, a threat of retaliation and of joint setback to the short-run Nash equilibrium. The tool for this we call a social institution, i.e., a social rule plus (a credible threat of an) endogenous sanction to generate the sacrifice of the short-run maximum. This terminology has long been established (e.g., Schotter, 1981; Axelrod, 1984/2006).

7 On the formal side of this expectation, see section 6.

8 See note 5.

9 Again, for more detail, see section 6.
10 For a formal illustration, again, see section 6.
11 See note 6.
12 Note that not simply a maximum memory length is required. But there may be evolutionarily advantageous combinations of both proper memory and forgetfulness under different levels of stability or turbulence (e.g., Dosi et al., 2017).
13 E.g., Dai and Liu, 2017 on e-mobility. On examples of such "agile production innovation" in China also Dai and Yang, 2017.
14 Also, again, see the chapters throughout this volume for many more aspects, theory, and evidence, and much more detail.
15 *World Values Survey* (WVS) data, for instance, showed an approximately 10%–point decline in so-called general trust from 1990 to 2007 in terms of yes-answers to the question: "Generally speaking, would you say that most people can be trusted or that you need to be very careful in dealing with people?" With another WVS question, "How much do you trust people you meet for the first time?" answers showed a 5%–point drop from 2007 to 2012 still (for more detail, e.g., Dai and Elsner, 2015).

References

Acemoglu, D., A. Ozdaglar and A. Tahbaz-Salehi (2017) "Microeconomic Origins of Macroeconomic Tail Risks." *American Economic Review* 107: 54–108.

Albin, P. S. and D. K. Foley (1992) "Decentralized, Dispersed Exchange without an Auctioneer: A Simulation Study." *Journal of Economic Behavior & Organization* 18(1): 27–52.

Antonelli, C. (2017a) *The Evolutionary Complexity of Endogenous Innovation: The Engines of the Creative Response*, Cheltenham, UK and Northampton, MA: Edward Elgar.

Antonelli, C. (2017b) *Endogenous Innovation: The Economics of an Emergent System Property*, Cheltenham, UK and Northampton, MA: Edward Elgar.

Arrow, K. J. and G. Debreu (1954) "Existence of an Equilibrium for a Competitive Economy." *Econometrica* 22: 265–290.

Arthur, W. B. (1989) "Competing Technologies, Increasing Returns, and Lock-in by Historical Events." *Economic Journal* 99: 116–131.

Ashby, W. R. (1956) *An Introduction to Cybernetics*, London, UK: Chapman & Hall.

Aspara, J., K. Pajunen, H. Tikkanen and R. Tainio (2014) "Explaining Corporate Short-Termism: Self-Reinforcing Processes and Biases among Investors, the Media and Corporate Managers." *Socio-Economic Review* 12(4): 667–693.

Axelrod, R. (1984) *The Evolution of Cooperation* (2nd ed.), New York: Basic Books, 2006.

Bak, P., C. Tang and K. Wiesenfeld (1987) "Self-Organized Criticality: An Explanation of 1/f Noise." *Physical Review Letters* 59(4): 381–384.

Barabási, A.-L. (2002) *Linked: The New Science of Networks*, Cambridge, MA: Perseus Publishing.

Barabási, A-L. and R. Albert (1999) "Emergence of Scaling in Random Networks." *Science* 284(5439): 509–512.

Battiston, S., G. R. Caldarelli, T. Roukny and J. E. Stiglitz (2015) "The Price of Complexity in Financial Networks." Available at http://papers.ssrn.com/sol3/papers.cfm?abstract_id=2594028 (accessed January 20, 2017).

Battiston, S., S. Vitali and J. B. Glattfelder (2011) "The Network of Global Corporate Control." *PLoS One* 6(10): e25995. Available at https://doi.org/10.1371/journal.pone.0025995 (accessed December 27, 2017).

Bednar, J., A. Jones-Rooy and S. E. Page (2015) "Choosing a Future Based on the Past: Institutions, Behavior, and Path-Dependence." *European Journal of Political Economy* 40: 312–332.

Beinhocker, E. (2012) "New Economics, Policy and Politics." T. Dolphin and D. Nash (eds.), *Complex New World: Translating New Economic Thinking into Public Policy*, London, UK: Institute for Public Policy Research, 134–146.

Bianconi, G. and C. Rahmede (2015) "Complex Quantum Network Manifolds in Dimension *d*>2 are Scale-Free." *Nature: Scientific Reports* 5: 13979. Available at doi:10.1038/srep139791 (accessed November 26, 2018).

Biggs, R., M. Schlueter and M. Schoon (2015) *Principles for Building Resilience*, Cambridge, UK: Cambridge University Press.

Bloom, N., P. Aghion, R. Blundell, R. Griffith and P. Howitt (2005) "Competition and Innovation: An Inverted U Relationship." *Quarterly Journal of Economics* 120(2): 701–728.

Boudreau, K. J., N. Lacetera and K. R. Lakhani (2008) "Parallel Search, Incentives and Problem Type: Revisiting the Competition and Innovation Link." Working Paper No. 09–041, Harvard Business School. Available at https://pdfs.semanticscholar.org/1687/4121bea49c69b7fd8252f83546271df02f08.pdf (accessed November 30, 2018).

Bush, P. D. (1999) "Recognized Interdependence." P. A. O'Hara (ed.), *Encyclopedia of Political Economy*, 2: 963–964, London, UK: Routledge.

Cao, X. and J. Gong (2017) "The Tradeoff of the Commons under Stochastic Use." *Journal of Public Economics* 145(1): 150–161.

Cetrulo, A., V. Cirillo and D. Guarascio (2018) "Weaker Jobs, Weaker Innovation: Exploring the Temporary Employment-Product Innovation Nexus." ISI Growth Working Paper 6/2018.

Chang, H-J. (2002) *Kicking Away the Ladder: Development Strategy in Historical Perspective*, London and New York: Anthem Press.

Chen, P. (2010) *Economic Complexity and Equilibrium Illusion: Essays on Market Instability and Macro Vitality*, London and New York: Routledge.

Chen, Z., Z. Wu and S. Xie (2000) *The Extent of Marketization of Economic Systems in China*, Huntington, NY: Nova Science Publishers.

Christensen, C. (1997) *The Innovator's Dilemma: When New Technologies Cause Great Firms to Fail*, Cambridge, MA: Harvard University Press.

Clement, J. and P. Puranam (2018) "Searching for Structure: Formal Organization Design as a Guide to Network Evolution." *Management Science* 64(8): 3879–3895.

Coad, A., P. Nightingale, J. Stilgoe and A. Vezzani (2018) "The Dark Side of Innovation." Special Issue Call for Papers for *Industry and Innovation*. Available at http://explore.tandfonline.com/cfp/bes/ciai-si-dark-side-of-innovation (accessed November 22, 2018).

Colander, D. and R. Kupers (2014) *Complexity and the Art of Public Policy: Solving Society's Problems from the Bottom Up*, Princeton, NJ: Princeton University Press.

Commons, J. R. (1934) *Institutional Economics: Its Place in Political Economy*, New York: Palgrave Macmillan (reprint New Brunswick, NJ: Transaction Publ., 1990).

Corak, M. (2013) "Income Inequality, Equality of Opportunity, and Intergenerational Mobility." *Journal of Economic Perspectives* 27(3): 79–102.

Dai, S. and W. Elsner (2015) "Declining Trust in Growing China." Working Papers in East-Asian Studies 101, University of Duisburg-Essen. Available at www.econstor.eu/bitstream/10419/109976/1/823908763.pdf (accessed December 27, 2017).

Dai, S. and G. Liu (2017) "Emergence of New Products and Agile Innovation in a Catching-up Economy: Evidence from the Low-speed Electric Vehicle Industry in the Shandong Province, China." Presentation at the 2017 EAEPE Annual Conference, Budapest, October.

Dai, S. and G. Yang (2017) "Does Social Inducement Lead to Higher Open Innovation Investment? An Experimental Study." Working Papers on East Asian Studies 112, University of Duisburg-Essen. Available at www.uni-due.de/imperia/md/content/in-east/about/publications_green_series/paper112-2017.pdf (accessed December 18, 2017).

David, P. A. (1985) "Clio and the Economics of QWERTY." *American Economic Review P&P* 75(2): 332–337.

Debreu, G. (1974) "Excess Demand Functions." *Journal of Mathematical Economics* 1(1): 15–21.

Dessi, R. and X. Zhao (2017) "Overconfidence, Stability and Investments." *Journal of Economic Behavior & Organization* 145: 474–494.

Dosi, G., L. Marengo, E. Paraskevopoulou and M. Valente (2017) "A Model of Cognitive and Operational Memory of Organizations in Changing Worlds." *Cambridge Journal of Economics* 41(3): 775–806.

Dosi, G., M. C. Pereira, A. Roventini and M. E. Vergillito (2018) "What if Supply-Side Policies Are Not Enough? The Perverse Interaction of Flexibility and Austerity." ISI Growth Working Paper 1/2018. Available at www.isigrowth.eu/2018/01/09/what-if-supply-side-policies-are-not-enough-the-perverse-interaction-of-flexibility-and-austerity/ (accessed May 15, 2018).

Dunbar, R. I. M. (1993) "Co-Evolution of Neocortex Size, Group Size and Language in Humans." *Behavioral and Brain Sciences* 16(4): 681–735.

Dunbar, R. I. M. (2008) "Cognitive Constraints on the Structure and Dynamics of Social Networks." *Group Dynamics: Theory, Research, and Practice* 12(1): 7–16.

Elsner, W. (1989) "Adam Smith's Model of the Origins and Emergence of Institutions: The Modern Findings of the Classical Approach." *Journal of Economic Issues* 23(1): 189–213.

Elsner, W. (2012) "The Theory of Institutional Change Revisited: The Institutional Dichotomy, Its Dynamic, and Its Policy Implications in a More Formal Analysis." *Journal of Economic Issues* 46(1): 1–43.

Elsner, W. (2017) "Complexity Economics as Heterodoxy: Theory and Policy." *Journal of Economic Issues* 51(4): 939–978.

Elsner, W. and T. Heinrich (2009) "A Simple Theory of 'Meso': On the Coevolution of Institutions and Platform Size." *Journal of Socio-Economics* 38: 843–858.

Epstein, J. and R. Axtell (1996) *Growing Artificial Societies: Social Science from the Bottom Up*, Cambridge, MA: The MIT Press.

Fontana, M. (2012) "Policy in Complex Social Systems." P. Heritier and P. Silvestri (eds.), *Good Government, Governance, Human Complexity*. Firenze, I: L.S. Olschki, 221–233.

Fontana, M. (2013) "Pluralism(s) in Economics: Lessons from Complexity and Innovation." *Journal of Evolutionary Economics* 24(1): 189–204.

Fu, T. (2017) "What Determines Firms' Access to Credit in the Absence of Effective Economic Institutions: Evidence from China?" *Economics* 11(2017–31). Available at http://dx.doi.org/10.5018/economics-ejournal.ja.2017-31 (accessed November 30, 2018).

Gallegati, M., A. Kirman and A. Palestrini (2007) "Implications of Scaling Laws for Policy-Makers." M. Salzano and D. Colander (eds.), *Complexity Hints for Economic Policy*, New York, NY: Springer, 291–302.

Garcia-Vega, M. and E. Huergo (2017) "Trust and Technology Transfers." *Journal of Economic Behavior & Organization* 142(C): 92–104.

Georgescu-Roegen, N. (1975) "Energy and Economic Myths." *Southern Economic Journal* 41(3): 347–381.

Geyer, R. and P. Cairney (2015) *Handbook on Complexity and Public Policy*, Cheltenham, UK and Northampton, MA: Edward Elgar.

Geyer, R. and S. Rihani (2010) *Complexity and Public Policy: A New Approach to Twenty-First Century Politics, Policy and Society*, London, UK: Routledge.

Gilles, R., E. Lazarova and P. Ruys (2015) "Stability in a Network Economy: The Role of Institutions." *Journal of Economic Behavior & Organization* 119: 375–399.

Glaeser, E. L., D. Laibson and B. Sacerdote (2002) "An Economic Approach to Social Capital." *Economic Journal* 112(483): F437–F458.

Godin, B. and D. Vinck (2017) *Critical Studies of Innovation: Alternative Approaches to the Pro-Innovation Bias*, Cheltenham, UK and Northampton, MA: Edward Elgar.

Goerner, S. (2017) "The Science of Flow Says Extreme Inequality Causes Economic Collapse." *Evonomics*. Available at http://evonomics.com/science-flow-says-extreme-inequality-causes-economic-collapse/ (accessed September 1, 2017).

Grant, D. and L. B. Moses (2017) *Technology and the Trajectory of Myth*, Cheltenham, UK and Northampton, MA: Edward Elgar.

Güth, W., S. Berninghaus and S. Bleich (2013) "The Consequences of (De)Regulation on Employment Duration and Efficiency-An Experimental Study." *Economic Inquiry* 51(1): 1050–1065.

Heinrich, T. (2013) *Technological Change and Network Effects in Growth Regimes: Exploring the Microfoundations of Economic Growth*, London and New York: Routledge.

Heinrich, T. (2016) "Evolution-Based Approaches in Economics and Evolutionary Loss of Information." *Journal of Economic Issues* 50(2): 390–397.

Heinrich, T. (2018a) "A Discontinuity Model of Technological Change: Catastrophe Theory and Network Structure." *Computational Economics* 51(3): 407–425.

Heinrich, T. (2018b) "The Rate of Change in Evolutionary Systems and Evolutionary Economic Modeling." *Journal of Economic Issues* 52(2): 570–579.

Heinrich, T. and H. Schwardt (2013) "Institutional Inertia and Institutional Change in an Expanding Normal-Form Game." *Games* 4: 398–425.

Helbing, D. (2013) "Globally Networked Risks and how to Respond." *Nature* 497: 51–59.

Herrmann-Pillath, C. (2017) *China's Economic Culture: The Ritual Order of State and Markets*, London and New York: Routledge.

Herrmann-Pillath, C. (2018) "The Case for a New Discipline: Technosphere Science." *Ecological Economics* 149: 212–225.

Hodgson, G. (2002) "Reconstitutive Downward Causation: Social Structure and the Development of Individual Agency." E. Fullbrook (ed.), *Intersubjectivity in Economics: Agents and Structures*, London and New York: Routledge, 159–180. Available at www.isigrowth.eu/2018/02/17/weaker-jobs-weaker-innovation-exploring-the-temporary-employment-product-innovation-nexus/ (accessed May 15, 2018).

Jayasinghe, P. (2017) "On Micro foundations of Macroeconomics." *Real-World Economics Review* 82: 60–75. Available at www.paecon.net/PAEReview/issue82/Jayasingh82.pdf (accessed November 30, 2018).

Jennings, F. (2005) "How Efficiency/Equity Trade-offs Resolve through Horizon Effects." *Journal of Economic Issues* 39(2): 365–373.

Kauffman, S. A. (1993) *The Origins of Order Self-Organization and Selection in Evolution*, New York: Oxford University Press.

Kauffman, S. A., D. Farmer, R. V. Solée, S. Valverde, M. R. Casals and N. Eldredge (2013) "The Evolutionary Ecology of Technological Innovations." *Complexity* 18(4): 15–27.

Kendall, G., X. Yao and S. Y. Chong (2007) *The Iterated Prisoner's Dilemma: 20 Years On*, Singapore: World Scientific.

Keynes, J. M. (1936) *The General Theory of Employment, Interest and Money*, London: Palgrave Macmillan (reprinted 2007).

Kingston, W. (2017) *How Capitalism Destroyed Itself: Technology Displaced by Financial Innovation*, Cheltenham, UK and Northampton, MA: Edward Elgar.

Kirman, A. P. (1992) "Whom or What Does the Representative Individual Represent?" *Journal of Economic Perspectives* 6(2): 117–136.

Kleinknecht, A., Z. Kwee and L. Budyanto (2016) "Rigidities through Flexibility: Flexible Labour and the Rise of Management Bureaucracies." *Cambridge Journal of Economics* 40(4): 1137–1147.

Komlos, J. (2016) "Has Creative Destruction become More Destructive?" *The B.E. Journal of Economic Analysis & Policy* 16(4): 1–12.

Langley, G. and J. Tulloch (2017) "Capitalism's Creation Myth Revisited." Available at https://projectm-online.com/risk/capitalisms-creative-destruction/ (accessed December 27, 2017).

Lin, J. Y. (2017) "Lessons from China's and East Asia's Catch Up: The New Structural Economics Perspective." V. Popov and P. Dutkiewicz (eds.), *Mapping a New World Order: The Rest beyond the West*, Cheltenham, UK and Northampton, MA: Edward Elgar, 53–70.

Lindgren, K. (1989) "Evolutionary Dynamics in Game-Theoretic Models." W. B. Arthur, S. Durlauf and D. Lane (eds.), *The Economy as an Evolving Complex System II*, Reading, MA: Addison-Wesley, 337–367.

Lipsey, R. G. and K. J. Lancaster (1956) "The General Theory of Second Best." *Review of Economic Studies* 24(1): 11–32.

List, F. (1841) *Das Nationale System der Politischen Ökonomie*, Stuttgart and Tübingen: Cotta'scher Verlag.

Loasby. B. (2012) "Building Systems." *Journal of Evolutionary Economics* 22(4): 833–846.

Lueders, M., T. W. Andreassen, S. Clatworthy and T. Hillestad (2017) *Innovating for Trust*, Cheltenham, UK and Northampton, MA: Edward Elgar.

Lux, T. and M. Marchesi (1999) "Scaling and Criticality in a Stochastic Multi-Agent Model of a Financial Market." *Nature* 397: 498–500.

Mandelbrot, B. and R. L. Hudson (2006) *The Misbehavior of Markets: A Fractal View of Financial Turbulence*, New York: Basic Books.

Mantel, R. R. (1976) "Homothetic Preferences and Community Excess Demand Functions." *Journal of Economic Theory* 12(2): 197–201.

Marlowe, F. W. (2005) "Hunter-Gatherers and Human Evolution." *Evolutionary Anthropology* 14: 54–67.

Marshall, A. (1890) *Principles of Economics* (8th ed.), London: Palgrave Macmillan, 1920.

Masiliunas, A. (2017) "Overcoming Coordination Failure in a Critical Mass Game: Strategic Motives and Action Disclosure." *Journal of Economic Behavior & Organization* 139: 214–251.

May, R. M. (1976) "Simple Mathematical Models with Very Complicated Dynamics." *Nature* 261(5560): 459–467.

Mazzucato, M. (2013) *The Entrepreneurial State: Debunking Public vs: Private Sector Myths*, London and New York: Anthem Press.

Mazzucato, M. (2016) "Innovation Policy as Creating Markets, Not Only Fixing Them: Implications for Complexity Theory." D. S. Wilson and A. Kirman (eds.), *Complexity and Evolution: Towards a New Synthesis for Economics*, Cambridge, MA and London: The MIT Press, 271–284.

McKelvey, M. and J. Jin (eds.) (2018) *Innovative Capabilities and the Globalization of Chinese Firms: Becoming a Leader in Innovation Spaces*, Cheltenham, UK and Northampton, MA: Edward Elgar.

Milonakis, D. (2017) "Formalising Economics: Social Change, Values, Mechanics and Mathematics in Economic Discourse." *Cambridge Journal of Economics* 41(5): 1367–1390.

Mirowski, P. (1989) *More Heat than Light: Economics as Social Physics, Physics as Nature's Economics*, Cambridge, UK: Cambridge University Press.

Mulgan, G. (2017) "Cognitive Economics: How Self-Organization and Collective Intelligence Works." *Evonomics*. Available at http://evonomics.com/cognitive-economics-intelligence-mulgan/ (accessed December 27, 2017).

Nowak, M. (2006) *Evolutionary Dynamics: Exploring the Equations of Life*, Cambridge, MA: Harvard University Press.

O'Boyle, B. and T. McDonough (2017) "Bourgeois Ideology and Mathematical Economics – A Reply to Tony Lawson." *Economic Thought* 6(1): 16–34.

OECD (2009) *Applications of Complexity Science for Public Policy: New Tools for Finding Unanticipated Consequences and Unrealized Opportunities*, Paris: OECD.

OECD (2011) *Divided We Stand: Why Inequality Keeps Rising*, Paris: OECD.

OECD (2017) *Debate the Issues: Complexity and Policy Making*, P. Love and J. Stockdale-Otárola (eds.), Paris: OECD.

Ormerod, P. (2012) "Networks and the Need for a New Approach to Policymaking." T. Dolphin and D. Nash (eds.), *A Complex New World: Translating New Economic Thinking into Public Policy*, London: Institute for Public Policy Research, 28–38.

Page, S. (2012) "A Complexity Perspective on Institutional Design." *Politics, Philosophy & Economics* 11(1): 5–25.

Pairolero, N. A. (2018) "Inventor Innovative Inequality in Software Technologies." Available at https://papers.ssrn.com/sol3/papers.cfm?abstract_id=3185727 (accessed November 22, 2018).

Pareto, V. (1897) *Cours d'Économie Politique*, Leipzig: Duncker & Humblot.

Payson, S. (2017) *How Economics Professors Can Stop Failing Us: The Discipline at a Crossroads*, Lanham, Boulder, New York and London: Lexington/Rowman & Littlefield.

Pogach, J. (2018) "Short-Termism of Executive Compensation." *Journal of Economic Behavior & Organization* 148: 150–170.

Polanyi, K. (1944) *The Great Transformation: The Political and Economic Origins of Our Time*, New York: Farrar & Rinehart (reprint Boston, MA: Beacon, 2001).

Pyke, F. (2018) "Managing Technological Change for Inclusive Growth." *Cambridge Journal of Economics* 42(6): 1687–1695.

Radzicki, M. J. (1990) "Institutional Dynamics, Deterministic Chaos, and Self-Organizing Systems." *Journal of Economic Issues* 24(1): 57–102.

Rasmus, J. (2016) *Systemic Fragility in the Global Economy*, Atlanta, GA: Clarity Press.

Robins, F. (2010) "China: A *new* Kind of 'mixed' Economy?" *Asian Business & Management* 9(1): 23–46.

Room, G. (2011) *Complexity, Institutions and Public Policy: Agile Decision-Making in a Turbulent World*, Cheltenham, UK and Northampton, MA: Edward Elgar.

Ruth, M. and S. Goessling-Reisemann (eds.) (2018) *Handbook on Resilience of Socio-Technical Systems*, Cheltenham, UK and Northampton, MA: Edward Elgar.

Salzano, M. and D. Colander (eds.) (2007) *Complexity Hints for Economic Policy*, Milan: Springer.

Sautua, S. I. (2017) "Does Uncertainty Cause Inertia in Decision Making? An Experimental Study on the Role of Regret Aversion and Indecisiveness." *Journal of Economic Behavior & Organization* 136: 1–14.

Schlossberger, J. (2017) "The Network Topology of Locally Interacting Agents and System-Level Distributions of Agent Actions." Available at https://papers.ssrn.com/sol3/papers.cfm?abstract_id=3085658 (accessed January 24, 2018).

Schotter, A. (1981) *The Economic Theory of Social Institutions*, Cambridge, UK: Cambridge University Press.

Schrepel, T. (2017) "Predatory Innovation: The Definite Need for Legal Recognition." Available at https://papers.ssrn.com/sol3/papers.cfm?abstract_id=2986246 (accessed December 27, 2017).

Sen, A. K. (1974) "Choice, Ordering and Morality." S. Korner (ed.), *Practical Reason*, Oxford, UK: Blackwell.

Sen, A. K. (1977) "Rational Fools: A Critique of the Behavioral Foundations of Economic Theory." *Philosophy & Public Affairs* 6(4): 317–344.

Simon, H. (1955) "A Behavioral Model of Rational Choice." *The Quarterly Journal of Economics* 69(1): 99–118.

Simon, H. (1962) "The Architecture of Complexity." *Proceedings of the American Philosophical Society* 106: 467–482.

Solari, S. and F. Gambarotto (2014) "Territorial Rooting as an Element of Wellbeing." *Review of Social Economy* 72(4): 504–522.

Sonnenschein, H. (1973) "Do Walras' Identity and Continuity Characterize the Class of Community Excess Demand Functions?" *Journal of Economic Theory* 6(4): 345–354.

Sraffa, P. (1926) "The Laws of Returns under Competitive Conditions." *The Economic Journal* 36(144): 535–550.

Swann, G. M. P. (2015) *Common Innovation: How We Create the Wealth of Nations*, Cheltenham, UK and Northampton, MA: Edward Elgar.

Tainter, J. A., D. Strumsky, T. G. Taylor, M. Arnold and J. Lobo (2018) "Depletion vs. Innovation: The Fundamental Question of Sustainability." R. Burlando and A. Tartaglia (eds.), *Physical Limits to Economic Growth*, London and New York: Routledge, 64–93.

Taleb, N. (2007) *The Black Swan: The Impact of the Highly Improbable*, London and New York: Penguin Books.

Veblen, T. B. (1899) *The Theory of the Leisure Class: An Economic Study of Institutions*, New York: Palgrave Macmillan.

Vega-Redondo, F. (2013) "Network Organizations." *Journal of Complex Networks* 1: 72–82.

Velupillai, V. (ed.) (2005) *Computability, Complexity and Constructivity in Economic Analysis*, Hoboken, NJ: Wiley Blackwell.

Velupillai, V. (2007) "The Impossibility of an Effective Theory of Policy in a Complex Economy." M. Salzano and D. Colander (eds.), *Complexity Hints for Economic Policy*, New York: Springer, 273–290.

Von Schomberg, R. and J. Hankins (eds.) (2018) *Handbook on Responsible Innovation*, Cheltenham, UK and Northampton, MA: Edward Elgar.

Watts, D. (1999) *Small Worlds: The Dynamics of Networks between Order and Randomness*, Princeton, NJ: Princeton University Press.

Wilson, D. S. (2016) "Two Meanings of Complex Adaptive Systems." D. S. Wilson and A. Kirman (eds.), *Complexity and Evolution. Toward a New Synthesis for Economics*, Cambridge, MA and London: The MIT Press, 31–46.

Young, A. A. (1928) "Increasing Returns and Economic Progress." *The Economic Journal* 38: 527–542.

2 Technology, social beliefs, and national system of innovation policies

Reflections on China's innovation policies after 2006

Shuanping Dai, Aleksandra Davydova, Yang Liu

1 Introduction

The "National Guidelines for the Medium- and Long-Term Plan for Science and Technology Development (2006–2020)" (No. 20051231. For simplicity, hereafter we code the policies referred to according to their date of publication. For details, see Appendix 2-A) and the "Decision on Implementing the Outline of the Scientific and Technological Plan and Enhancing Independent Innovation Capacity" (No. 20060126) are the landmark documents in China's innovation transformation. Prior to their implementation, government and firms adhered to the conventional way of importing, introducing, and imitating. They did not place great emphasis on indigenous innovation, doing so in order to enhance export products with higher technological value added faster. After having become a member of the World Trade Organization (WTO), China has had to abide by international rules and reduce illegal imitation. Furthermore, with the expansion and upgrade of trade and structural change at home, the former strategies no longer work well, and China must now enhance its own innovative capacity and competitive performance via a new strategy for innovation.

This stark transformation to indigenous innovation has attracted considerable interest from scholars – such as Liu et al. (2011) and Sun and Liu (2014) – who wish to understand, examine, and evaluate China's innovation policies. In terms of policymaking, China has experience in coordinating a portfolio of innovation policies such as science and technology (S&T) ones and industrial, financial, tax, and fiscal measures between ministries – rather than it heavily depending on the efforts of the Ministry of Science and Technology (MoST) (Liu et al., 2011). As a result of these efforts, China has successfully mobilized resources for S&T and consequently improved its performance in patent application and scientific publication, for instance – and on an unprecedented scale and with exceptional speed (OECD, 2008). Yet some necessary institutions that market-led innovation depends on still perform inadequately, such as those related to corporate governance, the research and development (R&D) financing system, technology-based entrepreneurship, and the enforcement of intellectual property rights (IPR) (OECD, 2008). Furthermore, it is a much more difficult task to establish an enterprise-based innovation system taking top-down approaches. Hence, the reforms within state-owned enterprises (SOEs) and public research institutes, which are considered to be the major strategic groups for improving China's innovation capacity, should be more fundamental still – even despite the impressive achievements that have already been realized in the country's policy realms (Hutschenreiter and Zhang, 2007).

With the increasing government efforts vis-à-vis innovation, most scholarly attention has focused on the topics of innovation outcomes – for example Boeing et al. (2016) and Guan and Yam (2015). However, with the exception of Benner et al. (2012) – who investigates priority setting in China's research policies and find that this is the interactive result of top-down decision making, with a response mechanism from the bottom up – little attention has been paid to how the central government sets different goals, agendas, and priorities in its policies. In order to fill this knowledge gap in a general sense, this chapter will review 83 of China's innovation policies published at the national level (i.e. by the State Council) since 2006. It will also take a close look at how these innovation policies evolve, and furthermore how the central government gradually has established and improved China's national innovation system.

We manually collected the policies of immediate relevance to technological innovation and national innovation strategy from the State Council's homepage on the internet, and calibrated our collection through the policy set published by the MoST. Due to the limitations of this aim setting, this chapter will therefore not evaluate and predict the effects of these policies – but applies instead a framework proposed by Dai (2016) for a national system of innovation policies, a subsystem of the national innovation system (NIS, hereafter), to review these. The general idea of this framework is to classify innovation policies into three groups: Policy I, which includes the immediate policies for S&T; Policy II, which refers to the set of policies that provide ancillary institutional support for Policy I; and Policy III, which is the core indicator by which to identify a national system of innovation policies and functions as the coordination mechanism within and between Policies I and II. Policy III is also a cognitive mechanism by which the actors involved can understand policies in a homogeneous way, which is reflected in the common tags of those generated by these actors.

The remaining parts of this chapter will be organized as follows. The next section will briefly introduce the "national system of innovation policies" review framework. On this basis, the third section will then summarize China's innovation policies implemented at the national level since the seminal indigenous innovation transformation strategy announced in 2006. This may provide us with a clear and comprehensive picture of how China's innovation policies across three levels have evolved since then. The fourth section will draw attention to some of the specific and most significant aspects of the policies' evolution, in order to understand the system of innovation policies in the context of China's NIS. The final section sets out our conclusions.

2 A framework of national system of innovation policies

For reviewing Chinese innovation policies, we suggest a comprehensive framework that reveals the interactive properties between them in the process of innovation (Dai, 2016). This suggested framework reflects better than conventional approaches (see, e.g., Edquist, 2006) do the modern reality of interconnectedness and interdependence between markets, actors, and the NIS, and adds a cognitive perspective to deal with how the policies systematically work. It refers to the relationship between the innovation process and innovation-related actors' behavior and cognition (Dai, 2016). Therefore, the framework for innovation policies comprises the following groups thereof: (Policy I) those that focus on specific areas of S&T; (Policy II) those that provide the necessary conditions for innovation activities; and, (Policy III) those that help actors, and in particular innovators, to have common cognition of Policies I and II, and to coordinate actors' shared understanding of them both.

Policy I represents a set of immediate policies for S&T. It reflects the initial attitude toward the NIS, which puts the S&T policies at the center of analysis (Lundvall, 1992). This group of policies covers regulatory measures, such as patent regulation, economic instruments, such as tax incentives for R&D, and direct investment support for research organizations. It also addresses other measures, such as creating technical standards and codes of conducts for firms operating in S&T fields (Borras and Edquist, 2013). These policies aim to correct market failures and encourage companies to invest in S&T (Dai, 2016). Thus, such policies help to generate new technologies and to enhance companies' learning, absorption, and innovation capacities (Metcalfe, 1995).

The Policy II set provides ancillary institutional support for Policy I. The effectiveness of measures that immediately target S&T activities is highly dependent on a favorable institutional environment being in place (Freeman, 1995). Policies not targeted directly at innovation are also very important for innovation development (Paraskevopoulou, 2012). Policy II therefore includes measures for economic market and competition regulation, labor market and human resources development, and public policies (Lundvall et al., 2002) as well. The main aim of these Policy II measures is to make Policy I successful under specific institutional conditions. Policy II provides innovators with adequate conditions for the implementation of Policy I measures, and encourages them to share their innovation resources voluntarily in order to improve the performance quality of innovation activities (Dai, 2016). Moreover, regulations in other policy fields may provide additional incentives for innovation. For example, in a situation where environmental policy bans some chemicals from being used in manufacturing then related firms are indirectly motivated to look for alternative solutions and are encouraged to technologically innovate so as to adjust to the regulations (Borras and Edquist, 2013). Thus, Policy II affects not only the process of innovation but also its integration and diffusion in the country's economy and society.

Policy III concerns two main aspects, specifically the coordination mechanism between policies and cognition of them. The coordination mechanism relates, first, to the idea of connecting Policies I and II in an appropriate way

(Dai, 2016) and, second, to coordinating and integrating policies between policy domains, as suggested in the "third generation of innovation policy" by the OECD (2005). Thus, Policy III concerns the creation of a specific mechanism for managing the complexity of innovation policies (Magro and Wilson, 2013). In general, different policies issued by the government are interrelating, and then the interconnectedness of the policies may produce results that differ from initial aims, without thoughtful coordination (Magro and Wilson, 2013). In addition, innovation policies are not always consciously chosen and designed but are dependent, for example, on lobbying activities, rather than on the evaluation of existing needs and objectives (Borras and Edquist, 2013). In the process of innovation policy creation and implementation, therefore, various problems and failures of coordination can occur (Magro and Zabala-Iturriagagoitia, 2014). A specific coordination mechanism being reflected in Policy III should help to overcome these two issues.

The idea behind the cognition aspect of Policy III is to provide innovation-related actors with as many shared tags for innovation policies as possible (Dai, 2016). Tags of policies reflect the attributes of the latter within certain underlying problem settings under individual subjective explorations (Dai, 2015). Shared tags for innovation policies are "R&D," "novelty," or "education" for example (Dai, 2016). Nevertheless, as we know from the institutional approach, policies might be interpreted differently depending on how actors pursue and understand them (Beckert, 2010). Thus, one person might have a somewhat shallow understanding of innovation and associate it with "improvement," "change," or even "imitation"; while for somebody else, innovation has a much deeper meaning and includes tags such as "open innovation" and "complexity" (Dai, 2016).

As another example, IPR protection may be a promising tool for people to formulate a perception of innovation's value and coordinate their behavior toward others' IPR; innovation will be respected and protected properly, with little violation of others' interests if the IPR laws are perfectly implemented. The idea behind Policy III is to provide shared tags of policies to make the structure of the innovation policy system more homogeneous and to eliminate any interaction problems in the design and implementation of innovation policies. Policymaking must therefore create channels and platforms for agents to learn, apply, and produce policy-relevant knowledge (OECD, 2005). We consider these policies to be especially important for long-term national innovation capacity development and for the identification of a NIS. In general, they contribute to the national value of innovation, to the coordinated cognition of innovative activities, and to the general innovative environment (Dai, 2016).

3 China's policies for establishing indigenous innovation

In this section, we highlight the main aspects of national-level innovation policies implemented in China between 2006 and 2017. The analysis is exploiting 72 related policy documents. We will not address all of these in detail, but instead will provide a general overview of the different policies' content – therein referring to the major features of Policies I, II, and III earlier outlined.

3.1 Policy I

According to the proposed framework, Policy I refers to the immediate measures for S&T. In the course of China's innovation development, the government has come up with a great many direct policies in order to boost S&T–related progress. First, the Chinese government has provided comprehensive numerical targets for S&T – such as for R&D, citation ranks, research centers and laboratories, patents, and so on – in order to achieve the goal of indigenous innovation. Policy No. 20051231 and No. 20160728 set aims, such as increasing national gross expenditure on R&D to 2.5% of gross domestic product (GDP), raising the S&T contribution to economic growth to more than 60%, reducing the dependence on imported technology by 30%, and increasing China's international science paper citation and ranking in patents granted to being the top five in the world by 2020. Policy No. 20111230 set, among other things, such indicators as the number of company-owned patents to double by 2015, which will be doubled again by 2020 according to No. 20160728. One hundred national engineering centers and several new national engineering and first-class science and research laboratories were to be built and a series of innovative companies to have entered the global top 500 by 2015, according to Policy No. 20130115.

Second, the Chinese government has supported and motivated domestic companies to innovate. To this end, the government has provided tax and financial incentives and has been actively involved in procurement and developing talents for S&T–related fields. Some of the tax incentives include before-income tax deductions, the accelerated depreciation of R&D equipment, and reduced import duties and value-added tax (VAT) exemption for S&T development products and key equipment (No. 20060207; No. 20120901). Examples of financial incentives are encouraging investment in innovative small and medium enterprises' technology fund, supporting the government institutions that provide loans for S&T projects, and promoting the commercial finance organizations that provide loans and financial services for S&T projects (No. 20060207). In government procurement, innovative products take priority according to the procurement catalog (No. 20060207). The government has also established talent development projects in the fields of fundamental and advanced technological research, in order to provide companies and research institutions with qualified specialists in S&T fields (No. 20051231; No. 20060207; No. 20110726; No. 20170901).

Third, and most importantly, the Chinese government pays special attention to particular sectors, in order to achieve its innovation goals more quickly and to establish and maintain global competitiveness. Sectoral policies have clearly reflected the central government's core concerns over the past decade. For instance, there are 11 important areas – including 68 breakthrough technologies – that enjoyed priority status, 27 cutting-edge technologies, 18 basic scientific research topics, and four national key scientific research programs that have received significant investment and support (No. 20051231; No. 20130223). Also recently, the central government stresses on the basic science research and devotes more efforts into it (No.20180119). This reflects the fact that China's government has not only wanted to achieve innovative goals in some areas in the short term but has also been keen to pay more attention to sustainability and competitiveness in the long run too.

With reference to the example of information technology (IT), in No. 20051231 this was set as one of the key innovation areas – with a focus on six priority breakthrough IT technologies, including next generation network, and high-definition, large-screen, flat-panel display technology. Years later, in 2011, China's companies had become key players in the global IT market and could keep pace with its leaders (Hout and Ghemawat, 2010). Thus, central government set IT as a strategic emerging industry (SEI, No. 20120709) and promoted new IT technologies such as cloud computing and storage (No. 20150106), the Internet of Things (IoT) (No. 20130205; No.20171119), Big Data (No. 20150831), and Artificial Intelligence (No. 20170708). It tried to combine this with the industrialization process, which has to do with the outlines of smart industrialization and Made in China 2025 (No. 20110704; No. 20150508). Based on the successes achieved in the initial period, IT was a key priority in sustainable innovation capacity-building programs (No. 20130115). The other sectors, focused on Biology (No. 20090602), New Energy Vehicles (No. 20120628), and Energy Saving and Environmental Protection (No. 20120616) were also supported by specific policies. This dynamic, adaptive adjustment of policy is often seen in other policy areas as well. Table 2.1 traces the evolution of the S&T industries and key sectors during the past ten years.

Thus we might conclude that Policy I is widely represented on the Chinese government agenda in the period from 2006 to 2017. The policies listed here represent only one part of the immediate measures adopted for S&T advancement in China. Yet, as noted in the analytical framework description, Policies II and III must provide stark support to Policy I, in order to be effective and to contribute to successful innovation in China.

3.2 Policy II

Policy II is responsible for providing favorable institutional support for Policy I measures. As mentioned in the analytical framework description, Policy II includes a very wide range of policies that may be innovation-orientated or not. Conventional policies in this group include fiscal, tax, and financial measures, and ones for human capital advancement, the standardization of IPR, as well as the promotion of high-tech industrialization measures.

First, fiscal and tax measures are the most effective way to stimulate innovative activities. Besides the direct fiscal support provided to S&T, as summarized in Policy I, firms in the technological and innovative sectors can apply for further

Table 2.1 Sector and Scientific Focuses in China's S&T since 2006

2005			*2011*	*2013*		*2015*
Important Areas	*Leading Sectors*	*Cutting-Edge Technologies*	*SEI*	*Important Areas*	*Scientific Focus*	*Made in China 2025*
Energy	Energy conservation technology; Clean energy technology	Advanced energy technology	Energy conservation	Energy conservation; new energy	Energy	
Water and mineral resources						
Environment			Environmental protection	Environmental protection	Earth system science and environment	
Agriculture	Agriculture			Agriculture		Farm machinery
Manufacturing	Equipment manufacturing Industry	Advanced manufacturing; laser technology	High-end equipment manufacturing	Manufacturing	Engineering technology	High-end numerically controlled machine tools and robots
						Electrical equipment
Transportation: low energy and NEV			New energy / automotive	Overall transportation; New energy / automotive		Energy-saving cars and new energy cars; high-end rail transportation equipment
IT and modern Service industry	IT Industry	IT	New-generation IT	New-generation IT; Modern service industry		New-generation IT
Population and health	Biology	Biotech	Biotech	Biotech	Life science	Biomedicine and high-end medical equipment
Urbanization and urban development						
Public security						
National defense	Aerospace	Aerospace			Aerospace and astronomy	Aerospace equipment
	New materials	New materials	New materials	New materials	Material science	New materials
	Marine technology			Ocean engineering equipment and high-end vessels		
					Particle physics and nuclear physics	

specific tax preferences and for public funding and services (No. 20051231). Compared to previous policies, this support has been reinforced and increased in recent ten years.

Second, financial market policies concern measures such as the construction and improvement of a multilevel capital market, the deepening of transaction reform (No. 20060207), and an increase in credit investment via the development and promotion of new financial products and services for firms (No. 20120901), to support firms' technological upgrades. These financial measures do not target directly at S&T, but they definitely provide companies with more efficient economic instruments with which to improve their innovation. The government is also increasing its support for international cooperation and exchange, which have potential spillover effects in terms of the innovation and technology capacity of Chinese companies. Among other things, the foreign investment management system has been developed to create a stable, transparent, and predictable business environment (No. 20150508).

Third, the Chinese government has many policies for improving the quality of human capital, optimizing infrastructure for talent creation, and improving personnel training methods so as to provide a continuous supply of human capital that meets market demands. For instance, the government has constantly improved the professional title system in order to encourage universities to cultivate scientific and professional talents (No. 20051231; No. 20060207; No. 20100401; No. 20100708; No. 20181226), and has worked with the vocational education system to provide appropriately trained personnel for industry (No. 20140502; No. 20190124). At the same time, the government has attempted to build strategic alliances between industry, research institutes, and universities – not only by promoting direct cooperation, but also by improving the mobility of personnel between public, academic, and business entities (No. 20100401; No. 20171205). Improvements in the social policy domains have also contributed to the further promotion of innovation. For example, the Hukou registration system has been adjusted to meet the demand for talented human capital. Policy No. 20060207 states that if companies hire university graduates and talent, the Hukou restrictions do not apply.

Fourth, the Chinese government has also focused on the promotion of high-tech industrialization. The measures to achieve this goal include the following: support for national high-tech industrial development zones, the establishment of technology exchange platforms and university science parks (No. 20051231), and scientific services (No. 20111212; No. 20141009). A further measure for industrial upgrading has been the creation of and support for S&T intermediary agency and engineering centers (No. 20110704).

Fifth, the field of IPR can be assigned to both Policies II and Policy III simultaneously. We suggest that IPR measures that refer to institutional support for innovation be included in Policy II, and those that regulate IPR protection and cover sanctions be assigned to Policy III – because the latter send a specific signal about the common cognition of IPR values. In the Policy II realm, the Chinese government has attempted to improve, for example, the institutional mechanisms for sharing the benefits from intellectual property ownership (No. 20100401) and has aimed to participate in the formulation of internationally accepted standards (No. 20051231; No. 20060207).

Finally, since 2015 the Chinese government has specifically highlighted the support and encouragement of entrepreneurship under the strategy of "mass entrepreneurship and innovation" (No. 20150302). An entrepreneurship service platform is currently being developed, and venture investment institutes cultivated (No. 20150302). The government is also attempting to eliminate those monopoly agreements and forms of unfair competition that are not conductive to entrepreneurship, as well as to deepen the reform of commercial institutions and to establish convenient market both entry and exit mechanisms (No. 20150611; No.20160916). Lately, education reform has emphasized the entrepreneurial spirit – while the university system is now being reorganized so as to boost entrepreneurship and innovation (No. 20150504).

This shows that the Chinese government is putting considerable effort into creating favorable institutional settings for innovation and to ensuring the success of Policy I measures, specifically by boosting the competitive environment, providing adequate human capital, and promoting high-tech industrialization and entrepreneurship.

3.3 Policy III

As mentioned in the analytical framework description, Policy III has two main components: namely coordination and cognition. The coordination aspect of Policy III refers to the different coordination mechanisms for connecting Policy I and Policy II in particular, as well as for managing innovation policies' complexity in general. We identify some of the elements that form the basis for the future development of Policy III. For instance, a unified national S&T reporting system – which concerns report submission, collection, and the data management and sharing system – is to be established by 2020 (No.20140831; No.20180317). The State Council has established a system of joint inter-ministerial meetings to coordinate the information exchanged between regions, departments, and firms (No.20150814). It has also launched projects that serve as a coordination platform for various different innovation entities (No. 20051231) and has proposed a coordination mechanism for innovation governance (No.20150924). Furthermore, the government is trying to improve the openness of innovation resources and to optimize the efficiency of their utilization within society. In 2014, the Chinese government put forward a reform proposal for building open research facilities and equipment sharing systems for innovators (No.20141231). The government has strived to create a national unified and open network management platform through which to share scientific resources and services, in order to achieve a higher utilization efficiency vis-à-vis these (No.20141231).

The cognition element of Policy III corresponds with the aspiration of the common interpretation and awareness of innovation policies by different actors, supports the enhancement of scientific competence among them, and creates an environment that respects and welcomes innovation. As mentioned in relation to Policy II, the Chinese government clearly has the aim of establishing an IPR protection system, of improving intellectual property regulations, and of increasing its efforts to sanction any infringements of IPR (No. 20060207; No. 20060327; No. 20080605; No. 20111113; No. 20140329). These measures contribute to the shared value of IPR protection. Moreover, the government has implemented "Chinese Citizens' Scientific Competence Action Plan." This facilitates the popularization of S&T; it also tries to promote the idea of a sustainable lifestyle as the foundation for the better acceptance of innovation policies as well as to create an innovation-friendly environment. Even though the scope of these policies is the whole of society, the government has identified some specific targets groups – such as young people, rural and urban workers, leading cadres, and civil servants – who it wishes to act as role models for a sustainable attitude toward life and work (No. 20060206; No. 20110619; No. 20160225).

4 Toward systemic innovation with new features

The national system of innovation policies is a subsystem of the NIS and is the core indicator of how the NIS evolves. We have learned that China has made incredible efforts at different policy levels to make the transformation to indigenous innovation. In this section, we will investigate how the different policies help China to achieve its goals regarding systemic innovation, and identify the country's specific national features in current economic and technology scenarios from the perspective of the national system of innovation policies.

4.1 China's NIS

China's NIS (No. 20051231; No. 20060126; No.20070123) is an interactive social system, which is led by government and fundamentally driven by the market mechanism for resource distribution, among the technological innovation subjects, in order to promote China as an indigenous innovator. The reform of the S&T system in 1985 was the origins of China's NIS, which includes technological, knowledge, defense technology, and regional innovation, as well as technology intermediary services. We summarize its different components in Figure 2.1.

Firms are at the core of China's NIS, and technological innovation is the major task for establishing an innovative China (e.g., No. 20051231; No. 20130128; No. 20160728). Universities and research institutes are the fundamental scientific pillars contributing knowledge to society, alongside them also interacting with firms and generating new technologies. Another area of innovation on which strong emphasis has been placed is that of defense technology. As a country with a population of over one billion people, defense and security are major national concerns but cost resources that are critical elsewhere. China has

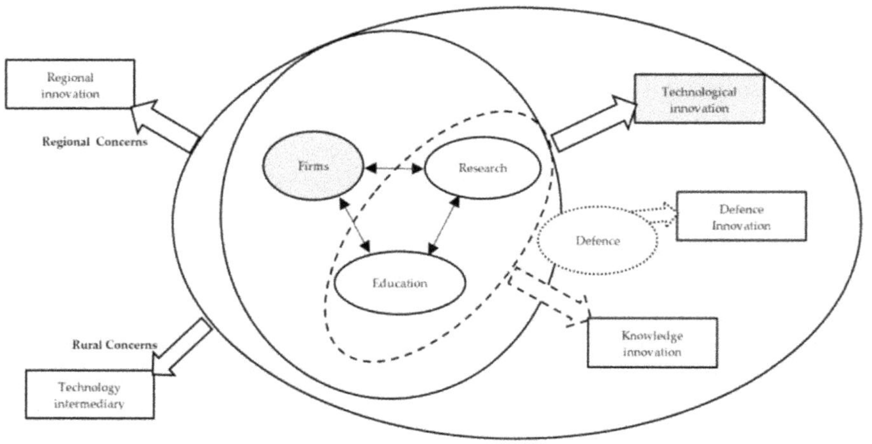

Figure 2.1 The conception of China's NIS in 2006

therefore started to coordinate military and civil technology development and encourage the two sectors to share technological resources.

To address regional disparities, China has also set different agendas in different regions; for example, it has been decided that the eastern provinces would pursue their indigenous innovation capacity whereas the western and middle regions would attempt to establish a technology infrastructure and prepare to achieve long-term innovation objectives. Technology intermediary services have also been targeted, with those for rural areas being the main element hereof (No. 20060427; No. 20060828). In parallel to these innovation initiatives, the government has played a visible role in leading and providing services for all.

Based on "the national system of political economy" first envisaged by Friedrich List (1841/1856), Lundvall (1992) proposed a new concept, the "national system of innovation," to specify how an economy could catch up in technology and development terms. The basic principles of the NIS are now widely accepted by scholars and practitioners worldwide. The system is "a set of institutional actors that, together, plays the major role in influencing innovative performance" (Nelson and Rosenberg, 1993, pp. 4–5); the core tools for innovation should be the efforts in science and technological investment, education and training systems, knowledge accumulation, learning from the developed economies, the promotion of strategic industries, and so forth. On the other hand, the coordination mechanisms behind these efforts must be carefully designed and distributed. Furthermore, Freeman (1995) has drawn attention to the emerging diffusion process of technical change at the level of firms and industries.

Formal innovation strategies and policies are, without doubt, fundamental; however, as the interdependence of firms, industries, and national economies increases – for example with the rise of transnational corporations – any concerns about specific technical innovation must take into account the issue of how such firms interact, learn from, and imitate each other. In this sense the NIS not only addresses the issues of specific innovation efforts as well as pertinent institutions and policies (Policies I and II) but also focuses on the changes and influences occurring at the micro level. What Chinese firms and governments have been doing since the 1980s – namely, copying, imitating, and buying technologies from abroad – is similar to the approach adopted by Japan in the 1950s and 1960s and by Germany in the 1870s. However, this does not imply that China will become as important an innovator as the others did. One explanation of Japan's success is that it focused on integrating industrial R&D, production, consumption, and management; the Soviet Union and Latin American countries – which had similar R&D investment levels – were unable to hit these heights, however (Freeman, 1995).

The NIS approach stresses the importance of interaction between institutions that help knowledge and innovation generation (OECD, 1997). Innovation hence is the result of continuing interaction between agents and institutions, rather than a linear output of R&D investment as driven by Policy I. Moreover, as the framework introduced in the second section showed, countries vary in terms of institutional context and have specific cultural features – the NIS must reflect these differences. Policymakers must also understand and define specificities, in order to establish the right NIS for enhancing innovative performance. However, often we may observe that catching-up economies place more emphasis on Policy I and less on the second level – while not having the patience to consider Policy III at all. That is exactly our opinion with regard to the Chinese NIS launched in 2006. Similarly, as Kroll et al. (2010) point out, aside from the efforts made in the field of technological development, government should also pay the same amount of attention to markets and consumers too – not to mention to organizational and process innovation as well.

The Chinese government has proposed that the critical breakthrough to achieving innovation-driven economic development is to promote systemically comprehensive innovation reform (No. 20150907). The experimental ideas and experiences have been introduced at national level since 2017 (No. 20170907; No. 20181223). Besides the coordination of innovation and economic development, this new approach places more emphasis on coordinating the innovations in technology, management, brand, organization, and in business models, on developing military technology that can also be used for civilian purposes, and on coordinating the introduction of technology from abroad alongside engaging in collaborative innovation with other countries.

Major efforts will be devoted to establishing mechanisms and rules in areas of fair competition (e.g., No. 20120923), IPRs (e.g., No. 20141210), S&T results transfer (e.g., No. 20110704; No.20150907; No.20170915; No. 20180318), financial innovation (e.g., No. 20120923), talent training and incentives (e.g., No. 20151024), open innovation (e.g., No. 20141231), and S&T management (e.g., No. 20140303; No. 20141203; No. 20180718). This new approach extends the original Chinese NIS in a much more comprehensive manner, with it now closer to the conventional understanding of NIS in that it precisely reflects the fact that the Chinese government has changed its understanding of innovation and the innovation system. It has also reflected the weakness of the system thus far, with its overemphasis on technological innovation. However, for those catching-up economies like China, it is a rational way to concentrate its limited resources and capacities on technological innovation – in order to achieve a leap forward in indigenous innovation. Nevertheless, this kind of opportunism with its huge possibilities may lead to a systemic failure when it comes to taking further steps in innovation if the policy system underpinning it is not established well.

Nevertheless challenges remain, although the Chinese government has had a clear blueprint for its NIS. The essential point of NIS is to create an interactive platform for firms and industries, and to provide a proper coordination mechanism at the national level to support their interaction. The Chinese economy is still currently dominated by SOEs, although the private sector has contributed most to the economy. Given the specific nexus between politics and economy, private enterprises are therefore unable to be treated equally in terms of financial support and policy favors, for instance, and as such may not be able to innovate effectively. Against this backdrop, it can be quite challenging to establish systemic linkages between (national and regional) sectors and firms, and, as a consequence, hundreds of thousands of innovation entities have been isolated and may not have achieved satisfactory innovation outcomes to date.

4.2 Toward an open and shared innovation system

The concept of open and shared innovation has been a major concern for China over the past ten years. Open innovation has never been adopted as a clear national strategy, although policymakers have attempted to establish an open and cooperative innovation environment (Fu and Xiong, 2011). The strategy of "going global and bringing in" is the basis on which China's firms have attempted to catch up and to embed themselves in the global value chain and industrial division since the 1980s reform, because domestic technological and knowledge accumulation was weak and could not satisfy market demands at that early stage. Of course, this strategy is too dependent on the availability of external technology and in the long run is not sustainable.

From 2006 or thereabouts, governmental policies have a clear stress on the open innovation strategy (e.g., No. 20051231; No. 20060126) – in which the fundamental ways of achieving indigenous innovation are now designated "integrated innovation" and "innovations on the basis of introduction, digestion, and absorption." Both ways clearly put emphasis on how to open up China's innovation system. At the same time, firms in China were encouraged to "go global," to acquire and invest in foreign companies, and to integrate into global innovation networks. However, until then, the term "open" in China's innovation models simply meant that the country should remain open to the advanced technology and developed economies and markets and integrate into global innovation tracks and technological progress. However later on, and especially with the governance of Premier Li Keqiang, the meaning of "open" was greatly extended. It not only now indicates that China's innovation attempts are open to the world but, in a much more important sense, also shows that all innovators operating in the system are able to easily access equipment and facilities as well as to share ideas, data, and other key resources.

In the seminal policies of No. 20120923 and No. 20150924, the Chinese government clearly advocates for establishing an "open, shared, and interactive innovation network" in which labs, resources, equipment, and research reports can be easily shared. This will allow the innovators – meaning firms, universities, and research institutes – to interact effectively at every stage of their projects. For example, the program of the 2011 Collaborative Innovation Center aims to coordinate the resources at the disposal of universities and research institutes to make research happen quicker and more effectively (No. 20130115). As China is increasing integrated in the global value chain, open and collaborative innovation will definitely become an influential business model in the country. For example "Made in China 2025" (No. 20150508), one of the Chinese government's most important innovation strategic declarations to date, stresses that the country should "utilize global resources and markets, enhance industrial global distribution, international coordination, and cooperation, obtain new comparative advantages, and upgrade to the open level in manufacturing" (for a specific example, see No. 20150513; No. 20180314).

Besides these conventional wisdoms, the central government also now stresses the significance of open source innovation. This may help people to coordinate their understanding about innovation (i.e. Policy III) in a straightforward manner. In a proposed plan on "Internet plus," for example, it is clearly stated that the Chinese government will:

> encourage firms, via the internet, to provide open-source access to software outcomes that are supported by national grants and firms' own funds; encourage education institutes, social groups, firms, and individuals to launch open-source programs, to actively join international open-source projects. . ., encourage firms to create a new business ecology, . . . and help the open-source community to coordinate and cooperate on standard regulation and intellectual property.
>
> (No.20150701)

China clearly has caught hold of the new trends in industrial innovation, according to the arguments found in Chesbrough and Crowther (2006) – which suggest that open innovation should focus not only on high-tech sectors but also on a wide range of different industries in the information and internet age.

4.3 An innovative and entrepreneurial society

The core capacity for sustainable economic growth must be at the mercy of greater productivity and innovation. China is now engaged in a major transformation from a labor-intensive to a technology-intensive model, its aim being to achieve higher value added as a developed country. Thus, an innovative and entrepreneurial society concept was established as the basis for a reform strategy designed to achieve this goal.

The concept of "Mass Entrepreneurship and Innovation" (MEI) was first proposed by Premier Li Keqiang in Davos in the summer of 2014, and was officially elaborated on in the "2015 Report of the Work of the Government," and was promoted again with more extensive support in 2018 (No. 20180918). The MEI not only aims to solve urgent problems such as unemployment in conditions of slowing economic growth and resource constraints, but also has a focus on making structural adjustments. In addition, the MEI will henceforth be a driving force for government reform of administrative institutions and regulations (No. 20150611; No. 20150814; No. 20150923; No. 20170721).

This innovation strategy specifies two elements – namely entrepreneurship and "the mass" – that once again reflect the new conception of China's NIS. First of all, the government may ease approvals of and regulations on start-ups and create a friendly environment for entrepreneurship and innovation. The process for obtaining administrative and non-administrative approval for business start-ups was an onerous one previously. Before this reform, for instance, the start-ups in some regions had to be approved by more than 100 administrative units, whereas afterward this was reduced to only one while the process could also now be completed online.

Secondly, this also acts an opportunity for business model innovation, because the MEI is successfully integrated with and supported by the development of e-commerce. For instance, "Internet plus" is typically the project that has been promoted in this context since 2015. We may observe another positive signal at the government level too, namely that, from the end of 2015, China's government started to emphasize "supply side" rather than "demand side" reform. The latter had been the dominant reform strategy for the two decades hitherto. Innovation and entrepreneurship are thus acting as the means to encourage suppliers to work toward this goal.

An entrepreneurial society refers to "places where entrepreneurship has emerged as a focal point for economic growth, sustainable job creation, and competitiveness in global markets" (Audretsch, 2009, p. 505), and has specific values, organizational skills, attitudes, and the like. The United States, which was in stagnation in the 1970s and lost competitiveness in its traditional physical capital-based industries in the 1980s, successfully became an entrepreneurial society from the 1990s onward. The critical driving force behind this was policy innovation, such as deregulation in the airline industry. Nevertheless, we should not conclude that China must learn from the US' policies and lessons. Instead, China must carefully create policies, and especially Policy III, so as to encourage people to start innovative businesses while simultaneously focusing attitudes and values on the entrepreneurial society, as the entrepreneurial context has been changing since 2000s (Dai et al., 2019).

4.4 Remaining questions

The China government has made substantial efforts to establish an indigenous innovative economy since 2006 and has gradually followed up on developed economies' own successful experiences. Nevertheless, we must ask whether China will ever actually achieve its goals and, if not, what the remaining shortcomings are to be overcome. In addition, even if China does achieve the goals defined for S&T then national overall averages can sometimes be misleading. This is because of the unbalanced distribution of innovative activities in China, which is still far from being a mature innovative country (Gu and Lundvall, 2006; Gu et al., 2016). Our answers therefore focus on the following aspects.

First of all, the Chinese government may reform its governance approaches and correspondingly improve administration skills. Based on the preceding policy overview, it is very impressive that the central government plays a significant role in promoting its national innovation strategy. However, it places too much emphasis on government intervention in individual innovative efforts, which may distort the incentive structures for individuals as they attempt to secure official support – for instance, governmental subsidies in certain sectors. Hence, central government may gradually change its conventional direct investment approach and widen its efforts to create an innovation-friendly environment.

Secondly, there is the matter of China's national system of innovation policies. As we argued earlier, the core aspect of defining a specific national system in a very strict way is to have a national Policy III, because Policies I and II are not in themselves sufficient to differentiate countries from each other systematically. Accordingly, the critical issue is to identify what kind of policy tools are available in policymaking. Without doubt, this is a long-term task – but one that nevertheless cannot be ignored. Of course, China has established policies in this field; if we want to define a Chinese national system of innovation policies, though, cultural factors must be considered.

5 Conclusion

As the policy review has shown, China has made significant efforts to establish an innovative economy and society since 2006, and all policies proposed before the end of 2018 have been continuously followed up on and improved in the past thirteen years. A China's NIS has been clearly elaborated and implemented, according to the innovation policies that have been adopted at the national government level.

One immediate conclusion is that China's innovation system may become open and attractive to ordinary people, and competitive too – if innovation investment remains sustainable through the support of the MEI strategy. Those innovative efforts are highly connected to current technological conditions, and in particular those of information and internet technologies. Open innovation shared between different actors will be a sound approach to helping these individuals form a common cognition on innovation and to coordinating their respective innovation activities. These features may be the critical elements for defining China's NIS.

After reviewing the national innovation policies, we found that the majority of them are still of the type Policy I or Policy II, and some evidence of type Policy III is existing, but these need to be developed further – for example policies on how to reform governmental regulation and governance in order to have an innovation-friendly environment. Alternatively, how to develop suitable tools in Policy III for the MEI strategy in the near future and for a Chinese national system of innovation policies in the long run.

References

Audretsch, D. B. (2009) "Emergence of the Entrepreneurial Society." *Business Horizons* 52(5): 505–511.

Beckert, J. (2010) "How Do Fields Change? The Interrelations of Institutions, Networks, and Cognition in the Dynamics of Markets." *Organization Studies* 31(5): 605–627.

Benner, M., L. Liu and S. S. Serger (2012) "Head in the Clouds and Feet on the Ground: Research Priority Setting in China." *Science and Public Policy* 39(2): 258–270.

Boeing, P., E. Mueller and P. Sandner (2016) "China's R&D Explosion – Analyzing Productivity Effects Across Ownership Types and Over Time." *Research Policy* 45(1): 159–176.

Borras, S. and C. Edquist (2013) "The Choice of Innovation Policy Instruments." *Technological Forecasting and Social Change* 80(8): 1513–1522.

Chesbrough, H. and A. K. Crowther (2006) "Beyond High Tech: Early Adopters of Open Innovation in Other Industries." *R and D Management* 36(3): 229–236.

Dai, S. (2015) *Networks of Institutions: Institutional Emergence, Social Structure and National Systems of Policies*, London, UK and New York: Routledge and Taylor & Francis Group.

Dai, S. (2016) "Innovation and National Systems of Innovation Policies: A Network Approach." Claudius Gräbner, T. Heinrich and H. Schwardt (eds.), *Policy Implications of Recent Advances in Evolutionary and Institutional Economics*, London, UK; New York: Routledge and Taylor & Francis Group.

Dai, S., Y. Wang and Y. Liu (2019) "The Emergence of Chinese Entrepreneurs: Social Connections and Innovation." *Journal of Entrepreneurship in Emerging Economies* 11(3): 351–368.

Edquist, C. (2006) "Systems of Innovation: Perspectives and Challenges." J. Fagerberg and D. C. Mowery (eds.), *The Oxford Handbook of Innovation*, Oxford: Oxford University Press, 182–205.

Freeman, C. (1995) "'The National System of Innovation' in Historical Perspective." *Cambridge Journal of Economics* 19(1): 5–24.

Fu, X. and H. Xiong (2011) "Open Innovation in China: Policies and Practices." *Journal of Science and Technology Policy in China* 2: 196–218.

Gu, S. and B-Å. Lundvall (2006) "China's Innovation System and the Move Towards Harmonious Growth and Endogenous Innovation." *Innovation: Management, Policy & Practice* 18(4): 413–440.

Gu, S., S. S. Serger and B-Å. Lundvall (2016) "China's Innovation System: Ten Years on." *Innovation: Management, Policy & Practice* 18(4): 441–448.

Guan, J. C. and R. C. M. Yam (2015) "Effects of Government Financial Incentives on Firms Innovation Performance in China: Evidences from Beijing in the 1990s." *Research Policy* 44(1): 273–282.

Hout, T. and P. Ghemawat (2010) "China VS the World: Whose Technology Is It?" *Harvard Business Review* 88(12): 94–103.

Hutschenreiter, G. and G. Zhang (2007) "China's Quest for Innovation-Driven Growth – The Policy Dimension." *Journal of Industry, Competition and Trade* 7(3): 245–254.

Kroll, H., M. Conlé and M. Schüller (2010) "China: Innovation System and Innovation Policy." R. Frietsch and M. Schüller (eds.), *Competing for Global Innovation Leadership: Innovation Systems and Policies in the USA, Europe and Asia*, Stuttgart: Fraunhofer Verlag, 241–264.

List, F. (1841) *National System of Political Economy*, Philadelphia: Lippincott.

Liu, F., Denis Fred Simon, Yu-Tao Sun and Cong Cao (2011) "China's Innovation Policies: Evolution, Institutional Structure, and Trajectory." *Research Policy* 40(7): 917–931.

Lundvall, B. Å. (ed.) (1992) *National Systems of Innovation: Towards a Theory of Innovation and Interactive Learning*, London, UK: Printer.

Lundvall, B-Å., Björn Johnson, Esben Sloth Andersen and Bent Dalum (2002) "National Systems of Production, Innovation and Competence Building." *Research Policy* 31(2): 213–231.

Magro, E. and J. R. Wilson (2013) "Complex Innovation Policy Systems: Towards an Evaluation Mix." *Research Policy* 42(9): 1647–1656.

Magro, E. and J. M. Zabala-Iturriagagoitia (2014) "Coordination-Mix: The Hidden Face of STI Policy." *Review of Policy Research* 31(5): 367–389.

Metcalfe, J. S. (1995) "Technology Systems and Technology Policy in an Evolutionary Framework." *Cambridge Journal of Economics* 19: 25–46.

Nelson, R. R. and N. Rosenberg (1993) "Technical Innovation and National Systems." R. R. Nelson (ed.), *National Inovation Systems: A Comparative Analysis*, Oxford, UK: Oxford University Press, 3–22.

OECD (1997) *National Innovation Systems*, Paris and France: OECD Publishing.

OECD (2005) *Governance of Innovation Systems: Volume 1: Synthesis Report*, Paris and France: OECD Publishing.

OECD (2008) *OECD Reviews of Innovation Policy: China*, Paris and France: OECD Publishing.

Paraskevopoulou, E. (2012) "Non-technological Regulatory Effects: Implications for Innovation and Innovation Policy." *Research Policy* 41(6): 1058–1071.

Sun, Y. and F. Liu (2014) "New Trends in Chinese Innovation Policies Since 2009: A System Framework of Policy Analysis." *International Journal of Technology Management* 65(1–4): 6–23.

Appendix 2-A

List of policies mentioned in this chapter

Policy Code	*Document Title*
No. 20051231	National Guideline for the Medium- and Long-Term Plan for Science and Technology Development (2006–2020)
No. 20060126	Decision on Implementing the Outline of the Scientific and Technological Plan and Enhancing the Independent Innovation Capacity
No. 20060206	The Outline of the National Scheme for Scientific Literacy (2006–2010–2020)
No. 20060207	Notice of the State Council on Implementation of Some Supporting Policies Concerning the 'Outline of the National Mid-term and Long-term Planning for Science and Technology Development' (2006–2020)
No. 20060327	Notice of the Action Guideline of Protecting Intellectual Property Rights
No. 20060427	Notice of the Opinions of Promoting Scientific and Technologic Change at the County (County Level Cities) Level
No. 20060828	Opinions on Deepening Reform and Strengthening the Construction of Agricultural Technology Introduction System
No. 20070123	Notice of the 11th Five-Year Plan of National Indigenous Innovation Capacity Building
No. 20080605	Outline of the National Intellectual Property Strategy
No. 20090602	Notice of Some Policies on Accelerating Biology Industry
No. 20100401	Outline of National Medium- and Long-Term Talent Development Plan (2010–2020)
No. 20100708	Outline of National Medium- and Long-Term Education Reform and Development Plan (2010–2020)
No. 20110619	Implementation Plan for the Outline of the National Action Scheme of Scientific Literacy for All Chinese Citizens (2011–2015)
No. 20110704	China's National S&T Development Plan for the 12th Five-Year Period 2011–2015
No. 20110726	National Medium- and Long-Term Scientific Talent Development Plan (2010–2020)
No. 20111113	Opinions on Further Improving Combating IPR Infringement and Manufacture and Sell of Fake and Shoddy Goods
No. 20111212	Guiding Opinions on Accelerating the Development of Hi-Tech Service
No. 20111230	Plan for Industrial Transformation and Upgrading (2011–2015)
No. 20120616	Notice of the 12th Five-Year Plan of the Energy Saving and Environmental Protection
No. 20120628	Notice of the Development Plan of the Energy Saving and New Energy Vehicles
No. 20120709	Notice of the 12th Five-Year Development Plan of National Strategic Emerging Industry

Policy Code	Document Title
No. 20120901	Guiding Opinions on Promoting Enterprise Technological Transformation
No. 20120923	Opinions on Deepening Scientific Institutional Reform and Accelerating the Establishment of National System of Innovation
No. 20130115	Notice of Developing National Indigenous Innovation Capacity in the 12th Five-Year Plan
No. 20130128	Opinions on Strengthening Firm's Dominating Role in Innovation and Comprehensively Advancing its Innovation Ability
No. 20130205	Guiding Opinions on Promoting Orderly and Healthy Development of the Internet of Things Industry
No. 20130223	Notice of the Medium- and Long-Term Development Plan for Key National Science and Technology Infrastructure (2012–2030)
No. 20140303	Several Opinions on Improving and Enhancing the Management of the Research Projects and Grants under Central Treasury
No. 20140329	Notice of the General Office of the State Council on Issuing the Essentials of the Nationwide Fight against IPR Infringement and the Manufacturing and Sales of Fake and Shoddy Goods
No. 20140502	Decision of the State Council on Accelerating the Development of Modern Vocational Education
No. 20140831	Notice of the General Office of the State Council Forwarding the Guiding Opinions of Ministry of Science on Accelerating the Establishment of the National Science and Technology Reporting System
No. 20141009	Several Opinions on Accelerating the Development of Scientific Service
No. 20141203	Notice of the Reform Plan on Deepening the Management of Scientific Plan (Special Grant, Fund, etc.) under Central Treasury
No. 20141210	Notice of Implementing Thoroughly National Intellectual Property Rights Strategic Action (2014–2020)
No. 20141231	Opinions on Major National Research Infrastructure and Large Scientific Instruments Open to the Public
No. 20150106	Opinions on Promoting Cloud Computing Industry and Cultivating New Industrial Formation of Information Technology
No. 20150302	Guiding Opinions on the Development of Maker Space to Promote Mass Entrepreneurship and Innovation
No. 20150504	Implementation Opinions on Deepening the Reform of the Education of Innovation and Entrepreneurship in Institutions of Higher Education
No. 20150508	Notice of "Made in China 2025"
No. 20150513	Guiding Opinions on Promoting International Cooperation on Production Capacity and Equipment Manufacture
No. 20150611	Opinions on Several Policies for Vigorously Promoting Mass Entrepreneurship and Innovation
No. 20150701	Guiding Opinions on Actively Promoting "Internet Plus" Actions
No. 20150814	Letter on Approving the Establishment of a Joint Inter-ministerial Meeting System to Promote Mass Entrepreneurship and Innovation
No. 20150831	Notice of the Action Guideline of Promoting Big Data Development
No. 20150907	Overall Plan for the Reform Experiment of Systematically Improving Comprehensive Innovation in Some Regions
No. 20150923	Guiding Opinions on Establishing Support Platforms for the Mass Entrepreneurship and Innovation
No. 20150924	Implementation Plan for Deepening Science and Technology Institutional Reform
No. 20151024	Notice of the Overall Plan on Advancing the Building of World-Class Universities and Disciplines

(*Continued*)

(Continued)

Policy Code	*Document Title*
No. 20160225	Implementation Plan for the Outline of the National Action Scheme of Scientific Literacy for All Chinese Citizens (2016–2020)
No. 20160728	Notice of National Innovation Plan in the 13rd Five-Year Plan
No. 20160916	Opinions on Improving Sustainable and Healthy Development of Entrepreneurial Investment
No. 20170708	Notice of the New Generation Artificial Intelligence Development Plan
No. 20170721	Opinions on Enforcing the Implementation of the Indigenous Innovation-Driven Strategy and Further Improving the Mass Entrepreneurship and Innovation
No. 20170901	Opinions on Further Activating Private Investment for Promoting Sustainable National Economic Development
No. 20170907	Notice of Spreading the Supporting Reform Measures on Innovation
No. 20170915	Notice of the Plan of Establishing National Technology Transfer System
No. 20171119	Guiding Opinions on Deepening "Internet + Advanced Manufacture" and Developing Industrial Internet.
No. 20171205	Opinions on Deepening the Integration of Industry and Education
No. 20180119	Opinions on Enhancing Basic Science Research
No. 20180314	Notice of Organizing International Plans and Projects on Big Science
No. 20180317	Notice of Scientific Data Management
No. 20180318	Acting Guidance for Outward IPR Transfer
No. 20180718	Notice of Some Measures for Research Management Optimization and Improving Research Efficiency
No. 20180918	Opinions on Promoting High Qualitied Entrepreneurship and Innovation and making Mass Entrepreneurship and Innovation Updated
No. 20181223	Notice of Spreading the Supporting Reform Measures on Innovation (Second)
No. 20181226	Notice of Implementation of Granting Greater Autonomy to Scientific Research Institutions and Personnel.
No. 20190124	Reform Program of National Vocational Education

3 China's research and development sector

Progress and outlook

Yanrui Wu

China has made considerable progress in science and technology in recent decades. In particular, the country has become a leading investor in research and development (R&D). If the current growth momentum is maintained, China could be transformed from the world's manufacturing powerhouse to a technological superpower (Sigurdson et al., 2005). This change would have important implications for the rest of the world. The objective of this chapter is to present a critical review of China's R&D policy and the role of key players in the sector, with a view to providing an assessment of the country's R&D sector. The rest of the chapter starts with a discussion of the trends in R&D activities in section 1. Then section 2 reviews the role of business sector in China's R&D. This is followed by an assessment of R&D in industrial subsectors in section 3. Subsequently, section 4 examines government support and university-industry collaboration and section 5 discusses China's offshore investment and its impact on domestic innovation. The outlook and challenges in the country's R&D sector are explored in section 6. Finally, section 7 concludes the chapter.

1 Trends in China's R&D activities

To guide the country's science and technology development in the coming decades, China's State Council released a major policy document in 2006. The policy goal is to make China an innovation-oriented society by the year 2020 and a world-leading innovator in the longer term (State Council, 2006). This development strategy was further emphasized in China's 12th Five-Year Program (FYP) 2011–2015. With the onset of the global financial crisis, indigenous innovation becomes even more important for Chinese firms to reduce production costs associated with rising wages and environmental protections and hence increase their international competitiveness. According to the official policy statement, coastal China will be transformed from the "world factory" to an R&D hub, high value-added manufacturing, and services (State Council, 2011). The 12th FYP designates seven strategic emerging industries as the drivers for China's future economic development. More recently, the 13th FYP (2016–2020) also focused on innovation and campaigned for "mass entrepreneurship and innovation."

In fact, China's investment in R&D has maintained a steady rate of growth for decades. In recent years, this growth was boosted by the new development policies. For example, during the period 2001–2018, the average growth rate of R&D investment reached 14.9% per annum which is much higher than the average growth rate of China's GDP over the same period.[1] Among the world's major spenders in R&D, China was ranked number two in 2016 with a total spending of $259 billion (in purchasing power parity terms according to the World Bank data) in comparison with $511 billion by the United States (number one in the world) and $169 billion by Japan (number three in the world). China also has the largest R&D research team with a total of about 1.59 million full-time equivalent (FTE) researchers in 2015 which was well ahead of 1.38 million in the United States.[2]

R&D expenditure as a proportion of the country's GDP or R&D intensity has risen from 0.90% in 2000 to 2.18% in 2018 as shown in Figure 3.1. This puts China on par with countries such as Belgium, Canada, the Netherlands, and Norway. Though China's R&D intensity is still behind those of major players such as the United States (2.74%), Germany (2.94%), and Japan (3.15%), it is well ahead of other large developing economies such as South Africa (0.80%) and Brazil (1.28%).[3]

The increased effort in R&D has boosted China's innovation capacity. For example, the number of invention patents granted in China doubled during the period of 2006–2009 and more than trebled during 2009–2017 (Figure 3.2). In particular, the share of domestically owned inventions increased from 43.4% in 2006 to 77.8% in 2017. Apart from the current R&D personnel, there are

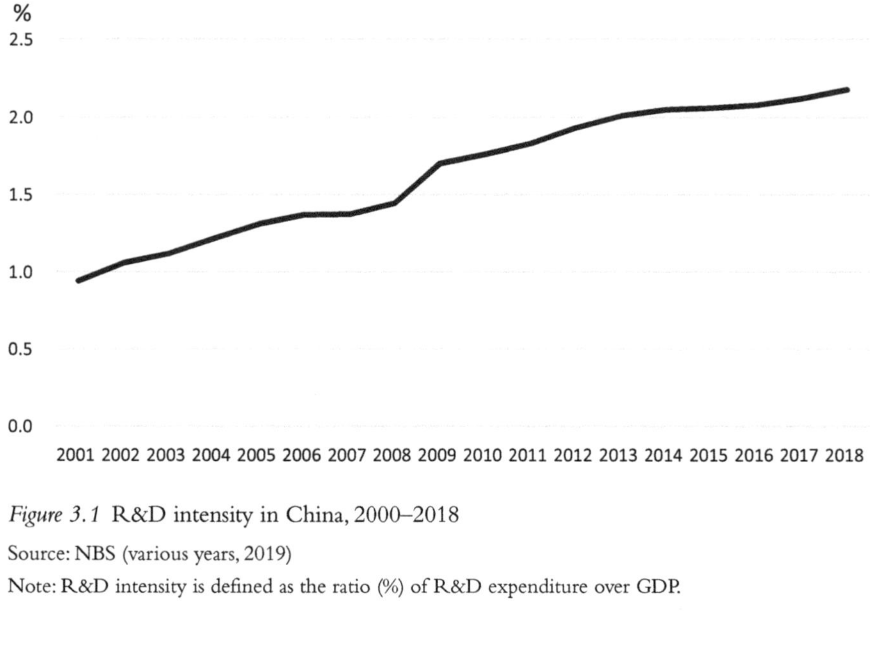

Figure 3.1 R&D intensity in China, 2000–2018

Source: NBS (various years, 2019)

Note: R&D intensity is defined as the ratio (%) of R&D expenditure over GDP.

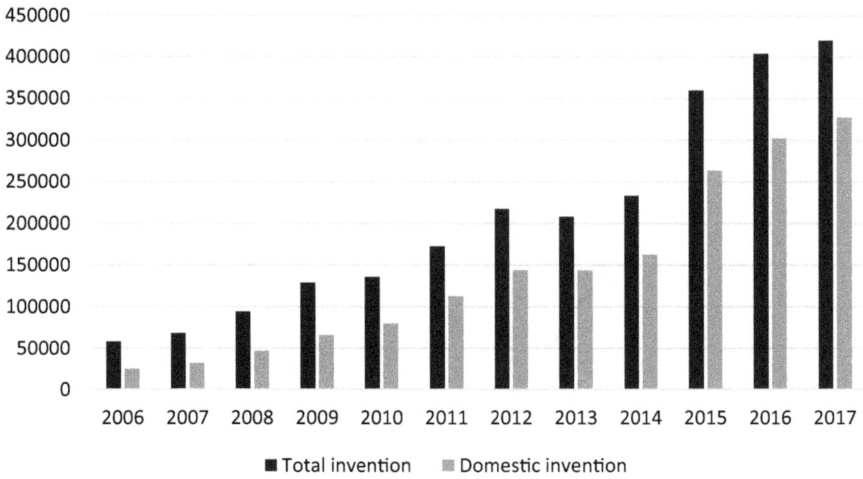

Figure 3.2 Granted invention patents, 2006–2017

Source: NBS (various years)

also about 27.5 million undergraduate students and 2.6 million postgraduate students who are studying in Chinese universities (NBS various years). Over 608,000 Chinese students also went overseas to study in 2017, and about 480,000 graduates from foreign institutions returned home in the same year according to the same source. These students will potentially add to the pool of R&D researchers and hence further strengthen China' innovation capacity in the coming years.

The increased role of indigenous R&D activities is well reflected in a study by Shi and Wu (2019) who examine China's input-output tables and considered product-embodied R&D expenditure. The authors further decompose the total R&D content in a sector into five components, namely the direct R&D expenditure of the industry, R&D incorporated in domestic intermediate inputs, domestic investment goods and services, imported intermediate inputs, and imported investment goods and services. Given this decomposition, the evolution of the five components of product-embodied R&D in terms of intensity is illustrated in Figure 3.3.

The prominence of the intensity of R&D embodiment in imported capital goods is captured by the sharp corner in the pentagon of year 2000 in Figure 3.3. The message is very clear that China's innovation system highly relies on the innovation spillover from imported capital goods. But this sharp point disappeared in 2005 and 2010. Instead, direct R&D of the industry and R&D embodied in domestic investment goods, and services take the dominant positions. This change implies that China's innovation system is becoming increasingly independent and self-enforced after a decade of development. In

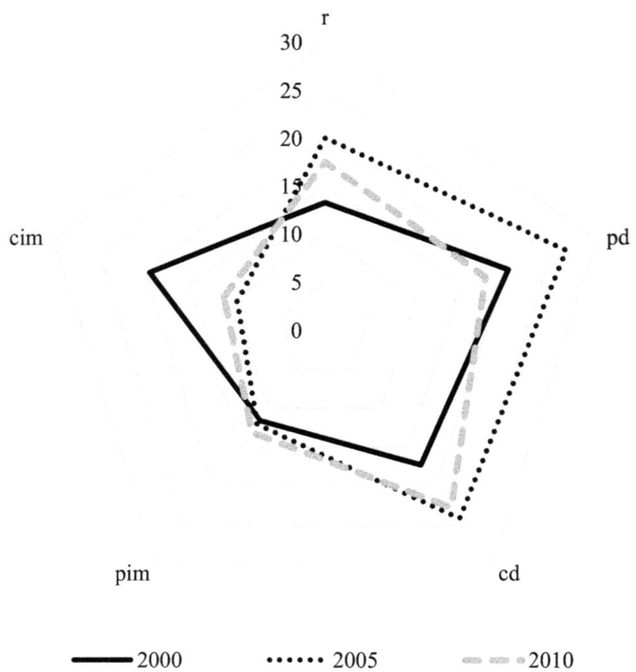

Figure 3.3 Five components of embodied R&D in selected years

Source: Shi and Wu (2019)

Note: The five components represent, respectively, the intensity of the direct R&D expenditure (r) of the industry, R&D incorporated in domestic intermediate inputs (pd), domestic investment goods and services (cd), imported intermediate inputs (cim) and imported investment goods and services (pim).

particular, many industries such as the traditional industries (agricultural, mining, and textiles) and high-tech industries are now less dependent upon the R&D embodiment in the imported capital goods (Shi and Wu, 2019).

However, considerable R&D is still embodied in imported dimensions namely the imported intermediate inputs and imported investment goods and services. In Figure 3.3, it is also noticed that the intensity of R&D incorporated in domestic intermediate inputs (pd) declined considerably during the period of 2005–2010. This change may reflect the disruption of the global financial crisis which triggered the release of the economic stimulus package of 4 trillion *renminbi*. Temporary credit expansion boosted Chinese firms' nominal earnings and hence led to a decline in R&D intensity (Shi and Wu, 2019).

In terms of intersectoral technology diffusion, intersectoral connection between Chinese industrial sectors has expanded dramatically. Shi and Wu (2019) adopt a network analysis approach and visualize the whole network's

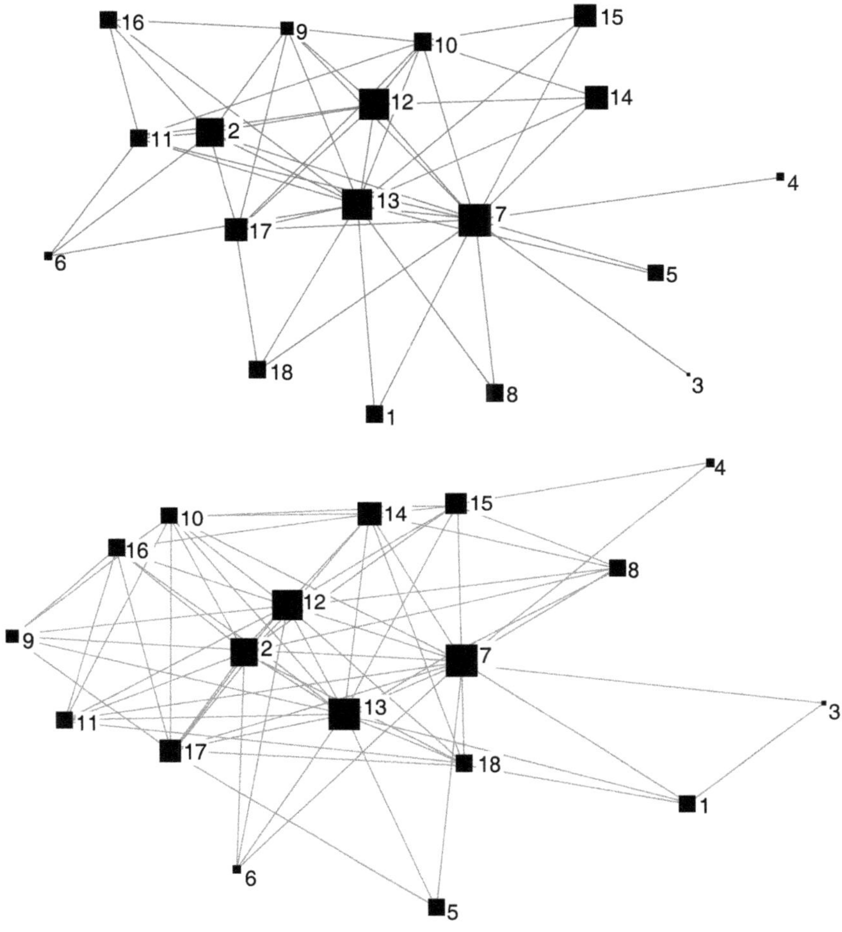

(b)

Figure 3.4 Domestic networks in 2000 vs. 2010

Source: Shi and Wu (2019)

structural change during 2000 and 2010. The top panel (a) of Figure 3.4 clearly shows that the network in 2000 is relative sparse, several sectors are distributed separately, and connectivity occurs mainly via some central sectors (sectors 7 – "chemicals and chemical products," 12 – "machinery and equipment, not elsewhere classified" and 13 – "electrical and optical equipment, transport equipment").[4] In 2010, however, the domestic network was quite well-connected. The same three industries (sectors 7, 12, and 13) completely possessed the central positions and acted as the most important R&D

sources. In comparison with the network in 2000, this kind of polycentric network is much better for technology diffusion (Shi and Wu, 2019). These findings imply that China's domestic innovation system is much better connected over time. Three industries in particular completely possess the central positions and act as the most important R&D sources surrounded by other industries.

2 The role of the business sector in China's R&D

Associated with the expansion in China's R&D capacity is the important role of the business sector including private businesses. Since the mid-1990s, Chinese business enterprises have become the leading players in the country's R&D activities. In 1997, Chinese firms together accounted for 42.9% of the country's R&D spending. However, this figure rose to 60.3% in 2000, 73.4% in 2010, and 76.4% in 2017 (NBS various years). It is now in line with the likes of Japan (78.5%), South Korea (75.4%), Sweden (70.5%), Switzerland (73.5%), and the United States (72.6%).[5]

The firms' increased role in R&D is also reflected in the changing share of patents applied by and granted to the enterprise sector over the national total. For example, the share of granted invention patent by firms over the national total increased from 37.6% in 2006 to 50.2% in 2010 and further to 61.4% in 2017.[6] Large and medium-sized manufacturing enterprises (LMEs), which account for 15.8% of all manufacturing firms, undertake 74.7% of total R&D expenditure and 60.7% of all invention patent applications by manufacturing firms.[7]

In terms of ownership, domestic firms were responsible for about 78.4% of R&D expenditure in 2017 with the rest being undertaken by firms with funds from Hong Kong, Macao, and Taiwan (HMT, 9.3%) and other foreign-invested firms (12.3%). These shares are consistent with the market shares of the three types of firms in the country (see Table 3.1). However, it appears that

Table 3.1 R&D Spending shares (%) by ownership, 2017

Ownership	*R&D spending*	*R&D personnel*	*Business revenue*	*Profits*
Domestic firms	78.4	77.5	78.1	75.4
State	7.6	6.7	8.6	7.0
Private	26.5	28.9	33.6	30.8
Shareholding	15.4	15.9	9.9	13.0
Limited liability	28.9	25.9	25.9	24.8
Others	0.0	0.1	0.1	0.0
Offshore firms	21.6	22.5	21.9	24.6
HMT	9.3	11.1	9.0	9.4
OECD	12.3	11.4	12.8	15.1

Source: The statistics in this table are calculated using information from NBS (2018)

the shareholding companies and limited liability firms tend to spend more on R&D relative to their market shares (revenue and profit shares).

In contrast, domestic privately owned firms were less keen to invest in R&D activities (Table 3.1). This situation may be the result of government policies or inherited from the pre-reform system in which SOEs and large firms were the key players. These findings were also reported in an empirical study using firm-level data by Wu (2017). Wu also shows that a high level of liability or debt burden is detrimental to innovation and that firms with heavy debts are less likely to invest in R&D or be persistent innovators if they do invest in innovation. These firms' R&D intensity is also likely to be lower. This was also observed in other economies such as Japan (Ogawa, 2007). Therefore, reducing company debt is vital for improvement in innovation. According to Wu (2017), Chinese innovative firms are in general large ones, exporters, and relatively more capital intensive. Siddharthan and Agarwal (1992) make the same observation about Indian firms.

3 R&D by sector

There are however considerable variations across the industrial subsectors in the Chinese economy. The top ten sectors with the largest R&D spending in 2017 (these sectors are listed in Table 3.2) accounted for about 75.8% of total R&D spending within all sectors. In particular, the top five sectors have a combined share of more than 50%. On average, these top players spend much more on R&D activities than other industrial subsectors. However, if the intensity is defined as the ratio of R&D spending over total revenue, three of the top spenders fall behind the industrial average. Thus there is still scope for growth in some sectors.

Table 3.2 R&D Spending by the top ten industrial sectors in 2017

Industrial sectors	*Spending shares (%)*	*Spending/ Profits (%)*	*Spending/ Revenue (%)*
Computers, communication etc	16.7	34.9	1.9
Transport equipment	13.3	20.3	1.6
Electrical equipment	10.4	26.7	1.7
Chemicals	7.6	15.6	1.1
General purpose machinery	5.8	22.3	1.5
Ferrous metals	5.3	18.6	1.0
Special purpose machinery	5.3	25.7	1.8
Pharmaceuticals	4.5	16.1	2.0
Non-ferrous metals	3.9	23.0	0.9
Nonmetallic mineral products	3.0	8.3	0.6
Top-ten sector	75.8	21.2	1.4
Economy-wide		16.0	1.1

Source: The statistics refer to enterprises with the designated scale or above and are drawn from NBS (2018).

As expected, the top ten sectors cover most of the so-called high technology (high-tech) industries, namely pharmaceuticals, medical equipment, computer, electronic and communication equipment, and aerospace. Not surprisingly, through the analysis of firm-level data, Wu (2017) observes that Chinese firms in these industries are more likely to invest in R&D. Investment in innovation may have boosted Chinese firms' competitiveness as China has done exceptionally well in the export of high-tech products. In 2006, the country became the world's largest exporter of high-tech products. In 2009, the value of China's high-tech exports amounted to US$348 billion, which is greater than the combined value (US$284 billion) of high-tech exports from Germany and the United States, or the world's second and third largest exporters of high-tech products, respectively. In 2010, China's exports of high-tech products further increased to US$492 billion. However, about 79% of the high-tech product exports were associated with China's processing trade, which is overwhelmingly dependent upon imported materials.[8]

Furthermore, China's processing trade is dominated by foreign-invested firms. As a result, foreign-invested firms accounted for 44% of China's high-tech exports in 2016 with an additional 33% being exported by firms with capital from HMT (Hong Kong, Macao, and Taiwan) (Figure 3.5). As foreign-owned firms are minor R&D players in China, China's success in high-tech product exports is not driven by indigenous innovation. Researchers have provided further evidence at the micro level to show that China has been very successful in attracting foreign high-tech enterprises and promoting exports but

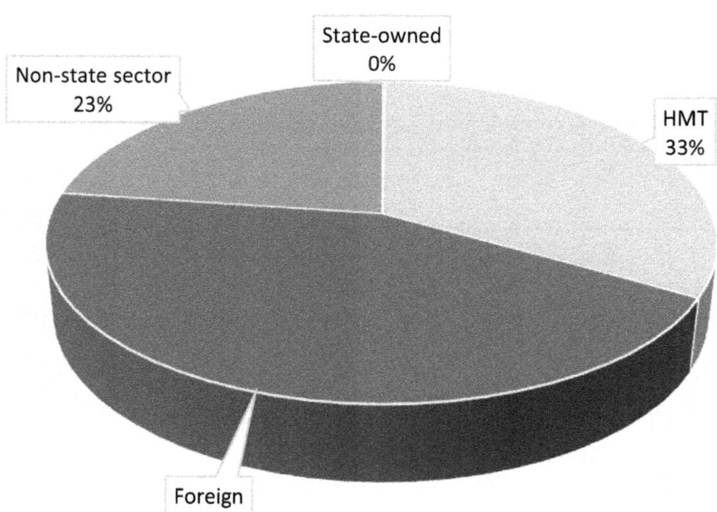

Figure 3.5 High-tech product exports by ownership, 2016

Source: The raw data are drawn from MoST (2017)

the country's domestic firms are still not competitive in the high-tech product market (Fu et al., 2012). Thus, it is cheap labor rather than innovation that is the key to the growth of China's high-tech product exports.

Even within the high-tech product sectors, considerable differences exist. Two sectors (electronic and communication equipment, and computers and office equipment) in particular accounted for 71% of total R&D spending and 94% of the total value of exports in the high-tech product sectors in 2010, though these numbers dropped slightly (to 67% and 92% respectively) in 2016. In addition, high-tech businesses are mainly located in the coastal areas, which have a 96% share of the export value and 84% of the R&D spending in the high-tech product sectors (YST various years).

4 Government support and university-industry collaboration

Since the release of the *Guideline for the National Medium- and Long-term Science and Technology Development Programs (2006–2020)* by the State Steering Committee of Science and Technology (S&T) and Education, the top innovation policy body in China, the Chinese government has initiated a series of national S&T programs. These programs are part of the drive for the country to reduce its reliance on the manufacture of labor-intensive goods and upgrade toward the production of higher value-added or skill-intensive goods (Woo, 2012). The national S&T programs are funded by the government and managed by the Ministry of Science and Technology of China (MoST) to support basic, applied, strategic, and demonstrative S&T research-oriented programs (Shi et al., 2019). Broadly these programs consist of fundamental programs and major programs. The fundamental programs include five sub-programs, namely, 973 Programs, 863 Programs, Supportive Programs, Infrastructure Platforms, and Policy-guiding Programs (PGP)[9]. Others like International Science and Technology Cooperative Special Programs (IS&TCSP) are specially designed for international collaborations. The major programs are designed to develop critical strategic products, key generic technology, and major construction projects. The national S&T programs are supported, organized, and implemented by the government to focus on several important areas. Participation in these programs is decided through competitive applications by the firms. The selection is made on the basis of the applicants' intended research areas, current technology competence, foundations and conditions in terms of investment, human resource allocation and infrastructure platform (as specified in the application forms of these programs).

The allocation of funds during 2006–2013 is demonstrated in Figure 3.6. It is clear that the Major Programs, 973 Programs, 863 Programs, and Supportive Programs account for the dominant share. In addition, the number of projects within each program also varies. In terms of the amount of money received per project on average, 863 Programs rank number one followed by the Supportive Programs and 973 Programs. Provincial governments also implemented

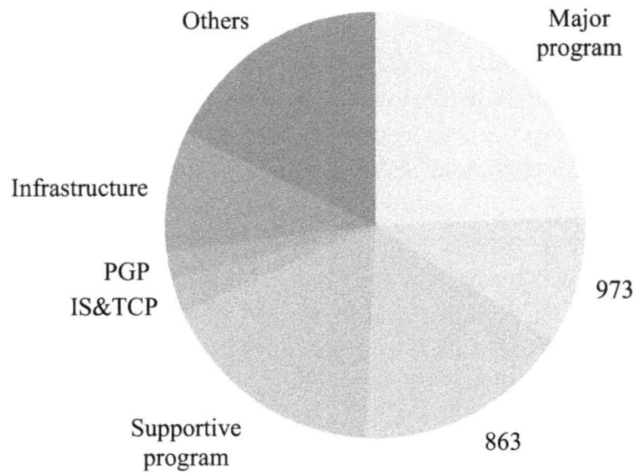

Figure 3.6 Allocation of fund during 2006–2013

Source: Shi et al. (2019)

S&T programs which are however different from the national ones in terms of their goals and selection criteria even though these programs are assumed to be complementary to national programs (Shi et al., 2019).

The selection of program participants is mainly based on firms' knowledge stock, knowledge infrastructure, and experience in undertaking or joining S&T programs. Shi et al. (2019) show that state-owned enterprises (SOEs) still have higher probability to participate in national S&T programs and argue that the preference of government has not changed much across programs and over time. The effect of national S&T is controversial. According to Shi et al. (2019), the effect of national S&T programs may be overestimated in general. The authors provided empirical evidence to support that government grants may crowd out private investment in R&D and hence lead to potential deterioration of innovation efficiency. At the firm level, the effect seems to be bigger for large firms and non-SOEs. Deeper engagement with S&T programs could accumulate the crowding out effect and therefore be detrimental to innovation performance. Shi et al. (2019) also observe a significantly positive effect on external R&D investment and patent applications through the participation of national S&T programs. However, these impacts on external R&D investment are not stable over time.

Associated with the implementation of national S&T programs, Chinese universities are encouraged to develop industrial links, expand their research funding and strengthen their applied research capacities. Project 211 and Project 985 are two examples among many initiatives and reforms, which aim to assist Chinese universities in research capacity building and collaboration with the industry sector. The effectiveness of these initiatives has attracted the attention of researchers. Shi, Wu and Fu (2019) present a study to investigate whether university-industry collaboration has contributed to efficiency improvements in Chinese firms. Their study is based on empirical analysis of panel data of 443 innovative firms covering the period of 2008–2011. The authors consider the impacts of university-industry collaboration at the two stages of the innovation process, namely the research and development (R&D) stage and commercialization stage.

Shi, Wu and Fu (2019) show that firms can benefit from the external knowledge obtained through collaborations with academic institutions. Although there are certain barriers particularly for SMEs to launch collaboration with universities, once started, collaborations between firms and universities have a very positive and significant effect on innovation. It is argued that the excessive exposure to the external environment may raise the risk of knowledge, but Shi, Wu and Fu (2019) find no empirical evidence of this adverse effect with the sample of Chinese innovative firms.

Shi, Wu and Fu (2019) however observe that, subject to regional institutional factors, university-industry collaboration may have different effects across the two innovation stages. Stringent enforcement of intellectual property rights (IPR) reinforces the barrier for imitation and raises the demand for more indigenous innovation investment. It may also exacerbate the conflicts over intellectual property due to collaboration (Bruneel et al., 2010), and hence reduce the post-innovation rents (Aghion et al., 2018). All these are harmful to efficiency improvement at the R&D stage. But the possibility of the knowledge leakage is likely small at the commercialization stage, and therefore the impact of collaboration is not affected significantly.

The impact of university-industry collaboration in regions with a higher level of openness tends to be smaller at the commercialization stage. Shi, Wu and Fu (2019) argue that, although the risk of knowledge leakage is much higher in a more open region, at the R&D stage firms still can benefit from the knowledge spillovers generated by foreign firms. However, at the commercialization stage firms may have to face more fierce market competition and worse conditions for appropriating innovation benefits.

In addition, Shi, Wu and Fu (2019) also observe that the impact of university-industry collaboration on firms' R&D efficiency will be greater in regions with a university sector of high quality since technology and innovation is biased toward skilled labor, particularly in science-based industries. However, this difference does not exist at the commercialization stage.

The findings mentioned here imply that regional governments should design and implement policies to build an innovation-supporting and collaboration-friendly institutional environment so that firms can fully benefit from university-industry collaboration.

5 Offshore investment and innovation effect

In the twenty-first century, China has become the world's third largest source country of foreign direct investment. The latest UNCTAD statistics show that China invested about US$125 billion globally in 2017, a ten-fold increase from about US$12 billion in 2005.[10] However, the bulk of the investment went to

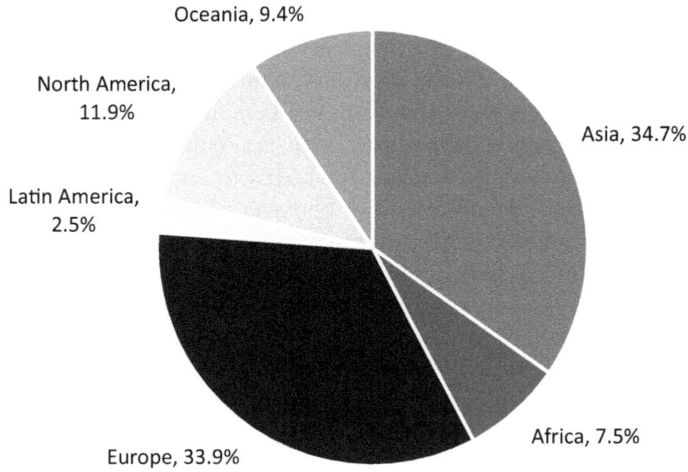

Figure 3.7 Distribution of Chinese OFDI in 2017

Source: Author's own work based on raw data from NBS (2018)

Note: Asia excludes Hong Kong and Latin America excludes Cayman Islands and British Virgin Islands.

Hong Kong. A large amount was also invested in Cayman Islands and British Virgin Islands. Investment in these places is highly suspicious and accounted for almost a half of China's total OFDI. If these tax havens are excluded, Chinese OFDI is mainly concentrated in Asia and Europe (Figure 3.7).

The dramatic growth in OFDI has partly been driven by the country's *Go Global* policy initiated at the start of this century (Wang and Miao, 2016). Researchers have for a long time been interested in the reverse technology spill-over effect, namely domestic firms improve their technological innovation and productivity due to overseas investment activities. Zhou et al. (2019) presented a case study of China by using a balanced panel dataset for 31 Chinese provinces and municipalities over the period 2004–2014. The authors focus on 21 main destinations of Chinese outward foreign direct investment (OFDI) which are divided into two groups, namely 11 developed economies and ten transitional and emerging economies.[11] Zhou et al. (2019) show that domestic innovation performance is positively related to OFDI in developed economies while it is negatively related to OFDI in transitional and emerging economies. The authors also observe that financial development and human capital could weaken these relationships between OFDI and domestic innovation performance. They argue that government policies should promote the structural reform of the Chinese state-owned banking system to reduce concentration and strengthen interbank competition. Otherwise, enterprises may face further difficulties in raising funds.

The conclusion by Zhou et al. (2019) is consistent with that by Hong et al. (2019). The latter goes further to look at the effect of technology gap between host and home countries. Hong et al. (2019) introduce the concepts of "observed technology gap" and "expected technology gap." An observed technology gap refers to the existing differences in technology between establishments (countries or regions) while an expected technology gap reflects the effort of imitating and learning from technology leaders. The authors conclude that regions with a large observed technology gap and a small expected technology gap can benefit more from OFDI. Therefore, a large observed technology gap provides home country firms with the potential to catch up with host country leaders or the so-called advantage of backwardness. This restates the importance of investment in technology-leading countries, on the one hand. On the other hand, a small expected technology gap provides the impetus for home country firms to assimilate and internalize cutting-edge technology. Thus government policies should also focus on narrowing the expected technology gap.

6 Outlook and challenges

With robust economic growth and strong government support, China's investment in R&D, as well as innovation capacity, is set to expand. From an international perspective, it seems that China's R&D spending pattern is to follow those of Japan and South Korea (Figure 3.8). Given the size of the Chinese

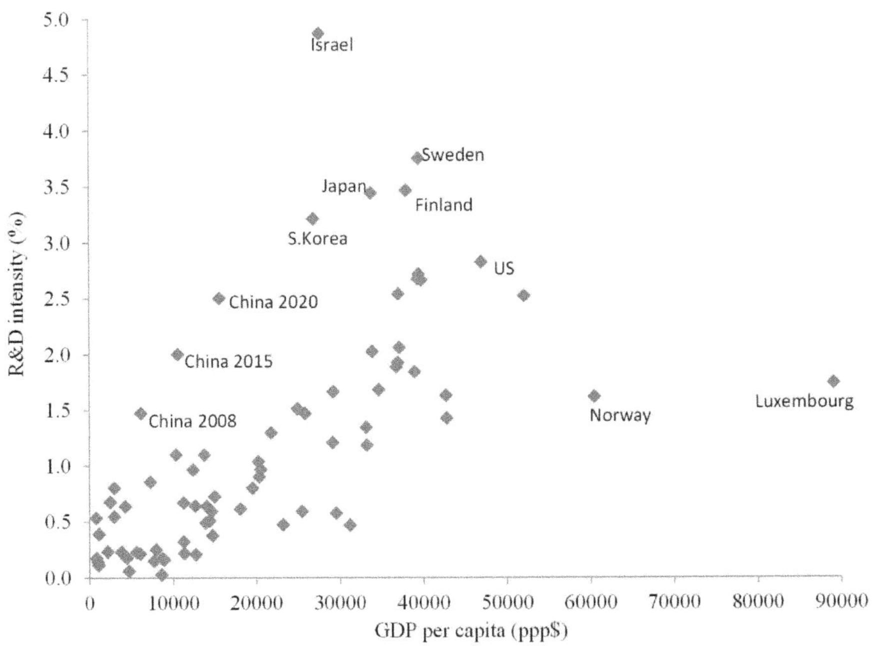

Figure 3.8 R&D intensity and GDP per capita in selected economies, 2008

Source: The raw data are drawn from the World Bank (2011)

economy, it can be anticipated that the country will become a technology leader in the world. Therefore, it can be concluded that within decades, China could become a modern and creative high-income society as advocated in the World Bank's China 2030 Report released on February 27, 2012.

However, several challenges will affect the sustainability of China's current growth momentum. First, there is huge disparity across the Chinese regions. Among the 31 administrative regions in China, the average R&D intensity in firms varies from under 6% in three regions to more than 20% in five regions in 2017 (Figure 3.9). This gap adds to the broad regional inequality which is now a major social issue faced by policymakers in the country.

Second, the structure and hence quality of China's R&D has changed in recent years. The combined share of basic and applied research expenditure over total R&D spending declined from 32% in 1995 to 17% in 2010 and further to 16% in 2017 while this figure is around 50% in major developed economies (OECD, 2009, YST various years). Thus, the expanded role of Chinese enterprises may have led to the rapid growth of market-driven R&D investment. The challenge ahead for policymakers is then to ensure that the market-oriented R&D activities would not grow at the expense of long-term innovation capacity building in the country.

Third, Figure 3.10 illustrates that private firms have the largest share of invention patent applications, which is consistent with their R&D investment share (see Table 3.1). Shareholding firms seem to perform better than other firms with disproportionately more patent applications. However, firms with offshore capital account for disproportionately less shares. Therefore, future policies should aim to provide more incentives for foreign firms and encourage them to invest more in R&D. Particularly strict enforcement of intellectual property protection is vital for foreign firms to register their inventions in China. Though China has made rapid progress and noteworthy achievements in IPR law reforms in the past decades, foreign investors are still concerned about China's enforcement of IPR regulations and laws. The lack of protection of IPRs is detrimental to indigenous innovation too. Thus, more efforts should be made to promote IPR knowledge and awareness in society, and enforce the related laws and regulations stringently.

In addition, large and medium enterprises (LMEs) spent proportionally more on R&D in China. In 2017, LMEs accounted for 74.7% of R&D spending while their market share is much smaller (63.7% and 68.6% in terms of revenue and profit shares) according to the National Bureau of Statistics (NBS, 2018). Thus, small firms may be disadvantaged in terms of access to R&D resources or lack of incentives for investment in innovation. This disparity should be corrected. This view was also expressed in the World Bank's China 2030 Report. While large and medium firms are important players in China's R&D sector, small enterprises could have the advantage of being potent and flexible in some fields of innovation, and hence should be encouraged to be more active in innovation (Tong and Zhu, 2009).

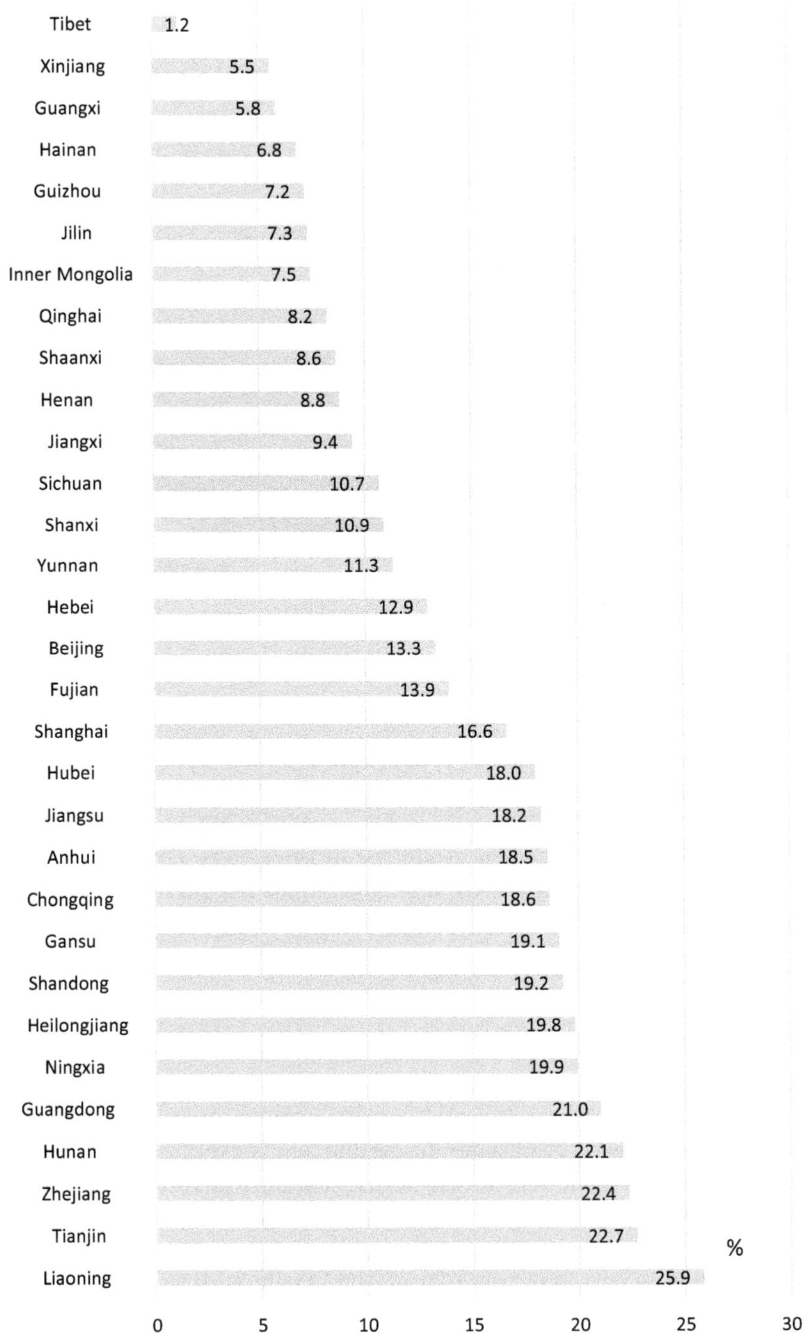

Figure 3.9 R&D intensity in Chinese regions, 2017

Note and source: R&D intensity is defined as the ratio (%) of R&D expenditure over profits by all firms with designated scale or above and is calculated using data from NBS (2018)

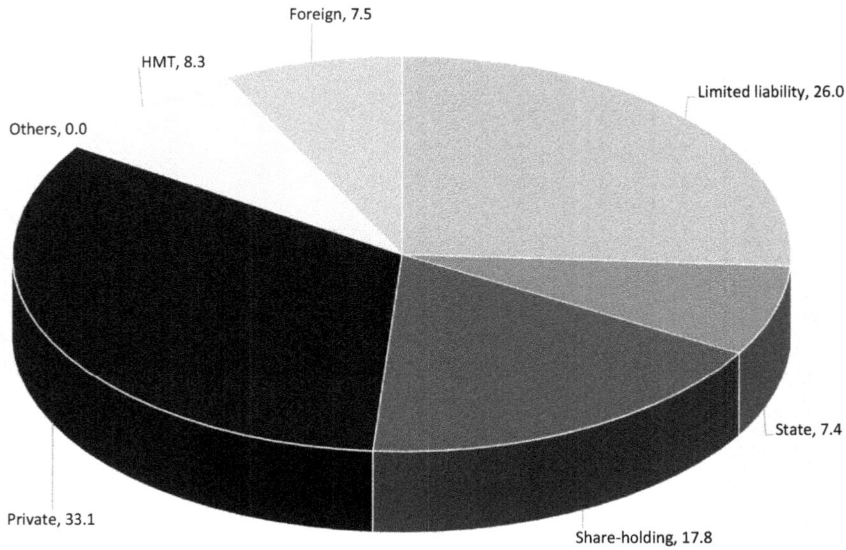

Figure 3.10 Shares of patent applications, 2017

Source: The raw data drawn from NBS (2018)

Finally, labor compensation as a proportion of total R&D costs in China was about 21% in 2007, 24% in 2010, and 30% in 2016 (YST various years). It is much lower than the OECD average of about 50% (OECD, 2009). Therefore, China still enjoys a considerable advantage in labor costs. However, low labor compensation could also make Chinese institutions less attractive in the internationally competitive labor market.

7 Conclusions

In summary, China has achieved considerably in the R&D sector in terms of investment, capacity building, and outcome. Growth in this sector has been particularly strong in recent years due to the support of government policies. China's economic power continues to expand and is expected to overtake the United States to become the world's largest economy in a decade. There is no doubt that China's R&D sector will grow. There are however some challenges ahead.

The business sector dominates China's R&D field with an investment share of over 70%. This phenomenon is reshaping the structure of China's R&D activities. The challenge to policymakers is to ensure that the quality of R&D and hence long-term capacity building would not be compromised due to the expansion of market-oriented activities. SOEs are still major investors in R&D, but they suffer from poor efficiency performance. The immediate concern is how to improve efficiency in the SOEs. In the long run, the role of private businesses in R&D should be strengthened. Chinese policymakers will also face challenges in reducing regional inequality and retaining skilled R&D researchers in an internationally competitive market.

Acknowledgments

This chapter is an extended version of Yanrui Wu, "China's Rapid Catch-up in Research and Development," EAI Background Brief No.711, East Asian Institute, National University of Singapore, March 2012. The author thanks Professor Yongnian Zheng and the East Asian Institute (NUS) for hosting him during his sabbatical leave from 14 November 2011 to 13 February 2012. He also thanks Paul Jensen, Sarah Tong, John Wong and participants of a seminar at CEPII Club (Paris) for their helpful comments on earlier drafts. The chapter also draws material from "Trends and Prospects in China's Research and Development Sector" (The Australian Economic Review, 45(4), 467–74). The author acknowledges the permissions from the publisher John Wiley and Sons.

Notes

1 This growth rate is based on the author's own calculation using data from the NBS (various years, 2019).
2 These numbers were derived by using data from the World Development Indictors, World Bank (www.worldbank.org, accessed Feb 2019).
3 Data are drawn from the World Development Indictors, World Bank (www.worldbank.org, accessed Feb 2019).
4 Shi and Wu (2019) classify the Chinese economy into 18 sectors, namely (1) Agriculture, hunting, forestry, and fishing; (2) Mining and quarrying; (3) Food products, beverages, and tobacco; (4) Textiles, textile products, leather, and footwear; (5) Wood and products of wood and cork, and Pulp, paper, paper products, printing, and publishing; (6) Coke, refined petroleum products and nuclear fuel; (7) Chemicals and chemical products; (8) Rubber and plastics products; (9) Other nonmetallic mineral products; (10) Basic metals; (11) Fabricated metal products except machinery and equipment; (12) Machinery and equipment, not elsewhere classified; (13) Electrical and optical equipment, Transport equipment; (14) Electrical machinery and apparatus, not elsewhere classified; (15) Manufacturing not elsewhere classified; recycling; (16) Electricity, gas, and water supply; (17) Construction; and (18) Total services. This industrial classification conforms to ISIC Rev. 3.0.
5 These are 2016 statistics reported online (https://stats.oecd.org).
6 Those shares are calculated by using data from NBS (various years). Chinese patents are officially classified into three categories, namely, invention, design, and utility patents.
7 These shares are derived by using statistics from NBS (various years).
8 In this paragraph, the 2009 statistics are drawn from the World Bank (2011) and the 2010 data are sourced from MoST (2011).
9 The full names of 973 Programs and 863 Programs are National Basic Research and Development Programs of China, and National High Technology Research and Development Programs of China, respectively (see the website of MoST for more details on these programs: www.most.gov.cn/kjjh).
10 These numbers were drawn from NBS (2019) and the United Nations Conference on Trade and Development (unctadstat.unctad.org) online database.

11 The 11 developed economies include the United States, Australia, Singapore, United Kingdom, France, Canada, Germany, the Netherlands, Sweden, Republic of Korea, and Japan. The ten transitional and emerging economies are the Russian Federation, Kazakhstan, Indonesia, South Africa, Mongolia, Pakistan, Iran, India, Thailand, and Brazil.

References

Aghion, P., L. Cassar, S. Bechtold and H. Herz (2018) "The Causal Effects of Competition on Innovation: Experimental Evidence." *The Journal of Law, Economics, and Organization* 34(2): 162–195.

Bruneel, J., P. d'Este and A. Salter (2010) "Investigating the Factors that Diminish the Barriers to University – Industry Collaboration." *Research Policy* 39(7): 858–868.

Fu, Dahai, Yanrui Wu and Yihong Tang (2012) "Does Innovation Matter for Chinese High-Tech Exports? A Firm-Level Analysis." *Frontiers of Economics in China* 7(2): 218–245.

Hong, Jin, Chongyang Zhou, Yanrui Wu, Ruicheng Wang and Dora Marinova (2019) "Technology Gap, Reverse Technology Spillover and Domestic Innovation Performance in Outward Foreign Direct Investment: Evidence from China." *China and World Economy* 27(2): 1–23.

MoST (2011) *China High-tech Industry Data Book 2011*, compiled by the Ministry of Science and Technology, Beijing. Available at www.sts.org.cn.

MoST (2017) *China High-tech Industry Yearbook 2017*, compiled by the Ministry of Science and Technology, Beijing: China Statistics Press.

NBS (2018) *China Statistical Yearbook 2018*, compiled by National Statistical Bureau, Beijing: China Statistics Press.

NBS (2019) *China Social and Economic Statistics Communiqué 2018*, compiled by National Bureau of Statistics, 28 February. Available at www.stats.gov.cn.

NBS (various years) *China Statistical Yearbook*, published annually by National Statistical Bureau, Beijing: China Statistics Press.

OECD (2009) "Measuring China's Innovation System: National Specificities and International Comparisons." STI Working Paper 2009/1, Statistical Analysis of Science, Technology and Industry, OECD, Paris.

Ogawa, Kazuo (2007) "Debt, R&D Investment and Technological Progress: A Panel Study of Japanese Manufacturing Firms' Behaviour During the 1990s." *Journal of Japanese and International Economics* 21(4): 403–423.

Shi, Xing and Yanrui Wu (2019) "Evolution of Product-embodied R&D in China." *Structural Change and Economic Dynamics* 49: 324–333.

Shi, Xing, Yanrui Wu and Dahai Fu (2019) "Does University-Industry Collaboration Improve Innovation Efficiency? Evidence from Chinese Firms." *Economic Modelling*, Forthcoming.

Shi, Xing, Yanrui Wu, Dahai Fu, Xiumei Guo and Huaqing Wu (2019) "Effects of National Science and Technology Programs on Innovation in Chinese Firms." *Asian Economic Papers* 18(1): 207–236.

Siddharthan, N. S. and R. N. Agarwal (1992) "Determinants Of R&D Decisions: A Cross-Section Study of Indian Private Corporate Firms." *Economics of Innovation and New Technology* 2(2): 103–110.

Sigurdson, Jon, Jiang Jiang, Xinxin Kong, Yongzhong Wang and Yuli Tang (2005) *Technological Superpower China*, Cheltenham: Edward Elgar Publishing.

State Council (2006) "Medium-to-Long Term Program of National Science and Technology Development 2006–2020." Available on the Chinese government website www.gov.cn.

State Council (2011) "12th Five-year Programme 2011–2015." Available on the Chinese government website www.gov.cn.

Tong, Sarah Y. and Jingjing Zhu (2009) "China's Rapidly Growing Enterprise-led Innovation System." EAI Background Brief No. 461, East Asian Institute, National University of Singapore.

Wang, Huiyao and Lu Miao (2016) *China Goes Global: How China's Overseas Investment is Transforming Its Business Enterprises*, Palgrave Macmillan Asian Business Series, Basingstoke: Palgrave Publishing.

Woo, W. T. (2012) "China Meets the Middle-Income Trap: The Large Potholes in the Road to Catching-up." *Journal of Chinese Economic and Business Studies* 10(4): 313–336.

World Bank (2011) *World Development Indicators 2011*, Washington, DC: The World Bank. Available at www.worldbank.org.

Wu, Yanrui (2017) "Propensity, Intensity and Persistence of R&D Spending in Chinese Firms." *China: An International Journal* 15(4): 179–203.

YST (various years) *China Statistical Yearbook of Science and Technology*, compiled by National Statistical Bureau and Ministry of Science and Technology, Beijing: China Statistics Press.

Zhou, Chongyang, Jin Hong, Yanrui Wu and Dora Marinova (2019) "Outward Foreign Direct Investment and Domestic Innovation Performance: Evidence from China." *Technology Analysis & Strategic Management* 31(1): 81–95.

4 Technological capabilities in China

Patterns of specialization toward a knowledge-intensive economy

Iciar Dominguez Lacasa, Mahmood Shubbak

1 Introduction

Technological development and innovation have long been a center of intensive research in economic and business studies (Fagerberg et al., 2010). There is an increasing unanimity in the literature on the role that technological development can play as the key factor for both economic growth and business competitiveness (Schumpeter, 1934; Pavitt, 1963; Freeman, 2004; Andries and Faems, 2013; Shubbak, 2018). Accordingly, growing empirical evidence highlights the vital role of accumulating domestic technological capabilities for developing economies in order to be able to absorb, adopt, and further develop advanced technologies (Mowery and Nelson, 2001; Malerba and Nelson, 2011; Shubbak, 2019). Successful catching-up processes in latecomer economies are usually accompanied by deep learning, knowledge accumulation, and technical change procedures (Lall, 1992; Ernst and Kim, 2002).

In this analysis, we consider the technological capability of a country as its ability to employ scientific and technical knowledge into cognitive and practical competences for absorbing, using, and developing new technologies. On this basis, countries can differ in the development of their technological capabilities due to various endogenous and exogenous factors. Technology upgrading can thus be seen as a multi-dimensional structural change process: technologically, industrially, and organizationally (Dominguez Lacasa et al., 2019; Radosevic and Yoruk, 2016).

In this chapter, we study the evolution of technological capabilities in China since 1980 using patent indicators. The main aim is to deepen our knowledge about the process of technological catching up taking place in China and to identify the interrelated processes of structural change therein directed toward becoming a knowledge-intensive economy in the period 1983–2012.

China has witnessed rapid improvements in its technological capability both vertically, in terms of its intensity, and horizontally, in terms of its diversity (Lee, 2018; Dominguez Lacasa et al., 2019). Nonetheless, this process seems to be quite recent. To capture the Chinese technological patterns of specialization and structural change, the chapter first analyzes specialization indicators over time, then it traces the dynamics of Chinese technological activities in different fields until 2012. The assessment considers global trends in technological development and the position of China and other emerging economies in a dynamic technological landscape.

The present chapter is organized in five sections. The next section explains the research methodology, data, and indicators used throughout the empirical analysis. Section 3 considers the development trends of Chinese technological capabilities with relevance to selected developed and emerging economies. In section 4, the technological specialization and dynamism indicators are discussed. Finally, we conclude in section 5 by synthesizing the main findings and providing outlooks for further research.

2 Data and indicators

To empirically capture the technological capability building processes and catching-up processes undertaken in China, this chapter is built upon the analysis of patent data. Patents represent a common form of intellectual property both in the business and academic realms (OECD, 2009). They have been created to grant their owner the exclusive legal right to commercially use and license their inventions for a limited period of time – usually twenty years. In return, patent owners disclose the technical details of their inventions to the public.

Despite the limitations for using patents as an indicator of technological innovation (Archibugi, 1992; Pavitt, 1985), patent indicators allow for covering long periods of time as well as large geographical areas. They also reveal detailed technical information about inventions along with their legal and intellectual owners (Dominguez Lacasa et al., 2018). Accordingly, the empirical analysis of patent filings can offer rich insight into the accumulated technological knowledge and its development trends over time. Pavitt (1985 p. 82) argued that "patent statistics reflect innovative – and not just inventive – activities," as they cover the entire development and commercialization cycle of new inventions and are directly related to the marketable exploitation of them.

In this section, we explain our data sources and indicators in detail. Accordingly, this section provides the reader with the sources of data used throughout the chapter and mathematical definitions of the empirical indicators introduced therein.

The patent data used in this chapter is extracted from the Worldwide Patent Statistical Database (PATSTAT, 2014), which is developed and maintained by the European Patent Office (EPO). We distinguish between two forms of technological capability: domestic technological capability pushing the technology frontier, and domestic technological capability for development behind the technology frontier, which triggers the adoption and improvement of technologies developed abroad. Such differentiation is empirically achieved using two types of patent applications:

A **Transnational patent applications** (TN) of domestic inventors are used as a proxy for technological capability pushing the technology frontier. TN patents can be defined as patent applications enforceable across the national borders of a single country.

This is the case of patent applications filed at the European Patent office through the regional phase (EPO Patents) as well as international patent applications filed under the Patent Cooperation Treaty (PCT Patents). Therefore, the number of TN patents is technically calculated by summing up EPO and PCT patent applications, avoiding double counting of applications that belong to the same patent family (Frietsch and Schmoch, 2010).

Since TN patents are cross-country enforceable, they are usually expected to hold a higher technological and economic value and are thus associated with a perceived novelty at the global level (technology frontier).

B **Priority Filings** (PF) are used in this research as a proxy for technological capability behind the global technology frontier. A priority filing is defined as the first patent application filed to protect an invention, usually in a national patent office.

The indicator was put forward to trace technological activities in developing countries and emerging economies (de Rassenfosse et al., 2013). It has further been used in development studies to capture the overall technological capability of a country (Dominguez Lacasa et al., 2019).

However, Dominguez Lacasa et al. (2019) found that, for developing and emerging countries, a significantly high share of the overall patented technological capability covers process innovations and improvements on foreign technologies. Accordingly, the fractional counts[1] of priority filings are used in this research as a proxy for technological capability behind the global technology frontier.

To compare the development trends of the Chinese technological capabilities with other developing and developed economies, we calculate the **patent intensity indicator** as the total number of patent applications (*App*) filed by the country's inhabitants in a specific year (y) over its population (N) in that year (Equation 4.1). We calculate the patent intensity (patent applications per capita) for both patent types – transnational and priority filings – independently.

$$Patent\ Intensity = \frac{App_{y}}{N_{y}} * 10^{6} \tag{4.1}$$

Population data[2] (N_y) is extracted from the World Bank's World Development Indicators database (World Bank, 2019). For practical purposes, the calculated intensity is multiplied by 10^6 so that it represents patent applications per million inhabitants.

Regarding the **temporal and spatial coverage** of our analysis, it covers 33 years over the timespan of 1980 to 2012[3]. Additionally, the technological specialization analysis considers three periods: 1983–1992, 1993–2002, and 2003–2012.

Besides China, the other emerging countries taken into consideration are Brazil, Russia, India, and South Africa. Furthermore, Japan, the United States of America, and the EU15 are considered as three baselines for the comparative analysis.

To capture the structural change process toward a knowledge-intensive economy in China, we trace the dynamics of its **technological inventive activities** relative to other countries. Empirically, we built upon the technological content of countries' patent portfolios. Patent statistics databases such as PATSTAT contain rich information on the technological fields under which novelty is claimed. The International Patent Classification (IPC) system is the most common system used for this purpose. It provides a detailed classification of patent filings' technological content through hierarchical levels: sections, classes, and groups (WIPO, 2019).

Based on the IPC system, Schmoch (2008) defines 35 technological fields grouped in five technological sectors: Chemicals, Electrical Engineering, Mechanical Engineering, Instruments, and Others (see Table 4.1). In our analysis of domestic technological specialization, we implement this definition to divide countries' priority-filing portfolios into technological sectors and fields.[4] Table 4.1 gives the counts of priority filings in each field and sector over three periods. The last column includes an indicator for capturing how the sectors and fields are developing related to each other or, in other words, how global specialization changes over time.

The **Technological Dynamics Indicator** captures the global shifts of technological specialization between the initial (R_i) and final (R_f) periods under consideration. Accordingly, the indicator is calculated here as the ratio of the global technological specialization of the sector (R) in the last period to that in the first period (Equation 4.2).[5]

$$Dynamism = \frac{R_f}{R_i};\ where\ R = P_{Wj} / P_{WT} \tag{4.2}$$

According to the patent data, "Electrical Engineering" and "Other Fields" were the sectors that gained relative importance in terms of inventive activities in the period 1983–2012. "Chemicals" maintained its relative importance over time while "Mechanical Engineering" and "Instruments" decreased their share in the total patent output.

We further track the specialization in each country in the different sectors and assess changes in specialization over time. To estimate the **relative technological specialization** in each country, we calculate the **Revealed Technological Advantage Index** (RTA), which was originally developed by Balassa (1965).

This indicator allows for the estimation of the relative technological specialization of a country (i) in a specific technology (j) within all technologies (T) of its patent portfolio vis-a-vis the global (W) technological specialization in a given period (see Equation 4.3, where P represents the fractional counting of transnational patent applications).

$$RTA = \frac{p_{ij} / p_{iT}}{p_{Wj} / p_{WT}} \tag{4.3}$$

Table 4.1 Priority filings in 35 technology fields and five technological sectors 1983–2012

Sector	No.	*Technological Field*	*1983–1992*		*1993–2002*		*2003–2012*		*Tech. dynamism**
			Filings	*Share*	*Filings*	*Share*	*Filings*	*Share*	
Electrical engineering	1	Electrical machinery, apparatus, energy	3,283,177	6.8%	3,638,303	6.5%	5,721,462	7.3%	1.1
	2	Audio-visual technology	2,884,693	6.0%	3,145,035	5.7%	3,830,756	4.9%	0.8
	3	Telecommunications	1,546,926	3.2%	2,170,269	3.9%	2,718,840	3.5%	1.1
	4	Digital communication	389,906	0.8%	1,052,599	1.9%	2,709,435	3.4%	4.3
	5	Basic communication processes	866,172	1.8%	653,628	1.2%	673,122	0.9%	0.5
	6	Computer technology	2,515,751	5.2%	3,261,782	5.9%	5,791,905	7.4%	1.4
	7	IT methods for management	60,247	0.1%	543,177	1.0%	1,189,037	1.5%	12.1
	8	Semiconductors	1,960,535	4.1%	2,389,294	4.3%	3,426,649	4.4%	1.1
			13,507,408	**28.0%**	**16,854,087**	**30.3%**	**26,061,207**	**33.2%**	**1.2**
Instruments	9	Optics	25,07,691	5.2%	2,816,545	5.1%	3,287,011	4.2%	0.8
	10	Measurement	2,901,561	6.0%	2,399,004	4.3%	3,724,947	4.7%	0.8
	11	Analysis of biological materials	163,536	0.3%	180,500	0.3%	291,879	0.4%	1.1
	12	Control	979,338	2.0%	1,034,473	1.9%	1,476,738	1.9%	0.9
	13	Medical technology	1,115,381	2.3%	1,631,701	2.9%	2,369,135	3.0%	1.3
			7,667,506	**15.9%**	**8,062,223**	**14.5%**	**11,149,710**	**14.2%**	**0.9**
Chemistry	14	Organic fine chemistry	918,712	1.9%	908,853	1.6%	1,231,774	1.6%	0.8
	15	Biotechnology	362,765	0.8%	513,627	0.9%	920,000	1.2%	1.6
	16	Pharmaceuticals	406,193	0.8%	764,885	1.4%	1,801,198	2.3%	2.7
	17	Macromolecular chemistry, polymers	965,966	2.0%	971,376	1.7%	1,122,837	1.4%	0.7
	18	Food chemistry	536,678	1.1%	794,065	1.4%	1,697,346	2.2%	1.9
	19	Basic materials chemistry	1,008,999	2.1%	1,162,264	2.1%	1,716,763	2.2%	1.0
	20	Materials, metallurgy	1,736,758	3.6%	1,299,173	2.3%	1,934,318	2.5%	0.7
	21	Surface technology, coating	991,722	2.1%	972,935	1.7%	1,323,186	1.7%	0.8
	22	Microstructural and nanotechnology	2,233	0.0%	26,277	0.0%	135,671	0.2%	37.3
	23	Chemical engineering	1,291,973	2.7%	1,205,170	2.2%	1,587,826	2.0%	0.8
	24	Environmental technology	675,957	1.4%	1,006,961	1.8%	1,364,232	1.7%	1.2
			8,897,957	**18.5%**	**9,625,584**	**17.3%**	**14,835,151**	**18.9%**	**1.0**

Mechanical Engineering	25	Handling	1,845,949	3.8%	2,085,144	3.7%	2,212,334	2.8%	0.7
	26	Machine tools	2,255,422	4.7%	1,789,115	3.2%	2,314,352	2.9%	0.6
	27	Engines, pumps, turbines	1,612,779	3.3%	1,615,819	2.9%	2,287,691	2.9%	0.9
	28	Textile and paper machines	1,602,205	3.3%	1,599,857	2.9%	1,720,702	2.2%	0.7
	29	Other special machines	2,169,126	4.5%	2,195,203	3.9%	2,511,712	3.2%	0.7
	30	Thermal processes and apparatus	1,205,471	2.5%	1,260,377	2.3%	1,660,663	2.1%	0.8
	31	Mechanical elements	1,505,991	3.1%	1,792,763	3.2%	2,329,592	3.0%	0.9
	32	Transport	1,836,127	3.8%	2,681,053	4.8%	3,769,165	4.8%	1.3
			14,033,070	**29.1%**	**15,019,330**	**27.0%**	**18,806,212**	**23.9%**	**0.8**
Other fields	33	Furniture, games	968,735	2.0%	1,869,552	3.4%	2,599,503	3.3%	1.6
	34	Other consumer goods	902,477	1.9%	1,369,117	2.5%	1,799,437	2.3%	1.2
	35	Civil engineering	2,242,854	4.7%	2,819,456	5.1%	3,289,939	4.2%	0.9
			4,114,066	**8.5%**	**6,058,125**	**10.9%**	**7,688,880**	**9.8%**	**1.1**
Total			**48,220,007**	**100.0%**	**55,619,349**	**100.0%**	**78,541,159**	**100.0%**	**1**

Source: PATSTAT, October 2014. Authors' calculations.

* Ratio between the shares in the first and last period (1983–1992 and 2003–2012).

Technical Notes: fractional counting on the IPC Class.

Accordingly, an RTA value of 1 corresponds to an equal share of a technology in a country's patent portfolio to the share of that technology in the world patent output. RTA indices larger than 1 means that the country was relatively more specialized in the considered technology compared to the world during the selected period. Likewise, when the RTA index is lower than 1, it means that the country was relatively less specialized in the considered technology.

3 The development of Chinese technological capabilities

The analysis of technological capabilities first considers the accumulated technological capabilities over the past three decades. Accordingly, the capabilities are considered as an aggregated figure, taking into account all technological sectors in order to figure out the position of China with relevance to other countries. First, we examine the development of the Chinese technological capabilities and other emerging economies by tracing their position in the global trends of patent intensity both at the technology frontier (considering transnational patents) and behind the frontier (considering priority filings).

Tracking the development trends of technological capabilities in China compared to other countries, Figures 4.1 and 4.2 show the priority filing – and transnational – patent intensities (patent applications per million inhabitants) respectively over the period 1980–2015.

The analysis shows a significant difference in patent intensity between the developed and emerging economies in both patent types: at the technology frontier and behind the technology frontier. Japan, EU, and the US have registered higher per capita patent applications over almost the whole period.

In what concerns technological capabilities behind the technology frontier, the analysis shows a relatively prominent development taking place in China. As shown in Figure 4.1, the country has experienced an exponential growth in its priority filings since 2000, increasing from less than ten patents per million inhabitants to more than 400 in almost one decade. It further exceeded the US and EU15 since 2010. However, it is still far behind Japan.

In comparison with other emerging economies under consideration, the analysis reveals that China has accumulated the largest stock of technological capabilities over the past two decades. Although its technological development started ten years later than that of Russia, it was able to catch up and further forge ahead thanks to its high growth rate.

Considering patent intensity at the global technology frontier (Figure 4.2), the difference between the BRICS (Brazil, Russia, India, China, South Africa) economies and the baseline countries is much clearer. Emerging economies are still lagging behind the developed countries in these types of technological capabilities. For instance, in 2015, the considered developed countries had, on average, a TN patent intensity of 250 compared with only 25 in China (the highest intensity achieved by the considered developing economies in the same year).

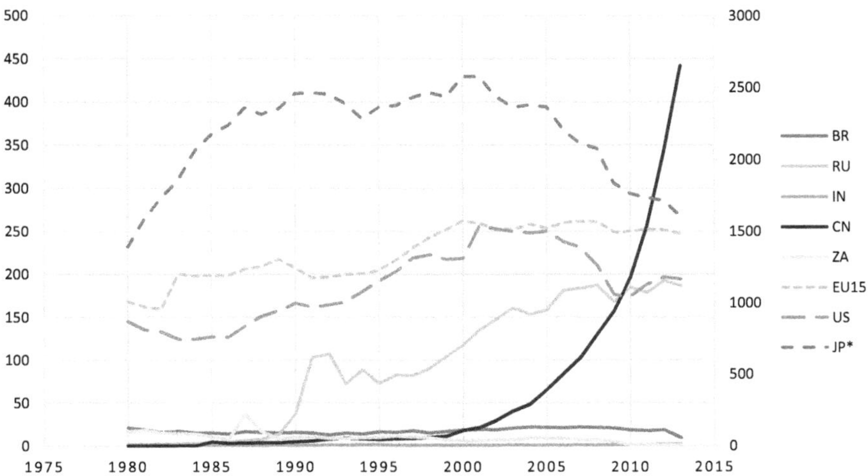

Figure 4.1 Behind-frontier patent intensity (priority patents per capita) 1980–2015 in China and in selected countries

Source: (PATSTAT, 2014; World Bank, 2019); Authors' calculations

* data scaled in the right-side axis

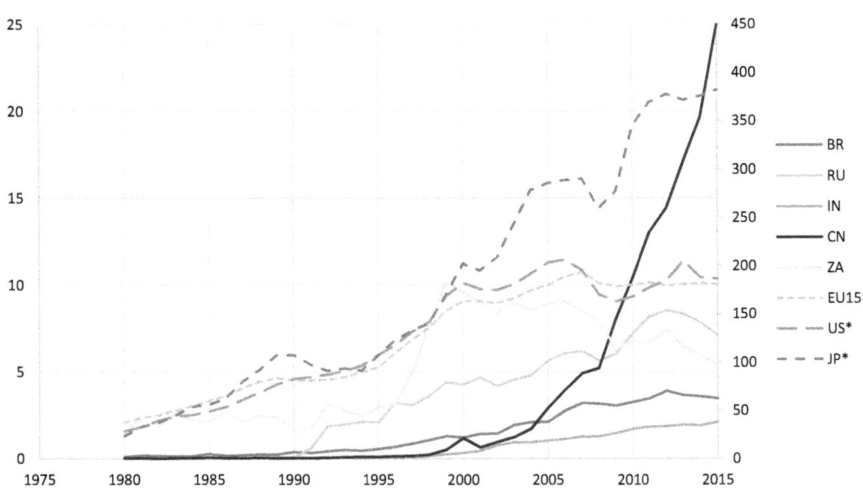

Figure 4.2 Frontier patent intensity (transnational patents per capita) 1980–2015 in China and selected countries

Source*:* (PATSTAT, 2014; World Bank, 2019); Authors' calculations

*data scaled in the right-side axis

Despite this large difference, the case of China is still prominent relative to the other emerging economies under consideration. Similar to priority filings patents, an exponential growth of transnational patent intensity can be found in China since 2000. It has exceeded both Russia and Brazil in its technological capabilities at the global frontier since 2009.

4 Technological specialization in China compared to other emerging economies

Next, we use the RTA index for different sectors and consider changes over time to investigate the technological specialization dynamics of the economies under consideration at the technological frontier in the period 1983–2012. We follow the empirical methodology put forward by Dominguez Lacasa et al (2017). By first calculating the RTA indices for the countries in five technological sectors, we then consider the shifts in the RTA index values in the initial (RTA_i) and final (RTA_f) periods. Accordingly, we identify four groups of technology capabilities at the technological frontier per country as follows:

1 Technological capabilities of ***continuous advantages***: when RTA > 1 in both periods
2 Technological capabilities ***newly gained advantages***: when $RTA_f > 1$ and $RTA_i < 1$
3 Technological capabilities ***lost advantages***: when $RTA_f < 1$ and $RTA_i > 1$
4 Technological capabilities of ***continuous disadvantages***: when RTA< 1 in both periods

Following this classification, we differentiate between the sectors for which technological capabilities are well-established in countries on one hand, and the sectors that are increasingly gaining new attention on the other. Such sectors are thus experiencing an expansion of the domestic absorptive capacity in the considered countries.

Table 4.2 shows, for each country, their sectors of continuous advantages, sectors of newly gained advantages, sectors of lost advantages and sectors of continuous disadvantage. The analysis combines the RTA in two periods 1983–89 and 2003–2012.

Until 2012 China shows a relative permanent specialization in the chemistry sector. The data does not give evidence for diversification efforts toward other new sectors. Most importantly, until 2012 China seems to have disregarded the Instruments and Electrical Engineering sectors, which have large technological opportunities.

The other emerging economies have a slightly more diversified profile specializing in more than one field (except for India, which does not display a continuous advantage in any sector). Most importantly, except for Russia and China, the emerging economies were diversifying toward new sectors. This

Table 4.2 Shifting sectors of RTA (five technological sectors) in China and other emerging economies 1983–89/2003–12

	RTA >1 (1983–92)	*RTA <1 (1983–92)*
RTA >1 (2003–12)	***Brazil:*** Mechanical Engineering, Other fields* ***Russia:*** Instruments, Chemistry*, Mechanical Engineering ***India:*** no sector ***China:*** Chemistry* ***South Africa:*** Chemistry, Other Fields* ***USA:*** Instruments ***Japan:*** Electrical Engineering*, Instruments ***EU15:*** Mechanical Engineering, Other Fields	***Brazil:*** Chemistry* ***Russia:*** no sector ***India:*** Electrical engineering* ***China:*** no sector ***South Africa:*** Mechanical Engineering ***USA:*** Electrical Engineering* ***Japan:*** Mechanical Engineering, Other Fields* ***EU15:*** no sector
	Sectors of continuous advantages	**Sectors newly gained advantages**
RTA <1 (2003–12)	***Brazil:*** no sector ***Russia:*** Other Fields* ***India:*** Chemistry*, Other Fields* ***China:*** Other Fields* ***South Africa:*** n/a ***USA:*** Chemistry*, Other Fields* ***Japan:*** no sector ***EU15:*** Chemistry*	***Brazil:*** Electrical Engineering*, Instruments ***Russia:*** Electrical Engineering* ***India:*** Instruments, Mechanical Engineering ***China:*** Electrical Engineering*, Instruments, Mechanical Engineering ***South Africa:*** Electrical Engineering*, Instruments ***USA:*** Mechanical Engineering ***Japan:*** Chemistry* ***EU15:*** Electrical Engineering*, Instruments
	Sectors of lost advantages	**Sectors of continuous disadvantages**

Source: PATSTAT October 2014. Authors' calculations

*Indicator for technological dynamism >1 (See Table 4.1)

development speaks for missing structural change in China, at least until 2012. India and Brazil seemed, however, to be more diversified and as if they were putting an emphasis on new dynamic sectors, specifically on Chemistry (Brazil) and on Electrical Engineering (India).

To capture the extent to which economies were contributing to technological change in the most dynamic sectors in the period 2003–2012 we extend the specialization analysis to the dynamism of the technological sectors (Figure 4.3) and fields (Table 4.3).

By considering explicitly the technological dynamism indicator of the sectors and fields, the analysis combines the direction of global technological change with the patterns of specialization of the countries. The indicator considers changes in the global direction of technological change between the initial and final periods by revealing which technological sectors (and fields) are gaining relative global importance and which are in stagnation. Taking this indicator as given by the indicator presented in Table 4.1 and the RTA in the most recent period we see whether countries were specialized in dynamic or in stagnated sectors (and fields). We translate these dynamic changes into the ability to benefit from technological opportunities. More specifically, we classify the sectors for each country into four categories for the most recent period:

- Sectors (or fields) of **static specialization**: sectors the region is specializing in (RTA > 1) while reporting decreasing technological dynamism (Dynamism < 1);
- Sectors (or fields) of **dynamic specialization**: sectors the region is specializing in (RTA > 1) while reporting increasing technological dynamism (Dynamism > 1);
- **Retreat** sectors (or fields): sectors with RTA<1 in the corresponding region that experience decreasing technological dynamism;
- Sectors (or fields) of **lost opportunities**: sectors with RTA < 1 in the corresponding region that reports increasing technological dynamism.

The graphs in Figure 4.3 combine the specialization rates RTA in 2003–2012 (y-axis) with the technological dynamism of the sectors (x-axis).

Interestingly, the data suggests that in the period 2003–2012 industrialized economies were quite diversified. The RTA in the different sectors is relatively close to 1. The US shows a slight dynamic specialization in "Electrical Engineering" (the sector with the largest technological opportunities in terms of growth) while the EU15 seemed to be losing opportunities in this dynamic sector.

In the same period, emerging economies showed a more heterogeneous picture. Some countries were specializing in very dynamic sectors (India in "Electrical Engineering" and South Africa and Brazil in "Other Fields" and in "Chemicals"); at the same time, Russia and China give a more static picture with a dynamic specialization in "Chemicals" only – a sector with relatively lower technological opportunities than "Electrical Engineering" and "Instruments." China was losing opportunities for specializing in the very dynamic sector of "Electrical Engineering," even though the loss was not as clear as in the case of Russia.

However, considering the level of specialization in 35 technological fields, the analysis shown in Table 4.3 provides interesting findings, especially for China. Again, the technological fields are classified as experiencing "Dynamic specialization," "Static specialization," "Lost Opportunities" or "Retreat." The arrows in the table give the different specialization types for each country and technological field.

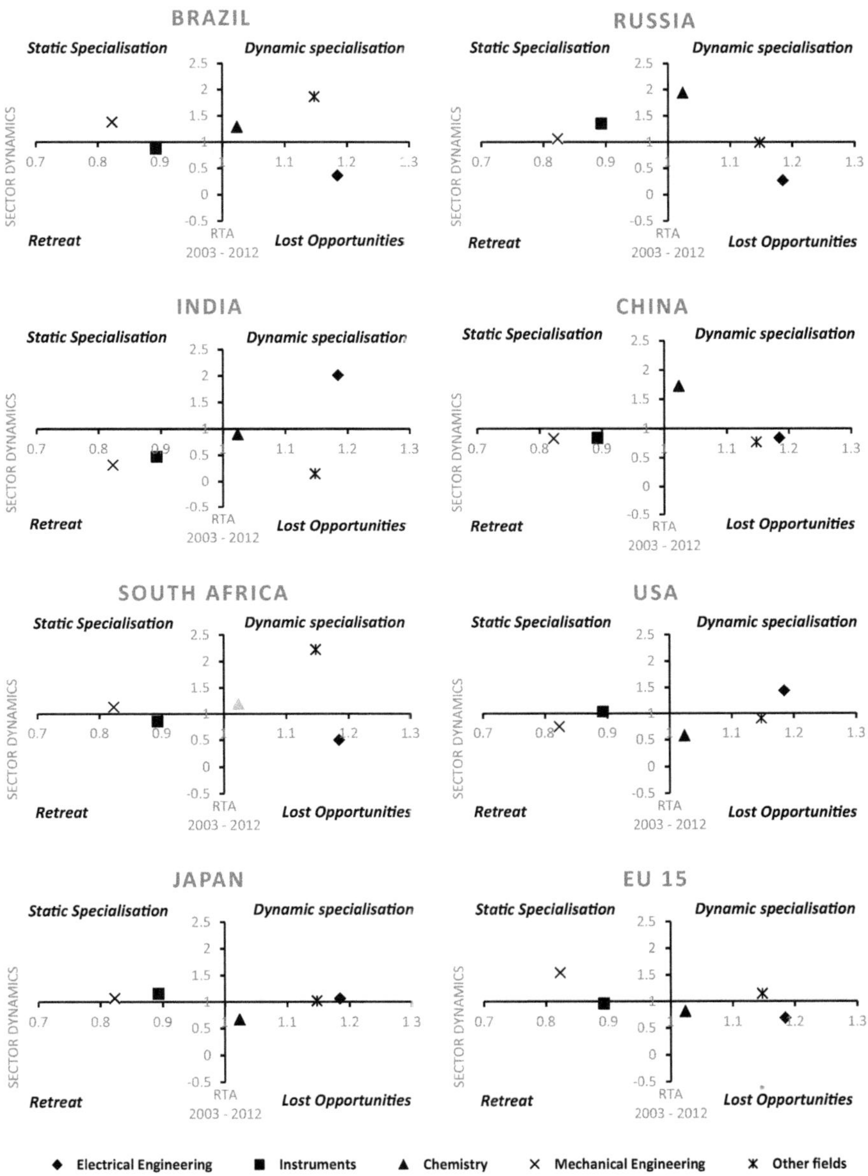

Figure 4.3 Classification of technological sectors in countries 2003–2012

Source: PATSTAT October 2014. Authors' calculations

Even though Brazil and China seem to not be benefiting from the technological opportunities in "Electrical Engineering" and in "Instruments" until 2012, when considering the 35 technological fields, the data suggests a path toward selected knowledge-intensive fields.

Table 4.3 Opportunity areas (35 technological fields) for countries 2003–2012

Technological Class	*BR*	*RU*	*IN*	*CN*	*ZA*	*EU15*	*US*	*JP*
Electrical engineering	↘	↘	↑	↘	↘	↘	↓	↑
1 Electrical machinery, apparatus, energy	↘	↘	↘	↘	↘	↘	↘	↑
2 Audio-visual technology	↓	↓	↓	↓	↓	↓	↓	↗
3 Telecommunications	↘	↘	↓	↘	↘	↘	↓	↓
4 Digital communication	↘	↘	↑	↓	↘	↘	↓	↘
5 Basic communication processes	↓	↗	↗	↓	↓	↓	↗	↗
6 Computer technology	↘	↘	↓	↘	↘	↘	↑	↘
7 IT methods for management	↘	↘	↑	↘	↘	↘	↑	↑
8 Semiconductors	↘	↘	↘	↘	↘	↘	↘	↑
Instruments	↓	↗	↓	↓	↓	↓	↗	↗
9 Optics	↓	↓	↓	↓	↓	↓	↓	↗
10 Measurement	↓	↗	↓	↗	↓	↗	↓	↓
11 Analysis of biological materials	↑	↑	↘	↑	↘	↑	↘	↘
12 Control	↗	↓	↗	↓	↗	↗	↗	↗
13 Medical technology	↑	↑	↘	↘	↑	↑	↑	↘
Chemistry	↑	↑	↘	↑	↑	↘	↘	↘
14 Organic fine chemistry	↗	↓	↗	↗	↗	↗	↓	↓
15 Biotechnology	↑	↑	↑	↑	↑	↘	↘	↘
16 Pharmaceuticals	↑	↑	↑	↑	↘	↘	↘	↘
17 Macromolecular chemistry, polymers	↓	↓	↓	↗	↓	↓	↓	↗
18 Food chemistry	↑	↑	↘	↑	↑	↘	↘	↘
19 Basic materials chemistry	↑	↑	↘	↑	↑	↘	↘	↘
20 Materials, metallurgy	↗	↗	↓	↗	↗	↓	↓	↓
21 Surface technology, coating	↓	↓	↓	↗	↓	↓	↗	↗
22 Microstructural and nanotechnology	↘	↑	↘	↑	↘	↑	↘	↘
23 Chemical engineering	↗	↗	↓	↗	↗	↗	↓	↓
24 Environmental technology	↑	↑	↘	↑	↘	↑	↘	↘
Mechanical Engineering	↗	↗	↓	↓	↗	↗	↓	↓
25 Handling	↗	↓	↓	↓	↗	↗	↓	↓
26 Machine tools	↓	↓	↓	↓	↓	↗	↓	↓
27 Engines, pumps, turbines	↗	↗	↗	↓	↓	↗	↓	↓
28 Textile and paper machines	↓	↓	↓	↓	↓	↓	↓	↗
29 Other special machines	↗	↓	↓	↓	↓	↗	↓	↓
30 Thermal processes and apparatus	↗	↓	↓	↗	↓	↓	↓	↓
31 Mechanical elements	↗	↘	↓	↓	↗	↗	↓	↗
32 Transport	↑	↘	↘	↘	↑	↑	↘	↑
Other fields	↑	↘	↘	↘	↑	↑	↘	↑
33 Furniture, games	↑	↘	↘	↘	↑	↘	↑	↑
34 Other consumer goods	↑	↘	↘	↘	↑	↑	↑	↘
35 Civil engineering	↗	↗	↓	↓	↗	↗	↓	↓

↑ Dynamic spec ↗ Static spec.
↓ Retreat ↘ Lost opportunities

Source: Author's calculations (PATSTAT, 2014)

According to the data available, Brazil is losing opportunities in all fields of "Mechanical Engineering." In what concerns the sector "Instruments," Brazil seems to be able to benefit from technological opportunities in selected growing fields. For instance, it shows a dynamic specialization in the growing technological fields of "Analysis of Biological Materials" and "Medical Technology" within the sector "Instruments." Interestingly, these fields relate to fields in the sector "Chemistry" (where Brazil displays an overall dynamic specialization) such as "Biotechnology," "Pharmaceuticals" and "Environmental Technology." The profile of Brazil speaks hence for a dynamic specialization in knowledge-intensive technological fields based in life sciences and in dynamic instrument technologies.

A similar profile with slight differences at the level of technological fields can be observed for China. As does Brazil, China shows a dynamic specialization in "Chemistry." Considering the 35 technological fields, the data speaks for a dynamic specialization in selected technologies in "Instruments" such as in the field of "Analysis of Biological Materials." Again, this field is related to knowledge-intensive technological fields in "Chemistry" where China has a dynamic specialization (such as "Biotechnology," "Pharmaceuticals," and "Microstructural and Nanotechnology"). In other words, China is benefiting from the technological opportunities in the "Instruments" sector in the fields with technological opportunities. Interestingly, within the sector "Electric Engineering," China shows a dynamic specialization in just one field ("Digital Communication"). Together with India (the only emerging economy with a dynamic specialization in "Electric Engineering" which is also held by the US and Japan), China once again seemed to be exploiting technological opportunities in a specific technological field within this sector until 2012.

5 Conclusions

The analysis of the technological capabilities of China using patent data suggests that, compared with other emerging economies, China has been able to accumulate a considerable stock of technological capabilities over the past decades. Despite its latecomer position, China has reached impressive levels of patenting activity both at the technological frontier and behind the technological frontier.

In terms of specialization and structural change, however, the results until 2012 are less impressive. According to the data available, until 2012 China was neither able to enter into new technological sectors nor contribute significantly to accumulated capabilities in most dynamic technological sectors such as "Electrical Engineering" and "Other fields" (including fields such as "Games," "Consumer Goods," and "Civil Engineering").

The data suggests that, until 2012, no major structural change had taken place in China. Other emerging economies, such as India, Brazil or South Africa, seemed to be better able to enter new technological fields and to benefit from the technological dynamism of fields in the "Electrical Engineering" sector or in "Other Fields" (which mainly include civil engineering, games, and other consumer goods). China was mainly specialized in the dynamic sector "Chemistry" and, more specifically, in the fields "Biotechnology," "Pharmaceuticals," "Chemical Food," and "Microstructural and Nanotechnology." At the sectoral level, the performance of China in terms of entering new dynamic sectors was quite disappointing.

Despite this general trend, until 2012 China had been able to benefit from the technological opportunities of selected dynamic fields in "Instruments" and in "Electrical Engineering." Even though these exceptions do not change the overall trend of a slow pace of structural change toward a knowledge-based economy until 2012, for selected fields in life sciences and in "Digital Communication," China was starting to move toward new dynamic technological fields.

Notes

1 For more information regarding patent indicators and counting methods, see (OECD, 2009).
2 The total population indicator used here is based on the de facto definition of population, which counts all the residents of a country regardless of their legal status or citizenship. The values are taken as midyear estimates (World Bank, 2019).
3 Considering the patenting administrative procedures, patent applications are made publicly available 18 months after their priority date. Accordingly, to avoid data misinterpretation, the most recent years were dropped from the analysis. Using PATSTAT, 2014 database, we acknowledge this data coverage limitation of our research.
4 In the case of priority filings classified under IPC classes that belong to different technological fields, our identification follows a fractional counting methodology.
5 Kindly notice that the global technological specialization ratio of a sector (R) (Equation 4.2) is calculated the same way as the denominator of the RTA (Equation 4.3).

References

Andries, P. and D. Faems (2013) "Patenting Activities and Firm Performance: Does Firm Size Matter?" *Journal of Product Innovation Management* 30(6): 1089–1098.

Archibugi, D. (1992) "Patenting as an Indicator of Technological Innovation: A Review." *Science and Public Policy* 19(6): 357–368.

Balassa, B. (1965) "Trade Liberalisation and 'Revealed' Comparative Advantage." *The Manchester School* 33(2): 99–123.

de Rassenfosse, G. et al. (2013) "The Worldwide Count of Priority Patents: A New Indicator of Inventive Activity." *Research Policy* 42: 720–737.

Dominguez Lacasa, I., A. Giebler and S. Radošević (2017) "Technological Capabilities in Central and Eastern Europe: An Analysis Based on Priority Patents." *Scientometrics* 111(1): 83–102.

Dominguez Lacasa, I., B. Jindra, S. Radosevic and M. Shubbak (2019) "Paths of Technology Upgrading in the BRICS Economies." *Research Policy* 48(1): 262–280.

Dominguez Lacasa, I. and M. Shubbak (2018) "Drifting Towards Innovation: The Co-evolution of Patent Networks, Policy, and Institutions in China's Solar Photovoltaics Industry." *Energy Research & Social Science* 38: 87–101.

Ernst, D. and L. Kim (2002) "Global Production Networks, Knowledge Diffusion, and Local Capability Formation." *Research Policy* 31(8–9): 1417–1429.

Fagerberg, J., M. Srholec and B. Verspagen (2010) "The Role of Innovation in Development." *Review of Economics and Institutions* 1(2): 1–29.

Freeman, C. (2004) "Technological Infrastructure and International Competitiveness." *Industrial and Corporate Change* 13(3): 541–569.

Frietsch, R. and U. Schmoch (2010) "Transnational Patents and International Markets." *Scientometrics* 82(1): 185–200.

Lall, S. (1992) "Technological Capabilities and Industrialization." *World Development* 20: 165–186.

Lee, K. (2018) *The Art of Economic Catch-Up: Barriers, Detours and Leapfrogging*, Cambridge, UK: Cambridge University Press.

Malerba, F. and R. Nelson (2011) "Learning and Catching up in Different Sectoral Systems: Evidence from Six Industries." *Industrial and Corporate Change* 20(6): 1645–1675.

Mowery, D. and R. Nelson (2001) *Sources of Industrial Leadership Studies of Seven Industries*, Cambridge, UK: Cambridge University Press.

OECD (2009) *OECD Patent Statistics Manual*, Paris: Organisation for Economic Co-operation and Development.

PATSTAT (2014) *EPO Worldwide Patent Statistical Database*. Available at www.epo.org/searching-for-patents/business/patstat.html (accessed February 14, 2019).

Pavitt, K. (1963) "Research, Innovation and Economic Growth." *Nature* 200: 206–210.

Pavitt, K. (1985) "Patent Statistics as Indicators of Innovative Activities: Possibilities and Problems." *Seientometrics* 7(1–2): 77–99.

Radosevic, S. and E. Yoruk (2016) "Why Do We Need a Theory and Metrics of Technology Upgrading?" *Asian Journal of Technology Innovation* 24(S1): 8–32.

Schmoch, U. (2008) "Concept of a Technology Classification for Country Comparisons." *Final Report to the World Intellectual Property Organisation (WIPO)*. Available at www.wipo.int/edocs/mdocs/classifications/en/ipc_ce_41/ipc_ce_41_5-annex1.pdf (accessed February 22, 2019).

Schumpeter, J. A. (1934) *Theory of Economic Development: An Enquiry into Profits, Capital, Interest and the Business Cycle*, Cambridge, MA: Harvard University Press.

Shubbak, M. (2018) "Innovation Capability, Network Embeddedness and Economic Performance: Profiling Solar Power Innovators in China." *International Journal Technological Learning, Innovation and Development* 10(3–4): 258–294.

Shubbak, M. (2019) "The Technological System of Production and Innovation: The Case of Photovoltaic Technology in China." *Research Policy* 48(4): 993–1015.

WIPO (2019) "International Patent Classification (IPC)." Available at www.wipo.int/classifications/ipc/ipcpub (accessed March 3, 2019).

World Bank (2019) "World Development Indicators." Available at https://databank.worldbank.org/data/source/world-development-indicators (accessed March 10, 2019).

5 Economic transition and innovation development in China from an evolutionary economics perspective

Jutta Günther and Julia Sinnig

1 Introduction

The rise of China's economy from being developmental to now one of the biggest in the world has been astonishing for many and somehow miraculous. The objections – namely open but yet highly government-regulated markets – which determine the business and innovation environment as well as its continuous strong growth is a fascinating topic to analyze.

The question of how economies develop and what leads to economic growth is a central theme in economic theorizing. Economic theory offers a variety of approaches to explain growth or – more widely speaking – economic development. One relatively young and innovative approach lies in evolutionary economics. With a strong resemblance to evolutionary theory (Nelson and Winter, 1982; Santangelo, 2003; Hodgson and Huang, 2010) in biology, of course not transferring their concepts entirely, evolutionary economists aim to explain economic development from a different angle than the widely acknowledged growth theory in the tradition of Solow (1956) and Swan (1956); theories which further developed into endogenous growth models (Grossman and Helpman, 1992; Romer, 1986, 1990). Evolutionary thinking is, at least for two reasons, a promising – and possibly more suitable – approach to shed light on China's astonishing development success. First, evolutionary theorizing explicitly follows a history-friendly approach, and we believe that the economic development in China cannot be understood without historical considerations. Second, the evolutionary economic approach explicitly takes into account the importance of institutions, which underwent deep changes in China and play a very significant role in the increasing economic growth and change of the entire economy (Ten Brink, 2013).

The purpose of this chapter is to reflect the rapid economic and technological developments in China since the late 1970s from an evolutionary economic perspective. Thereby, we will pay particular attention to the economic environment and international opening of China for foreign investors. The astonishing development of China is especially interesting to analyze, as it grew from a developing country to the second biggest economy in the world in a relatively short period of time. It is even expected that China will soon surpass the

United States as the worldwide leading economy (World Economic Forum, 2017). The focal point of this chapter is that China's strategic transition from imitation to innovation contributes to this enormous economic development (Li, 2010; Yip and McKern, 2016). It will be illustrated using time series of foreign direct investment (FDI) and research and development (R&D), as well as patent data later in this chapter.

This chapter will be structured as follows. Section 2 will deal with crucial aspects of evolutionary economic theory. It will discuss some of the core principles of evolutionary economics, including an excursion into the concept of "Routines." Section 3 forms the empirical part. It reviews China's reform policies and aspects of economic history, starting with the opening of China to the world economy. It further draws out the economic environment and business strategies before turning to selected indicators of technological development over time. Finally, section 4 will draw conclusions and highlight future research topics.

2 Evolutionary thinking – an alternative approach to understand economic development

General considerations

At its core, evolutionary theory looks at the economy as an ever-changing system with a permanent dynamic instead of an equilibrium-prone system in the neoclassical sense. Moreover, and different from the neoclassical approach of endogenous growth models, the evolutionary theory explicitly considers political, social, and cultural change (Guha, 1981). Neoclassical theorists rather neglect those factors or – if at all – expect them as given. Therefore, evolutionary theorists challenge two main concepts of neoclassical economics: the notion of equilibrium and the concept of the rational actor who operates under maximizing assumptions (Nelson and Winter, 1982). They do not believe that every actor on every relevant market possesses full information about all alternatives and is able to choose the most promising or "optimal" alternative given his utility maximizing behavior (Nelson and Winter, 1982). Moreover, they claim that a fully rational and "know it all" actor who makes no systematic mistakes does not exist. Furthermore, they state there is a lack in providing an answer to the question of *how* an optimal decision is developed. This is *not* part of a neoclassical approach to economics. The act of learning is not considered at all; every agent in the market *just knows* the optimal strategy to perform under given circumstances (Dosi and Nelson, 1994; Nelson and Winter, 1982; Santangelo, 2003). Besides that, as Santangelo (2003, p. 205) claims, the "reliance on equilibrium analysis . . . neglects phenomena associated with historical change." Even more so, to expecting every market to be in equilibrium, even under uncertain and unpredictable surroundings, is totally unrealistic (Silva and Teixeira, 2009). Instead, an economic theory that explains actors' decision making, and thus economic growth from the viewpoint of "satisfactory behaviour" like evolutionary theory, will of course involve structural, technological, cultural, and institutional change (Hodgson and Huang, 2010). As a consequence, it will also pay attention to the differences of countries and industries with respect to their development progress and growth patterns instead of applying a "one fits all" model (Nelson and Winter, 2002).

Although aspects from biology were already introduced into social sciences and into economic theory in the 1880s to 1890s, the concept of evolutionary theory fell into oblivion during the postwar period when neoclassical theory approached (Silva and Teixeira, 2009). It was not until the mid-1970s that evolutionary economics had a comeback due to the work of authors like Richard Nelson and Sidney Winter. Their work "An Evolutionary Theory of Economic Change" published in 1982 marks a starting point of evolutionary economics and gave rise to many further publications in the field.

Despite the fact that a core model or dominant approach does not exist and various strands within the evolutionary economic theory arose, there are still certain commonalities which the community agrees with. Although Hodgson and Huang note that "there is nothing in the etymology or usage of the term "evolution" that necessarily connotes Darwinism or any particular doctrine" (2010, p. 351) the roots and key elements of evolutionary economics lay undeniably in Darwin's work. Of course, every author is aware of the differences between biological and social evolution. However, evolutionary economics is based on concepts of variation, mutation, and adaption within a highly uncertain environment in which a selection principle prevails (Santangelo, 2003). It is the "Survival of the Fittest," meaning that firms will only persist when they are able to adapt within an uncertain environment (mutation) by deriving certain behavioral routines to compete against others (variety; Santangelo, 2003).

Variety in a closer sense means the number of actions, which have been actually tried and from which success finally derived, rather than all the actions, which would have been theoretically possible within a neoclassical set of perfect actions (Alchian, 1950; Nelson and Winter, 2002). In the end, the selection principle comes to the fore by showing through experience which firms are profitable (through their actions and behavior) and which are not, with the more profitable ones driving the less profitable firms out of the market (Nelson and Winter, 1974, 1982; Verspagen, 2005). However, economists agree that behavior differs from industry to industry and from firm to firm. No uniform behavior succeeds, but the one that manages to adapt as "best" as possible to a certain situation or environment will prevail (Nelson and Winter, 1974; Santangelo, 2003).

Regarding the highly uncertain and therefore unpredictable economic environment of any firm, especially Nelson and Winter (1982) stress the stochastic elements in the determination of decisions as well as in the decision outcomes. The economic system is thereby understood as a "complex and evolving system, which is out of equilibrium at any time" (Silva and Teixeira, 2009, p. 5). However, Hodgson and Huang point out one crucial dilemma: are markets to be treated as universal of human interaction or do they depend on other institutions such as the state? And, whose evolution has to be explained? This question is especially interesting when reviewing China's economic development in section 3.

A core piece: routines

As shown in the previous part how the selection principle from evolutionary biology has been transferred to economic theorizing, one can find another analogy for the units of selection: genes (Dosi and Nelson, 1994). Genes in the evolutionary economic sense are looked at as "routines" (Nelson and Winter, 2002), which are defined as "repetitive pattern of activity in an entire organization" (Santangelo, 2003, p. 207) and serve as "general term for all regular and predictable[1] behavioral patterns of firms" (Nelson and Winter, 1982, p. 14). It is acknowledged that routines form out of actions on the basis of habits, customs, and beliefs by individuals and firms in the economic environment. Economic actors do not act "optimally" as presumed in neoclassical theory. Their actions are just the best they can do (Dosi and Nelson, 1994).

The analogy to genes draws from the heritable, durable, and replicable character routines imply (Silva and Teixeira, 2009). This means that firms whose routines have proven to be successful will pass them on to further generations whereas firms with ineffective behavioral patterns will fail in the industry, and thus – via selection principle – will finally be driven out of the market (Nelson and Winter, 1982). This derives from the fact that in an ever-changing, unstable, and uncertain environment the development of routines and their successful and stable performance over time requires "continuous learning and adaption" (Santangelo, 2003, p. 207). Routines, therefore, serve as a way of dealing with these complex surroundings while they still bear the risk of competing instead of supporting each other (Andersen, 1994).

Nelson and Winter (1982) as well as later Dosi and Nelson (1994) aimed to categorize routines into three classes. First, there are "standard operating procedures," which determine short-run behavior and how much a firm produces. Secondly, there are those routines based on general behavioral patterns, which affect the growth and decline of a firm. Third – and in context of this chapter the most interesting category – there are routines that define search processes for "better ways of doing things" (Dosi and Nelson, 1994).

While neoclassical theorists believe that knowledge, and generally all techniques, are available everywhere, at every time and zero costs, in evolutionary theory knowledge has to be gathered through search processes, for example, R&D activities. Thus, learning and knowledge creation causes (large) costs (Nelson and Winter, 2002). The attraction of foreign direct investment (FDI) has been a frequent tool especially in emerging and developing countries to reduce the expenses of learning and to transfer knowledge and technology internationally (Findlay, 1978; Keller, 1996). China's economic development relied heavily on the accumulation of FDI, which will be shown in more detail through empirical data in section 3. Concepts of evolutionary thinking have been included in the theory of multinational companies, stressing that local embeddedness and networks of knowledge creation matter for technologically positive effects (Cantwell, 1989, 1995).

Furthermore, Nelson and Winter state that the "concept of search obviously is the counterpart of that of mutation in biological evolutionary theory" (1982,

p. 18). Thus, these search processes should at best gather new knowledge about better production processes, technologies etc. and are thought of as routinized or as embedded within organizational routines. However, the knowledge gathered from these search processes and from resulting routines thereof has a strong tacit dimension and cannot be extracted and passed on easily (Dosi et al, 1994). This leaves firms with successful routines in a predominant position while at the same time firms with "weaker" routines will face difficulties with imitation plans. In addition to this, since gathering new knowledge that might lead to new or slightly different future routines is costly, not all firms enter into the search process. They will only do so when their profitability will fall under a certain expected level (Silva and Teixeira, 2009).

Innovation from an evolutionary perspective

Evolutionary thinking is very suitable to explain economic development as a dynamic process where the economy is constantly changing. At its core lies innovation in the sense of new products or production processes, which keep an economy in motion. Product and process innovations are well defined in the economic literature as functionally new products or processes introduced into the market. This classical distinction between product and process innovation dates back to Schumpeter's famous work "Theory of Economic Development" (1911) where he refers to innovation (new combinations) as the driving force of economic development. Besides product and process innovation, he also introduced the exploitation of new markets, access to new resources, and new organizational structures as innovations. This understanding or definition of innovation shapes the economic literature through today (Schmookler, 1966).

The evolutionary literature emphasizes that innovation is a process, not just a single event at a certain point in time or "manna from heaven." In this sense, innovation includes a learning process that involves the supply side (technology push) and the market or demand side alike (Kline and Rosenberg, 1986; Di Stefano et al., 2012; Von Hippel, 2005). Thinking in these categories means that innovation is an uncertain and complex process, not just subject to an act of optimization (cost minimizing).

Going further, the evolutionary perspective also encourages a systemic understanding of innovation in the sense that innovation is not only subject to business enterprises but also involves other actors, such as scientific organizations, research laboratories, and public agencies (Nelson, 1993; Lundvall, 1992; Edquist, 2005). The system of innovation is composed of different actors, and the institutional environment they are operating in matters strongly for the functioning and the results of an innovation system. There is a vast empirical literature in innovation economics based on systemic considerations, focusing on the dynamics of interaction between entities that belong to the system (Allen, 1983; Hagedoorn et al., 2000; Pavitt, 2005; Kudic and Guenther, 2017).

The innovation system approach – conceptionally closely related to evolutionary principles – has traditionally been applied to innovation analyses related to established market economies. However, for developing and emerging as well as transition economies, which are often characterized by a completely different historical development, the evolutionary-systemic perspective seems particularly suitable (Malerba and Nelson, 2012; Lundvall et al., 2009). A crucial advantage is that evolutionary and systemic approaches take into consideration the importance of institutions and their own interconnection (von Jacobi, 2017), which is also expressed in the concept of network alignment (von Tunzelmann et al., 2010; von Tunzelmann, 2004). To analyze and understand innovation-driven economic development in emerging and transition economies, these approaches are particularly valuable because they pay attention to the complexity of economic and technological processes and imply a differentiated view with respect to better practice and policy issues (Guenther, 2015).

Concluding reflections

As evolutionary economic theory is a combination of behavioral, institutional, and Schumpeterian economics, its central theses remain vague (Dopfer and Potts, 2004) instead of making up a fully-fledged theory. There is no core model in evolutionary theory that would serve as a fundamental building block for the entire field. Currently, there is no sign that the internal heterogeneity is going to converge, let alone disappear (Hodgson and Huang, 2010). There is an ongoing discourse among evolutionary economists. Silva and Teixeira (2009, p. 1) talk about an "over concern with formalization issues among evolutionary researchers." Dopfer and Potts (2004, p. 196) state,

> The latent difficulties in piecing together the individual empirical studies and theoretical developments across the scope of evolutionary economics have made it exceedingly difficult to invest heavily in the development of deep theory, and therefore, to coordinate large-scale empirical investigations.

Economists are trying to fill the lack of empirical analyses in evolutionary economics with relatively new approaches, such as Evolutionary Game Theory or Evolutionary Realism, as well as further studies regarding different ontologies within evolutionary economics.

However, it remains an open question whether the critique about the heterogeneity of evolutionary theorizing is more an inferiority complex of its proponents being confronted with the full-fledged neoclassical theory than a problem *per se*. If economics is about explaining real-world phenomena and solving real-world problems, then what is more important: a precisely formalized, homogenous block of theoretical models or a history-friendly and "closer to reality" collection of theoretical pieces trying to explain economic change embedded in a social context? This will remain subject to an ongoing discussion in the discipline of economics.

The next section will take a closer look into the real world based on selected empirical insights into China's economic and technological development. The empirical insights will be reflected against the theoretical aspects of evolutionary thinking, such as the emergence of (new) routines in business activity or FDI as a strong driver of innovation.

3 Economic and technological development in China

Economic reforms and international opening

China's metamorphosis from a centralized economy to one of the biggest economies in the world began in the late 1970s. By this time, peasants in rural areas where allowed to rent formerly communally owned land and establish private farms (Wu and Fan, 2014; Lin et al., 2003), eventually rising the value of agricultural output by 61% until the mid-1980s (Wu and Fan, 2014). At the same time, more power was steadily given to the state-owned enterprises (SEOs), thus granting them more autonomy (Lin et al., 2003).

Further steps to gradually open the markets to the world economy were undertaken by the "Open Door" policy, which eventually created the "Law of the People's Republic of China on Joint Ventures Using Chinese and Foreign Investment" and thus granted foreign direct investment (FDI) legal status (Broadman and Sun, 1997; Chen et al., 1995). It furthermore included the establishment of four special economic zones along the south-eastern coastal area, which were designed to attract foreign capital, but were also testing grounds for planned economic reforms (Vietor, 2007; Friedman, 2014; Chen et al., 1995).

As discussed in section 2, FDI is a strong vehicle for technology transfer and a driver for economic growth, and therefore, it is highly important for the development of China. At the beginning, foreign investments only trickled into the Chinese economy. This was due to various constraints foreign investors faced when trying to explore business opportunities in China. These constraints included factors like the nonconvertibility of the Chinese currency, uncertain property rights and a poorly defined legal environment for FDI activities in general and long and complicated processes of bureaucratic approval (Broadman and Sun, 1997; Chen et al., 1995).

However, the situation massively improved once incentives for FDI activities were established. Potential investors now faced easier approval procedures, tax incentives, better access to workforces, land, and were granted electricity use and benefited from a newly founded currency exchange market for joint ventures (Vietor, 2007; Chen et al., 1995). The concept of "Special Economic Zones" (SEZ) was then extended to 14 more coastal cities, the Yangtze river delta, the Pearl river delta, the south of Fujian province (the region opposite Taiwan) and finally the Shanghai Pudong new area (Chen et al., 1995; Wu and Fan, 2014).

This led – almost instantly – to a massive inflow of FDI. From 1991 to 1993 foreign investment rose to US$67.53 billion, which is nearly the total sum of the years 1979 to 1990 (Chen et al., 1995). China held 40% of overall FDI share of all developing countries by 1997 (Broadman and Sun, 1997).

With respect to international trade, imports and exports grew strongly from 1978 to 2000, with imports from US$10.89 billion to US$225.1 billion and exports from US$9.75 billion to US$249.2 billion (Lin et al., 2003). Eventually, China entered the World Trade Organization (WTO) in 2001, beginning its membership effectively in January 2002. It took 15 years of negotiations. A compromise for China's membership of the WTO was found when the government agreed to reduce trade barriers and eliminate import quotas among other guidelines that followed (Wu and Fan, 2014; Vietor, 2007). The entry to the WTO further spurred imports and exports, and China has become an important player in international trade relations today.

China exhibited an enormous growth of its gross domestic product (GDP) since the late 1970s. According to the World Bank, average GDP growth accounted to 9.66% since 1978[2]. In absolute figures, GDP grew from US$294 billion (constant 2010 US$) in 1978 to US$9.51 trillion (constant 2010 US$) in 2016, making China one of the fastest growing economies in the world.

The inflow of international capital and increase of private businesses was followed by an increase in the standard of living of the Chinese population. The consumption level per head rose from RMB 184 in 1978 to RMB 3,397 in the year 2000. The consumption structure changed as well, manifested in preferred consumer durable goods chosen: from mainly watches and bicycles in the 1970s, to telephones, video cameras, and recorders in the 1990s, to more costly goods in the beginning of the 2000s, such as cars (Lin et al., 2003).

The "China Model" is formally a "state capitalism with strong government intervention" (Wu and Fan, 2014). The tremendous economic transformation in China took place "[w]ithout democracy, or virtually any political freedom" as Vietor notes (2007, p. 79). China has come a long way since first opening their markets in the late 1970s, but the economic liberalization has not spread to every sector. The state still imposes absolute, or at least strong control, over "pillar industries" and "backbone enterprises" like machinery, electronics, telecommunications, coal, civil aviation, automobile industry, construction, and various others (Wu and Fan, 2014; Vietor, 2007).

Today, the Chinese system is a market-based, capitalistic economy combined with an absolute, communist leadership in politics. Whether this will prevent China from becoming a world economic power in the future remains controversial (Ten Brink, 2013).

Economic environment, business strategies, and industry shifts

Referring to evolutionary thinking, Nelson and Winter (2002, p. 26) state that historical change on socio-economic systems enforces "constant exogenous change," confronting firms with a continuous stream of new and unfamiliar problems. This is certainly true for the Chinese economic development. The economic system has not just changed, as explained in the previous section – it has been turned over. Investors and entrepreneurs, who intent to turn their business activities to the Chinese markets face not only the usual difficulties

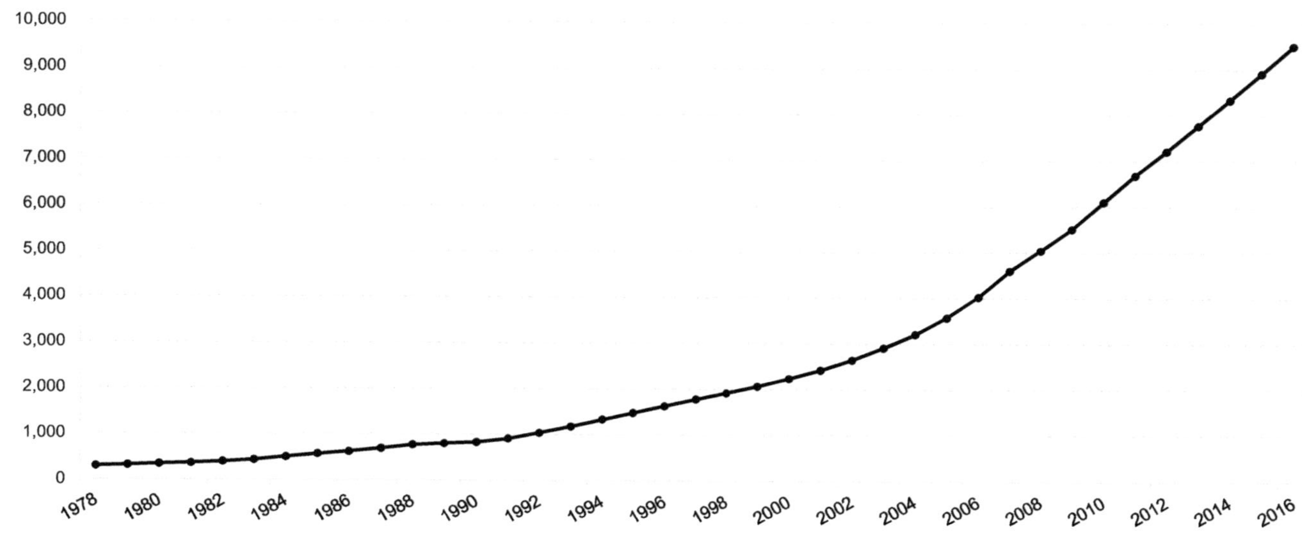

Figure 5.1 Annual GDP of China 1978 to 2016 in constant bn. 2010 US$

Source: World Bank, 2017 (World Development Indicators)

as in Western markets, e.g., uncertainties about strategies from competitors or unknown customer needs and demands. They also struggle with more Chinese-specific constraints (Sull and Wang, 2005). An overview of these special factors is provided by Sull and Wang (2005), who define them as:

- Unpredictable regulation and industrial policy: this means that laws and regulations set by the government are enforced differently by the communes, thus putting enterprises in the same industry under different intensities of pressure.
- Uncertainty from integration into global markets: this especially regards SOEs that are threatened by strong MNEs as competitors, as they often integrate into the market with more capital and are favored by governmental investment incentives.
- Uncertain cost of capital and access to it: China's banks are state-run, thus allocation of funds to centralized and given preferably to SOEs. Private firms do not have access to funds continuously, rather they are given to them periodically.
- Unclear and shifting property rights: often, the "basic question of who owns what on a business" cannot be answered, as property rights are unspecific and shifting over time.

Overall, unpredictability occurs out of these dynamic and ever-changing contexts, which make it impossible for economic agents to foresee future events. This is exactly what evolutionary economists propose. Contrary to Western economies, however, since large parts of the economy are controlled by the state, changing political regulations impose even more unknown variables. Enterprises, regardless of being domestic (and state-owned) or multinational thus have to adopt to these continuously changing environments and find strategies – or routines, for that matter – which are successful.

Empirical studies have shown that China's economic growth relied heavily on the attraction of foreign capital and certainly became a crucial part of economic development in China (Friedman, 2014). While Chen et al. (1995, p. 691) state that FDI has a positive impact on economic growth by raising efficiency of an economy through accelerating developmental processes, inland provinces lacked behind their economic development, developing less than their coastal counterparts. Inward FDI flows as can be seen in Figure 5.2 increased over the entire transition period. However, there are strong regional disparities with respect to the attraction of FDI. The largest part went to the coastal areas and river deltas, which were the first to open up to international business due to their status as SEZs (Broadman and Sun, 1997).

This circumstance led to different growth performances and an increasing economic gap between the inland and coastal area and caused some severe inequality during the economic transition process. Coastal provinces proceeded to grow faster and increase economically as they continued to further attract FDI (Démurger, 2000). This shift did not only put a heavier strain on inland

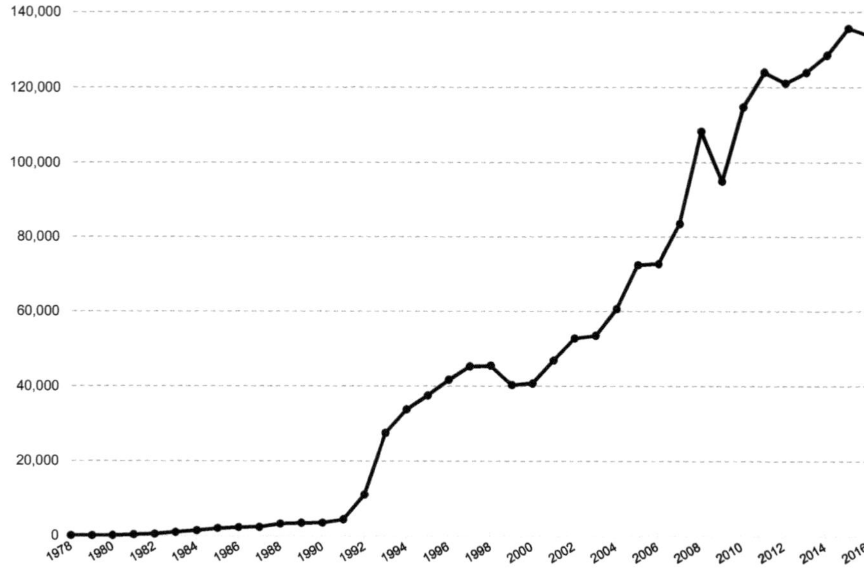

Figure 5.2 Annual inflow of foreign direct investment to China 1978 to 2016 (current million US$)

Source: United Nations Conference on Trade and Development (UNCTAD, 2017)

provinces compared to coastal areas, it also showed that FDI incentives was not the most important factor in attracting foreign business. It was rather undeveloped infrastructure networks and the uneven improvement of infrastructure itself that negatively affected investment decisions (Broadman and Sun, 1997; Démurger, 2000; Lin, 2014).

However, empirical results have found that the main reason for the economic spurt of the coastal areas lies in the "long commercial and industrial traditions and geographical and ethnic links with Hong Kong, Macao and Taiwan" (Wei et al., 1999, p. 865). Even today, this still has not changed. According to the Ministry of Commerce of the People's Republic of China, in 2015 Hong Kong by far dominated the list of top regions with investment in China, accounting for almost three-quarters of the whole sum of investments into China (MOFCOM, 2016).

However, inward FDI to catching-up transition economies is typically influenced by factors such as the level of international trade, GDP growth of the home and host economy as well as labor cost (Günther and Kristalova, 2016). As the inland areas are clearly missing this geographical advantage, these factors gain even more importance and illustrate strategy options for the government to maintain growth and close this developmental gap (Wei et al., 1999).

One could think that China's efforts toward international opening would mean that external investors were favored over domestic ones as has often been the case in catching up, transition economies (Günther and Kristalova, 2016).

Conversely, Chen et al. (1995) argue that in China the opening of the trade and the attraction of FDI "forced domestic manufacturers to compete globally," eventually demanding "plant managers and government officials [to] develop and adopt rules and laws of market economy." Hence, domestic manufacturers have to improve management, increase their variety, lower production costs and achieve better economic results (Chen et al., 1995). These strategies to stay and succeed in an industry or market can be seen as an expression of developing and adopting routines in a strongly selective environment. From an evolutionary perspective, this is exactly the competition or selection process in which actors observe, learn, and change their behavior continuously.

It is found that successful companies were able to respond to their environment quickly and effectively, seizing opportunities almost instantly when they came up, and securing themselves a strong position while they forced competitors out of business (Sull and Wang, 2005).

Domestic firms are mostly concentrating their business toward the domestic market, including the Chinese communities Hong Kong, Taiwan, and Macao. On the one hand, they are uncomfortable taking their business outside their comfort zone of their own language and business practices (Orr and Roth, 2012). On the other hand, a practice called "*guanxi*" exists. The principles of *guanxi* are quite difficult to abstract, but it officially means the "cultivation of relationships" and is crucial to any sort of economic transaction in China. There is a fine line between *guanxi* and corruption, which can cause difficulties for international investors to enter into certain businesses (Vietor, 2007). This argument may be supported by the example Sull and Wang (2005) provide: while global brand leaders such as Procter & Gamble and Coca-Cola faced rigid competition from local brands in China, Danone could enter the market more successfully. It committed partnerships with leading and already established Chinese firms and benefitted from their market-specific knowledge leading to quite successful revenues of US$ 1 billion in 2003.

Orr and Roth (2012) acknowledge that different challenges and opportunities for MNE and domestic enterprises exist and therefore recommend slightly different strategies to succeed. Like Sull and Wang (2005), they strongly advise MNEs to gain knowledge of local consumers, as firms who are established in China and are able to closer connect with their Chinese networks tend to be more successful than those who manage their subsidiaries from their home countries. Success gained from this strategy does not so much rely on technological knowledge, but rather it implies the importance of tacit knowledge.

Today, China has become one of the largest exporters of goods in the world. The economic transition led to a shift away from the formerly dominant agricultural sector to manufacturing sectors (Lin, 2014), retail trades, IT and software, and other service sectors. This trend is reflected in the sectoral distribution of FDI as well. We illustrate this by the number of FDI projects carried out in China. Accordingly, the most attractive economic sectors in the year 2015 are wholesale and retail trades, followed by manufacturing projects, leasing and business services, and financial services as can be seen in Figure 5.3.

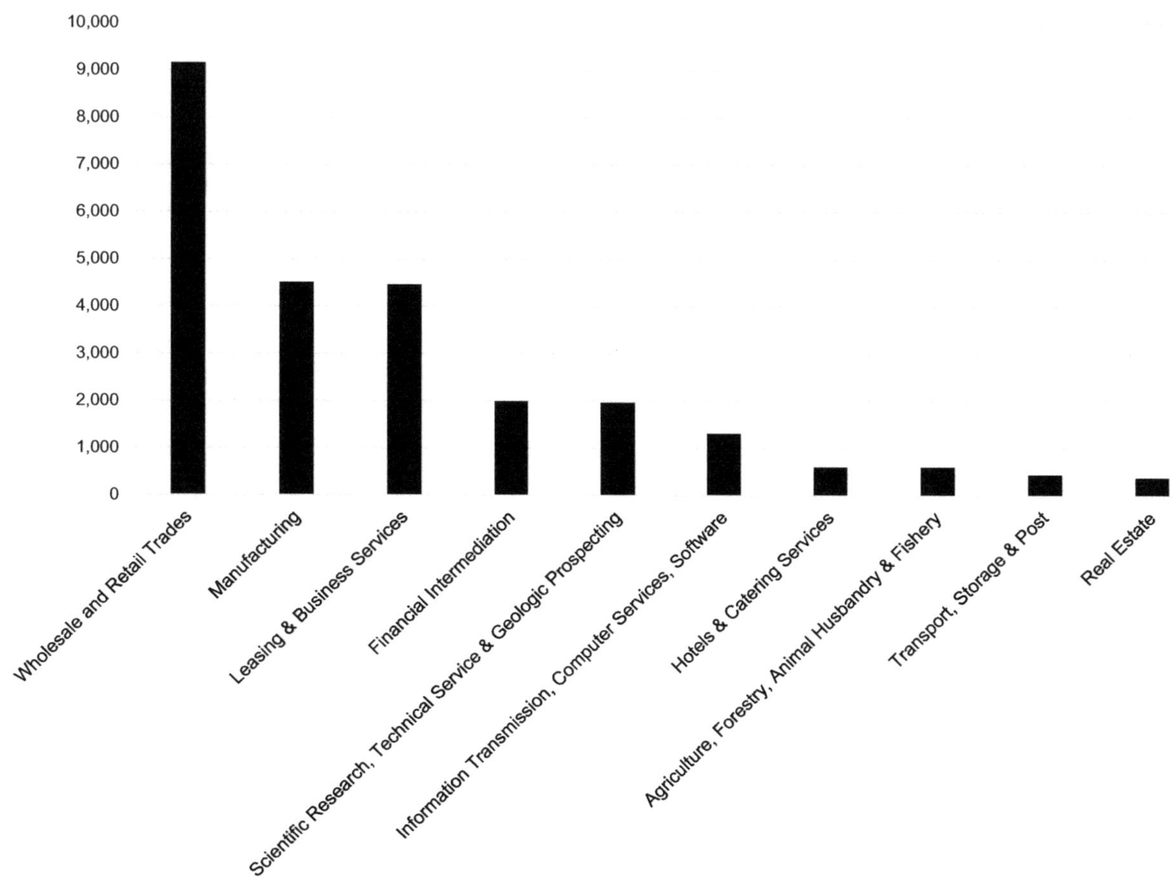

Figure 5.3 Top ten sectors according to the number of FDI projects 2015

Source: National Bureau of Statistics of China (2016)

Overall, the economic transition in China led to a heavy structural change of the entire economy, whereby service sectors have gained strong importance.[3]

Technological developments and innovation

The success of many Chinese businesses is based on advantages gained from relative local advantages, such as low-cost labor and inexpensive land (Orr and Roth, 2012). However, as indicated previously, with the structural change toward more knowledge-based sectors, the importance of technological activities has strongly increased in China too. The concentration on a continuous stream of innovation (Lin, 2014) to "survive and grow in a highly competitive environment and [adapt] to the transition of institutional environment" (Kotabe et al., 2011, p. 166) matters for companies active in the Chinese economy.

Technological activities like systematic research and development, targeted or spontaneous inventive activity, and finally innovation are an integral part of business activity. We will illustrate this by two frequently used indicators, which are patent applications and expenditure for R&D (as percent of GDP).

The R&D intensity of China has strongly increased since the mid-1990s. Looking at the total expenditure for R&D as percent of GDP, the R&D intensity has increased from 0.56% in 1996 to more than 2.0% in 2015 (see Figure 5.4). Not only did the intensity of R&D expenditure triple between 1996 and 2015, but the intensity of R&D personnel (R&D workers per million population) also grew threefold since 1996 according to World Bank statistics. While in

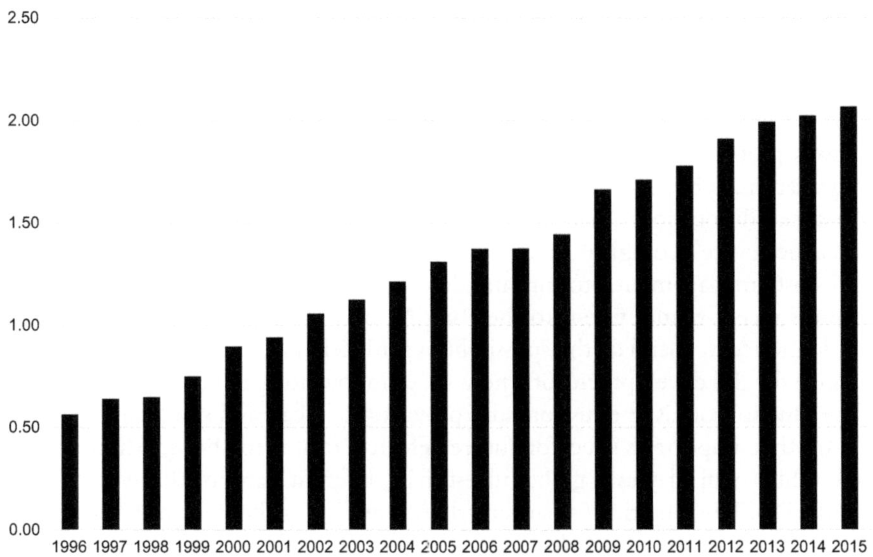

Figure 5.4 R&D expenditure (as % of GDP) in China 1996 to 2015

Source: World Bank, 2017 (World Development Indicators)

1996 the number of R&D personnel per million population amounted to 442, it was 1,177 in 2015.

Not every R&D activity leads to an innovation or a successful innovation in the sense of a market success. Firms with a positive attitude toward risk taking are expected to be more likely to eventually develop an innovation (Orr and Roth, 2012). An alternative indicator expressing the capacity of an economy to be inventive is the number of patent applications. Looking at this indicator for China, it shows that patent applications were for long time no major issue in the Chinese economy. With the structural changes as described earlier, the patenting activity increased tremendously, especially over about the last ten years (see Figure 5.5). Interestingly, the importance of residential patent applications has gained tremendously since the late 2000s and outperformed the number of nonresidential patent applications by far.

4 Open questions and future research

Since its opening and reforms in the 1970s, China has experienced a tremendous economic and technological development as expressed by standard indicators presented in this chapter, such as GDP, trade, R&D and patent statistics. The uniqueness of the "case of China" derives not only out of the high speed of developments, but also out of the fact that a market-based economic system is combined with a communist political leadership. While at first glance this contradictive combination can be viewed as a catalyst of the economic development, it is questionable on the other hand whether China will be able to further move ahead like this in the world economy (Ten Brink, 2013).

In this section, we outlined selected developments of the Chinese economy, leaving out many aspects and details of course. While the figures presented are impressive, there are shadowy sides of all these achievements too. Wu and Fan (2014, p. 70) state that China's rapid economic growth has led to "increasingly serious problems of resource depletion, energy shortages, and environmental degradation." They also mention the widening gap between rich and poor and the social dislocations (Wu and Fan, 2014). Will the country be able to cope with the severe ecological problems regarding air, water, and ocean pollution, and waste management, erosion, and deforestation (Vietor, 2007) in the future? China's recent commitment to the Paris Agreement of 2015 (Dimitrov, 2016) could induce new and further possibilities for R&D investments and might be a chance for the development of a new set of innovations and routines regarding the reduction of CO2 emissions and provision of clean and sustainable energy.

Another important issue for future research relates to the question which role China will play as a global investor in different parts of the world (outward FDI). This question is particularly interesting in the light of China's role as a major investor in developing countries, especially in sub-Saharan Africa. Although state-owned Chinese investments are often combined with development aid programs (Kaplinsky and Morris, 2009), China's interest for these investments is rooted in the "need to supply a growing industrial sector" (Zafar, 2007, p. 104; Cheung et al., 2012). It will be interesting to observe how these

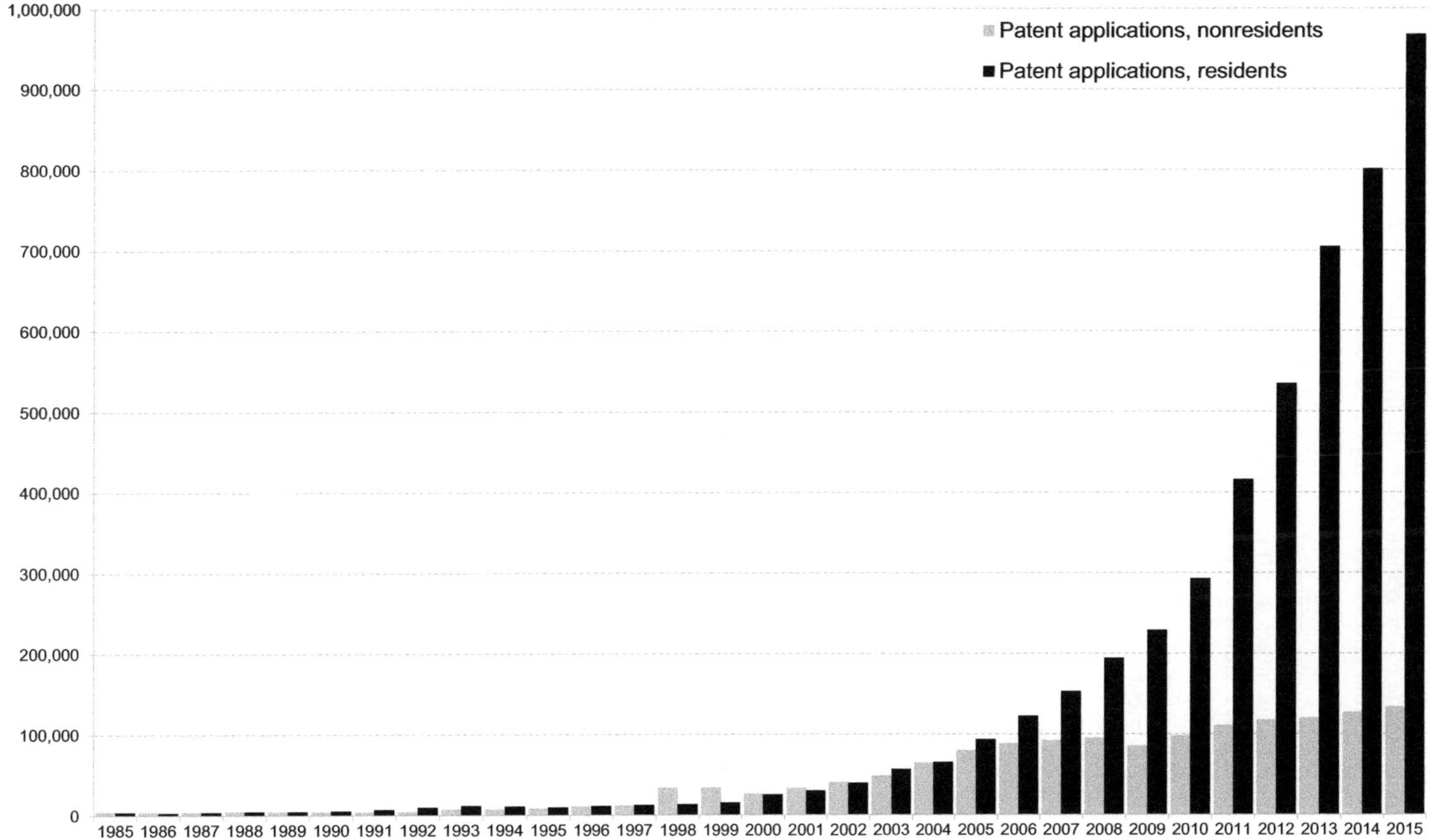

Figure 5.5 Patent applications in China 1985 to 2015

Source: World Bank, 2017 (World Development Indicators)

Note: Resident patent applications are those for which the first-named applicant or assignee is a resident of the state or region concerned. Nonresident patent applications are from applicants outside the relevant state or region.

investments will evolve in the future, when there might be a shift to a more sustainable economy due to the obligations made in the Paris Agreement of 2015.

The "case of China" turns well-established patterns of economic thought upside down. It is obvious that the "case of China" cannot easily be explained within an existing (new) growth theory if at all. A powerful state with ever-changing regulations causes much uncertainty for actors in private business. As discussed in section 2, new procedures or products (innovations) are eventually found through a trial and error principle instead of a cost-benefit based consideration. The adaptation of new business strategies through learning and change is another key element of evolutionary theory that fits the real world situation in China much better than an optimization strategy. As expressed throughout section 3 of this chapter, evolutionary thinking helps to explain certain phenomena that grow out of the "case of China."

A major advantage of the evolutionary perspective is that its concepts are closer to reality. First and foremost are bounded rationality and routines instead of rationality and optimization. The understanding of markets as an ever-changing construct with firms as constantly modifying their activities offers an explanation of China's rapid economic development that goes beyond standard cost-benefit argumentation. In the light of evolutionary thinking, foreign investors, for example, do not only enter the Chinese market because of (transaction) cost calculations, but also to accumulate knowledge and to benefit from a network of cross-border relationships. We would like to draw attention to the circumstance that standard neoclassical arguments are not enough to understand such a complex yet surprisingly quick economic development like in China. So far this chapter does not claim to provide a comprehensive or fully-fledged alternative, but it would like to invite to a discussion of the Chinese success story a theoretically broader perspective, including the rich insights from evolutionary economic theory.

Notes

1 Nonetheless, Nelson and Winter (1982) clarify that certainly not all behavior is routine. The term is rather used for behavior that has a repetitive and predictable character only.

2 Information is based on World Bank statistics. However, that exact figure might slightly differ from figures provided by other authors. Lin et al. (2003), for example, state an average annual GDP growth rate of 9.5%.

3 This process refers to the Industry Life Cycle (ILC), a recurring topic within the literature on evolutionary economics (Klepper, 1997). The ILC is a suitable concept to explain how well different industries in China have developed in the past and are developing in the present. It is furthermore understood that with economic development and growth of economic sectors, cities, and regions via aggregation, the growth of the whole economy can be explained by the ILC (Potter and Watts, 2011).

References

Alchian, A. A. (1950) "Uncertainty, Evolution, and Economic Theory." *Journal of Political Economy* 58(3): 211–221.

Allen, R. C. (1983) "Collective Invention." *Journal of Economic Behaviour and Organization* 4: 1–24.

Andersen, E. S. (1994) *Evolutionary Economics: Post-Schumpeterian Contributions*, London, UK: Pinter.

Broadman, H. G. and X. Sun (1997) "The Distribution of Foreign Direct Investment in China." *The World Economy* 20(3): 339–361.

Cantwell, J. (1989) *Technological Innovation in Multinational Corporations*, Oxford, UK: Blackwell.

Cantwell, J. (1995) "The Globalization of Technology: What Remains of the Product Cycle Model?" *Cambridge Journal of Economics* 19(1): 155–174.

Chen, C., L. Chang and Y. Zhang (1995) "The Role of Foreign Direct Investment in China's Post-1978 Economic Development." *World Development* 23(4): 691–703.

Cheung, Y.-W, J. de Haan, X. Qian and S. Yu (2012) "China's Outward Direct Investment in Africa." *Review of International Economics* 20(2): 201–220.

Démurger, S. (2000) "Infrastructure Development and Economic Growth: An Explanation for Regional Disparities in China?" *Journal of Comparative Economics* 29(1): 95–117.

Di Stefano, G., A. Gambardella and G. Verona (2012) "Technology Push and Demand Pull Perspectives in Innovation Studies: Current Findings and Future Research Directions." *Research Policy* 41(8): 1283–1295.

Dimitrov, R. S. (2016) "The Paris Agreement on Climate Change: Behind Closed Doors." *Global Environmental Politics* 16(3): 1–11.

Dopfer, K. and J. Potts (2004) "Evolutionary Realism: A New Ontology for Economics." *Journal of Economic Methodology* 11(2): 195–212.

Dosi, G. and R. R. Nelson (1994) "An Introduction to Evolutionary Theories in Economics." *Journal of Evolutionary Economics* 4(3): 153–172.

Dosi, G., D. J. Teece, R. Rumelt and S. Winter (1994) "Understanding Corporate Coherence: Theory and Evidence." G. Dosi (ed.), *Innovation, Organization and Economic Dynamics: Selected Essays*, Cambridge, UK: Cambridge University Press, 264–293.

Edquist, C. (2005) "Systems of Innovation: Perspectives and Challenges." J. Fagerberg, D. C. Mowery and R. R. Nelson (eds.), *The Oxford Handbook of Innovation*, Oxford: Oxford University Press, 181–208.

Findlay, R. (1978) "Relative Backwardness, Direct Foreign Investment and the Transfer of Technology: A Simple Dynamic Model." *Quarterly Journal of Economics* 92(1): 1–16.

Friedman, E. D. (2014) "Economic Development and Sectoral Unions in China." *ILR Review* 67(2): 481–503.

Grossman, G. M. and E. Helpman (1992) *Innovation and Growth in the Global Economy*, Cambridge, MA: The MIT Press.

Guenther, J. (2015) "Innovation." J. Hölscher and H. Tomann (eds.), *Palgrave Dictionary of Emerging Markets and Transition Economies*, London, UK: Palgrave Macmillan, 360–371.

Guha, A. S. (1981) *An Evolutionary View of Economic Growth*. Oxford, UK: Clarendon Press.

Günther, J. and M. Kristalova (2016) "No Risk no Fun? Foreign Direct Investment in Central and Eastern Europe." *Intereconomics – Review of European Economic Policy* 51(2): 95–99.

Hagedoorn, J., A. N. Link and N. S. Vonortas (2000) "Research Partnerships." *Research Policy* 29(4–5): 567–586.

Hodgson, G. M. and K. Huang (2010) "Evolutionary Game Theory and Evolutionary Economics: Are They Different Species?" *Journal of Evolutionary Economics* 22(2): 345–366.

Kaplinsky, R. and M. Morris (2009) "Chinese FDI in Sub-Saharan Africa: Engaging with Large Dragons." *The European Journal of Development Research* 21(4): 551–569.

Keller, W. (1996) "Absorptive Capacity: On the Creation and Acquisition of Technology in Development." *Journal of Development Economics* 49: 199–227.

Klepper, S. (1997) "Industry Life Cycles." *Industrial and Corporate Change* 6(1): 145–182.

Kline, S. and N. Rosenberg (1986) "An Overview of Innovation." C. Edquist and M. McKelvin (eds.), *Systems of Innovation: Growth, Competitiveness and Employment*, Cheltenham, UK: Edward Elgar.

Kotabe, M., C. X. Jiang and J. Y. Murray (2011) "Managerial Ties, Knowledge Acquisition, Realized Absorptive Capacity and New Product Market Performance of Emerging Multinational Companies: A Case of China." *Journal of World Business* 46: 166–176.

Kudic, M. and J. Guenther (2017) "Understanding the Complex Nature of Innovation Network Evolution." A. Pyka and U. Cantner (eds.), *Foundations of Economic Change – A Schumpeterian View on Behaviour, Interaction and Aggregate Outcomes*, Wiesbaden: Springer, 501–524.

Li, Y. (2010) *Imitation to Innovation in China: The Role of Patents in Biotechnology and Pharmaceutical Industries*, Cheltenham, UK: Edward Elgar.

Lin, J.Y. (2014) "Economic Growth and Development." G. C. Chow and D. H. Perkins (eds.), *Routledge Handbook of the Chinese Economy*. New York: Routledge, 55–75.

Lin, J.Y., F. Cai and Z. Li (2003) *The China Miracle, Development Strategy and Economic Reform* (3rd ed.), Hong Kong: The Chinese University Press.

Lundvall, B-A. (1992) *National Systems of Innovation: Towards a Theory of Innovation and Interactive Learning*, London: Pinter Publishers.

Lundvall, B. A., K. J. Joseph, C. Chaminade and J. Vang (2009) *Handbook of Innovation Systems and Developing Countries: Building Domestic Capabilities in a Global Setting*, Cheltenham, UK: Edward Elgar.

Malerba, F. and R. R. Nelson (2012) *Economic Development as a Learning Process: Variation Across Sectoral Systems*, Cheltenham, UK: Edward Elgar.

Ministry of Commerce People's Republic of China (MOFCOM) (2016) "Statistics of FDI in China in January-December 2015." Available at http://english.mofcom.gov.cn/article/statistic/foreigninvestment/201602/20160201260821.shtml (accessed January 2, 2018).

National Bureau of Statistics of China (2016) "Foreign Direct Investment by Sector: Number of Projects." Available at http://data.stats.gov.cn/english/easyquery.htm?cn=C01 (accessed January 3, 2018).

Nelson, R. R. (1993) *National Innovation Systems: A Comparative Analysis*, Oxford: Oxford University Press.

Nelson, R. R. and S. G. Winter (1974) "Neoclassical vs. Evolutionary Theories of Economic Growth: Critique and Prospectus." *The Economic Journal* 84(336): 886–905.

Nelson, R. R. and S. G. Winter (1982) *An Evolutionary Theory of Economic Change*, Cambridge: Harvard University Press.

Nelson, R. R. and S. G. Winter (2002) "Evolutionary Theorizing in Economics." *The Journal of Economic Perspectives* 16(2): 23–46.

Orr, G. and E. Roth (2012) "A CEO's Guide to Innovation in China." *McKinsey Quarterly*, February. Available at https://www.mckinsey.com/featured-insights/asia-pacific/a-ceos-guide-to-innovation-in-china.

Pavitt, K. (2005) "Innovation Processes." J. Fagerberg, D. C. Mowery and R. R. Nelson (eds.), *The Oxford Handbook of Innovation*. Oxford: Oxford University Press, 86–114.

Potter, A. and D. H. Watts (2011) "Evolutionary Agglomeration Theory: Increasing Returns, Diminishing Returns, and the Industry Life Cycle." *Journal of Economic Geography* 11: 417–455.

Romer, P. (1986) "Increasing Returns and Long Run Growth." *Journal of Political Economy* 94: 1002–1037.

Romer, P. (1990) "Endogenous Technological Change." *Journal of Political Economy* 98: 71–102.

Santangelo, G. D. (2003) "The Evolutionary Perspective on Growth." N. Salvadori (ed.), *The Theory of Economic Growth: A "Classical" Perspective*, Cheltenham, UK: Edward Elgar Publishing Limited, 204–220.

Schmookler, J. (1966) *Invention and Economic Growth*, Cambridge, MA: Harvard University Press.

Silva, S.T. and A. A. C. Teixeira (2009) "On the Divergence of Research Paths in Evolutionary Economics: A Comprehensive Bibliometric Account." *Journal of Evolutionary Economics* 19: 605–624.

Solow, R. M. (1956) "A Contribution to the Theory of Economic Growth." *The Quarterly Journal of Economics* 70(1): 65–94.

Sull, D. N. and Y. Wang (2005) *Made in China: What Western Managers Can Learn from Trailblazing Chinese Entrepreneurs*, Boston, MA: Harvard University Business School Press.

Swan, T. W. (1956) "Economic Growth and Capital Accumulation." *Economic Record* 32: 334–361.

Ten Brink, T. (2013) *China's Kapitalismus. Entstehung, Verlauf, Paradoxien*, Frankfurt, NY: Campus Verlag.

UNCTAD (2017) "Foreign Direct Investment: Inward and Outward Flows and Stock, Annual, 1970–2016." Available at http://unctadstat.unctad.org/wds/ReportFolders/reportFolders.aspx (accessed January 3, 2018).

Verspagen, B. (2005) "Innovation and Economic Growth." J. Fagerberg, D. C. Mowery and R. R. Nelson (eds.), *Oxford Handbook of Innovation*, Oxford: Oxford University Press, 487–513.

Vietor, R. H. K. (2007) *How Countries Compete – Strategy, Structure, and Government in the Global Economy*, Boston, MA: Harvard University Business School Press.

Von Hippel, E. (2005) *Democratizing Innovation*, Cambridge, MA and London: The MIT Press.

Von Jacobi, N. (2017) "Institutional Interconnections: Understanding Symbiotic Relationships." *Journal of Institutional Economics* 14(5): 853–876.

Von Tunzelmann, N. (2004) "Network Alignment in the Catching-Up Economies of Europe." F. McGowan, S. Radosevic and N. von Tunzelmann (eds.), *The Emerging Industrial Structure of the Wider Europe*, London: Routledge, 23–37.

Von Tunzelmann, N., J. Günther, K. Wilde and B. Jindra (2010) "Interactive Dynamic Capabilities and Regenerating the East German Innovation System." *Contributions to Political Economy* 29(1): 87–110.

Wei, Y., X. Liu, D. Parker and K. Vaidya (1999) "The Regional Distribution of Foreign Direct Investment in China." *Regional Studies* 33(9): 857–867.

World Bank (2017) "Data Bank: World Development Indicators China." Available at http://databank.worldbank.org/data/reports.aspx?source=2&country=CHN (accessed December 20, 2017).

World Economic Forum (2017) "The World's 10 Biggest Economies 2017." Available at www.weforum.org/agenda/2017/03/worlds-biggest-economies-in-2017/ (accessed April 12, 2018).

Wu, J. and S. Fan (2014) "China's Economic Reform – Processes, Issues, and Prospects (1978–2012)." G. C. Chow and D. H. Perkins (eds.), *Routledge Handbook of the Chinese Economy*, New York: Routledge, 55–75.

Yip, G. S. and B. McKern (2016) *China's Next Strategic Advantage: From Imitation to Innovation*, Cambridge: The MIT Press.

Zafar, A. (2007) "The Growing Relationship between China and Sub-Saharan Africa: Macroeconomic, Trade, Investment, and Aid Links." *The World Bank Research Observer* 22(1): 103–130.

6 Architecture-based innovation strategies in the development of China's passenger vehicle sector

Marcus Conlé

1 Introduction

Three decades of rapid growth have allowed China to join the ranks of the largest economies in terms of GDP. Nonetheless, the sources of the rapid growth and its sustainability remain an issue. State-directed investment as a means to maintain the country's growth momentum continues to be the focal point of the debate (Naughton, 2017; Holz, 2018). On the other hand, analyses of the growth phenomenon that focus on qualitative changes of knowledge, organization, and outputs have been relatively few. However, the situation is changing quickly in recent years. The success of some Chinese industries in the world market, and the frequent challenges that global lead firms face in China's domestic market, have increasingly led scholars (Breznitz and Murphree, 2011; Conlé, 2011; Fu, 2015; Zhou et al., 2016 to name just a few) to turn away from arguments solely emphasizing the availability of cheap resources and adopt perspectives focusing on the ways resources are being created and employed instead. Accordingly, there exists by now plenty of research concentrating on the specific nature of China's efforts of upgrading design and manufacturing capabilities as well as on the country's innovation patterns. Although these efforts are hitherto undertaken in a rather disparate fashion, there arguably exists a common theme to the different perspectives – one that can be productively linked to the broader literature on national competitiveness.

Patterns of industrial leadership are widely associated with firms successfully playing out the advantages of their proximate environment. Moving away from the early economists' emphasis on natural endowments, advantages are today argued to result from the cultural, structural, and institutional characteristics of the national setting and to translate into specific patterns of innovation (e.g., Porter, 1990; Soskice, 1997; Lundvall, 1998). In innovation studies, the relationship between the national setting, firms' innovation strategies, and competitive success in various industries is theorized in three different ways: one of them, the "technological paradigm" view, suggests that sustained industry leadership is associated with the learning economies that incumbent firms can reap along an industry's technological trajectory (Dosi, 1982). The emergence of novel technologies, in turn, opens up windows of opportunity that allow new entrants to successfully disrupt previous industry leadership structures (Perez and Soete, 1988). Accordingly, the readiness of national innovation systems and policies to respond to radical changes of technology and seize the resulting opportunities is considered to constitute a relevant competitive advantage (Lee and Lim, 2001). The "comparative institutional analysis of innovation" (Casper, 2010), on the other hand, insists that interdependencies between national institutions provide for a limited adaptability of national innovation systems toward technological change. Instead, two types of coherent national institutional configurations are argued to stand out for advantaging domestic firms in seizing changes in sectoral opportunity conditions and in gaining leadership positions in industries that are characterized by either radical or incremental innovation. Finally, Fujimoto (2007) has outlined a third approach of architecture-based comparative advantage that shares common ground with the comparative approach concerning the variation of organizational capabilities across national economies. In place of distinguishing outputs in terms of a product technology's relative novelty (radical vs. incremental), Fujimoto's approach adopts a design perspective that distinguishes industries according to prevalent types of product architectures (integral vs. modular designs, in particular).

The competitiveness literature provides a good starting point for scrutinizing the nature of innovative activities and catching-up development in China. To begin with, the paradigm view directs attention toward examining the opportunity conditions for innovative activities. Research on China has shown that although innovative activities frequently take place in industries experiencing rapid development because of radical technological breakthroughs, a "Western techno-fetishism of novelty" (Breznitz and Murphree, 2011, p. 195) is unhelpful in tracing Chinese innovation strategies – in contrast to perspectives that focus on the creative utilization of given technology. The comparative literature calls attention to how institutions enable or hinder distinct types of innovative activities. Following concurrent trends in that literature (Allen, 2013), China scholars have pointed out the relevance of institutional multiplicity and its effect on the emergence and interaction of a variety of organizational forms (e.g., Conlé, 2011; Lüthje et al., 2013). As the outgrowth of the relevant actions and interactions is difficult to capture with the simple radical/incremental dichotomy, further concepts have come to be explored in the China literature to characterize prevalent innovation strategies in the Chinese economy. The most salient characterization of such strategies relies on Henderson and Clark's (1990) extended typology of innovation which augments said radical/incremental dichotomy with a third type – architectural innovation (Ernst and Naughton, 2008; Kaplinsky et al., 2009; Conlé, 2011). Adopting the concept effectively forges a link to Fujimoto's design-based perspective that has been fruitfully adopted to describe innovation in the Chinese context (Ge and Fujimoto, 2004; Wang, 2008). Other concepts that have been used to define Chinese innovation strategies such as "open innovation" (Fu, 2015) or "manufacturing innovation" (Bonvillian, 2013; Nahm and Steinfeld, 2014) point to issues that are related to those captured by Fujimoto.

While it might be easy to agree with the previous literature that architectural innovation is a useful concept to characterize prevalent innovation strategies within the Chinese context, it needs to be pointed out that the link between architectural innovation, the country's institutional and organizational setup, and domestic corporate performance in the relevant industries is far from fully elaborated. The purpose of this contribution is to explore these connections and their implications in greater detail. This requires a distinction between the concept and the more conventionally used types of innovation. In the present contribution, we will argue against understanding architectural innovation as a simple add-on to the two commonly used innovation types. Instead, it sets a few entirely new focal points. First of all, architectural innovation constitutes a potentially disruptive strategy that is not necessarily connected to a lead in the creation of radically new product technology but can also involve the creative utilization of available component technology. Accordingly, architectural innovation is not only undertaken by technology leaders but it is also a feasible strategy for follower firms. Second, whereas radical and incremental innovations are generally associated in the comparative literature with distinctive organizational forms, this is not the case with architectural innovation. As the literature on the so-called "mirroring hypothesis" holds, there exists an interrelationship between organizational architectures and product architectures.[1] Organizational architectures encompass a firm's internal organization and its external organization – that is, its forms of interaction with other firms in its industrial ecosystem. The gist of the argument advanced here is that product architectural technology and business organization coevolve, with the utilization of particular forms of architectural technology facilitating the employment of particular forms of business organization, and vice versa. Accordingly, architectural innovation, as defined in the present chapter, relates to the exploitation of nationally distinctive sectoral opportunities that open up because of ongoing adaptations between organizational structures and product architectures. More specifically, we will show that the prevalent forms of innovation in China can be explained in terms of an interplay of fragmented domestic industry architectures and a general trend in many industries toward the modularization of product architectures. We argue that, as a distinctive feature of China's pattern of architectural innovation, the prevalent domestic conditions allow firms to source product components and mix and match them in unparalleled ways.

The rest of this chapter is structured into three more sections. Section 2 introduces the concept of architectural innovation. While subsection 2.1 reviews Henderson and Clark's (1990) seminal contribution in order to discuss the concept in relation to radical and incremental innovation, subsection 2.2 introduces two dimensions according to which different architecture-based innovation strategies may vary. In this connection, strategies refer to generic organizational approaches toward the modularization or integration of product architectures. Section 3 then provides a case study that seeks to illustrate the Chinese innovation pattern. While similar patterns can be observed in a whole range of sectors such as, for instance, color TVs, air conditioners, and mobile phones (e.g., Watanabe, 2014), the passenger vehicle sector was chosen because it exemplifies the distinctiveness of China's approach toward modularization compared to the leading car-producing nations. Following a brief introduction of the sector's main trajectory in subsection 3.1, subsection 3.2 deals with the Chinese development path. Section 4 concludes.

2 Defining architectural innovation

2.1 The concept

The concept of innovation is intimately connected not only to novelty in the form of new and/or improved technology but, even more importantly, to its impact on economic organization. Generally speaking, innovation may have an effect on both the innovating firm's position in the competitive order and the position of the innovator's (extant) competitors. It is this double impact – the availability of new or improved technology for society at large as well as the potentially disruptive effect on the sectoral order – that is at the core of the predominant definitions of the forms of innovation. Schumpeter's original distinction between radical and incremental innovation follows along these lines. Consequently, radical innovations have entered the spotlight. Tushman and Anderson (1986), for instance, associate radical innovation with infrequently occurring major technological discontinuities that, depending on the required changes to the prevailing skills, knowledge, and capabilities, may be either competence-enhancing or competence-destroying from the point of view of incumbent firms. In the latter case of a competence-destroying radical innovation, the sectoral changes that are induced by the innovation(s) might involve new market segmentations and substantial changes in the status ordering of the firms within the broader sector. Accordingly, competence-destroying innovations are argued to provide "windows of opportunity" for breaking into sectors or for tearing down existing sectoral segmentations. The opening up of windows of opportunity are central to the most salient discussions on entry and catching-up development (Perez and Soete, 1988).

		Disruptive to the Sector's Status Ordering	
		Yes	**No**
Disruptive to the Sector's Core Technologies	**Yes**	Radical Innovation (competence-destroying)	Radical Innovation (competence-enhancing)
	No	Architectural Innovation	Incremental Innovation

Figure 6.1 Types of innovation according to their disruptive effects

It is against the backdrop of associating the failure of incumbent firms mainly with radical innovation that Henderson and Clark (1990) advance the concept of architectural innovation. Their fundamental argument is presented in Figure 6.1. According to the conventional understanding, if a given sector is described in terms of its knowledge base, then large changes to this knowledge base create significant adaptive challenges for incumbent firms that might be readily exploited by unencumbered entrants with the requisite knowledge and capabilities. The thrust of Henderson and Clark's argument is that shifts in the knowledge base are indeed sufficient to explain sectoral disruptions, but, contrary to the conventional understanding, they are not necessary. Instead, innovations that do not affect the sector's knowledge base may also have similar consequences to a sector and its incumbent firms. Henderson and Clark substantiate their argument by distinguishing between conceptual knowledge and architectural knowledge. In this connection, conceptual knowledge is understood as the standard "toolbox" of principles and methods that are utilized to implement the functions of a product's components. Architectural knowledge, on the other hand, is understood as the knowledge of arranging the functional elements into physical components and linking them to generate the product's overall performance. This distinction allows differentiating between changes in the sector's toolbox and changes in the product architecture including the functional components and their interfaces. Consequently, radical (incremental) innovation is concretized as a fundamental (minor) change in both the toolbox and the product architecture, whereas architectural innovation involves a significant change of the product architecture using the standard toolbox of conceptual principles and methods. As in the case of competence-destroying radical innovations, architectural innovations pose severe challenges to incumbent firms due to the destruction of the incumbents' architectural knowledge.

Following their study on architectural innovations in the semiconductor lithographic alignment equipment industry, Henderson and Clark (1990) hint at the possibility that the innovation of product architectures might be related to distinct organizational structures and information-processing procedures. This so-called "mirroring hypothesis" was further extended by Sanchez and Mahoney (1996). They suggest that product architectures tend to be reflected in organizational structures and industry architectures (see also Sanchez and Mahoney, 2013). As different product architectures are associated with different possibilities of decomposing design tasks, different architectures effectively allow for variations in industrial ecosystems in terms of market and nonmarket coordination. In emphasizing the relationship between coordination modes and patterns of innovation, this literature, in turn, invites drawing connections to the literature of the comparative institutional analysis of innovation. In his groundbreaking paper, which presents his reading of Porter's (1990) study of national competitive advantage, Soskice (1997) argues that the globally leading industrial economies show distinct patterns of innovation. Whereas radical innovation strategies seem to be prevalent in Anglo-Saxon economies with their market-liberal organizational patterns, the Northern European countries (and Japan), with their coordinated forms of market organization, appear to excel in incremental innovation (see also Hall and Soskice, 2001). At first glance, the concept of architectural innovation provides the opportunity to add a third type of innovation to the existing dichotomy to increase the variety of possible outcomes in the comparative framework. In this connection, Ernst and Naughton (2008) were the first ones to describe the innovation strategies of Chinese firms in terms of architectural innovation – followed by others (e.g., Conlé, 2011). More generally, Nahm and Steinfeld (2014, p. 289) point out that, in characterizing prevalent forms of innovation in China, China scholars typically have come to "bear the influence of the seminal theoretical work of Henderson and Clark."

While architectural innovation might indeed be a suitable concept to pinpoint prevalent patterns of innovation in China, the concept is, however, not as easily aligned with the comparative frameworks as it superficially appears. This is because architectural innovation might be connected to various forms of business organization and industry architectures whereas the comparative frameworks suggest a one-to-one mapping of forms of organization and innovation types. Providing the most concrete definitions in the relevant literature, Casper (e.g., Casper and Soskice, 2004; Casper and Whitley, 2004; Casper, 2010) associates radical innovation with disruptive, competence-destroying technological change and incremental innovation with cumulative, competence-enhancing change. To succeed in sectors characterized by either of the two technological settings, firms are argued to require the institutional means to adapt their innovation strategies accordingly. In disruptive technological settings, supportive institutional environments allow a rather flexible organization of resources and capabilities within and across firms, whereas in cumulative technological settings, beneficial institutions originate organizational patterns that enforce a more sustained coordination and long-term orientation. These relationships are used to explain the industrial leadership of firms from particular countries in a range of industries featuring particular technological opportunity conditions and innovation patterns.

According to Henderson and Clark, architectural innovations potentially have disruptive effects, too. However, this does not necessarily imply that they take place in settings that are inherently characterized by major technological discontinuities. Still, the competitive challenges of firms within different sectors can be distinguished according to the character of the ongoing technological change, although there is no straightforward connection between the nature of technological change and the level of uncertainty involved in the creation of technology and/or the appropriation of the returns from introducing new technology. Instead, the focus shifts to the specific ways technology is created, adapted, utilized, and implemented in the creation of products. Products are typically *combinations* of technology. While none of the technologies might be disruptive, the architectural innovation strategies that forge distinct connections between the technologies might very well be. As product architectures move into the spotlight, different focal points are set in connection with the nature of the sectoral knowledge base. Especially the structural organization (coupling) of the development and utilization of knowledge and capabilities moves into the spotlight. Considering the systemic interrelationship between product architectures and organization architectures, as it expresses itself in the mirroring hypothesis, differences in business organizations and industrial ecosystems across countries will provide firms with different options in pursing particular product innovation strategies. Consequently, different national industry architectures might provide the basis for distinct patterns of organizational learning and architectural innovation. It is in this context that Fujimoto's (2007) approach of architecture-based comparative advantage comes into play.

2.2 Architecture-based innovation strategies

The existence of differences among countries, especially Japan and the US, with regard to the use of product architectures has certainly not been missed (e.g., Langlois and Robertson, 1995, Sako and Murray, 2000). Above all, Fujimoto (2007) has pioneered an architecture-based perspective on national competitive advantage that connects to Henderson and Clark's mirroring hypothesis for the comparison of national innovation patterns. In line with the modularity literature, he defines product architecture as a scheme consisting of three features: the decomposition of the product's overall functionality into discrete functional elements (e.g., "store data"); the assignment of the functional elements to a number of physical components (e.g., a data storage component); and the specification of the interfaces across which the components interact (Ulrich, 1995, Baldwin and Clark, 1997). Fujimoto also adopts the two conventional distinctions between modular and integral as well as open and closed product architectures. Accordingly, modularity concerns the codification and standardization of interface specifications with the intent of increasing the decomposability and the configurability (the ability to "mix and match") of the overall product system. Openness, on the other hand, refers to the creation and sharing of interface specifications among firms within a larger industrial ecosystem (Sanchez and Collins, 2001). Fujimoto combines these two dichotomies to arrive at three distinct types of product architectures: closed-integral, closed-modular, and open-modular. His proposition is that whereas Japan leads in closed-integral architectures, the US has a competitive advantage in open-modular architectures.

In distinguishing product design outcomes, Fujimoto seeks to simultaneously state something about the organization of the design and manufacturing process. However, drawing on Nobeoka (2005), two problems need to be considered in regard to linking organizational and product architectures. To begin with, while Japan is widely considered to be good at designing integral product architectures, Japanese companies have obviously no problems coming up with admirable modular product designs. Representing all the modular electronic products made in Japan, the Sony Walkman is easily among the most cited modular products in the vast modularity literature (e.g., Sanderson

	Scope	Degree
Extent of Task Decomposition	Extent of organizational separation of tasks and functions (strict vs. loose)	Extent of interactions among organizations (strong vs. weak)
Extent of Task Externalization	Scope of task externalization (peripheral vs. core systems)	Degree of task externalization (co-developed vs. off-the-shelf)

Figure 6.2 The two dimensions of design and manufacturing tasks

and Uzumeri, 1995; Ulrich, 1995; Sanchez and Mahoney, 1996). The second problem is that the "dominant designs" (Abernathy and Utterback, 1978) of industry sectors tend to change over time. It is these design transitions that are usually associated with the biggest disruption to existing sectoral structures. Some evolutionary theorists, most forcefully Langlois (Langlois and Robertson, 1995; Langlois, 2003), see a general trend toward modularity through an industry's development. However, movements in the reverse direction, from modular to integral architectures, have also been documented (e.g., Ernst, 2005). An illustrative example of this shift is the Japanese bicycle component producer Shimano's transforming a formerly competitive market into a near monopoly by introducing a more integral architecture (Fixson and Park, 2008). Still, various sectors that have traditionally featured more integral designs – including the automotive sector that we will use as an example in the present book chapter – have recently experienced a move toward more modular architectures. If national patterns were related to specific types of architectures, incumbent Japanese firms in those sectors would fail simply due to their incapacity to increase the modularity of their architectures. However, seeing the interaction between organizational and product architectures in this way would not only seriously understate the design capabilities of many Japanese firms but also underestimate the plurality of possibilities to modularize product architectures.

While there is clearly a point in looking at variations in the properties of product designs, the most pronounced differences between firms from various national institutional environments are arguably not so much found in the particular choices between product modularity and integrality. Instead, the differences concern the firms' strategies toward generating and/or adapting to sectoral trends – that is, for instance, their specific approaches toward modularization or integration.[2] At the national level, these approaches tend to present themselves in distinct patterns of innovation. If so, it can be expected that national differences are captured more systematically in organizational instead of (product-related) technological terms. This requires a slight rephrasing of Fujimoto's terminology. From an organizational point of view, the dimensions used by Fujimoto relate to the configuration of design and manufacturing tasks as well as to the organizational locus of capability building and the provision of relevant tasks. Figure 6.2 specifies these two dimensions more concretely. The first dimension, the extent of design task decomposition, refers to the ways that tasks are specified and assigned to particular organizations (or their subunits). Tasks may be clearly specified and circumscribed so as to allow an independent search for solutions for the separate tasks, or they may be more tightly coupled so that more coordination is required to solve the problems emanating from the interdependences among the tasks involved. A high scope of task decomposition implies that tasks and functions are separated relatively strictly among different organizational units. In the case of a high degree of design task decomposition, the tasks are moreover structured in a way that minimizes the amount of information and other resources that need to be exchanged among tasks and units. On the other hand, the task externalization dimension pertains to the extent that tasks are delegated to independent others rather than vertically controlled by the focal actor. A high scope of task externalization indicates that external collaborators are not only engaged in tasks related to noncritical technology and product components but also in tasks that include the design and development of core technology. If the degree of task externalization is low, then the involvement of a focal firm in the tasks is relatively strong – and its organizational capabilities are rather broad – whereas, at the other end of the spectrum, the implementation of tasks are bought "off-the-shelf" as ready-made solutions from capable outside suppliers.

Architecture-based innovation strategies thus rest on the organizational structures that enable firms to create and access specific capabilities. The organizational structures channel innovation strategies as they determine the options available to firms for partitioning and assigning tasks and, therefore, the feasibility of implementing particular product architectures (Sanchez and Mahoney, 2013). Architecture-based innovation strategies have the potential to disrupt sectoral orders if the related product designs are successful in the market while incumbent market leaders are unable to change the relevant organizational patterns to accommodate similar product designs. The disruption of sectoral status orders through architectural innovation might involve changing the extent of integration or modularization. It might also involve intensifying integration or modularization by closing or (further) opening the product architecture. The relevant level at which innovative activities and the development of capabilities concerning the creation and implementation of distinct product designs take place might be the firm. However, especially in the context of national innovation patterns, architecture-based strategies frequently need to be considered in the context of larger industrial ecosystems. A focal firm is then not all by itself in pursuing a particular strategy while the firm's strategy is related to, and fundamentally dependent on, still other firms probing essential complementary strategies. In these cases, the economic opportunity conditions are strongly conditioned by the prevalent organizational capability structures. As the structures evolve and channel the process of modularization or integration, they give rise to distinct industrial trajectories – and distinct national patterns of innovation. The following case study of the passenger vehicle industry places the Chinese trajectory within the current sectoral trend toward modular architectures and differentiates the Chinese innovation pattern from patterns in the leading car-producing countries. It demonstrates the usefulness of describing these differences in terms of the extent of task decomposition and the extent of task externalization.

3 Patterns of architectural innovation in China's passenger vehicle industry

3.1 The sector's main trajectory

The automotive industry is at present specifically associated with the development of the internal combustion engine (ICE) and the model case for an industry featuring integral product designs. However, both features have only gradually come to characterize the industry, and the likelihood has lately increased that the very features may not characterize the sector in the future. When the automotive industry emerged in the late nineteenth century, competition initially came to be based on modular designs accommodating a wide range of components from existing segments of the passenger transport sector, such as bicycles, horse carriages, and locomotives. The core concept of the emergent industry was still in flux and a large number of competitors were probing the feasibility of carriage-like (the dominant US approach) and locomotive-like (the succeeding French approach) designs in addition to different types of powertrain technologies encompassing the eventually triumphant ICE as well as electric motors and steam engine propulsion systems (Langlois and Robertson, 1989; Mowery and Rosenberg, 1998). Massive entry into the sector provided an increasing source of creative opportunities and competition. Particularly, the United States stood out with an initially steady increase in the number of entering firms, typically with a background in bicycle manufacture, and a consistently large population of considerably over a hundred auto firms until well into the 1920s (Klepper, 2002).

After the automobile sector had settled on an ICE–based dominant design, a number of connected shifts in product and process technologies have gradually transformed the sector; first, from one featuring an open-modular to a closed-modular and, then, to a closed-integral product architecture. The original shift is closely related to Henry Ford's introduction of the Model T whose modular architecture and component sharing with other models allowed the entrepreneur to tap the large low-income demand of his fellow citizens (Alizon et al., 2009). As the Model T evolved, the manufacture of an increasing number of components was brought in-house. Concurrent with similar changes going on at Ford's major competitors, most notably General Motors (GM), the American auto industry made a strong move toward closed-system approaches (Langlois and Robertson, 1989). A similar tendency toward integration was observed in the other major auto-producing countries, but the forms of integration differed in terms of the organizational separation of tasks and the extent of delegating tasks to independent suppliers. When the source of competitive success in the automobile sector shifted from designs for easing component access and scale-up toward performance-related designs concerning, inter alia, velocity, safety, and drivability, more integral design approaches came to enjoy an advantage over strategies featuring a higher extent of task decomposition. Especially Japan's successful entry and expansion in the global auto industry is associated with the integrative coordinative capabilities that are embedded in its firms' organizational forms (e.g., Hemmert, 1999).

More recently, the sector has yet experienced a trend toward modularization. Despite similarities with Henry Ford's approach of driving down production costs through the simplification of production processes and the exploitation of economies of scale at the component level, the present approach differs. Because of the rapid progress in computer-aided design and manufacturing methods, modularity has entered the automobile sector as a promise of a low-cost approach toward increasing product variety as well as a feasible option for increasing outsourcing in order to reduce costs and tap external sources of design knowledge (MacDuffie, 2013). While the highly visible development of the computer industry has contributed to the emergence of this new cognitive frame, other stimuli in the immediate sectoral context have also played a significant part in its emergence and diffusion. First, after decades of incremental improvements in performance, there appears to be little to be gained in terms of customer appreciation from further improvements in the performance of the classical functions, such as for instance, an increase in velocity. Rather, adaptability to environmental changes in demand and technology have gained an increasing degree of attention. In advanced (primarily Western) economies, a new generation of (especially urban) consumers with different lifestyles and different attitudes toward car usage and ownership appears to form, while developments in emerging economies have given rise to a large pool of potential customers. On the other hand, concerns about air pollution and climate change have provided for expectations of a radical technological change of the core powertrain technology. Finally, the diffusion of information and communication technologies throughout the economy is expected to continue to change the design and functions of the car.

The increasingly uncertain state of the sectoral competitive order – and the sectoral environment more generally – has created ample space for divergent innovation strategies. As expected, companies from various regions have shown a different pattern and inclination with regard to modularization (Takeishi and Fujimoto, 2001; Sako, 2003). While American and European firms tend to embrace modularization specifically as a means toward raising the extent of outsourcing, Japanese companies appear more reluctant to change the structure of their quasi-vertical organizational forms although they have introduced organizational changes to accompany increasing design modularity. German auto firms aggressively pursue modularized platform designs for downsizing the main assembly, improving mass customization, and adapting to the technological uncertainties.[3] Just like the major US automakers, the German firms source many car modules from the leading supplier firms. In contrast to their US rivals, which have been particularly responsive to core-competence slogans, the German firms have kept a larger range of capabilities in-house. As outsourcing has played an increasing role in the sector, supplier firms have become a more salient factor. In the United States, GM and Ford have spun off two large "turn-key suppliers" (Sturgeon, 2002), Delphi and Visteon, respectively. The Japanese and German organizational forms, on the other hand, had never shown a comparatively high level of ownership integration, despite their relatively intimate interaction with suppliers such as Denso and Bosch. Because of the recent sectoral development, a transnational population of competing independent supplier firms has emerged (Sturgeon et al., 2009).

In addition to the strategies of the incumbent carmakers, several companies from outside the sector have recently explored the industry's changing opportunity structure. Among the advanced economies, entry attempts (and rumors) are particularly pronounced in the United States. Since the electronics and information content of automobiles has increased tremendously, firms from related sectors have probed the feasibility of entering the industry as suppliers and even as competing integrators. The consumer electronics giant Apple, for instance, is rumored to develop an own-branded electric passenger vehicle (e.g., Wakabayashi and Ramsey, 2015). It would follow in the footsteps of Silicon Valley company Tesla motors (and other less successful companies such as Fisker Automotive). Tesla has managed to enter the sector by relying heavily on the (external) design capabilities of other companies. Tesla's first car, the Roadster, was based on a combination mainly of Tesla's proprietary electric powertrain and a chassis that was designed and provided by Lotus Cars (e.g., Davies, 2010).

As MacDuffie and Fujimoto (2010) point out, the complexity of a modern car serves as a powerful barrier to entry that protects industry leaders from emerging rivals. However, as the dominant concept of the car is under pressure, opportunities for entrants open up in various regions of the sectoral landscape. Most of all, electric cars may be more prone to modularization and simplification (e.g., Christensen, 2011). As the electrification of the car gathers momentum, accompanying moves toward modularity are likely to lead to open designs that provide access points for independent developments by emerging supplier firms. In addition, existing component makers will try to seize opportunities to extend the range of their design activities in order to capture more value. Because of outsourcing, the large supplier firms have already developed strong design capabilities. Until recently, however, the persistent integrality of the car and, perhaps even more so, the carmakers' determination to keep control of their product systems appear to inhibit a more independent design part by the suppliers (Zirpoli and Camuffo, 2009; Cabigiosu et al., 2013; MacDuffie, 2013). The incumbents' efforts of precluding "Intel inside" type of sectoral trajectories (like in the modular ICT sector) might, however, be thwarted by the open-modular development path characterizing China's sectoral innovation pattern.

3.2 Development and change in China's passenger vehicle sector

China has a comparatively brief history of automotive development. While various small auto shops existed (predominately in Shanghai) before the establishment of the People's Republic in 1949, the mass production of vehicles started only in 1956 with the establishment of the No. 1 Motor Vehicle Manufacturing Plant (now First Auto Works, FAW), one of the most important Sino-Soviet development projects. Because of the collaboration with the Soviet Union, China adopted a "vertically divided division of labor" (Marukawa, 1995). Accordingly, firms specialized in a very narrow range of final products, while they were insisting on carrying out in-house the major upstream activities such as machining, metal stamping, casting, and forging. Therefore, economies of scale relating to the various activities could not be reaped. This problem was aggravated as Chinese auto companies multiplied, especially during the major decentralization phases of the Great Leap and the Cultural Revolution. While several firms that entered during the Great Leap – including Shanghai Automotive (SAIC) – survived the abandonment of the campaign, numerous additional firms entered the sector in the 1970s, several of which turned into viable companies. As Lyons (1987) calculates, at the start of the 1980s, the Chinese auto industry featured more than a hundred assembly plants with similarly thin product foci but highly diverging capacities and production methods. Among them, the No. 1 Plant accounted for about a third of overall national manufacturing output, while the No. 2 Plant (now Dongfeng Motor), a Third-Front project that was established in a mountainous region of inland Hubei province, had not achieved regular operations until the late 1970s. While FAW and Dongfeng were mainly involved in the production of heavy trucks, two provincial-level plants, SAIC and Nanjing Auto (now a subsidiary of SAIC) had emerged as manufacturers of light vehicles. Additionally, more than 2,000 manufacturing units were involved in vehicle parts production. The locus of coordination and control of all these manufacturing and assembly units was scattered among different ministries, ministerial bureaus, organizations of the People's Liberation Army (PLA), provincial and local-level bureaus as well as rural communes (Lyons, 1987; Noble et al., 2005).

When the passenger car segment became the key focus of the Chinese government in the 1980s, two measures appeared to signal a departure from the previous development trajectory. First, entry into the passenger car segment became more strongly regulated as only eight manufacturers received a license to operate in that segment. Moreover, the VW-SAIC joint venture heralded the beginning of the "market access for technology" approach toward international development cooperation that has since characterized several other medium to high-technology sectors, particularly in the 1990s (e.g., Kroll et al., 2008). Until the turn of the century, the selected Chinese passenger car companies were matched with all relevant foreign transnational car manufacturers that were flocking to China in order to participate in the emerging market. The influx of incumbent international car companies had particularly positive effects on the development of component manufacturing as well as the supplier firms' organizational development including their project execution capabilities (Thun, 2006; Nam, 2011). The most popular car models of the late 1990s – the (Shanghai VW) Santana, the (FAW Tianjin) Xiali, the (FAW-VW) Jetta, and the (Dongfeng Peugeot-Citroen) Fukang – achieved localization rates of more than 80% (Xi et al., 2009). Yet, if the development of indigenous design capabilities had been the primary motivation, then the performance was bleaker. The activities of the joint ventures remained focused on the manufacturing of imported designs (Liu and Tylecote, 2009).

Due to the efforts of the Chinese government at both national and local levels, the output of passenger vehicle production increased tremendously. Above all, a vibrant domestic car component industry developed and strongly simplified the local sourcing of parts and components. Especially the Yangtze River Delta gained from the early VW-SAIC JV and the concerted effort of Volkswagen and the Shanghai government to develop a functioning value chain (Thun, 2006). Yet, the contours of Chinese innovation arguably emerged in the less regulated vehicle segments such as light vans and trucks as well as motorcycles. In these segments, competition soon grew fierce as de facto industry standards developed through an early government-sponsored diffusion of truck technology in the 1970s, the uncontrolled diffusion of licensed technology from the Japanese companies Suzuki and Daihatsu in trucks (and small cars), as well as the drainage of licensed technology from the leading Japanese motorcycle companies Honda, Suzuki, and Yamaha (Ge and Fujimoto, 2004; Noble et al., 2005; Marukawa, 2013). New companies predominately entered those segments by relying on the established supply chains of the incumbent vehicle makers. Apart from the entry of new firms, the large numbers of existing firms were now free to explore new forms of specialization in order to realize some of the economies that they had foregone before. The component manufacturers, moreover, increasingly reacted by broadening their product offerings in order to extend the range of their customers. Initially, the availability of components for competing firms was mainly due to a widespread practice among Chinese firms to run a company with a similar product profile next to their joint ventures with foreign companies. This practice allowed those component firms to exploit the emergent demand from new entrants by offering similar components at customized price-quality ratios (Brandt and Thun, 2010).

The secondary segments of the passenger vehicle sector have entered the spotlight particularly after the country's accession to the WTO in 2001. In fact, when regulation on entry into the passenger car segment was eased, several Chinese companies had already begun with the production of those cars. Now they were granted licenses, although many entrants continued to pursue the strategy of entering into ownership relations with a firm to acquire (or share) the production license. Among the most salient entrants, two companies integrated forward from component manufacturing. One of the firms – Chery Automobile, a company established on local-government initiative in 1997 in the relatively backward Anhui province – moved into car manufacturing after having developed its first engine. The second firm – BYD, a company that had first ventured into rechargeable battery manufacturing to become the largest producer of nickel-cadmium (NiCd) and lithium-ion (Li-ion) batteries – had integrated horizontally into battery electric motors and then integrated forward into passenger car manufacturing. However, still another company, Geely Auto, provides a more common blueprint of the development strategies of new domestic entrants to the passenger car sector. Similar to later entrants such as Lifan Industry, Geely started with motorcycle production and then moved horizontally into four-wheel passenger cars. In doing so, the company used a then-popular Chinese car, the FAW Xiali (itself based on the Daihatsu Charade), as a "reference design" for producing its own car. According to Wang (2008), Geely's first model shared about 70%of the components with the archetype model. Like the mentioned Chery Automobile, Geely was able to purchase most of the components from the original producer's (FAW Tianjin's) fully developed supplier network. But unlike the former company,[4] and in stark contrast to the leading foreign companies (Marukawa, 2014), Geely even (out-) sourced the core component, the engine, from FAW Xiali's supplier, Tianjin Toyota Automotive Engine, a joint venture between Toyota and Tianjin Auto. Only later, when it succeeded in the market, and Toyota sought to limit the technological externalities, Geely integrated backward into core component manufacturing (Wang, 2008).

This strategy appears to be pervasive in the Chinese auto industry after the turn of the century. As Marukawa (2013, 2014) explains, in 2004, more than half of the numerous auto manufacturers fully lacked engine design and manufacturing capabilities and sourced all of their engines from the market. Shenyang Aerospace Mitsubishi Engine (SAME), a Mitsubishi JV, for instance, supplied engines to more than 20 companies. Increasingly, foreign companies have started to see the trend of the industry architecture as a large opportunity for exploiting their design capabilities in ways that are elsewhere still frustrated by the transnational auto companies. For instance, whereas in transactions with foreign firms, Visteon merely supplies modules based on their customers' instructions, it is requested to design the modules for their Chinese customers itself. Component manufacturers such as SAME have also turned to offer (integral) sets of interacting components (for instance, engines and transmissions) (Marukawa, 2014). Other firms such as Delphi have specifically reworked the interfaces of their engine management systems in order to increase the matching capacity of their product with the market-dominating SAME engines (Wang and Kimble, 2010). These decentralized design activities by (often international) component manufacturers are supplemented by the entry of national and international design houses.[5]

The adoption of designs from international competitors, component manufacturers, and design houses is yet merely part of the story. In order to make extensive use of components from the market, complementary changes in product and industry architectures need to occur. As Geely's car manufacture expanded, for instance, the product architecture was designed with the explicit intent of increasing the possibilities for mixing and matching components to be sourced from the market (Wang, 2008). Accordingly, the modularization process in the Chinese passenger car segment does not only consist of (knowledgeable) component manufacturers adapting and extending their products to penetrate the upstream market consisting of predominately unexperienced system integrators. While the technological sophistication of the domestic system integrators is clearly inferior to that of their (international) suppliers (Marukawa, 2014), the domestic integrators still perform an important task in the process by seeking ways (with the help of design houses) to increase the parts and components to choose from. These efforts become especially interesting as companies entering the sector from unexpected pathways are probing some new (re)combinations. The widening of technological possibilities through the increased questioning of the ICE technology and the growing (re)consideration of electric mobility has added to a growing vehicle variety in the Chinese setting, particularly in the mini and microcar segment.

China's electric microcar segment – the smallest automobile class consisting of low-mass, low-speed vehicles – has grown considerably in recent years. Many entrants into that segment share their background in motorcycle production with Geely. Some of them have yet taken a detour to the vibrant electric bike segment that has taken off since the mid-1990s. The Chinese production of e-bikes has virtually exploded, increasing from 40,000 in 1998 to ten million in 2005 and accounting for more than 90% of the global market (Weinert et al., 2007; Tyfield et al., 2014). Having left a mark on the e-bike architectures, the entrants' origin of traditional bikes or motorcycle manufacture is represented in the generic e-bike forms: as bicycle or scooter style e-bikes (Weinert et al., 2007). As Marukawa (2014) has observed, while firms in advanced economies would start by developing the major components, typically in collaboration with selected suppliers, the Chinese e-bike makers have simply experimented with existing bicycle and motorcycle parts and adding existing component (e.g., battery) technology. Moreover, when conventional parts did not perform their function in connection with other functions of the bike (e.g., when brakes would not perform at higher speed), then the component manufacturers would be approached to search for appropriate solutions. Until recently, the evolution of the open-modular architecture of the e-bike has brought a number of changes and upgrades in the components, which have vastly increased the functionality and decreased the price of the overall product (Weinert et al., 2007).

In addition to e-bikes, another Chinese approach to the passenger vehicle sector is via low-speed vehicles. While the e-bike makers target the urban population, and specifically the growing number of commuters of China's expanding cities, the low-speed vehicles have mainly emerged from agriculturally related utility vehicles such as low-speed trucks and three-wheelers. Backed by the local government of Shandong province, home of the domestically leading three-wheeler industry, several firms have experimented with electric propulsion systems since very early in their development. As both two-wheeler and three-wheeler firms have more recently sought to expand into the electric microcar segment, they have done so under the low-speed (electric) vehicle banner. Electric LSVs typically have strongly simplified powertrains (Kimble and Wang, 2013). In their basic version, their product architecture is broadly similar with that of the street-legal golf carts that mainly constitute the LSV segment in the US (e.g., Saporito, 2011). However, despite the restrictions that the firms face from the Chinese government,[6] the level of sectoral variety creation is arguably much higher in China than in other countries. In fact, Chinese LSV producers have not only experimented with golf cart designs but have also probed other kinds of (modular) architectures. This has also brought LSV makers closer to the minicar segment. Exploring the feasibility of creating simplified versions of prevalent minicars, LSV makers have come up with several models that are designed on the SMART or, more often, the vastly popular Chery QQ, itself a derivative of the Daewoo Matiz/Chevrolet Spark. As in other parts of China's vast passenger vehicle ecosystem, industry-wide component sharing drives these developments to a considerable extent. While these developments have prevented a speedy consolidation of the domestic market, it has brought about a high degree of variation – as evidenced by the unprecedented number of brands and models from which customers can choose.

4 Conclusions

A country's innovative capacity and its competitiveness is frequently assessed based on indicators showing how strongly domestic actors contribute to the creation of (measurable) scientific or engineering knowledge, particularly in the most dynamic technological domains. The notion of architectural innovation, as it is understood in the present chapter, seeks to broaden this perspective. It does so by pointing out that fundamentally new knowledge is important but not necessary to induce consequential changes in the segmentation and status ordering of existing sectors. While radical innovations can very well reinforce the position of incumbent industry leaders, innovations that do not significantly alter the sector's knowledge base can have quite disruptive effects. Even when it does not dislodge the incumbent industry leaders, it is often sufficient to help firms establish a viable position within the sector, while it may impose new market segmentations and a new division of labor. Architecture-based innovation strategies are frequently embedded in broader sectoral ecologies. If so, then distinct national patterns of architectural innovation can result from (initial) differences in industry structures. These differences are not only effective in providing domestic firms the means to alter general sectoral trends but also to push trends further than elsewhere or into particular directions.

While innovative activities in the Chinese context have not altered established sectoral paradigms, the domestic setting allows firms to push ongoing sectoral trends toward an exceptional degree of openness – as evidenced by the comparatively high level of design and manufacturing task externalization. China's distinct pattern of architectural innovation has emerged as an effect of the interplay of three factors. First, modularization has taken hold as the dominant cognitive frame in many industrial sectors, including the focal passenger vehicle sector. This ongoing general trend by itself entails an increasing disintegration of relevant tasks and a search for outsourcing opportunities by the leading system integrators. Second, the domestic development of a comprehensive population of supplier firms, including local branches of virtually all major transnational leaders and a wide range of domestic firms, accompanied by very high localization rates and high levels of competition have rendered it easy to shop domestically for all product-related parts and components. Third, the effective feasibility of using existing car models as reference designs has introduced a system of de facto standards that enables industry-wide component sharing. The resulting modular markets are generated and reinforced by the innovative efforts of component producers and newly appearing system integrators alike.

Although it would be far-fetched to argue that the Chinese innovation strategies in the automotive sector will help domestic firms to displace the global industry leaders in the near future, it would be grossly negligent to underestimate their effect on the segmentation of the sector and the position of component suppliers in the sector's dominant division of labor. The ferment of companies with similar mix-and-match architectural strategies bears the potential to reconceptualize the car for a low-income demand that is located at "the bottom of the pyramid" (Prahalad, 2006) and lacks a strong "automobile culture" (Kimble and Wang, 2013; Tyfield et al., 2014). If improvements lead to increases in quality and performance, the cars might even become a choice for consumers in advanced countries, especially in connection with car-sharing offers and other arrangements responding to contemporary changes in consumer behavior. As new system integrators attempt to establish themselves within the sector, they provide opportunities for component makers to extend the range of their design activities and value capture possibilities. While leading automakers try to prevent losing control of their product systems, the Chinese industrial dynamics might counteract these efforts by helping to introduce "Intel inside" strategies. It is exactly these diverse threats and opportunities that characterize China's innovative setting which no relevant firm can afford to miss.

Notes

1 The mirroring hypothesis concerns the following remark made by Henderson and Clark (1990, p. 27): "We have assumed that organizations are boundedly rational and, hence, that their knowledge and information-processing structure come to mirror the internal structure of the product they are designing." See also Sanchez and Mahoney (1996) who focus on organizational development in regard to product modularity. Sanchez and Mahoney (2013) provide an extensive review of the relevant literature.

2 MacDuffie (2013) uses this distinction to describe architectural change in the global automotive industry. See also Sako (2003) with a similar argument on the relationship between organizational architecture and product architecture.

3 Volkswagen's (VW) novel toolkit, for instance, spans several of the VW group member firms' platforms and does not only provide the customer with a range of choices based on

a minimum of component variations but also accommodates a groundbreaking number of different propulsion systems (Altenburg, 2014).

4 According to Marukawa (2014), Chery initially only built one (1596 cc) engine and sourced all other engines from companies such as SAME, Harbin Dongan (both of them Mitsubishi JVs), FAW-Daewoo, and Tritec Motors (a Brazilian BMW-Chrysler JV). Only gradually, it developed more indigenous engines with the help of Austrian engineering company AVL.

5 Harbin Hafei Auto, a car company with a background in military vehicle manufacturing and a daughter of Changan Auto since 2009, appears to have been the first company to outsource the product design, in this case to the Italian design house Pininfarina. Already in the mid-1990s, the Italian company started the cooperation by helping to design a new model of a truck based on the diffused Daihatsu platform. Later, Hafei also outsourced the chassis design to British company Lotus Cars (Xi et al., 2009). Many other companies followed suit.

6 Whereas LSVs (US) and "motorized quadricycles" (EU) are allowed to use designated streets with specific speed limits, Chinese national laws still prohibit LSVs from using public roads. Only Shandong province has made arrangements to bring LSVs on the road (Kimble and Wang, 2013). However, as with e-bikes that featured explosive growth despite efforts to ban them (Fairley, 2005), the sales of LSVs outstrip by far the conventional electric cars that are available in China. According to Wang (2015), over 300,000 LSVs were sold in China in 2014. If the Chinese government's prior history of pragmatic policymaking provides any indication for the future, then the government's opposition to the emergence of the LSV sector will not last long.

References

Abernathy, William J. and James M. Utterback (1978) "Patterns of Industrial Innovation." *Technology Review* 80(7): 41–47.

Alizon, Fabrice, Steven B. Shooter and Timothy W. Simpson (2009) "Henry Ford and the Model T: Lessons for Product Platforming and Mass Customization." *Design Studies* 30: 588–605.

Allen, Matthew M. C. (2013) "Comparative Capitalisms and the Institutional Embeddedness of Innovative Capabilities." *Socio-Economic Review* 11(4): 771–794.

Altenburg, Tilman (2014) "From Combustion Engines to Electric Vehicles: A Study of Technological Path Creation and Disruption in Germany." *GDI Discussion Paper 29/2014*, Bonn: German Development Institute. Available at www.die-gdi.de/uploads/media/DP_29.2014.pdf (accessed: November 13, 2018).

Baldwin, Carliss Y. and Kim B. Clark (1997) "Managing in an Age of Modularity." *Harvard Business Review*, September-October, 84–93.

Bonvillian, William B. (2013) "Advanced Manufacturing Policies and Paradigms for Innovation." *Science* 342: 1173–1175.

Brandt, Loren and Eric Thun (2010) "The Fight for the Middle: Upgrading, Competition, and Industrial Development in China." *World Development* 38(11): 1555–1574.

Breznitz, Dan and Michael Murphree (2011) *Run of the Red Queen: Government, Innovation, Globalization and Economic Growth in China*, New Haven and London, UK: Yale University Press.

Cabigiosu, Anna, Francesco Zirpoli and Arnaldo Camuffo (2013) "Modularity, Interfaces Definition and the Integration of External Sources of Innovation in the Automotive Industry." *Research Policy* 42: 662–675.

Casper, Steven (2010) "The Comparative Institutional Analysis of Innovation: From Industrial Policy to the Knowledge Economy." Glenn Morgan, John L. Campbell, Colin

Crouch, Ove Kaj Pedersen and Richard Whitley (eds.), *The Oxford Handbook of Comparative Institutional Analysis*, Oxford, UK: Oxford University Press, 335–362.

Casper, Steven and David Soskice (2004) "Sectoral Systems of Innovation and Varieties of Capitalism: Explaining the Development of High-Technology Entrepreneurship in Europe." Franco Malerba (ed.), *Sectoral Systems of Innovation: Concepts, Issues and Analyses of Six Major Sectors in Europe*, Cambridge, UK: Cambridge University Press, 348–387.

Casper, Steven and Richard Whitley (2004) "Managing Competences in Entrepreneurial Technology Firms: A Comparative Institutional Analysis of Germany, Sweden and the UK." *Research Policy* 33(1): 89–106.

Christensen, Thomas Budde (2011) "Modularised Eco-Innovation in the Auto Industry." *Journal of Cleaner Production* 19: 212–220.

Conlé, Marcus (2011) "Towards a New C-system of Innovation." Cornelia Storz and Sebastian Schäfer (eds.), *Institutional Diversity and Innovation: Continuing and Emerging Patterns in Japan and China*, London, UK and New York: Routledge, 154–217.

Davies, Joshua (2010) "How Elon Musk Turned Tesla into the Car Company of the Future." *Wired*, September 27. Available at www.wired.com/2010/09/ff_tesla (accessed June 5, 2015).

Dosi, Giovanni (1982) "Technological Paradigms and Technological Trajectories: A Suggested Interpretation of the Determinants and Directions of Technical Change." *Research Policy* 11(3): 147–162.

Ernst, Dieter (2005) "Limits to Modularity: Reflections on Recent Developments in Chip Design." *Industry and Innovation* 12(3): 303–335.

Ernst, Dieter and Barry Naughton (2008) "China's Emerging Industrial Economy: Insights from the IT Industry." Christoper A. McNally (ed.), *China's Emergent Political Economy: Capitalism in the Dragon's Lair*, London, UK and New York: Routledge, 39–59.

Fairley, Peter (2005) "China's Cyclists Take Charge: Electric Bicycles Are Selling by the Millions Despite Efforts to Ban Them." *IEEE Spectrum*, June, 54–59.

Fixson, Sebastian K. and Jin-Kyu Park (2008) "The Power of Integrality: Linkages between Product Architecture, Innovation, and Industry Structure." *Research Policy* 37: 1296–1316.

Fu, Xiaolan (2015) *China's Path to Innovation*, Cambridge, UK: Cambridge University Press.

Fujimoto, Takahiro (2007) "Architecture-Based Comparative Advantage – A Design Information View of Manufacturing." *Evolutionary and Institutional Economics Review* 4(1): 55–112.

Ge, Dongsheng and Takahiro Fujimoto (2004) "Quasi-Open Product Architecture and Technological Lock-in: An Exploratory Study on the Chinese Motorcycle Industry." *Annals of Business Administrative Science* 3(2): 15–24.

Hall, Peter A. and David Soskice (2001) *Varieties of Capitalism: The Institutional Foundations of Comparative Advantage*, Oxford, UK: Oxford University Press.

Hemmert, Martin (1999) "'Intermediate organization' Revisited: A Framework for the Vertical Division of Labor in Manufacturing and the Case of the Japanese Assembly Industries." *Industrial and Corporate Change* 8(3): 487–517.

Henderson, Rebecca M. and Kim B. Clark (1990) "Architectural Innovation: The Reconfiguration of Existing Product Technologies and the Failure of Established Firms." *Administrative Science Quarterly* 35(1): 9–30.

Holz, Carsten A. (2018) "China's Investment Rate: Characteristics and Implications." Working Paper May 13 Version. Available at SSRN: https://ssrn.com/abstract=2696760 or http://dx.doi.org/10.2139/ssrn.2696760 (accessed November 13, 2018).

Kaplinsky, Raphael, Joanna Chataway, Norman Clark, Rebecca Hanlin, Dinar Kale, Lois Muraguri, Theo Papaioannou, P. Robbins and Watu Wamae (2009) "Below the Radar:

What Does Innovation in Emerging Economies Have to Offer other Low-Income Economies?" *International Journal of Technology Management and Sustainable Development* 8(3): 177–197.

Kimble, Chris and Hua Wang (2013) "China's New Energy Vehicles: Value and Innovation." *Journal of Business Strategy* 34(2): 13–20.

Klepper, Steven (2002) "The Capabilities of New Firms and the Evolution of the US Automobile Industry." *Industrial and Corporate Change* 11(4): 645–666.

Kroll, Henning, Marcus Conlé and Margot Schüller (2008) "China: Innovation System and Innovation Policy." Fraunhofer ISI, GIGA and Georgia Tech STEP (eds.), *New Challenges for Germany in the Innovation Competition*, Karlsruhe: Final Report, 169–242.

Langlois, Richard N. (2003) "The Vanishing Hand: The Changing Dynamics of Industrial Capitalism." *Industrial and Corporate Change* 12(2): 351–385.

Langlois, Richard N. and Paul L. Robertson (1989) "Explaining Vertical Integration: Lessons from the American Automobile Industry." *Journal of Economic History* 49(2): 361–375.

Langlois, Richard N. and Paul L. Robertson (1995) *Firms, Markets and Economic Change*, London, UK: Routledge.

Lee, Keun and Chaisung Lim (2001) "Technological Regimes, Catching-up and Leapfrogging: Findings from the Korean Industries." *Research Policy* 30(3): 459–483.

Liu, Jiajia and Andrew Tylecote (2009) "Corporate Governance and Technological Capability Development: Three Case Studies in the Chinese Auto Industry." *Industry and Innovation* 16(4–5): 525–544.

Lundvall, Bengt-Ake (1998) "Why Study National Systems and National Styles of Innovation?" *Technology Analysis & Strategic Management* 10(4): 403–422.

Lüthje, Boy, Siqi Luo and Hao Zhang (2013) *Beyond the Iron Rice Bowl: Regimes of Production and Industrial Relations in China*, Frankfurt, Germany: Campus.

Lyons, Thomas P. (1987) "Spatial Aspects of Development in China: The Motor Vehicle Industry, 1956–1985." *International Regional Science Review* 11(1): 75–96.

MacDuffie, John Paul (2013) "Modularity-as-Property, Modularization-as-Process, and 'modularity'-as-Frame: Lessons from Product Architecture Initiatives in the Global Automotive Industry." *Global Strategy Journal* 3(1): 8–40.

MacDuffie, John Paul and Takahiro Fujimoto (2010) "Why Dinosaurs Will Keep Ruling the Auto Industry: Get Ready for the Complexity Revolution." *Harvard Business Review*, June, 23–25.

Marukawa, Tomoo (1995) "Industrial Groups and Division of Labor in China's Automobile Industry." *The Developing Economies* 33(3): 330–355.

Marukawa, Tomoo (2013) "Why Are There So Many Automobile Manufacturers in China?" *China: An International Journal* 11(2): 170–185.

Marukawa, Tomoo (2014) "The 'make of buy' Decision and Supply-Chain Governance." Mariko Watanabe (ed.), *The Disintegration of Production: Firm Strategy and Industrial Development in China*, Cheltenham, UK: Edward Elgar, 51–73.

Mowery, David C. and Nathan Rosenberg (1998) *Paths of Innovation: Technological Change in 20th-Century America*, Cambridge, UK: Cambridge University Press.

Nahm, Jonas and Edward S. Steinfeld (2014) "Scale-up Nation: China's Specialization in Innovative Manufacturing." *World Development* 54: 288–300.

Nam, Kyung-Min (2011) "Learning through the International Joint Venture: Lessons from the Experience of China's Automotive Sector." *Industrial and Corporate Change* 20(3): 855–907.

Naughton, Barry (2017) "Is China Socialist?." *Journal of Economic Perspectives* 31(1): 3–24.

Nobeoka, Kentaro (2005) "Competitiveness of Japanese Companies in Products with Modular Architecture: Limitation of Chinese Digital Appliance Manufacturers with Capabilities to Assemble." *Keizai Sangyo Journal*. Available at www.rieti.go.jp/en/papers/research-review/028.html (accessed May 29, 2015).

Noble, Gregory W., John Ravenhill and Richard F. Doner (2005) "Executioner or Disciplinarian: WTO Accession and the Chinese Auto Industry." *Business and Politics* 7(2), Article 1.

Perez, Carlota and Luc Soete (1988) "Catching up in Technology: Entry Barriers and Windows of Opportunity." Giovanni Dosi, Christopher Freeman, Richard Nelson, Gerald Silverberg and Luc Soete (eds.), *Technical Change and Economic Theory*, London: Pinter, 458–479.

Porter, Michael E. (1990) "The Competitive Advantage of Nations." *Harvard Business Review*, March-April, 73–93.

Prahalad, C. K. (2006) *The Fortune at the Bottom of the Pyramid: Eradicating Poverty through Profits*, Upper Saddle River, NJ: Wharton School Publishing.

Sako, Mari (2003) "Modularity and Outsourcing: The Nature of Co-evolution of Product Architecture and Organization Architecture in the Global Automotive Industry." Andrea Prencipe, Andrew Davies and Michael Hobday (eds.), *The Business of Systems Integration*, Oxford, UK: Oxford University Press, 229–253.

Sako, Mari and Fiona Murray (2000) "Modules in Design, Production and Use: Implications for the Global Automotive Industry." Paper prepared for the International Motor Vehicle Program (IMVP) Annual Sponsors Meeting, October 5–7, 1999, Cambridge MA. Available at http://citeseerx.ist.psu.edu/viewdoc/summary?doi=10.1.1.125.3249 (accessed November 13, 2018).

Sanchez, Ron and Robert P. Collins (2001) "Competing – and Learning – in Modular Markets." *Long Range Planning* 34: 645–667.

Sanchez, Ron and Joseph T. Mahoney (1996) "Modularity, Flexibility, and Knowledge Management in Product and Organization Design." *Strategic Management Journal* 17(S2): 63–76.

Sanchez, Ron and Joseph T. Mahoney (2013) "Modularity and Economic Organization: Concepts, theory, Observations, and Predictions." Anna Grandori (ed.), *Handbook of Economic Organization: Integrating Economic and Organization Theory*, Cheltenham, UK: Edward Elgar, 383–399.

Sanderson, Susan and Mustafa Uzumeri (1995) "Managing Product Families: The Case of the Sony Walkman." *Research Policy* 24(5): 761–782.

Saporito, Bill (2011) "Slow Riders: Souped-up Golf Carts Hit the Streets." *Time* 187(7): 52.

Soskice, David (1997) "German Technology Policy, Innovation, and National Institutional Frameworks." *Industry and Innovation* 4(1): 75–96.

Sturgeon, Timothy J. (2002) "Modular Production Networks: A New American Model of Industrial Organization." *Industrial and Corporate Change* 11(3): 451–496.

Sturgeon, Timothy J., Olga Memedovic, Johannes van Biesebroeck and Gary Gereffi (2009) "Globalisation of the Automotive Industry: Main Features and Trends, International Journal of Technological Learning." *Innovation and Development* 2(1–2): 7–24.

Takeishi, Akira and Takahiro Fujimoto (2001) "Modularisation in the Auto Industry: Interlinked Multiple Hierarchies of Product, Production and Supplier Systems." *International Journal of Automotive Technology and Management* 1(4): 379–396.

Thun, Eric (2006) *Changing lanes in China: Foreign Direct Investment, Local Governments, and Auto Sector Development*, Cambridge: Cambridge University Press.

Tushman, Michael L. and Philip Anderson (1986) "Technological Discontinuities and Organizational Environments." *Administrative Science Quarterly* 31(3): 439–465.

Tyfield, David, Dennis Zuev, Ping Li and John Urry (2014) "Low Carbon Innovation in Chinese Urban Mobility: Prospects, Politics and Practices." STEPS Working Paper 71,

Brighton: STEPS Centre. Available at http://eprints.lancs.ac.uk/73503/ (accessed November 13, 2018).

Ulrich, Karl (1995) "The Role of Product Architecture in the Manufacturing Firm." *Research Policy* 24: 419–440.

Wakabayashi, Daisuke and Mike Ramsey (2015) "Apple Gears up to Challenge Tesla in Electric Cars." *Wall Street Journal*, February 13. Available at www.wsj.com/articles/apples-titan-car-project-to-challenge-tesla-1423868072 (accessed June 5, 2015).

Wang, Hua (2008) "Innovation in Product Architecture – A Study of the Chinese Automobile Industry." *Asia Pacific Journal of Management* 25: 509–535.

Wang, Hua and Chris Kimble (2010) "Low-Cost Strategy through Product Architecture: Lessons from China." *Journal of Business Strategy* 31(3): 12–20.

Wang, Joey (2015) "Sales of Low-Speed Electric Vehicles Are Booming in China." *CarNewsChina.com*. Available at www.carnewschina.com/2015/03/05/sales-of-low-speed-electric-vehicles-are-booming-in-china (accessed June 18, 2015).

Watanabe, Mariko (2014) *The Disintegration of Production: Firm Strategy and Industrial Development in China*, Cheltenham, UK: Edward Elgar.

Weinert, Jonathan, Chaktan Ma and Christopher Cherry (2007) "The Transition to Electric Bikes in China: History and Key Reasons for Rapid Growth." *Transportation* 34: 301–318.

Xi, Liang, Lin Lei and Guisheng Wu (2009) "Evolution of the Chinese Automobile Industry from a Sectoral System of Innovation Perspective." *Industry and Innovation* 16(4–5): 463–478.

Zhou, Yu, William Lazonick and Yifei Sun (eds.) (2016) *China as an Innovation Nation*, Oxford, UK: Oxford University Press.

Zirpoli, Francesco and Arnaldo Camuffo (2009) "Persistent Integrality: Product Architecture and Inter-Firm Coordination in the Auto Industry." Paper presented at the International Motor Vehicle Program (IMVP) Automotive Research Conference, June 8–9, Rochester MI. Available at https://iris.unive.it/retrieve/handle/10278/23813/22226/Zirpoli_Camuffo_IMVP_ARC_2009_ugov.pdf (accessed November 13, 2018).

7 Moral capital and organizational legitimacy

Evidence from the private sector in China

Jun Li

Introduction

China is at the crossroads of change. After four decades of economic reform and opening to the outside world, China's per capita income on purchasing power parity hit $16,760 in 2017[1] and China has overtaken Japan to become the world's second largest economy. Yet, the growth model is now widely seen as too energy-hungry, too skewed to an export-driven growth model, and too dependent on massive state spending (Li and Wang, 2014). Serious concerns have grown about the sustainability of this growth model, particularly in an era when globalization is giving way to protectionism in the United States and many other countries. The consensus in China is that the country needs to raise its game in innovation (Ding and Li, 2015). Firms that gain the most from innovation are those that adopt strategies that give them legitimacy in the eyes of stakeholders (Rao et al., 2008). Compared with their counterparts in market economies, private enterprises in China have to fight harder for legitimacy in the light of the legacy of the planned economic regime.

Every business faces a social judgment of its acceptance, appropriateness, and desirability in the marketplace. Those that elicit a positive social judgment can claim to have established an organizational legitimacy (Zimmerman and Zeitz, 2002). Legitimacy is crucial since it enables organizations to access other resources needed to innovate, survive, and grow. Legitimacy also provides a means to overcome the "liability of newness" that is the cause of failure for so many new businesses (Stinchcombe, 1965).

In a transition economy like China, legitimacy building is even more critically important for private enterprises. Despite continued improvements in institutional environments in which private enterprises operate, private enterprises remain constrained by various institutional difficulties and constantly face challenges posted by prejudice against them (Chen et al., 2006; Gibb and Li, 2003; Peng, 2004; Atherton, 2008; Wu et al., 2018). Unlike their state-owned counterparts, private enterprises are continually subjected to ideological discrimination and have endured an unfavorable economic environment. In the state's decisions on resource distribution, political considerations can easily outweigh economic ones (Atherton, 2008; Li and Matlay, 2006; Walder, 1991). Politically legitimate state-owned enterprises (SOEs) under the oversight of central or local governments often enjoyed preferential treatment, while private enterprises, being less legitimate, have been discriminated against in terms of obtaining access to government-controlled resources (Li and Li, 2014; Wu et al., 2018; Zhang et al., 2008; Zhou, 2009). Even in recent years, government policies have drifted from time to time to favor the state sector, resulting in wide concerns that SOEs crowded out private enterprises (Huang et al., 2017). Access to key resources (e.g., external finance) is especially critical to the emergence and growth of Chinese private enterprises (Bhaumik and Estrin, 2007; Cull and Xu, 2005; Li, 2002). Hence, private enterprises have been found to display an inherent drive to build legitimacy (Tsang, 1996). A private enterprise's ability to build legitimacy in a relatively "hostile" environment has become the core of entrepreneurial success in China (Ahlstrom and Bruton, 2001; Atherton and Newman, 2017; Tsang, 1996).

Tsang (1996) finds private enterprises used four main strategic responses to build legitimacy. These included (1) concealment as the cover-up of private identity, (2) co-option as the move to co-opt local authorities in order to neutralize institutional opposition and enhance legitimacy, (3) influence as engagement in charitable activities and lobbying, and (4) escapism as focus on short-term profits for consumption at the expense of long-term growth or deliberate limitation of business growth and expansion. Since the enactment of the SME Promotion Law in 2002, the importance of the private sector has been explicitly recognized and use of concealment as a legitimacy-building strategy has become irrelevant. Nonetheless, both strategies of co-option and influence remain as relevant as ever.

Up to now, the co-option strategic response has received a lot of attention and more studies in the literature have been attributed to investigation into the impact of political capital on private enterprises in terms of business performance (Li and Zhang, 2007; Sheng et al., 2011; Yan and Chang, 2018), bank financing (Zhao and Lu, 2016; Zhou, 2009), new venture performance (Li and Zhang, 2007), and preferential treatment (Chen and Touve, 2011). A consensus from the evidence of this literature suggests positive impacts of political capital resulting from either *political networking* measured as entrepreneurs' ties with government officials or *political participation* measured as entrepreneurs' membership in the communist party or legislative bodies.

However, political participation is not an open route to every private enterprise, and political networking is not without its downside. The rise and fall of business tycoon Huang Guanyu, founder of Gome Electrical Appliances Holding, clearly shows that the political capital he once carefully cultivated opened so many doors for him to build his business empire and made him the richest man of the country. Ironically, the same political capital also crushed him to pieces when political ties turned sour. This story illustrates that adoption of a co-option strategy through the development of political connections has its inherent risks, as ties with government officials can be volatile and more transaction-oriented (Wedeman, 2013). As highlighted in Tsang (1996) and Ahlstrom and Bruton's (2001) research, a strategic response of influence, for which charitable giving is a key tool, can be equally effective for private enterprises in China to cope with institutional uncertainty and to pursue legitimacy. Use of charitable giving can help private enterprises build moral capital and subsequently moral legitimacy (Ahlstrom and Bruton, 2001). Yet, the role of moral capital in legitimacy building by private enterprises is overwhelmingly under-researched.

Zimmerman and Zeitz (2002) argue that legitimacy is a resource important for acquiring other resources. From a moral legitimacy theoretical perspective, this chapter builds on extant research to argue that private enterprises with more moral capital can tap into their moral legitimacy to improve access to resources and that moral capital may complement political capital to legitimize private enterprises. To test these arguments, I used private enterprises' charitable giving as a proxy for moral capital and access to bank loans by private enterprises as a proxy for organizational legitimacy. Logistic regressions were carried out to analyze a dataset from the 2012 National Survey of Chinese Private Enterprises. I find evidence to support the argument that moral capital has a positive effect on organizational legitimacy. Contrary to expectation, I also find tentative evidence suggesting that moral capital can be a substitute for political capital in building organizational legitimacy.

This chapter is structured as follows. In the next section, the theory of organizational legitimacy is used to derive hypotheses. This is followed by a description of the dataset and research methodology. Results are then presented and the hypotheses are tested. The final section discusses the results and concludes.

Entrepreneurs' moral capital and organizational legitimacy

Legitimacy is of importance to entrepreneurial firms (Becker-Blease and Sohl, 2015; Delmar and Shane, 2004). Organizational legitimacy is referred to as acceptance, appropriateness, and desirability of an action taken by an organization (Zimmerman and Zeitz, 2002). In order for entrepreneurial firms to succeed, they must be perceived as legitimate to those institutions and individuals with which they hope to engage in exchanges (Tornikoski and Newbert, 2007). They may attain legitimacy by conforming themselves to the passive characteristics deemed by the environment as typical of a legitimate organization ("conforming legitimacy"); they may also manipulate and deploy evocative symbols to actively garner legitimacy ("strategic legitimacy") (Zimmerman and Zeitz, 2002). So often, organizations obtain legitimacy through some combination of both approaches (Tornikoski and Newbert, 2007).

The legitimating processes have a strong cultural dimension (Deephouse and Suchman, 2008). Social legitimacy reflects a generalized perception that the actions of the organization are desirable, proper, or appropriate (Suchman, 1995). The social judgment of organizations is pervasive since they are embedded in normative systems and surrounded by implicit rules of what is perceived as appropriate behavior in society (Scott, 2008). The interplay between evaluations of values and actions results in moral legitimacy if actions are deemed to be morally "good" in society (Kibler and Kautonen, 2016; Überbacher, 2014). Thus, organizations engaging in the moral legitimation process attain moral capital and subsequently organizational legitimacy. Moral capital is defined as "the resources that sustain a moral community" (Haidt, 2012, p. 292).

Analyzing the history of entrepreneurship in the US, Acs (2013, 2015) demonstrates that philanthropy, as the art of putting wealth to work for the common good, was an important means for capitalist ventures to create moral capital. Philanthropy was shown to provide a mechanism for dismantling accumulated wealth that was made in the past and reinvesting it in ways that would strengthen future equality of opportunity (Acs, 2015). As such, philanthropy conferred moral capital on entrepreneurs that in turn legitimized their entrepreneurial undertakings. When moral capital is absent, societies will see persistent concentration of wealth, flourishing of rent-seeking, and suffering of innovation and entrepreneurship and democracy (Baumol et al., 2007).

Due to the importance of moral capital and moral legitimacy, organizations are using charitable giving in a more strategic manner, as those donations are helpful to enhance firm image and further improve firm performance (Brammer et al., 2006). Saiia et al. (2003, p. 170) define strategic philanthropy as the practice of "giving of corporate resources to address non-business community issues that also benefit the firm's strategic position and, ultimately, its bottom line."

The organizational legitimacy of private enterprises in China has been at the center of controversy for years. It is widely noted that the private sector in China was often treated as ideologically inferior to the state-owned sector, thereby lacking full organizational legitimacy (Peng, 2004). Lack of organizational legitimacy partly explains why private enterprises have difficulty in getting a variety of critical resources, most of which are still controlled by the state (Wu et al., 2018; Zhou, 2009).

In order to mitigate the consequences of a lack of organizational legitimacy, private enterprises have employed a number of legitimacy-building strategies as mentioned previously. One well-grounded argument is that Chinese entrepreneurs actively participated in politics in order to overcome the legal and regulatory constraints (Ahlstrom and Bruton, 2001; Tsang, 1996; Zhou, 2009). A less understood fact concerns corporate philanthropy as a legitimacy-building strategy. Godfrey (2005) argues that corporate philanthropy can generate positive moral capital among communities and stakeholders, resulting from building a reservoir of goodwill, more stable relations with the government and the community, and a good reputation. Such a legitimacy-building strategy via corporate philanthropy is to use active behavior to attain moral capital and eventually strategic legitimacy.

With reference to the Chinese context, Ahlstrom and Bruton (2001) identify charitable giving as one of the nine legitimacy-building strategies adopted by Chinese private enterprises. Outcomes of strategic philanthropy may reflect on the company's relations with the community and the government. For the former, corporate giving develops a positive corporate image and improves community relations in eliciting an organization's implicit and explicit acceptability (Ahlstrom and Bruton, 2001). For the latter, since governments typically encourage donations by private enterprises for public goods, companies' engagement in philanthropic activities align themselves well with the cause of governments, leading to a congruence between an organization and its wider political environment. In Jamali and Mirshak's (2006) research, the principles that were most frequently mentioned by the interviewed executives as motivating the responsible behavior of the firm were the principle of legitimacy. Philanthropic activities of private enterprises in China include disaster relief giving, poverty relief giving, environmental protection giving, and other charitable giving (Gao, 2011; Yin and Zhang, 2012).

Drawing from the psychology and social psychology literature, Coombs et al. (2008) propose generativity, immortality striving, and legacy creation as the antecedents of entrepreneurs' philanthropy. With regard to the distinct features of institutional environment in a transition economy, Ma and Parish (2006) argue that Chinese private entrepreneurs' charitable contributions are motivated to elicit social and political benefits. Consistent with the literature concerning the institutional environment in China, they maintain that uncertainty over privileges and government regulations caused private entrepreneurs to remain anxious about access to the government bureaucracy. Private contributions funneled through government agencies helped allay some of this anxiety.

Building moral capital is clearly a manipulation strategy, similar to building political capital, to serve the purpose of pursuit of legitimacy, as suggested by Godfrey (2005). However, there are differences between these two legitimation strategies. With regard to the mechanism for capital building, the development of political capital on the part of private entrepreneurs has a very narrow focus on developing relationships with the political machine through either political networking or political participation.

Political networking – i.e., entrepreneurs' ties with government officials – represents a unique type of social capital in China's transition economy (Li and Atuahene-Gima, 2001). Because the government still controls significant portions of strategic factor resources and has considerable power to approve projects and allocate resources, entrepreneurs deem to benefit from a disproportionately greater contact with government officials they can cultivate through political networking. Extant research has identified a number of reasons that explains why political capital can benefit the private sector from coping with the challenges facing them. For example, the emergence of the private sector has been at odds with the ruling party's ideology for a long time, and hence there were regulatory restrictions on the development of private enterprises primarily as a result of the question of its political legitimacy (Zhou, 2009). It was also noted that there is an absence of a level playing field between private enterprises and state-owned enterprises (Tsai, 2002; Xin and Pearce, 1996; Zhou, 2009). The state still arbitrarily keeps the private sector at a subordinate status. Another problem is the weak protection of private property rights (Zhou, 2009).

Empirical evidence confirms that managers' networking with local officials leads to better performance of new ventures in China (Li and Zhang, 2007). Peng and Luo (2000) show that managerial ties with government officials are positively related to firm performance in China. In their examination of high-technology industries in China, Li and Atuahene-Gima (2002) find that new ventures with extensive networking with government officials can rely on such networking to obtain information and funding, which can contribute to their performance.

Evidence in the literature seems to suggest that Chinese entrepreneurs' political capital investment behavior can be seen as a rational strategy to manage their external dependencies on government-controlled agencies, as the majority of formal financial institutions still are under the legal and regulatory constraints (Zhou, 2009). The political capital gained from Communist Party membership or legislative membership may benefit the entrepreneur not only politically, such as elevating his or her political status, but also economically, because it helps break the legal and regulatory constraints, thus mobilizing critical resources such as bank financing through enhancing the organizational legitimacy and the institutionalized social networks of the private firm and entrepreneur.

Greater stock of political capital can bring political legitimacy, thus helping solve the resource acquisition problem. A Communist Party membership or legislative membership signals the recognition of the entrepreneur's contribution to the economy and socio-political order by the state. Therefore, entrepreneurs with Communist Party membership or legislative membership have generally been treated differently from other entrepreneurs when the state allocates resources, and, thus, they may obtain government-mandated loans from the local branches of state-owned banks.

Bai et al. (2006), Chen et al. (2012), and Li et al. (2008) find that in China, access to bank loans was significantly easier for entrepreneurs that belong to the People's Congress (PC), yet membership of the People's Political Consultative Conference (PPCC) and the Chinese Communist Party (CCP) had a limited effect on access to bank loans. However, in contrast to previous studies, recent work by Chen and Touve (2011) find a positive relationship between membership of the Communist Party and access to loans from state-owned banks. Overall, this body of evidence indeed suggests that various forms of political participation may help SMEs to obtain assistance from financial institutions under government direction.

In addition to political legitimacy, the underdevelopment of institutions in China manifests additional need for moral legitimacy on the part of entrepreneurs in working through an uncertain and risky environment that lowers trust among people (Luo, 2003). Private enterprises are frequently locally owned, and this embeddedness in local communities provides incentives for generous giving to local causes, thus generating moral capital that can be complementary to political capital. Niehm et al. (2008) suggest that socially responsible actions by a community-based firm will be reciprocated over time by support from loyal customers, employees, suppliers, and other stakeholders. Reciprocal economic exchange is influenced by prevailing social norms, values, and expectations of stakeholders. Ye and Zhang's (2011) research shows that state-controlled banks assign a larger weight to corporate social responsibility information when they make loan decisions because they are more concerned about the strategic goals of the government, such as job creation, poverty alleviation, and environmental protection. Private enterprises' charitable giving manifests itself at the community level through the development of trust, commitment, reciprocity, and a sense of shared vision. Thus, the impact of moral capital is much more sustainable, since it resides on firms' relationships primarily with local communities and, to a lesser extent, with the political machine. Taken together with the previously mentioned arguments, I posit three hypotheses in this research:

- H1: In China, the development of political capital is an important strategy that enhances the legitimacy of private enterprises.
- H2: In China, the development of moral capital is an important strategy that enhances the legitimacy of private enterprises.
- H3: In China, moral capital in complementarity with political participation is an important strategy that enhances the legitimacy of private enterprises.

Data and methods

Sample and data collection

The data for this study came from the 2012 National Survey of Chinese Private Enterprises, which was designed and administered by a joint research team from the Department of United Front of the Central Committee of Chinese Communist Party (CCP), All China Federation of Industry and Commerce (ACFIC), Chinese Society of Research on Private Economy (CSRPE), and Chinese Academy of Social Sciences (CASS). The 2012 survey was the tenth in the biennial surveys which started in 1993, and like its precedents, it included only private enterprises that had at least eight employees and was owned by private entrepreneurs. The private enterprise was so defined in compliance with the official definition specified by the central government in the Tentative Stipulations on Private Enterprises promulgated in 1988. In the Chinese context, entrepreneurial activity in the private sector is categorized into two groups: (1) individual household (*Getihu*), a business employing less than eight people; and (2) private enterprise (*Siyin qiye*), a business employing more than eight persons (Tsang, 1996). Therefore, private enterprises represent the more important segment of the private sector in terms of size, resources, capabilities, and impacts.

The surveys in different years shared a large proportion of questions that constitute the core of the questionnaire but added additional questions in each specific survey to reflect changes in both political-economic circumstances of China and specific objectives of the survey. Using stratified random sampling method, the survey in 2012 selected a national representative sample of 5,073 private enterprises, and a total of 31 questions were asked face-to-face with both the entrepreneurs and accountants of the firms to collect information about the entrepreneurs and their firms in 2011. The surveys generate detailed information on private entrepreneurs and private enterprises, e.g., socio-demographic characteristics, pre-startup career history of the entrepreneurs, economic and financial statuses of their enterprises, employment, organization forms and governance, relationships between private enterprise and governments at all levels, and their future expectation (see Chen et al., 2006; Zhou, 2009 for a more detailed description of this data source). The data collection administered by three formal and authoritative organizations in China is widely considered to be representative, internally consistent, and valid for empirical entrepreneurship research (Zhao and Lu, 2016). The dataset from a succession of surveys has been used to examine various aspects of the private enterprise sector in China (e.g., Degryse et al., 2016; Li et al., 2008; Marquis and Qiao, 2018; Zhao and Lu, 2016; Zhou, 2009).

Measures

Dependent variables

Organizational legitimacy. In this research, I used two objective measures that indicate private enterprises' successful access to bank loans as proxies for organizational legitimacy. The justification of such measures is twofold. First, China's entry into the World Trade Organization (WTO) in 2001 triggered dramatic reshaping of the banking sector. The banking reform measures since 2003 have included financial capital injections, shareholding restructures, the introduction of foreign strategic investors, the listing of banks' share capital on foreign and Chinese exchanges, and the establishment of a system for the boards of directors (Dong et al., 2014). Comparatively, these reforms have improved the governance quality, changed banking behaviors, and injected competition into the financial sector. Commercial banks gradually have incentives to improve process efficiency and financial performance. Wang et al.'s (2014) research on the efficiency of operational processes of the banking system (i.e., deposit producing and profit-earning subprocesses) provides evidence to confirm this. They find that the Chinese banking reform improved its overall efficiency over the 2003–2011 period. There is also evidence to suggest that good performing firms have better access to bank finance (Ayyagari et al., 2010; Cheng and Degryse, 2010). Second, owing to local governments' ideological imprint that persistently affects decision making, state-owned banks are more likely to lend to large and established state-owned enterprises. Nonetheless, banks may legitimize their decision to lend to private enterprises with moral capital because moral capital is compatible with their ideological imprint. Therefore, reliance on bank loans as the primary source of financing for either short-term working capital or long-term business development suggests that the firm has fewer bank financing obstacles, thereby greater organizational legitimacy. For private enterprises in China, access to financial resources has been critical to their survival and growth. Evidence from extant research (for example, Li, 2002; Zhou, 2009) has shown that bank financing is the second most important source of capital for private enterprises, next only to internal sources, namely founders' own capital and retained earnings. To a great extent, access to bank loans by private enterprises is the manifestation of organizational legitimacy. For the two proxies, working capital primarily relying on bank loans is a binary variable, which is coded 1 if the firm relied on bank loans as its most important source of working capital, and 0 otherwise. Likewise, business development capital primarily relying on bank loans is a binary variable, which is coded 1 if the firm relied on bank loans as the most important source of business development, and 0 otherwise.

Independent variables

POLITICAL CAPITAL

Consistent with prior studies on the political capital of Chinese firms (e.g., Li et al., 2008; Zhao and Lu, 2016; Zhou, 2009), I used two proxies to measure political capital, that is, founders' membership in the Communist Party (CP), and founders' membership in People's Congress (PC) and/or in the People's Political Consultative Conference (PPCC). I followed Zhao and Lu's (2016) two steps of constructing an executive-position weighted ordinal measure of political capital. First, I created an administrative-level based membership score for members of CP and PC/PPCC (for CP members, scales: 4 = provincial, 3 = municipal; 2 = county, and 1 = township or city district; PC members, scales: 5 = national, 4 = provincial, 3 = municipal; 2 = county, and 1 = township, and for PPCC members, scales: 5 = national, 4 = provincial, 3 = municipal; 2 = county). Second, I constructed an executive-position–based score to capture the important political positions some founders take up in these organizations such as chairman, vice chairman or standing member. I assigned a score of 3 to a chairman position, 2 to a vice chairman, and 1 to a standing member. Then, I added both scores to obtain two final measures of political capital. "Political capital 1" is a measure of the entrepreneur's political connection with the Communist Party. "Political capital 2" is a measure of the entrepreneur's political connection with other political parties.

MORAL CAPITAL

Consistent with Acs (2015), I argue that private enterprises, when undertaking philanthropic activities, enhance social betterment and in the process attain moral capital that sustains moral community. Also, as noted by both Griffin and Mahon (1997) and Hempel and Gard (2004), size-adjusted corporate giving can be interpreted as a measure of firm generosity. Accordingly, I used the total contributions as a percentage of net profit as a proxy for moral capital. I computed the measure as the amount of giving by the company divided by the firm's net profit as reported in the same period.

Control variables

Following prior private enterprise studies, I included a set of variables concerning the characteristics of both the entrepreneur and the private enterprise to control for alternative explanations. First, I controlled for the founder's gender. It is a binary variable coded 1 if the founder was male and 0 otherwise. I also controlled for the founder's human capital. I used the highest qualification of education a founder had before starting his or her current business to measure his or her human capital. The six categories of qualification are "primary school," "secondary school," "high school," "diploma," "undergraduate," and "postgraduate." In addition, I controlled for firm age and firm size. Firm age was measured as the number of years the firm has been established. Firm size was measured by the natural logarithm of the number of people the firm employed. I also controlled for firm performance. Following prior research (Li and Zhang, 2007), firm performance was measured as net profit as a percentage of sales.

Additionally, I controlled for the effect of sector and region. Region of the firm, that is, whether it was located in the eastern, central, or western region, was controlled to capture possible institutional differences among these three regions. Two dummy variables were created with the eastern region as the reference category. Furthermore, 18 dummy variables were created with the agricultural sector as the reference category.

Results

Table 7.1 presents correlations of all variables along with the mean and standard deviations. I performed two checks on the correlational properties of the

Table 7.1 Correlation matric

	Mean	*SD*	*N*	*1*	*2*	*3*	*4*	*5*	*6*	*7*	*8*	*9*	*10*
1 Working capital as % of bank loans	0.32	0.47	5073	1.00									
2 Business development capital as % of bank loans	0.24	0.43	5073	0.45***	1.00								
3 Gender	1.16	0.37	5073	−0.08***	−0.06***	1.00							
4 Education	3.95	1.11	5073	0.01	0.05***	0.01	1.00						
5 Firm age	9.07	5.18	5073	0.13***	0.12***	−0.09***	0.07***	1.00					
6 Firm size	218.6	1122.24	5073	0.05***	0.06***	−0.02	0.08***	0.12***	1.00				
7 Profitability	−159.06	20081.16	5073	0.01	0.01	0.01	0.01	0.01	0.002	1.00			
8 Political capital 1	0.33	0.47	5073	0.1***	0.08***	−0.11***	0.13***	0.15***	0.05***	0.01	1.00		
9 Political capital 2	1.07	1.43	5073	0.18***	0.2***	−0.11***	0.17***	0.29***	0.16***	0.01	0.13***	1.00	
10 Moral capital	0.482	0.5	5073	0.12***	0.13***	−0.06***	0.03*	0.17***	0.02	0.01	0.09***	0.23***	1.00

*** significant (2-tailed) at $p < 0.001$; ** significant (2-tailed) at $p < 0.01$; * significant (2-tailed) at $p < 0.05$

data before testing the hypotheses. First, I reviewed the correlations among the independent variables in Table 7.1. The highest correlation coefficient was 0.29. Second, I examined the variance inflation factors (VIFs) of each independent variable. The largest VIF in regressions was 1.2, which is much lower than the threshold value of 10, indicating no serious multicollinearity problem (Neter et al., 1990).

Because the survey collected the information for the dependent and independent variables from the same respondent, a common method bias may occur. I used Harman's one-factor test to check for the presence of common method variance (Podsakoff and Organ, 1986). I subjected all the key measures to a factor analysis and then determined the number of factors accounting for the variance in the measures. A factor analysis of the nine items resulted in a solution which accounted for 76.41% of the total variance; the first factor accounted for 19.14% of the variance. The results of the tests indicate that no single factor accounted for a majority of the variance and thus common method bias is unlikely to be a concern for the data (Li and Zhang, 2007).

To test the hypotheses, I conducted fixed effects logistic regression analyses. The results of the analyses are presented in Table 7.2 and Table 7.3. As shown in both tables, Model 1 includes only the control variables. Model 2 adds political capital. In Model 3 moral capital is added. In Model 4, the interactive terms of political capital and moral capital are added.

H1 posits that in China the development of political capital is an important strategy that enhances the legitimacy of private enterprises. The regression results in Table 7.3 show that political capital measured as either CP membership or PC/PPCC memberships has a significant and positive relationship with firms whose working capital was primarily reliant on bank loans (significant at $p < 0.1$ and at $p < 0.001$), confirming the importance of political capital in legitimizing private enterprises. Results in Table 7.4 show that political capital measured as PC/PPCC memberships has a significant and positive relationship with firms whose working capital was primarily reliant on bank loans (significant at $p < 0.001$). However, the relationship between political capital measured as CP membership and organizational legitimacy is not significant. Taken together, the evidence lends support to H1.

Moral capital is the primary variable of interest. H2 posits that in China the development of moral capital is an important strategy that enhances the legitimacy of private enterprises. Results in Tables 7.2 and 7.3 consistently show that moral capital has a significant and positive relationship with firms whose working capital and development capital were primarily reliant on bank loans (significant at $p < 0.001$), confirming that moral capital plays an important role in legitimizing private enterprises. Hence, H2 is supported.

H3 proposes that in China moral capital in complementarity with political capital is an important strategy that enhances the legitimacy of private enterprises. Results in Tables 7.3 and 7.4 show that there is no statistically significant evidence with regard to the complementary effect between moral capital and political capital measured as PC/PPCC memberships on the organizational

Table 7.2 Logistic regression results: dependent variable = YES (working capital primarily relying on bank loans)

	Model 1		*Model 2*		*Model 3*		*Model 4*	
	Coefficient (std. error)	*Wald*	*Coefficient (std. error)*	*Wald*	*Coefficient (std. error)*	*Wald*	*Coefficient (std. error)*	*Wald*
Control variables								
Gender	−0.2★	4.66	−0.18^	3.52	−0.18^	3.59	−0.18^	3.6
	(0.09)		(0.09)		(0.09)		(0.09)	
Education	−0.07★	5.22	−0.09★★	8.56	-0.08★★	8.02	−0.08★	8.04
	(0.03)		(0.03)		(0.03)		(0.03)	
Firm age	0.01	2.39	0.01	0.53	0.01	0.29	0.01	0.27
	(0.01)		(0.01)		(0.01)		(0.01)	
Firm size	0.29★★★	170.23	0.24★★★	102.96	0.24★★★	97.81	0.24★★★	96.27
	(0.02)		(0.02)		(0.02)		(0.02)	
Profitability	0.17	2.91	0.15	2.27	0.1	1.02	0.11	1.03
	(0.1)		(0.1)		(0.1)		(0.1)	
Industry					Controlled			
Region					Controlled			
Independent variables								
Political capital 1			0.13^		0.13^	3.34	0.16	2.5
			(0.07)		(0.07)		(0.1)	
Political capital 2			0.12★★★		0.12★★★	22.55	0.12★★★	10.35
			(0.03)		(0.03)		(0.04)	
Moral capital					0.23★★★	11.6	0.25★★	6.79
					(0.07)		(0.1)	
Political capital 1 × Moral capital							−0.07	0.23
							(0.13)	
Political capital 2 × Moral capital							0.01	0.00
							(0.05)	
N	5703		5703		5703		5703	
Model χ^2 [df]	469.35★★★		500.33★★★		511.91★★★		512.14★★★	
−2 Log likelihood	5924.54		5893.56		5881.98		5881.74	
R^2	0.088		0.094		0.096		0.096	

★★★ significant at $p < 0.001$; ★★ significant at $p < 0.01$; ★ significant at $p < 0.05$; ^ significant at $p < 0.1$

Table 7.3 Logistic regression results: dependent variable = YES (business development capital primarily relying on bank loans)

	Model 1		*Model 2*		*Model 3*		*Model 4*	
	Coefficient (std. error)	*Wald*	*Coefficient (std. error)*	*Wald*	*Coefficient (std. error)*	*Wald*	*Coefficient (std. error)*	*Wald*
Control variables								
Gender	−0.06 (0.1)	0.34	−0.04 (0.1)	0.12	−0.04 (0.1)	0.14	−0.04 (0.1)	0.16
Education	0.01 (0.03)	0.19	−0.01 (0.03)	0.02	−0.01 (0.03)	0.01	0.01 (0.03)	0.01
Firm age	0.01 (0.01)	2.08	0.01 (0.01)	0.34	0.01 (0.01)	0.14	0.01 (0.01)	0.09
Firm size	0.29*** (0.02)	146.22	0.24*** (0.03)	84.36	0.23*** (0.03)	79.79	0.23*** (0.03)	77.54
Profitability	0.56*** (0.12)	20.1	0.53*** (0.12)	35.443	0.47*** (0.13)	13.94	0.47*** (0.13)	13.97
Industry				Controlled				
Region				Controlled				
Independent variables								
Political capital 1			0.06 (0.07)	0.61	0.05 (0.07)	0.5	0.21^ (0.11)	3.55
Political capital 2			0.15*** (0.03)	34.14	0.14*** (0.03)	28.72	0.13*** (0.04)	10.46
Moral capital					0.26*** (0.07)	12.54	0.33** (0.11)	9.64
Political capital 1 × Moral capital							−0.27^ (0.15)	3.46
Political capital 2 × Moral capital							0.02 (0.05)	0.16
N	5703		5703		5703		5703	
Model χ^2 [df]	416.03***		450.58***		463.13***		466.63***	
−2 Log likelihood	5167.1		5132.55		5120		5116.5	
R^2	0.079		0.085		0.087		0.088	

*** significant at $p < 0.001$; ** significant at $p < 0.01$; * significant at $p < 0.05$; ^ significant at $p < 0.1$

legitimacy of private enterprises. Interestingly, however, for organizational legitimacy when measured as development capital primarily relying on bank loans, there is weak evidence (significant at $p < 0.1$) that suggests a substitution effect between moral capital and political capital measured as CP membership. Taken together, H3 is not supported.

Discussion and conclusion

China needs more firms that are willing and able to innovate. Yet, a common challenge facing innovative firms is resource constraint (Ding et al., 2008; Li, 2015). Firms that obtain resources for innovation are those that adopt strategies to legitimize themselves in the eyes of stakeholders (Gao et al., 2010). It is in this context that this chapter examines the role of moral capital in legitimacy building by private enterprises in China. Three questions are proposed in this chapter: Does political capital help private enterprises build organizational legitimacy? Does moral capital help private enterprises build organizational legitimacy? Does moral capital complement political capital in helping private enterprises build organizational legitimacy? I used private enterprises' charitable giving as a measure of moral capital and access to bank loans by private enterprises as an indicator of organizational legitimacy to test the hypotheses.

For the effect of political variables, the results presented in this chapter largely confirm what has been consistently found in the political connection literature that political capital has a positive effect on firms' access to finance. In addition, the results of this chapter appear to suggest that political capital as measured by PC membership and PPCC membership have a greater effect than CP membership on organizational legitimacy of private enterprises. Hence, political capital as measured by PC membership and PPCC membership is more conducive to organizational legitimacy. Again, this finding is consistent with evidence in the literature (Bai et al., 2006; Li et al., 2008; Chen et al., 2012).

Most interestingly, this chapter finds that the relationship between moral capital and organizational legitimacy is statistically strong. The finding is consistent in two different measures of organizational legitimacy. The compelling evidence confirms that moral capital is conducive to moral legitimacy that allows private enterprises to have better access to resources.

The evidence, albeit weak, that moral capital can be a substitute for political capital measured as CP membership in building organizational legitimacy is intriguing. To the best of my knowledge, this is a new finding in the literature. Zhao and Lu (2016) argue that in the Chinese political system, a CP membership is not as important and prestigious as the membership of either PC or PPCC, mainly because almost every citizen is eligible to apply and be admitted to the Communist Party, while only a small handful can become a member of PC or PPCC. The result of this research provides some support to this view. Nonetheless, this research uses an executive-position–weighted ordinal measure of political capital and captures more than simply the status of a CP membership. The potential substitution effect could have a positive implication. Despite the compelling impact of developing relationships with the political machine through either political networking or political participation, such political capital can be vulnerable. This is because political capital, like other types of social capital, is built on the intimacy and strength of interpersonal relationships. Underpinning political capital is the contractual trust (Sako, 1992) that is clearly transaction oriented. Private entrepreneurs' shortcut route to the political power machine affords them the anticipated influence on key decision-makers and thus direct benefits owing to the overwhelming power of governments. The downside of the intimate relationship is its vulnerability to a change of political personnel and gray practices leading to charges of corruption (Kong et al., 2017). If the substitution effect holds true, private enterprises can do well by doing good. The reciprocal effect of moral legitimacy can be beneficial to private enterprises and society alike. Undoubtedly, this is an area in which more research needs to be done.

In conclusion, this chapter finds evidence to support the argument that moral capital has a positive effect on organizational legitimacy as measured by private enterprises' access to bank loans for either working capital or business development capital. Political capital is also found to be an important strategy to enhance the legitimacy of private enterprises. There is also tentative evidence to suggest that moral capital has a substitution effect on political capital in facilitating legitimacy. Taken together, research in this chapter suggests that private enterprises in China will perform well in innovation if they are able to leverage political capital and moral capital to establish legitimacy and win support from stakeholders.

Note

1 https://data.worldbank.org/indicator/NY.GNP.PCAP.PP.CD

References

Acs, Z. J. (2013) *Why Philanthropy Matters: How the Wealthy Give, and What It Means for Our Economic Well-Being*, Princeton, NJ: Princeton University Press.

Acs, Z. J. (2015) "Moral Capital in the Twenty-First Century." Working Paper 36, Swedish Entrepreneurship Forum. Available at https://entreprenorskapsforum.se/wp-content/uploads/2015/08/WP_36.pdf (accessed August 9, 2018).

Ahlstrom, D. and Bruton, G. (2001) "Learning from Successful Local Private Enterprises in China: Establishing Legitimacy." *Academy of Management Executive* 15(4): 72–83.

Atherton, A. (2008) "From 'fat pigs' and 'red hats' to a 'new social stratum': The changing Face of Enterprise Development Policy in China." *Journal of Small Business and Enterprise Development* 15(4): 640–655.

Atherton, A. and A. Newman (2017) *Entrepreneurship in China: The Emergence of the Private Sector*, London: Routledge.

Ayyagari, M., A. Demirgüç-Kunt and V. Maksimovic (2010) "Formal Versus Informal Finance: Evidence from China." *The Review of Financial Studies* 23(8): 3048–3097.

Bai, C. E., J. Lu and Z. Tao (2006) "Property Rights Protection and Access to Bank Loans: Evidence from Private Enterprises in China." *Economics of Transition* 14(4): 611–628.

Baumol, W., R. Litan and C. Schramm (2007) *Good Capitalism, Bad Capitalism*, New Haven: Yale University Press.

Becker-Blease, J. R. and J. E. Sohl (2015) "New Venture Legitimacy: The Conditions for Angel Investors." *Small Business Economics* 45(4): 735–749.

Bhaumik, S. K. and S. Estrin (2007) "How Transition Paths Differ: Enterprise Performance in Russia and China." *Journal of Development Economics* 82(2): 374–392.

Brammer, S., C. Brooks and S. Pavelin (2006) "Corporate Social Performance and Stock Returns: UK Evidence from Disaggregate Measures." *Financial Management* 35(3): 97–116.

Chen, G., J. Li and H. Matlay (2006) "Who Are Chinese Private Entrepreneurs? A Study of Entrepreneurial Attributes and Business Governance." *Journal of Small Business and Enterprise Development* 13(2): 148–160.

Chen, Y. and D. Touve (2011) "Conformity, Political Participation, and Economic Rewards: The Case of Chinese Private Entrepreneurs." *Asia Pacific Journal of Management* 28(3): 529–553.

Chen, Z., Y. Sun, A. Newman and W. Xu (2012) "Entrepreneurs, Organizational Members, Political Participation and Preferential Treatment: Evidence from China." *International Small Business Journal* 30(8): 873–889.

Cheng, X. and H. Degryse (2010) "The Impact of Bank and Non-Bank Financial Institutions on Local Economic Growth in China." *Journal of Financial Services Research* 37(2–3): 179–199.

Coombs, J. E., A. J. Shipp and L. J. Christensen (2008) "Entrepreneur as Change Agent: Antecedents and Moderators of Individual-Level Philanthropic Behaviour." *Frontiers of Entrepreneurship Research* 28(21), Article 1.

Cull, R. and L. C. Xu (2005) "Institutions, Ownership, and Finance: The Determinants of Profit Reinvestment among Chinese Firms." *Journal of Financial Economics* 77(1): 117–146.

Deephouse, D. L. and M. C. Suchman (2008) "Legitimacy in Organizational Institutionalism." R. Greenwood, C. Oliver and K. Sahlin et al. (eds.), *The Sage Handbook of Organizational Institutionalism*, Thousand Oaks, CA: Sage, 49–77.

Degryse, H., L. Lu and S. Ongena (2016) "Informal or Formal Financing? Evidence on the Co-funding of Chinese Firms." *Journal of Financial Intermediation* 27: 31–50.

Delmar, F. and S. Shane (2004) "Legitimating First: Organizing Activities and the Survival of New Ventures." *Journal of Business Venturing* 19(3): 385–410.

Ding, X., J. Li and J. Wang (2008) "In Pursuit of Technological Innovation: China's Science and Technology Policies and Financial and Fiscal Incentives." *Journal of Small Business and Enterprise Development* 15(4): 816–831.

Ding, X. D. and J. Li (2015) *Incentives for Innovation in China: Building an Innovative Economy*, London and New York: Routledge.

Dong, Y., C. Meng, M. Firth and W. Hou (2014) "Ownership Structure and Risk-Taking: Comparative Evidence from Private and State-Controlled Banks in China." *International Review of Financial Analysis* 36: 120–130.

Gao, J., J. Li, Y. Cheng and S. Shi (2010) "Impact of Initial Conditions on New Venture Success: A Longitudinal Study of New Technology-Based Firms." *International Journal of Innovation Management* 14(1): 41–56.

Gao, Y. (2011) "Philanthropic Disaster Relief Giving as a Response to Institutional Pressure: Evidence from China." *Journal of Business Research* 64(12): 1377–1382.

Gibb, A. A. and J. Li (2003) "Organizing for Enterprise in China: What Can We Learn from the Chinese Micro, Small, and Medium Enterprise Development Experience." *Futures: Journal of Policy, Planning and Futures Studies* 35(4): 403–421.

Godfrey, P. C. (2005) "The Relationship between Corporate Philanthropy and Shareholder Wealth: A Risk Management Perspective." *Academy of Management Review* 30(4): 777–798.

Griffin, J. J. and J. F. Mahon (1997) "The Corporate Social Performance and Corporate Financial Performance Debate: Twenty-Five Years of Incomparable Research." *Business and Society* 36(1): 5–31.

Haidt, J. (2012) *The Righteous Mind: Why Good People Are Divided by Politics and Religion*, New York: Pantheon Books.

Hempel, J. and L. Gard (2004) "The Corporate Givers." *Business Week*, November 29, 100–104.

Huang, Y., M. Pagano and U. Panizza (2017) "Local Crowding Out in China." Working Paper No. 450, Centre for Studies in Economics and Finance, University of Naples. Available at https://papers.ssrn.com/sol3/papers.cfm?abstract_id=2820682, (accessed June 11, 2018).

Jamali, D. and R. Mirshak (2006) "Corporate Social Responsibility (CSR): Theory and Practice in a Developing Country Context." *Journal of Business Ethics* 72: 243–262.

Kibler, E., and T. Kautonen (2016) "The Moral Legitimacy of Entrepreneurs: An Analysis of Early-Stage Entrepreneurship Across 26 Countries." *International Small Business Journal* 34(1): 34–50.

Kong, D., L. Wang and M. Wang (2017) "Effects of Anti-corruption on Firm Performance: Evidence from a Quasi-natural Experiment in China." *Finance Research Letters* 23: 190–195.

Li, H. and K. Atuahene-Gima (2001) "Product Innovation Strategy and the Performance of New Technology Ventures in China." *Academy of Management Journal* 44(6): 1123–1134.

Li, H. and K. Atuahene-Gima (2002) "The adoption of agency business activity, product innovation, and performance in Chinese technology ventures." *Strategic Management Journal* 23(6): 469–490.

Li, H., L. Meng, Q. Wang and L. A. Zhou (2008) "Political Connections, Financing and Firm Performance: Evidence from Chinese Private Enterprises." *Journal of Development Economics* 87(2): 283–299.

Li, H. and Y. Zhang (2007) "The Role of Managers' Political Networking and Functional Experience in New Venture Performance: Evidence from China's Transition Economy." *Strategic Management Journal* 28: 791–804.

Li, J. (2002) *Financing China's Rural Enterprises*, London and New York: Routledge Curzon.

Li, J. (2015) "Bridging the Equity Funding Gap in Technological Entrepreneurship: The Case of Government-Backed Venture Capital in China." Javed G. Hussain and Jonathan M. Scott (eds.), *Research Handbook on Entrepreneurial Finance*, Cheltenham, UK: Edward Elgar, 185–205.

Li, J. and H. Matlay (2006) "Chinese Entrepreneurship and Small Business Development: An Overview and Research Agenda." *Journal of Small Business and Enterprise Development* 13(2): 248–262.

Li, J. and L. M. Wang (eds.) (2014) *China's Economic Dynamics: A Beijing Consensus in the Making?* London and New York: Routledge.

Li, Z. and J. Li (2014) "State-Owned Enterprises (SOEs) in China's Transition to an Innovation-Oriented Economy." J. Li and LM. Wang (eds.), *China's Economic Dynamics: A Beijing Consensus in the Making?* London and New York: Routledge, 193–203.

Luo, Y. (2003) "Industrial Dynamics and Managerial Networking in an Emerging Market: The Case of China." *Strategic Management Journal* 24(13): 1315–1327.

Ma, D. and W. L. Parish (2006) "Tocquevillian Moments: Charitable Contributions by Chinese Private Entrepreneurs." *Social Forces* 85(2): 943–964.

Marquis, C. and K. Qiao (2018) "Waking from Mao's Dream: Communist Ideological Imprinting and the Internationalization of Entrepreneurial Ventures in China." *Administrative Science Quarterly*. Available at https://doi.org/10.1177/0001839218792837.

Neter, J., W. Wasserman and M. H. Kutner (1990) *Applied Statistical Models* (3rd ed.), Boston, MA: Irwin.

Niehm, L. S., J. Swinney and N. J. Miller (2008) "Community Social Responsibility and Its Consequences for Family Business Performance." *Journal of Small Business Management* 46(3): 331–350.

Peng, M. W., and Y. Luo (2000) "Managerial Ties and Firm Performance in a Transition Economy: The Nature of a Micro-Macro Link." *Academy of Management Journal* 43(3): 486–501.

Peng, Y. (2004) "Kinship Networks and Entrepreneurs in China's Transitional Economy." *American Journal of Sociology* 109: 1045–1074.

Podsakoff, P. M. and D.W. Organ (1986) "Self-reports in Organizational Research: Problems and Prospects." *Journal of Management* 12: 531–544.

Rao, R. S., R. K. Chandy and J. C. Prabhu (2008) "The Fruits of Legitimacy: Why Some New Ventures Gain More from Innovation than Others." *Journal of Marketing* 72(4): 58–75.

Saiia, D. H., A. B. Carroll and A. K. Buchholtz (2003) "Philanthropy as Strategy: When Corporate Charity 'Begins at Home'." *Business and Society* 42(2): 169–201.

Sako, M. (1992) *Price, Quality, and Trust: Inter-Firm Relations in Britain and Japan*, Cambridge: Cambridge University Press.

Scott, W. R. (2008) *Institutions and Organizations: Ideas and Interests* (3rd ed.), Thousand Oaks, CA: Sage.

Sheng, S., K. Z. Zhou and J. J. Li (2011) "The Effects of Business and Political Ties on Firm Performance: Evidence from China." *Journal of Marketing* 75(1): 1–15.

Stinchcombe, A. L. (1965) "Social Structure and Organizations." J. G. March (ed.), *Handbook of Organizations*, Chicago: Rand McNally, 142–193.

Suchman, M. C. (1995) "Managing Legitimacy: Strategic and Institutional Approaches." *Academy of Management Review* 20(3): 571–610.

Tornikoski, E. T. and S. L. Newbert (2007) "Exploring the Determinants of Organizational Emergence: A Legitimacy Perspective." *Journal of Business Venturing* 22(2): 311–335.

Tsai, K. S. (2002) *Back-Alley Banking*, Ithaca and London: Cornell University Press.

Tsang, E. W. K. (1996) "In Search of Legitimacy: The Private Entrepreneur in China." *Entrepreneurship Theory and Practice* 21(1): 21–30.

Überbacher, F. (2014) "Legitimation of New Ventures: A Review and Research Programme." *Journal of Management Studies* 51(4): 667–698.

Walder, A. G. (1991) "Local Bargaining Relationships and Urban Industrial Finance." *Bureaucracy and Policy Making in Post-Mao China*, Berkeley, CA: University of California Press.

Wang, K., W. Huang, J. Wu and Y. N. Liu (2014) "Efficiency Measures of the Chinese Commercial Banking System Using an Additive Two-Stage DEA." *Omega* 44: 5–20.

Wedeman, A. (2013) "The Dark Side of Business with Chinese Characteristics." *Social Research* 80(4): 1213–1236.

Wu, H., S. Li, S. X. Ying and X. Chen (2018) "Politically Connected CEOs, Firm Performance, and CEO Pay." *Journal of Business Research* 91: 169–180.

Xin, K. R. and J. L. Pearce (1996) "Guanxi: Connections as Substitutes for Formal Institutional Support." *Academy of Management Journal* 39(6): 1641–1658.

Yan, J. Z. and S. J. Chang (2018) "The Contingent Effects of Political Strategies on Firm Performance: A Political Network Perspective." *Strategic Management Journal* 39(8): 2152–2177.

Ye, K. and R. Zhang (2011) "Do Lenders Value Corporate Social Responsibility? Evidence from China." *Journal of Business Ethics* 104(2): 197–206.

Yin, J. and Y. Zhang (2012) "Institutional Dynamics and Corporate Social Responsibility (CSR) in an Emerging Country Context: Evidence from China." *Journal of Business Ethics* 111(2): 301–316.

Zhang, G., X. Peng and J. Li (2008) "Technological Entrepreneurship and Policy Environment: A Case of China." *Journal of Small Business and Enterprise Development* 15(4): 733–751.

Zhao, H. and J. Lu (2016) "Contingent Value of Political Capital in Bank Loan Acquisition: Evidence from Founder-Controlled Private Enterprises in China." *Journal of Business Venturing* 31(2): 153–174.

Zhou, W. (2009) "Bank Financing in China's Private Sector: The Payoffs of Political Capital." *World Development* 37(4): 787–799.

Zimmerman, M.A. and G.J. Zeitz (2002) "Beyond Survival: Achieving New Venture Growth by Building Legitimacy." *Academy of Management Review* 27(3): 414–431.

8 The interdependency of innovation obstacles in Chinese manufacturing firms

Jun Hou

1 Introduction

In developing countries, most firms have engaged in innovation through imitating or adapting existing production technologies to local conditions rather than creating new technologies (Cooper, 1989). Innovation studies in the developing country context have paid particular attention to examine the determinants, sources, and capability of innovation, and their contribution to firm's performance (Basant and Fikkert, 1996). Few studies, however, have investigated obstacles which block innovation or cause innovation failures.

Limited by their inadequate resources and experiences, firms in developing countries are likely to face barriers to innovation compared to ones from advanced economies. At the initial stage, obstacles may emerge to prevent firms from engaging in innovative activities (e.g., R&D investment). This happens more often in developing countries when firms decide to undertake innovation investment. They might choose not to invest due to inadequate financial sources, the lack of channels to acquire information about technologies or market, or the shortage of qualified high-skilled employees, among other reasons. After firms pass the initial line and engage in innovation competition, they may face different patterns of obstacles before turning innovation input into products or process innovation (Baldwin and Hanel, 2002; Mohnen and Röller, 2005). Obstacles during this process may represent a major determinant of the decision to abandon an ongoing innovation project or simply delay and limit the innovation outcomes. Like analyses of innovation determinants and acquisition strategies, gaining a thorough understanding of the nature and composition of barriers would also help firms and governments to better position corresponding innovation strategies and supportive policies (Hadjimanolis, 2003; Ferriani et al., 2008).

This study attempts to estimate the impact of innovation obstacles on firms' innovation performance. Special attention will be paid to the potential complementarities between obstacles, which are of particular relevance for accurately calculating their individual impacts and for drawing practical implications regarding the sequence of removing obstacles. A firm level dataset from Chinese manufacturing industries is used for the empirical analysis. The results reveal the potential interdependent relationship between obstacles and help to explain why some obstacles should be removed simultaneously and others should be tackled individually. To further investigate the sequence of eliminating the identified barriers, the marginal effects of each barrier are also estimated while controlling for the interactive effects. It is suggested that the net innovation gains of removing obstacles should also take into account the complementarities among them. In addition, policy choices should be specific to particular firm characteristics and development context.

The next section outlines the nature of obstacles to innovation and their impact on the innovation output. Section 3 specifies the model underlying the empirical analysis. Data and descriptive statistics are introduced in section 4. Section 5 reports and discusses the empirical findings. Section 6 concludes the chapter and draws policy suggestions.

2 Innovation obstacles across Chinese manufacturing firms

China's rapid economic ascendance and fast catching up with the leading industrial countries have become a remarkable economic force influencing the world economy. In 2006, China declared indigenous innovation to be a strategic priority. Then, a series of science and technology policies were made to remove potential innovation obstacles and consequently enhance the country's technological capability (Fu et al., 2016). As an outcome of these initiatives, R&D spending increased at an average annual real growth rate of almost 20%. This has made China the third largest global investor in R&D in 2012, just behind the United States and Japan, but ahead of individual economies of the EU.

Innovation has been recognized as a core driver of the economic transition in China over the past two decades. During the catch-up process, China has not only imitated and assimilated technologies from advanced countries but has also striven to establish indigenous innovation capabilities in order to sustain long-term economic growth. Upgrading the country's technological level and improving innovation performance requires persistent commitments in investing in R&D and supporting skills, as well as identifying and removing the potential obstacles to innovation.

An obstacle to innovation is defined as any factor that undermines the innovation process (Piatier, 1984). Obstacles may represent a major determinant of the decision to abandon ongoing innovation projects or simply delay the innovation outcomes (Baldwin and Hanel, 2003) while the obstacles faced by firms are perceived differently throughout the innovation process (Hadjimanolis, 2003). Even after the firm successfully becomes an innovator, obstacles may emerge and limit the levels of innovation (Mohnen and Röller, 2005).

The potential interactive effects among obstacles are particularly appealing from a policy perspective. For example, if there exist complementarities among obstacles, a policy that focuses only on one obstacle will be assumed to be insufficient. Policy packages will be more effective and appropriate in this context. Mohnen and Röller (2005) use the Community Innovation Survey (CIS) from four European countries to prove that a policy package is necessary to increase the propensity of becoming an innovator due to the identified complementarity, whereas a more individually targeted choice of corresponding government policies is suggested to eliminate obstacles in order to improve the innovation output for those who are already innovators. Another study regarding the complementary between innovation obstacles was written by Galia and Legros (2004). The authors investigate innovation obstacles faced by French manufacturing firms by using CIS French data. Their findings suggest that there might be interactions and reinforcement among obstacles, and a more targeted choice among corresponding government policies is expected to improve the innovation performance. Although there are emerging studies on the obstacles of innovation (Dougherty, 1992; Tourigny, 2004; Mohnen and Röller, 2005; Savignac, 2008), the literature in developing countries context remains scarce. Our understanding of the underlying factors impeding firms' technological catch-up and the system in which these factors are interconnected is limited.

3 Model specifications

3.1 Complementarity between obstacles versus complementarity between policies

In search of complementarity in obstacles and their corresponding policy responses, two notations need to be distinguished: the "positive complementarity" and the "negative complementarity." The former is applied for situations where the complementary activities are expected to be positively correlated with the outcomes; for example, the complementarity between human resource practices and information technology infrastructures, and the complementarity between internal and external technological acquisition strategies in fostering innovation. The presence of these activities tends to enhance innovation performance and complementarity is signalized as a significantly positive sign of the interaction term. The "negative complementarity" describes an interactive effect between activities that are likely to exacerbate the undermining impact on an economic outcome. The sign of the interaction term is expected to be negative. A good example is the complementarity between innovation obstacles. However, if complementarity is strictly interpreted as when "the presence of one factor increases the marginal return of the other factor," which is based on the standard notation given by Milgrom and Roberts (1995), then complementarity between obstacles indicates a positive interactive effect, regardless of a positive or negative correlation between these obstacles and the economic outcome. The definition of "negative complementarity" given earlier would accordingly be interpreted as substitutability in this conventional understanding. Figure 8.1 geometrically depicts the complementarity between obstacles and also the complementarity between corresponding policies. As the figure shows, the complementarity between two obstacles can be depicted in two different patterns, which can lead to two different interpretations in terms of policy responses. On the one hand, in the presence of both obstacles (−O1 and −O2), if the undermining effect of one obstacle (−O1) reinforces the other obstacle (−O2) by worsening the total effect on the outcome (point D), we define it as "negative complementarity." The policy response (O1 and O2) should at least remove one of the obstacles to avoid appearing together. The complementarity between these two obstacles reflects a substitutive relation between two corresponding policies, as shown by point B in Figure 8.1. On the other hand, on the basis of the conventional definition, the complementary between −O1 and −O2 should be interpreted as: the presence of one obstacle (−O1) increases the marginal return of the other obstacle (−O2) by mitigating the negative effects (shifting to point E). In another word, when one obstacle has already caused a deterring impact on innovation, having an additional obstacle would not matter anymore. The complementarity of obstacles then reflects a mutual-reinforcing relationship between two policy responses since tackling only one obstacle would magnify the hampering effect of the other. Differences between these two interpretations are critical for correctly formulating an economic model and interpreting the results. In the following sections, we use the latter

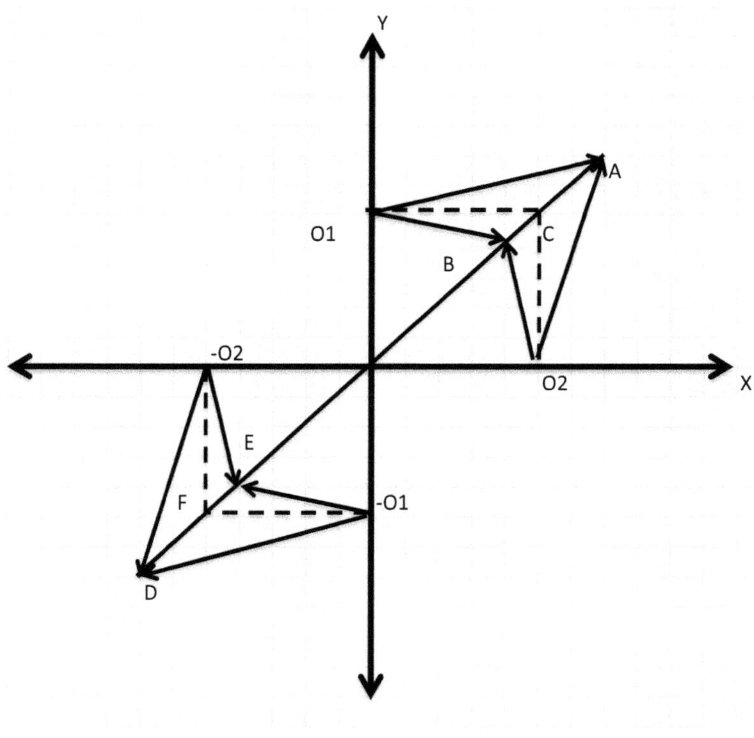

Figure 8.1 Positive complementarity versus negative complementarity[1]

definition: complementarity means that if one obstacle is present and hampers innovation, the second obstacle's hampering effect is alleviated.

3.2 Obstacles to innovation performance

In addition to identify the hampering factors to innovation performance (Dougherty, 1992; Mohnen and Röller, 2005; Mohnen et al., 2008), the current study also aims to accurately examine the corresponding marginal effects of obstacles by taking into account the potential complementarity between them.

The complementarity of our interest will be assessed in the productivity approach proposed by Athey and Stern (2002). This approach has been widely acknowledged in previous studies (Cassiman and Veugelers, 2006; Lokshin et al., 2008; Mohnen and Röller, 2005; Hou and Mohnen, 2013) by directly testing the impacts on the economic outcome of adopting two practices jointly. The Tobit model[2] will be employed and innovation performance will be measured by the intensity of new product sales. A latent variable will be incorporated to correct the potential censoring bias since the sales of new products will only be observed if a firm has achieved innovation of new products or services during the period under review (Heckman, 1976, 1979; Johnston and DiNardo, 1997; Verbeek, 2000; Greene, 2003; Kleinknecht and Mohnen, 2002; Mohnen and Röller, 2005). Ordinary Least Squares alone may fail to generate consistent estimates in this case. The introduced latent variable – whether a firm has gained new products or services – will absorb both the process of participation in product innovation and the outcome of interest. By including obstacles and their interactions in the innovation function, we will be able to systematically examine the potential complementarities.

$$PD_i^0 = A + \beta_f Firmspecifics_i + \beta_s Size_i + \beta_i Industry_i + \varepsilon_i$$
$$PD_i^0 = \begin{cases} 0 if & PD_i^* < 0 \\ PD_i^0 & otherwise \end{cases} \tag{8.1}$$

$$\begin{aligned} A = {} & \delta_1 x_1 + \delta_2 x_2 + \delta_3 x_3 + \delta_4 x_4 + \delta_{12} x_1 x_2 + \delta_{13} x_1 x_3 + \delta_{14} x_1 x_4 \\ & + \delta_{23} x_2 x_3 + \delta_{24} x_2 x_4 + \delta_{34} x_3 x_4 - \delta_{123} x_1 x_2 x_3 + \delta_{124} x_1 x_2 x_4 \\ & + \delta_{134} x_1 x_3 x_4 + \delta_{234} x_2 x_3 x_4 + \delta_{1234} x_1 x_2 x_3 x_4 \end{aligned} \tag{8.2}$$

where PD_i^o in Equation 8.1 indicates the outcome of innovation: sales of new products or services[3]. A is composited of four types of obstacles[4], $x_i, l = (1,2,3,4)$. PD_i^* is the latent value of new product sales for firm i. It tells whether a firm produces any new products or services during the period under review. We observe the outcome PD_i^o only if the latent selection variable PD_i^* is non-negative. It is assumed that the error term η_i and ε_i follow a joint normal distribution (Greene, 2003). "Firmspecifics" captures a vector of firm characteristics that influence firms' innovation and δ is a vector of estimated coefficients (for a detailed explanation of variables, see next section). Size and Industry are two sets of dummies to control for size and industry specificities of firm i. ε_i denotes the disturbance term.

3.3 Testing complementarity between pair-wise obstacles

Turning to the obstacles, x_l, l = (1,2,3,4) in Equation 8.2 are dichotomous choice variables which correspond to four types of obstacles in regard to a firm's perception of hampering factors it faces. x_l equals to one if the corresponding obstacle is reported as a major obstacle by the firm, otherwise it equals zero[5]. δ is a vector of coefficients that needs to be estimated. Obstacles here are treated as exogenous variables that do not correlate with the residuals. According to the notion of complementarity (Milgrom and Roberts, 1995), we conclude that x_i and x_j are complementary if the following conditions hold.

$$\begin{aligned} &f(x_i=1,x_j=1\mid Z)+f(x_i=0,x_j=0\mid Z)\geq \\ &f(x_i=1,x_j=0\mid Z)+f(x_i=0,x_j=1\mid Z) \end{aligned} \tag{8.3}$$

With more than two obstacles, consistently testing the complementarity between pairs of obstacles requires the full set of cross-terms in Equation 8.3 to be included. Specifically, the complementarity between x_1 and x_2 can only be posited if all of the following four inequality conditions are satisfied and with at least one inequality holding strictly.

$$\begin{cases} f_{1,2}(x_1x_2\mid x_3=0,x_4=0)=\delta_{12}\geq 0 \\ f_{1,2}(x_1x_2\mid x_3=1,x_4=0)=\delta_{12}+\delta_{123}\geq 0 \\ f_{1,2}(x_1x_2\mid x_3=0,x_4=1)=\delta_{12}+\delta_{124}\geq 0 \\ f_{1,2}(x_1x_2\mid x_3=1,x_4=1)=\delta_{12}+\delta_{123}+\delta_{124}+\delta_{1234}\geq 0 \end{cases} \tag{8.4}$$

Supposing all inequalities having the inverse sign in Equation 8.4, we would conclude substitutability[6]. The same formula can be adopted for testing pair-wise complementarity for x_1 and x_3 ; x_1 and x_4 ; x_2 and x_3 ; x_2 and x_4 ; x_3 and x_4. Estimation without controlling for the full cross-terms (the third- and fourth-order interactions) would lead to biased or inconclusive results (Mohnen and Röller, 2005; Lokshin et al., 2008) such as those based on δ_{12} by ignoring the potential third-order (δ_{123}, δ_{124}, and δ_{134}) and the fourth-order interactions (δ_{1234}) in equation (3). With multiple inequality restrictions imposed on δ, the one-sided multivariate hypotheses are used for computing the test statistics:

$$\text{Hypothesis Test 1} \qquad H_0: R\delta = 0 \ \text{ vs } \ H_1: R\delta \geq 0 \tag{8.5}$$

$$\text{Hypothesis Test 2} \qquad H_0: R\delta \geq 0 \ \text{ vs } \ H_1: R\delta ! \geq 0 \tag{8.6}$$

R is a matrix with a dimension of ($p \times k$) which defines the inequality restrictions imposed on the estimated parameters. p is the number of inequality constraints that have to be tested simultaneously. HT1 (Hypothesis Test 1) tests equality against at least one inequality strictly holding. HT2 (Hypothesis Test 2) tests if all $R\delta$ are larger or equal to zero against at least one violation in the null hypothesis (not all $R\delta$ are larger or equal to r)[7]. The "!" sign symbolizes "not." We emphasize a test procedure that takes into account both HT1 and HT2 herein, which have better statistical power than the test procedures that only consider one of them. Likelihood ratio tests (Gouriéroux et al., 1982) are used as the hypothesis testing method[8].

4 Data and variables

4.1 Data

The firm-level data as presented in the Investment Climate Survey (ICS)[9] conducted by the World Bank covers a broad range of topics including infrastructure, economic performance, and investment environments. Data collected from China in 2012 is used for the current study. The survey collects information from 25 major cities in China and includes questions about new product and process innovations, R&D activities, and, of particular relevance to this study, information with respect to obstacles facing by the Chinese manufacturing firms.

The main focus on innovation as defined by the ICS is consistent with other surveys, such as Community Innovation Surveys (CIS). Innovation is defined according to the successful implementation of new technological knowledge, either in the form of new (or significantly improved) products or services (product innovations) or new processes (process innovations). However, it is worth noting that innovations may refer to technologies that are novel or significantly improved only to the firm in which they are implemented and need not necessarily represent a new invention in the market. Table 8.1 defines the variables and provides corresponding statistics in summary. After the removal of inadequate values[10], our final sample includes 1,289 firms distributed across a wide range of regions and industries.

4.2 Measures for innovation performance

Innovation performance, the dependent variable in Equation 8.1, is measured by the percentage of new products and services sales in total turnover[11]. This share-in-sales indicator is the direct link between the innovation effort and the commercial success and has been widely used as output indicator in recent years (Klomp and Van Leeuwen, 1999; Mairesse and Mohnen, 2001). R&D is calculated by the share of a firm's R&D investment to the total sales during the period under review. The second and third columns of Table 8.2 show the average R&D and innovativeness across firms in different technology levels[12] and size groups[13]. In view of the new product sales, Chinese firms in non–high-tech and small-sized groups are less likely to succeed in

Table 8.1 Variables definition and summary (mean and SD)

Variable	*Definition*	*Mean*	*Std. Dev.*	*Min*	*Max*
Dependent variable					
New product sales	Percentage of annual sales accounted for by new products or services in 2012, in percentage	0.114	0.175	0	1
Explanatory variables					
R&D	Percentage of R&D expenditures in total annual sales in 2012	0.016	0.038	0	0.300
R&D^2	Square of percentage of R&D expenditures in total annual sales in 2012	0.002	0.008	0	0.090
Scale_sale	Total annual sales of 2012, in logarithm	3.122	1.659	−1.966	10.597
Fin_obs	Binary variable equals to 1 if "Access to finance" is recognized as a major or serious obstacle in a firm	0.612	0.487	0	1
Com_obs	Binary variable equals to 1 if "Practices of competitors in the informal sector" is recognized as a major or serious obstacle in a firm	0.609	0.488	0	1
Tax_obs	Binary variable equals to 1 if "Tax rates" is recognized as a major or serious obstacle in a firm	0.534	0.499	0	1
Lab_obs	Binary variable equals to 1 if "Inadequately educated workforce" is recognized as a major or serious obstacle in a firm	0.587	0.493	0	1
Control variables					
Foreign_own	Percentage of foreign ownership of firm, in percentage	0.050	0.191	0	1
Export_dum	1 if a firm is an exporter, dummy variable	0.321	0.467	0	1
University	Percentage of employees having university or above degree	0.328	0.470	0	1.000
Age	Age of the firm by the end of 2012, in logarithm	2.444	0.506	0	4.828
Manager_exp	Number of years of experiences that a firm's manager has, in logarithm	2.812	0.440	0.693	3.871
Certificate	1 if a firm has purchased any technology certificates. Dummy variable	0.697	0.460	0	1
Hi-tech	Three technology levels according to OECD technology classification. Dummy				
Size dummy	< 50, 50–100, > 100				
City dummy	included				
Industry dummy	included				

innovation. High-tech firms have a higher value (13.2 %) compared with firms in medium- or low-tech sectors, 10.2% and 10.8% respectively. Meanwhile, the small-sized firms tend to be less in proportion of commercialized innovation. A similar pattern has been exhibited for R&D intensity. In total, the average level of innovation sales is about 11.4% and the share of R&D in total sales is 1.6%. It is important to note that the product innovation in developing countries such as China may not refer to novelty inventions but imitative innovations that are only new to the firm itself, not necessarily new to the market. In addition, technological acquisitions which eventually transfer to new product sales may not only through in-house R&D efforts, they can also be achieved via a variety of channels such as embedded machinery and equipment purchasing, licensing, training, etc. Given the limited information from the data, this study will not address much of the acquisition strategies, and hopefully it will be compensated by controlling for the obstacles and other observed firm specifics.

4.3 Obstacle measures

There are in total 15 different obstacles investigated in the ICS-China 2012 survey. All respondents were asked how intensely each obstacle has affected their firm during the period under review. We have chosen the top four important barriers based on the question: which is the biggest obstacle faced by firm? (see Appendix 8-A). They are obstacles in relation to finance, skilled labor, informal competition, and tax, respectively. Four dichotomous variables are constructed according to another separate set of questions to indicate whether the firm assesses each as a major impediment (see Appendix 8-B). Questions are asked about obstacles to innovation on a four-point Likert scale. The corresponding obstacle variable takes the value 1 if the answer is marked as a major or very severe obstacle (scores 3 and 4) and takes the value zero otherwise.

The obstacles described in the ICS are impediments faced by a firm in its entire production and business operation process. Therefore, it is rational to argue that obstacles to a firm's operation would also be perceived as factors which undermine its innovation performance, especially when a firm intends to become an innovator[14].

Obstacles can be classified in different ways. The most common is to differentiate from the perspectives of internal and external to the firm (Piatier, 1984; Hadjimanolis, 2003). Internal obstacles refer to factors that are generated internally and related to the organizational characteristics, employees' quality and the management structure. External obstacles are related to supply, demand, and the environment (Hadjimanolis, 1999); for example, difficulties in acquiring external technological information, incorrect perception of the target market, and government regulations.

Difficulty in securing finance is recognized as one of the most severe internal barriers to innovation. Financial constraints as internal hampering factors to innovation have been extensively dealt with in previous literature. Himmelberg and Petersen (1994) use small firms in the high-tech industries to show a significant positive relationship between internal finance and firms' R&D. Stockdale (2002) reports that financial constraints are the second most important impeding factor for innovation for active firms in the UK, after high innovation costs. Similar results also have been obtained by other studies (e.g., Mulkay et al., 2001; Savignac, 2006; Tiwari et al., 2008; Mohnen et al., 2008).

Lack of skilled labor is another major internal obstacle that hampers innovation (Hadjimanolis, 1999). Innovation cannot be achieved without efficient utilization of R&D by qualified human capital. Skilled labor is also required in the production process to absorb and transfer ideas into new products. The concept of "absorptive capacity" proposed by Cohen and Levinthal (1990) also suggests that high levels of skills are necessary within a firm to facilitate the assimilation of external knowledge.

Considered as an external obstacle, competition from the informal sector is ranked as one of the top four obstacles by the sampled Chinese manufacturing firms (12.18%). Informal competition may damage innovation since the cost advantage that informal firms[15] enjoy is a result of ignoring regulations (e.g., intellectual property regulations). While regulation is a major determinant of the intensity of competition from the informal sector, severe obstacles caused by competition from the informal sector may indicate the poor regulatory and institutional quality that prevails in the market. Estimates by Schneider (2005) over 145 countries across the globe show that informality is an issue correlated with low-income countries.

Corporate taxation may influence firms' investment strategy and profit. Classified as another external obstacle, the tax rate has been ranked as the biggest obstacle to firms' production in Chinese manufacturing firms. High corporate taxes may reduce incentives for innovations by reducing their post-tax returns. Hence, a negative effect of corporate taxes on firm level innovation is expected (Arrow, 1962). The issue of taxation and innovation is complex in the sense that innovative activity of firms is associated with many aspects and levels of taxation. Favorable taxation regimes are expected to create additional and important incentives for innovation (Mohnen, 2000).

Savignac (2008) suggests that a positive correlation between the obstacles and innovation performance might be raised by firms that are not willing to innovate. Hence, it is important to distinguish between firms which opted not to become innovators and those who could not because of obstacles standing in their way. We try to filter out the former by excluding firms that do not aim at innovation, and, at the same time, have no perception of obstacles in their production and innovation process (Savignac, 2008).[16]

4.4 Patterns of innovation and obstacles

The fourth to seventh columns in Table 8.2 show the four types of obstacles in different technology levels and size groups.

Table 8.2 R&D and innovation output status of all and across each group (mean values)

	Innovation	*R&D*	*Fin_obs*	*Com_obs*	*Tax_obs*	*Lab_obs*	*Freq.*	*Percent*
Technology Level								
Low-tech	0.108	0.012	0.608	0.631	0.528	0.560	398	30.88
Medium-tech	0.102	0.015	0.624	0.644	0.483	0.579	449	34.83
High-tech	0.132	0.021	0.604	0.554	0.590	0.620	442	34.29
Size (Number of Employee)								
5 < × < 25	0.080	0.013	0.590	0.676	0.494	0.596	324	25.14
26 < × < 100	0.124	0.018	0.627	0.612	0.525	0.597	528	40.96
>100	0.128	0.016	0.611	0.556	0.574	0.570	437	33.9
Total	0.114	0.016	0.612	0.609	0.534	0.587	1,289	100

Technology levels

Given the fact that high-tech firms are in general more active in seeking new sources of innovation, it is likely they encompass potential innovation barriers easily than low-tech firms which are less active in engaging in innovation activities. Yet, less active in innovation activities does not mean they do need to innovate. Just as in the high-tech firms, managers in the low- and medium-tech Chinese manufacturing industries are also constantly seeking opportunities to upgrade technology to improve product quality. In addition, the relatively low level of investment in R&D and lack of innovation experience make it even harder for them to become innovators and obstacles also tend to be more profound in these industries. As shown from Table 8.2, low- and medium-tech firms' perception of innovation obstacles is more related to inadequate finance and competition caused by informal sectors while high-tech firms tend to be more pressured by the tax- and labor-related obstacles. Specifically, the low- and medium-tech groups are pressured by inadequate finance and more than 60% of the firms rate it as a severe obstacle, which are about 0.4 and 2 percentage points higher than the high-tech group. The barrier incurred by informal competition also seems to severely hamper firms' operation in the medium-tech firms. The labor- and tax-related obstacles more often appear in high-tech firms. Nearly 60% of the firms from that group perceive tax burden as a major obstacle and the corresponding figure for the labor-related obstacles is above 62%.

Firm size

Piatier (1984) explains that the patterns of obstacles faced by firms differ greatly associated with their size as well. The bottom panel of Table 8.2 exhibits that bigger size firms (the number of employees above 100) are less likely to encounter obstacles except for the tax barriers. This can be explained by the fact that large firms normally need to get involved in more complicated tax issues and suffer high tax contribution compared to small-sized firms. Barriers caused

Table 8.3 Obstacles across R&D and innovativeness (mean values and percentages)

	Fin_obs	*Com_obs*	*Tax_obs*	*Lab_obs*	*Freq.*	*Percent*
R&D investment						
No	0.570	0.608	0.477	0.566	765	59.35
Yes	0.674	0.611	0.616	0.618	524	40.65
New products or services						
No	0.553	0.586	0.487	0.588	674	52.29
Yes	0.676	0.634	0.585	0.587	615	47.71
Total	0.114	0.016	0.612	0.609	1,289	100

by informal competition and the lack of skilled workers seem to be more profound in constraining small firms (with a number of employees between five and 25). Firms with employees between 26 and 100 have the highest frequency of reporting inadequate finance and skills as obstacles, – 63% and 60% respectively.

Table 8.3 summarizes the presence of obstacles across different levels of innovation. To sum up, firms investing in R&D are inclined to be burdened by all four types of obstacles, whereas product innovators tend to suffer from factors in relation to finance, competition, and tax burdens.

4.5 Firm specificities

A set of control variables that captures the firm characteristics will be included in the function (1). Scale-sale which denotes the scale of a firm is reckoned by the logarithm of total turnover. Firms with a larger scale are expected to have more assets and resources to allocate to innovation. Age indicates the number of years a firm has been operating since it started. On the one hand, age may adversely affect innovation outcome (Tushman and Anderson, 1986; Henderson, 1993; Katrak, 1997) because younger firms are more creative and entrepreneurially dynamic. On the other hand, longer operation experience gives a firm prior expertise, already-established financial resources, and other complementary assets. Accordingly, one may also expect that older firms are more likely to successfully tackle obstacles that stand in their way (Schoonhoven et al., 1990; Tripsas, 1997).

International experiences have been proved to be crucial to innovation performance. Two indicators are used to capture the international experiences of firms. Export_dum take value 1 if a firm has participated in exporting activities during the period under review. Competing with international firms would force firms to gain competitiveness through innovation and establishing linkages with partners in the global supply chain could help firms to access advanced know-how; therefore, exporting firms are expected to be more innovative compared with non-export firms. However, in the case of the Chinese manufacturing sector, firms might compete in the global market with a price advantage of already existing products on the basis of their comparative advantage – relatively cheaper labor and materials. In this context, cost-efficient process innovation instead of creating new products might be favored in exporting firms. The effect of Export_dum on innovation is therefore ambiguous. Foreign_own indicates the percentage of foreign ownership. Foreign owned firms are characterized by higher capital intensity, high quality of human capital and efficient managerial mechanism. Some studies suggested that foreign owned firms are more productive (Globerman et al., 1994; Doms and Jensen, 1998; Kimura and Kiyota, 2007) while others argued that foreign owned firms tend to concentrate their R&D in their home countries (OECD, 2003).

The University variable records the percentage of employees who have completed 12 years of education. The education level of employees has been adopted as a measure for evaluating the inter-firm efficiency (Cohen and Levinthal, 1990; Furman et al., 2002; Kiley, 1999). From the innovation perspective, it would be the efficiency of assimilating technologies and transformation innovation into new products. Employees with a higher level of education assist a firm to obtain a large volume of innovation sales. Manager_exp is another indicator used to capture firms' absorptive capacity as experienced managers are likely to have better insights into future innovation opportunities, products, and technologies (Helfat and Lieberman, 2002). It measures how many years of experiences in the similar industries a firm's manager has. Given a higher degree of understanding about the market, experienced managers are usually more accurate and prompt in making correct decisions regarding a firm's production and innovation. Hence, the number of a manager's experiences is expected to be positively correlated with innovation performance. An additional set of variables are included in the innovation production function to control the technological capability of a firm. Certificate is a dichotomous variable to indicate whether a firm has an internationally recognized quality certification. Complying with international standards is evidence to show that a firm has already accumulated an adequate amount of technological capabilities. Under such circumstances, a firm is believed to be more innovative. Finally, three sets of dummies are included to control for size, industry, and country specific effects.

5 Obstacles to innovation: empirical results

5.1 Determinants of innovation performance

This section demonstrates how patterns of obstacles appear differently across size groups and technology levels in Chinese manufacturing firms. In addition, the complementary relationships between pairs of obstacles are tested in the innovation output function while controlling for firm and industry specificities.

As one of the major drivers of innovation, higher levels of R&D investment tend to result in better innovation performance, as shown in Table 8.4. The significant effects across all subgroups of our sample, except for the service

Table 8.4 Tobit Estimation results: full sample, size and technology levels

Variables	*Full Sample*	*Size of firms*			*Technology Levels*		
		Small-sized	*Medium-sized*	*Large-sized*	*Low-tech*	*Medium-tech*	*High-tech*
Explanatory var.							
R&D	6.247***	5.847***	7.260***	5.417***	5.935***	5.859***	6.345***
	(0.504)	(0.923)	(0.837)	(0.832)	(1.074)	(0.859)	(0.744)
R&D^2	−19.730***	−19.734***	−22.159***	−18.155***	−16.698***	−17.658***	−20.802***
	(2.468)	(4.505)	(4.018)	(4.253)	(5.476)	(4.172)	(3.617)
Sales, log	0.021***	0.017*	0.029**	0.012	0.027**	0.026**	0.019**
	(0.006)	(0.010)	(0.014)	(0.009)	(0.013)	(0.012)	(0.010)
Obstacle var.							
Fin_obs	−0.180***	−0.248**	−0.263**	−0.043	−0.488***	−0.053	−0.048
	(0.063)	(0.104)	(0.116)	(0.093)	(0.123)	(0.114)	(0.098)
Com_obs	−0.279***	−0.454***	−0.255**	−0.201**	−0.266***	−0.295***	−0.270***
	(0.060)	(0.101)	(0.102)	(0.100)	(0.103)	(0.112)	(0.092)
Tax_obs	−0.277***	−0.385***	−0.266***	−0.200**	−0.251**	−0.360***	−0.226***
	(0.054)	(0.101)	(0.098)	(0.077)	(0.098)	(0.102)	(0.081)
Lab_obs	−0.370***	−0.521***	−0.345***	−0.278***	−0.453***	−0.253***	−0.404***
	(0.055)	(0.094)	(0.097)	(0.082)	(0.096)	(0.098)	(0.089)
Fin_Com	0.121	0.185	0.216	−0.015	0.352**	0.028	0.061
	(0.082)	(0.139)	(0.145)	(0.130)	(0.154)	(0.148)	(0.127)
Fin_Tax	0.250***	0.236	0.359**	0.079	0.434***	0.284*	0.111
	(0.080)	(0.144)	(0.145)	(0.118)	(0.157)	(0.151)	(0.118)
Fin_Lab	0.342***	0.304*	0.422***	0.188	0.719***	0.026	0.316**
	(0.083)	(0.158)	(0.147)	(0.124)	(0.157)	(0.155)	(0.129)
Com_Tax	0.376***	0.573***	0.218	0.318**	0.216	0.567***	0.369***
	(0.081)	(0.133)	(0.152)	(0.131)	(0.147)	(0.150)	(0.123)
Com_Lab	0.335***	0.570***	0.285*	0.180	0.278**	0.213	0.506***
	(0.082)	(0.128)	(0.146)	(0.145)	(0.141)	(0.155)	(0.136)
Tax_Lab	0.438***	0.618***	0.273*	0.445***	0.447***	0.581***	0.381***
	(0.083)	(0.144)	(0.148)	(0.124)	(0.153)	(0.177)	(0.117)

Fin_Com_Tax	−0.143	−0.253	−0.085	0.013	−0.175	−0.259	−0.134
	(0.110)	(0.188)	(0.201)	(0.175)	(0.204)	(0.201)	(0.173)
Fin_Com_Lab	−0.202*	−0.161	−0.321	−0.011	−0.369*	0.093	−0.362**
	(0.112)	(0.194)	(0.197)	(0.186)	(0.204)	(0.207)	(0.178)
Fin_Tax_Lab	−0.487***	−0.441*	−0.622***	−0.274	−0.726***	−0.411*	−0.454***
	(0.118)	(0.225)	(0.209)	(0.174)	(0.236)	(0.237)	(0.167)
Com_Tax_Lab	−0.411***	−0.834***	−0.063	−0.398*	−0.160	−0.513**	−0.749***
	(0.127)	(0.219)	(0.225)	(0.217)	(0.225)	(0.252)	(0.203)
Fin_Lab_Com_Tax	0.233	0.481	0.160	0.023	0.093	0.181	0.670***
	(0.162)	(0.294)	(0.284)	(0.264)	(0.301)	(0.309)	(0.255)
Control Var.							
Certificate	0.067***	−0.010	0.077**	0.167***	0.125***	0.070*	−0.015
	(0.021)	(0.032)	(0.036)	(0.041)	(0.038)	(0.038)	(0.035)
University, perc	0.015***	0.024	−0.004	0.030***	−0.015	−0.032	0.038***
	(0.002)	(0.034)	(0.032)	(0.008)	(0.039)	(0.035)	(0.006)
Export_dum	0.021	0.068	0.047	0.022	−0.001	0.135*	0.005
	(0.034)	(0.062)	(0.062)	(0.050)	(0.057)	(0.071)	(0.054)
Foreign_own	0.045	−0.105	0.097	0.035	0.012	0.058	0.009
	(0.043)	(0.099)	(0.070)	(0.066)	(0.081)	(0.070)	(0.077)
Age, log	−0.037**	−0.056	−0.012	−0.063**	−0.009	−0.045	−0.055*
	(0.019)	(0.037)	(0.034)	(0.027)	(0.036)	(0.033)	(0.028)
Manager, log	0.034**	0.093**	−0.004	0.020	0.089**	−0.009	0.018
	(0.012)	(0.042)	(0.035)	(0.035)	(0.042)	(0.037)	(0.035)
Observations	1,289	324	528	437	398	449	442

Note: Standard errors in parentheses. *** $p < 0.01$, ** $p < 0.05$, * $p < 0.1$. Industry dummies and city dummies are included.

firms, confirm that R&D investment fosters sales due to the new products. It also shows that the marginal returns of R&D spending to innovation intensity are diminishing across different sizes and income levels. Firms with a higher turnover are expected to be more innovative compared with firms with small scales of turnover. The estimated coefficients for turnover are significant at 90% across all groups except for the large-sized firms. It is in line with others (Hou and Mohnen, 2013) that a relatively higher turnover increases the percentage of sales due to new products and services of a firm. This effect is more profound in the low-tech sample, given a higher magnitude of the corresponding coefficient.

Mature firms are less innovative, which is consistent with the argument that old firms are less dynamic in terms of changes and innovation (Katrak, 1997; Beck et al., 2008). In contrast, the positive sign of Export_dum implies that the intensity of new products innovation is strengthened by participating in export activities, especially among medium-tech firms. Foreign ownership was expected to foster innovation, but the effects are insignificant in our sample. The possible explanation is that foreign-owned firms tend to conduct R&D and innovation in their homeland rather than set up an R&D center or carry out innovation activities in the host country. University and Manager are indicators to partially represent the absorptive capacity of a firm. With more educated labor, innovation would be effectively assimilated within a firm and eventually translate into new products and services. Such an effect has been uncovered in the full sample as well as the large-sized and high-tech firms. The manager's previous experiences affect innovation performance only found in firms from the group of small-sized and low-tech firms. Certificate is indexed to capture the technological capability of firms. Products and services with internationally recognized certificates represent higher levels of technology experiences. Firms having been granted with such certificate are in general more productive in innovation, as shown by the estimated coefficients of Certificate.

To sum up, the findings present a clear pattern of the determinants to innovation across sectors. Due to the different nature and operation mechanism across different sizes and technology levels, firm-specific variables have shown rather heterogeneous effects on innovation performance.

5.2 Complementarity between obstacles to innovation

Turning to the intrinsic relationships between pairs of obstacles, Table 8.5 presents the complementarity test results. The test results are based on the likelihood ratio test at the 90% significant level[17]. Overall, the results exhibit a clear pattern of connections among obstacles in different size groups and technology levels. In general, the presence of complementarity between obstacles dominates the pattern with respect to sales due to new products and services. This finding is in line with previous studies (Mohnen and Röller, 2005; Galia and Legros, 2004), which confirms the hypothesis: there exists complementarity between labor- and tax-related obstacles in the innovation function. A complementarity

Table 8.5 Complementarity test results

Dependent variable	*Full Sample*	*Size groups*			*Technology Levels*		
		Small (5–25)	*Medium (26–100)*	*Large (>100)*	*Low-tech*	*Medium-tech*	*High-tech*
New product sales							
Fin_Com	N	N	N	N	Y	N	N
Fin_Tax	Y	N	Y	N	Y	Y	N
Fin_Lab	Y	Y	Y	N	Y	N	Y
Com_Tax	Y	Y	N	Y	N	Y	Y
Com_Lab	Y	Y	Y	N	Y	N	Y
Tax_Lab	Y	Y	Y	Y	Y	Y	Y

Note:Y: the presence of complementarity was confirmed; N: complementarity was not confirmed

suggests that the presence of one obstacle attenuates the deterring effect of the other obstacle. A more intuitive interpretation here would be that an additional obstacle does not matter anymore if existing obstacles are already preventing a firm from becoming a product innovator. A policy package that is on target for removing all complementary obstacles would be favored.

Findings also confirm that complementary or substitutive relationships between obstacles are less frequent for firms in high-tech or with a larger number of employees. Firms from high-tech or with large scales are comparatively more resource abundant, in skilled labor or through their past experience. They are less likely to encounter obstacles during the course of innovation, as well as interactions between obstacles. In this circumstance, a policy package would make few impacts on innovation performance compared to policies which are implemented separately.

5.3 Sequence of eliminating obstacles: conditional marginal gains

Rather than merely investigating the interdependent relationship between obstacles to innovation performance across Chinese manufacturing firms, a step further is to compute the marginal effects of having one extra obstacle while other obstacles are present. Table 8.6 gives the average marginal effects of each obstacle to innovation performance conditional on the censored sample. The marginal effects are calculated controlling for the potential complementarity among them. For example, the marginal effect of facing finance barrier for "Full Sample" composites eight elements, which are the estimated coefficients of Fin_obs and the other seven corresponding coefficients[18] with the presence of "Fin": Fin_Com, Fin_Tax, Fin_Lab, Fin_Com_Tax, Fin_Com_Lab, Fin_Tax_Lab, and Fin_Lab_Com_Tax. In total, there would be a decline of 1.4 percentages of sales due to the new products if a firm faces Finance barrier to innovation.

As exhibited in Table 8.6, obstacles faced by firms vary across sectors, income levels, and size groups. The finding verifies that high-income and large-sized firms encounter fewer obstacles compared to those of lower income and relatively smaller sized firms. Tax burdens seem to be the only obstacle faced by large-sized firms, while "inadequate skills" has also been perceived as an evident factor to hinder innovation for high-tech firms. As one may notice, some of the marginal effects of finance-related barrier turn out to be positive. This is a result of having a greater interactive effect that exists between finance obstacles and other obstacles, which cancels out the negative effect induced by "Finance" alone. The presence of the finance barrier would not matter anymore to inhibit the new products sales if the other three obstacles already exist.

Without adequate resources allocated to tackle obstacles together, effective strategies need to be formed with reference to the sequence of removing obstacles. This is of particular relevance for firms in China and other less developed countries. Due to the potentially interdependent relationship among them, the sequence of eliminating obstacles should be carefully scrutinized. A wrong sequence may result in removing obstacles which actually ease the undermining effects of others, and consequently lead to a further loss on innovation performance. Given a higher undermining effect imposed on innovation performance, labor and tax barriers should be first removed. Then barriers related to inadequate finance should follow and informal competition barriers should be the last ones to be removed in the full sample. Table 8.7 shows the suggestive sequence of eliminating obstacles across different sample groups. The sequence suggested in this table corresponds to the marginal effects given in Table 8.6. Obstacles exerting relatively higher undermining effect on innovation are

Table 8.6 Marginal effects, calculated with mean values of each obstacle

	Full Sample	*Small-sized*	*Medium-sized*	*Large-sized*	*Low-tech*	*Medium-tech*	*High-tech*
Finance	−0.014*	−0.019*	0.001	−0.020	−0.026	−0.015	0.047
Compet	−0.011**	−0.008**	0.029**	−0.058	0.009	−0.026	−0.021
Tax	−0.037**	−0.024**	−0.003**	−0.070**	−0.048**	−0.112*	−0.043
Labor	−0.045**	−0.036**	−0.077**	−0.034	−0.015**	−0.028**	−0.092**

*** $p < 0.01$, ** $p < 0.05$, * $p < 0.1$.

Table 8.7 Sequence of eliminating obstacles with respect to the marginal gains to innovation

	Full Sample	*Small-sized*	*Medium-sized*	*Large-sized*	*Low-tech*	*Medium-tech*	*High-tech*
First	Labor	Labor	Labor	Tax	Tax	Tax	Labor
Second	Tax	Tax	Tax	Compet	Finance	Labor	Tax
Third	Finance	Finance	Finance	Labor	Labor	Compet	Compet
Last	Compet	Compet	Compet	Finance	Compet	Finance	Finance

suggested to be removed before those with lower marginal effect. Take the "Full sample" as an example; "the shortage of skilled labour" appeared to severely undermine innovation performance in comparison to the other three obstacles, and thus, it needs to be tackled as a priority when designing government policies. The marginal effect of "Tax burden" is −0.037, which takes second place and is followed by "Finance" and "Competition."

6 Conclusion and policy remarks

The national innovation system which was proposed by Lundvall (1992) and Nelson (1993) highlighted the complexity of the innovation process and the potential barriers and interactions between these barriers at different levels and stages within firms, organizations or a country. In view of innovation policy, it is crucial to gain a better understanding of structures beneath these obstacles faced by firms. Appropriate policies could thereby be instigated to attenuate barriers which may lead to failures in innovation. Investigating the potential complementarity and substitutability between obstacles enables us to obtain a clear picture on how obstacles interact with each other in determining firms' innovation performance.

The development path of China has important implications for the world, not only in terms of its economic impact, but also in terms of the experiences in guiding and promoting the growth process for other developing countries. Not only emphasized in the substantial role of knowledge inputs – R&D – in helping a firm become an innovator, the empirical results also exhibited that obstacles facing by firms vary across sectors, income levels and size groups. The complementarity test suggests that four types of obstacles are complementary factors in strengthening innovation of Chinese manufacturing firms. Such an interdependent relationship implies that an additional obstacle does not matter if existing obstacles are already preventing a firm from becoming a product innovator. Hence, policy instruments should be designed to eliminate obstacles altogether rather than removing them individually. Under such circumstances, the presence of one obstacle (e.g., inadequate skills and high tax rate) would exacerbate the undermining effects induced by other obstacles (e.g., inadequate internal finance). In addition, most developing countries are incapable of coping with all innovation barriers simultaneously due to the shortage of internal and external resources. Effectively removing innovation barriers requires firms and governments to carefully design rational strategies. The empirical analyses have shown that eliminating obstacles should be considered to be sequentially done in order to achieve the optimal innovation performance.

Without obtaining the full information on process innovation, the current study is constrained to look only at product innovation. Other technological sourcing is also critical for firms in China since only 1.6% of firms engage in R&D and there are about 11.4% of firms that claim to have product innovation. About 10% of sampled firms adopt other channels as technological sourcing than R&D investment, which might cause a potential missing variable bias in estimating the innovation function. Another limitation of this study is that some firms might learn to cope with obstacles by innovating instead of realizing obstacles beforehand, which could explain the positive coefficients for obstacle variables in the innovation intensity function. Last, concrete policy suggestions on the sequence of removing obstacles could be obtained by computing the marginal effects of each obstacle by taking the potential complementarity into account.

Notes

1 The dash lines, where C and F lie, refer to the situation in which complementarity or substitutability are absent. In comparison to C and F, A and D refer to the situation where complementarity or substitutability are present.

2 The sample data reports all information even for firms who claimed not having innovation during the period under survey. Therefore, it is assumed sample selection bias will not appear in such circumstances and we choose Tobit type I instead of the Tobit type II (Heckman, 1979) model.

3 Due to the fact that R&D is not the only technological sourcing to innovation, other sourcing channels such as technology licensing, embedded machinery and imitation (these information are not available from the current data source) may also present and contribute to innovation output. R&D will not be used as indicator for the selection equation in the Heckman model. Based on the data in the empirical part, there are about 36.55% of firms which claims to be product innovators without R&D investment.

4 In Equation 8.2, subscript i has been deleted to ease the writing.

5 See section 3 for more details on the measurement of obstacles.

6 Previous studies of Athey and Stern (2002) and Mohnen and Röller (2005) refer to as "strictly complementary" if the greater or equal sign "≥" is replaced by a strictly greater sign ">."

7 HT1 is not defined to be exhaustive. The null hypothesis of HT1 is equality only.

8 The Wald Test has also been used in testing hypotheses (5) and (6) and results are consistent with the ones derived by using likelihood ratio test, results of Wald Test are available upon request. The empirical estimation was done by using statistical program R.

9 Enterprise Surveys (www.enterprisesurveys.org), The World Bank.

10 Firms with fewer than five employees (3.6%) have been deleted from our sample. Firms that do not aim at innovating are also filtered out from sample (D'Este et al., 2008, Mohnen and Röller, 2005; Savignac, 2008). Specifically, firms not aiming at innovating do not carry out innovation activities at all and are more likely to ignore obstacles to innovation. We assume that non-innovative firms which experienced failure of innovation would encounter at least one of four types of obstacles. Hence, we drop firms which have no new or updated products/services, and at the same time, report none of the chosen obstacles. It accounts for 6.2% of the total sample.

11 Process-innovation–related measurements are not covered by the current questionnaire, so the influence of obstacles to process innovation will not be studied here.

12 The classification of the technology level is based on the OECD classification. For a detailed definition, please see: www.oecd.org/sti/sci-tech/43281062.pdf.

13 As shown in Table 8.2, there are about 66% of firms with a size of smaller than 100 employees. The total sample is divided into three groups according to the distribution of the size of firms: 5–25 (25% of total sample), 26–100 (42% of total sample) and above 100 (34% of total sample).

14 By filtering out firms that do not intend to become an innovator (see note 10), it helps us to rule out the potential non-innovation related obstacles.

15 Informal firms (sectors) refer to firms (sectors) which are neither taxed nor monitored by any form of government.

16 This is done in order to correct for a sample selection problem (Mohnen and Röller, 2005; Savignac, 2008). In particular, the survey includes two questions asking whether the firm has achieved new products/service innovation and upgraded their products/services during the period under review. If a firm responded negatively to these two questions, we classified it as a non-potential products innovator. The underlying rationale is that non-innovating firms that did not experience any obstacle to innovation are unlikely to have the intention to innovate.

17 A multivariate one-sided hypothesis test is used in testing complementarity versus substitutability between two obstacles. Since our results show that a method combining HT1 and HT2 in general gives more efficient conclusion, the results in Table 8.5 are based on both HT1 and HT2. For instance, complementarity between two obstacles can be concluded only when one rejects the null hypothesis in HT1 and at the same time accepts the null hypothesis in HT2.

18 In order to calculate the marginal effects induced by one obstacle, the mean values of obstacle variables, which appear in the interaction term, are multiplied with the estimated coefficient. Specifically, the marginal effect of "Finance" barrier equals: _b[Fin_obs] + _b[Fin_Com] * mean[Com] + _b[Fin_Tax] * mean[Tax] + _b[Fin_Lab] * mean[Lab] + _b[Fin_Com_Tax] * mean[Com] * mean[Tax] + _b[Fin_Com_Lab] * mean[Com] * mean[Lab] + _b[Fin_Tax_Lab] * mean[Tax] * mean[Lab] + _b[Fin_Lab_Com_Tax] * mean[Lab] * mean[Com] * mean[Tax], where "b" symbolizes the estimated coefficient and "mean[]" indicates the value at mean. Standard errors are computed by using delta method, which is based on the first order approximation around the mean. For more details, see Oehlert (1992).

References

Arrow, K. J. (1962), "Economic Welfare and the Allocation of Resources for Invention." R. R. Nelson (ed.), *The Rate and Direction of Inventive Activity*, Princeton, NJ: Princeton University Press, 609–625.

Athey, S. and S. Stern (2002) "An Empirical Framework for Testing Theories about Complementarity in Organizational Design." NBER Working Paper No. W6600, NBER, Cambridge.

Baldwin, J. and P. Hanel (2003) "Innovation and Knowledge Creation in an Open Economy." *Canadian Industry and International Implications*, Cambridge: Cambridge University Press.

Baldwin, J. and Z. Lin (2002) "Impediments to Advanced Technology Adoption for Canadian Manufacturers." *Research Policy* 31: 1–18.

Basant, R. and B. Fikkert (1996) "The Effects of R&D, Foreign Technology Purchase, and Domestic and International Spillovers on Productivity in Indian Firms." *Review of Economics and Statistics* 78(2): 187–199.

Beck, T., A. Demirgüc-Kunt, L. Laeven and R. Levine (2008) "Finance, Firm Size and Growth." *Journal of Money, Credit and Banking* 40(7): 1379–1405.

Cassiman, B. and R. Veugelers (2006) "In Search of Complementarity in the Innovation Strategy: Internal R&D and External Knowledge Acquisition." *Management Science* 52: 68–82.

Cohen, W. and D. Levinthal (1990) "Absorptive Capacity: A New Perspective on Learning and Innovation." *Administrative Science Quarterly* 35(1): 128–152.

Cooper, C. (1989) *Technology and Innovation in International Economy*, Maastricht, The Netherlands: United Nation University Press.

D'Este P., S. Iammarino and N. Tunzelmann (2008) "What Hampers Innovation? Evidence from the UK CIS4." *Science and Technology Policy Research* 168.

Doms, M. and J. B. Jensen (1998) "Comparing Wages, Skills and Productivity between Domestically and Foreign-Owned Manufacturing Establishments in the United States." R. E. Baldwin, R. E. Lipsey and J. D. Richardson (eds.), *Geography and Ownerships as Basis for Economic Accounting*, Chicago: University of Chicago Press.

Dougherty, D. (1992) "Interpretive Barriers to Successful Product Innovation in Large Firms." *Organization Science* 3(2): 179–202.

Ferriani, S., E. Garnsey and D. Probert (2008) "Sustaining Breakthrough Innovation in Large Established Firms: Learning Traps and Counteracting Strategies." J. Bessant and T. Venables (eds.), *Creating Wealth from Knowledge*, Cheltenham, UK: Edward Elgar.

Fu, X., W. Woo and J. Hou (2016) "Technological Innovation Policy in China: The Lessons, and the Necessary Changes Ahead." *Economic Change and Restructuring* 49(2): 139–157.

Furman, J. L., M. E. Porter and S. Stern (2002) "The Determinants of National Innovative Capacity." *Research Policy* 31(6): 899–933.

Galia, F. and D. Legros (2004) "Complementarities between Obstacles to Innovation: Evidence from France." *Research Policy* 33(8): 1185–1199.

Globerman, S., J. Ries and I. Vertinsky (1994) "The Economic Performance of Foreign Affiliates in Canada." *Canadian Journal of Economics* 27: 143–156.

Gouriéroux, C., A. Holly and A. Monfort (1982) "Likelihood Ratio Test, Wald Test, and Kuhn-Tucker Test in Linear Models with Inequality Constraints on the Regression Parameters." *Econometrica* 50(1): 63–80.

Greene, W. H (2003) *Econometric Analysis* (5th ed.), Upper Saddle River, NJ: Prentice Hall.

Hadjimanolis, A. (1999) "Barriers to Innovation for SMEs in a Small Less Developed Country." *Technovation* 19: 561–570.

Hadjimanolis, A. (2003) "The Barriers Approach to Innovation." *The International Handbook on Innovation*, New York: Pergamon.

Heckman, J. J. (1976) "The Common Structure of Statistical Models of Truncation, Sample Selection and Limited Dependent Variables and a Simple Estimator for Such Models." *Annals of Economic and Social Measurement* 5(4): 475–492.

Heckman, J. J. (1979) "Sample Selection Bias as a Specification Error." *Econometrica* 47(1): 153–161.

Helfat, C. E. and M. B. Lieberman (2002) "The Birth of Capabilities: Market Entry and the Importance of Pre-History." *Industrial and Corporate Change* 11: 725–760.

Henderson, R. (1993) "Underinvestment and Incompetence as Responses to Radical Innovation: Evidence from the Photolithographic Alignment Equipment Industry." *Rand Journal of Economics* 24: 248–270.

Himmelberg, C. and B. Petersen (1994) "R&D and Internal Finance: A Panel Study of Small Firms in High-Tech Industries." *Review of Economics and Statistics* 76: 38–51.

Hou, J. and P. Mohnen (2013) "Complementarity between in-House R&D and Technology Purchasing: Evidence from Chinese Manufacturing Firms." *Oxford Development Studies* 41(3): 347–371.

Johnston, J. and J. DiNardo (1997) *Econometric Methods* (4th ed.), New York: McGraw-Hill.

Katrak, H. (1997) "Developing Countries' Imports of Technology, in-House Technologies Capabilities and Efforts: An Analysis of the Indian Experience." *Journal of Development Economics* 53: 67–83.

Kiley, M. T. (1999) "The Supply of Skilled Labour and Skill-Biased Technological Change." *Economic Journal* 109: 708–724.

Kimura, F. and K. Kiyota (2007) "Foreign-Owned Versus Domestically-Owned Firms: Economic Performance in Japan." *Review of Development Economics* 11: 31–48.

Kleinknecht, A. and P. Mohnen (2002) *Innovation and Firm Performance: Econometric Explorations of Survey Data*, New York: Palgrave Macmillan.

Klomp, L. and G. van Leeuwen (1999) *The Importance of Innovation for Firm Performance*, Amsterdam: Statistics Netherlands.

Lundvall, B. (1992) *National Systems of Innovation: Towards a theory of Innovation and Interactive Learning*, London: Pinter Publishers.

Lokshin, B., R. Belderbos and M. Carree (2008) "The Productivity Effects of Internal and External R&D: Evidence from a Dynamic Panel Data Model." *Oxford Bulletin of Economics and Statistics* 70(3): 399–413.

Mairesse, J. and P. Mohnen (2001) "To Be or not to Be Innovative: An Exercise in Measurement." Working Paper 8644: 35, Cambridge, MA: NBER.

Milgrom, P. and J. Roberts (1995) "Complementarities and Fit Strategy, Structure, and Organizational Change in Manufacturing." *Journal of Accounting and Economics* 19(2–3): 179–208.

Mohnen, P. (2000) "R&D Tax Incentives: Issues and Evidence." D. Neven and L. Röller (eds.), *The Political Economy of Industrial Policy in Europe and the Member States*, Berlin: Ed. Sigma, 183–199.

Mohnen, P., F. Palm, S. Van Der Loeff and A. Tiwari (2008) "Financial Constraints and Other Obstacles: Are they a Threat to Innovation Activity?" *De Economist* 156(2): 201–214.

Mohnen, P. and L.-H. Röller (2005) "Complementarities in Innovation Policy." *European Economic Review* 49: 1431–1450.

Mulkay, B., B. H. Hall and J. Mairesse (2001) "Firm Level Investment and R&D in France and the United States." Deutsche Bundesbank (ed.), *Investing Today for the World of Tomorrow*, Berlin: Springer Verlag.

Nelson, R. (1993) *National Innovation Systems: A Comparative Analysis*, Oxford: Oxford University Press.

OECD (2003) *Towards a Knowledge-Based Economy*, Paris: OECD.

Oehlert, G. W (1992) "A Note on the Delta Method." *American Statistician* 46: 27–29.

Piatier, A. (1984) *Barriers to Innovation*, London: Frances Pinter Publishers Ltd.

Savignac, F. (2006) "The Impact of Financial Constraints on Innovation: Evidence from French Manufacturing Firms." *Cahiers de la Maison des Sciences Économiques* v06042, Université Panthéon-Sorbonne working paper (Paris I).

Savignac, F. (2008) "Impact of Financial Constraints on Innovation: What Can Be Learned from a Direct Measure?" *Economics of Innovation and New Technology* 17(6): 553–569.

Schneider, F. (2005) "Shadow Economies Around the World: What do We Really Know?" *European Journal of Political Economy* 23(1): 598–642.

Schoonhoven, C., K. Eisenhardt and K. Lyman (1990) "Speeding Products to Market: Waiting Time to First Product Introduction in New Firms." *Administrative Science Quarterly* 35: 177–207.

Stockdale, B. (2002) "UK Innovation Survey 2001" *Economic Trends* 580: 36–42.

Tiwari, A. K., P. Mohnen, F. C. Palm and S. Schim van der Loeff (2008) "Financial Constraints and R&D Investment Evidence from CIS." C. van Beers, A. Kleinknecht, R. Ortt and R. Verburg (eds.), *Determinants of Innovative Behaviour: A Firm's Internal Practices and Its External Environments*, London: Palgrave Publishers, 217–242.

Tourigny, D. and C. D. Le (2004) "Impediments to Innovation Faced by Canadian Manufacturing Firms." *Economics of Innovation and New Technology* 13(3): 217–250.

Tripsas, M. (1997) "Unravelling the Process of Creative Destruction: Complementary Assets and Incumbent Survival in the Typesetter Industry." *Strategic Management Journal* 18(Summer Special Issue): 119–142.

Tushman, M. L. and P. Anderson (1986) "Technological Discontinuities and Organizational Environments." *Administrative Science Quarterly* 31: 439–465.

Verbeek, M. (2000) *A Guide to Modern Econometrics*, Chichester: John Wiley & Sons.

Appendix 8-A

The identification of the top four obstacles to firms in EECA countries is based upon the question "Which of the following elements of the business environment, if any, currently represents the biggest obstacle faced by this establishment?"

Obstacles	*Obs.*	*Percentage*
Access to finance (Finance)	***274***	***21.26***
Access to land	62	4.81
Business licensing and permits	3	0.23
Corruption	14	1.09
Courts	2	0.16
Crime, theft, and disorder	8	0.62
Customs and trade regulations	19	1.47
Electricity	73	5.66
Inadequately educated workforce (Labor)	***234***	***18.15***
Labor regulations	26	2.02
Political instability	8	0.62
Practices of competitors in the informal sector (Informal competition)	***157***	***12.18***
Tax administration	55	4.27
Tax rates (Tax)	***250***	***19.39***
Transport	87	6.75
Does not apply	17	1.32
Total	1,289	100

Appendix 8-B

Constructing the obstacle variables are based up on the following questions individually. Questions are asked about obstacles to innovation on a four-point Likert scale. The corresponding obstacle variable takes the value 1 if the answer is marked as a major or very severe obstacle (scores 3 and 4) and takes the value zero otherwise.

Finance: Is access to finance, which includes availability and cost, interest rates, fees, and collateral requirements, No Obstacle (0), a Minor Obstacle (1), a Moderate Obstacle (2), a Major Obstacle (3), or a Very Severe Obstacle (4) to the current operations of this establishment?

Labor: Is an inadequately educated workforce No Obstacle (0), a Minor Obstacle (1), a Moderate Obstacle (2), a Major Obstacle (3), or a Very Severe Obstacle (4) to the current operations of this establishment?

Information competition: Are practices of competitors in the informal sector No Obstacle (0), a Minor Obstacle (1), a Moderate Obstacle (2), a Major Obstacle (3), or a Very Severe Obstacle (4) to the current operations of this establishment?

Tax: Are tax rates No Obstacle (0), a Minor Obstacle (1), a Moderate Obstacle (2), a Major Obstacle (3), or a Very Severe Obstacle (4) to the current operations of this establishment.

9 Innovation in the digital age

An opportunity for China's catching up

Yongmin Wu and Yushan Ji

1 Introduction

Driven by emerging technological revolutions in information and communications technology (ICT) and artificial intelligence (AI), innovation in the digital age shows a brand-new feature. Intangible information is now more valuable than traditional production factors. Thus, the mode of production and organization is emerging in a new, more agile way which is called flexible production as well (Rigby et al., 2016; Cooper and Sommer, 2016). The "platform" mode, in which firms may cocreate values with customers through a variety of internet-based mechanisms, will gradually become the mainstream mode, and the boundaries of firms will become increasingly blurred (Sawhney et al., 2005). Compared with the traditional production system, the cost of R&D, production, and sales in the digital economy is greatly reduced, and the entire product life cycle is also shortened (Sawhney et al., 2005; Rigby et al., 2016; Cooper and Sommer, 2016). Pressured by the ICT environment, the division of labor in the world will continue to deepen (Klinenberg, 2016), and all fields of R&D, production, and sales can all be integrated ports in the "whole-industry-chain" (WIC). All links in the WIC will jointly create, pass, and share values together. For example, Xiaomi Company has formed a "user-information-organization" three-dimensional flexible value network, which realizes "value co-production" under the WIC. The manufacturing value chain with the traditional "smile curve" shape (Shih, 1996) will be subtly reshaped. As a catch-up economy, China has devoted tremendous efforts to improve its innovative capabilities in the wake of the next industrial revolution. In particular, China has made substantial investments in core technologies such as the Internet, big data, and AI. Compared with the previous three industrial revolutions, the innovative characteristics of the digital era have given China great potential to take advantage of the technological needs in the new industrial revolution and catch up with the developed countries.

This chapter explores "opportunity windows" by analyzing the innovative features in the digital era and suggests that China's comprehensive competitive advantage might enable technological catch-up. Section 2 summarizes and puts forward a general theoretical framework for developing countries to achieve technological catch-up within an evolutionary frame of thinking and discusses the policy implications of the developing economies. Section 3 discusses the "opportunity window" in China through the analysis of the innovative features in the digital age based on the theoretical framework. Section 4 illustrates the comprehensive competitive advantage to achieve technological catch-up in China compared with other countries and explains why digitalization may provide Chinese firms with a window of opportunity.

2 The theoretical framework of technological catch-up

Technological catch-up means that developing countries or regions gradually eliminate technological gaps with developed countries through their own efforts in the process of technological development, transcending developed countries (Perez and Soete, 1988). At present, China is still in a period of rapid technological catch-up as a whole. However, innovation in the digital age has more sophisticated evolutionary characteristics and provides a good "opportunity window" for China to catch up quickly. Under this background, this section will summarize and put forward a general theoretical framework for developing countries to achieve technological catching up, comprehensively sort out the technological catch-up theory from classicism to evolutionary economics, reveal the logic of evolutionary economics on technological catch-up, and summarize the basic ideas and policies about technological catch-up.

2.1 Technological catch-up and trajectory switches

Economic studies on developing countries catching up with developed countries can be traced back to the catching-up to Britain by Germany, Austria, and other countries in the process of industrialization (Mathews, 2002). Scholars (e.g., Lin et al., 1996) using the theory of comparative advantage uphold Ricardo's comparative advantage theory in trade theory and Heckscher-Ohlin's factor endowment theory that the differences in the initial resource endowments at the national level lead to significant cost differences in the same product across countries. A country's industrialization and economic development should follow this cost comparative advantage. Therefore, developing countries should stick to the low-cost advantage of production factors (such as labor force in China) and promote economic growth through developing less tech-intensive and labor-intensive industries (Lin et al., 1996; Steil et al., 2002), rather than relying on comparative advantage in order to realize dynamic upgrading from labor-intensive to technology-intensive industries, eventually achieve economic development and technological catch-up, and converge with the developed countries.

Gerchenkron's (1962) classical "advantage of backwardness" theory suggests that the developing countries' posterior status in the process of industrialization can bring some unique benefits and advantages, such as learning business models and imitating technologies, from the advanced economies. This is partly due to the particular fact that developing countries can introduce mature production technologies at relatively low cost while the developed countries heavily rely on extensive R&D investment in emerging technologies (Nolan and Lenski, 1985; Thurow, 1993, Shin, 2017; Lee and Ki, 2017). On the other hand, it shows that developing countries can thoroughly learn from the experience and lessons of the economic development and institutional changes in the developed countries and avoid detours (Fan, 1998). This backward advantage, however, can be applied neither by the developed countries nor by developing countries through their efforts and is completely symbiotic with the backward development. Therefore, as long as developing countries accumulate necessary capabilities in education, management, and research, they can achieve more manageable and faster economic growth than the developed countries can.

Although both comparative advantage and backward advantage propose the possibility of technological catch-up, few cases in practice have achieved catch-up by merely relying on these frameworks. This is because comparative advantage may lead countries to a "comparative advantage trap" and thus inhibits the development of capital, entrepreneurial spirit, and technological capabilities in developing countries (Kshetri, 2017). Furthermore, the preference for backward advantage also tends to lead developing countries to rely on a path of technological introduction and fall into the technological development cycle of "backwardness-introduction-backwardness-introduction" (Mazzucato, 2017). As an alternative, countries pay attention to the historical imitation of the system structure in catch-up, and they can fully achieve the replacement of economic and technological leadership (Freeman, 1987).

Evolutionary economics (Dosi, 1982; Perez, 2009) regards innovation as the core driving force of economic development and opens up new ideas of technological catch-up research centered on the concept of innovation in the sense of creative destruction. On the one hand, these studies inherit Schumpeter's economic cycle and the "creative destruction" of technological innovation. On the other hand, they widely draw on Darwin's evolution theory, and argue that technological evolution in the economic system is not simply a process of "input-output" but rather a process similar to "biological evolution" formed by different stages of initial optimization, incremental innovation, maturity, and decline (Steil et al., 2002). Technological evolution begins with a number of radical innovations, which lead to a series of new products and new approaches, followed by continuous improvement and development through a series of cumulative incremental innovations, and finally to maturity and recession. In this process, radical innovation has an obvious historical contingency. Only such a "devastating" radical innovation can be bred in the long economic depression (Dosi, 1982). However, once radical innovations emerge, the direction and speed of technological evolution follow similar "trajectories" and show accumulative nature (Dosi, 1982; Deng, 1993; Yu et al., 2015). Therefore, technological catch-up involves the initial position of a country on a fixed-technology trajectory and the relative speed of technological development. That is to say, latecomers in the technological track need to bridge the technological gap with the leaders through faster technological progress and catch up with them under certain conditions. Alternatively, a country may pass over certain technological stages and create different technological trajectories. In other words, achieving a technological change in leadership among countries may have a different kind of non-linear technological path (Perez, 2009). The conventional technological catch-up often links with technological introduction and imitation or pursuing the same technology development track. Some scholars (e.g., Lee and Lim, 2001), through studying emerging industrial economies in Asia, argue that developing countries can significantly enhance their own productivity and technological capabilities by introducing, imitating, and re-innovating advanced technologies from developed countries in the short term, so as to achieve the goal of technological catch-up. The radical technological catch-up suggests technological leaps or jumps in the existing technological trajectory, which is based on the evolution of the technology itself. Developing countries, with sufficient technological capabilities and infrastructure, can achieve technological catch-up by moving ahead of the developed countries into the emerging technological trajectories at the early proliferation stages (Perez and Soete, 1988). Alternatively, they pay attention in order to tap their potential and jump some of the development stages of technological trajectory; they even create their technological trajectory to catch up with the developed countries (Field, 1992; Hobday, 1995).

According to Perez (2009), who assumes that technological catch-up is not a linear process, it is unrealistic for developing countries to adopt rapid technological development to achieve the replacement of technological leadership among countries on a mature technological trajectory. This is because, on the one hand, the cumulative effect of learning and the external effects of incremental innovation in the established technological trajectory give the incumbent leader a clear advantage over the followers; most developing countries can only organize some small-scale continuous innovations or localize new technologies in developed countries through assimilation and absorption (Shin, 2017). On the other hand, with the promotion of economic globalization, the developed countries have captured the manufacturing enterprises of developing countries, locked their tracks of technological innovation through the global value chain, and controlled the international division of labor system. The developing countries can only follow the existing mature technologies when they carry out technological innovation, and their technological catch-up can just always move toward the technological frontier but will never reach the technological frontier (Shin, 2017). Getting into the new technological trajectory, or creating another one, only offers the possibility of catching up because it depends on the "opportunity window" provided by economic and technological systems (Perez, 2001).

Nevertheless, as the developed countries mainly dominate the existing economic structure and technological system, developing countries are only likely to lead the new technological trajectory, or create another technological trajectory, if economic restructuring and changes in the existing technological trajectory occur. Otherwise, catch-up will only have a disruptive impact on the country's economic structure and technological system, thus leading to a "structural crisis" (Shin, 2017). How to evade the above two crises has become an unavoidable challenge for developing countries in technological catch-up. Along the path Schumpeter pioneered, Bowles (2004) argues that the periodic alternation of stability and "creative destruction" in the process of moving among equilibria leads to an "intermittent equilibrium" in global technological evolution. In this process, some essential discontinuities in technological evolution can determine the scope of changes in technological systems and the magnitude of global economic structural readjustment.

The technological catch-up of developing countries depends on these changing opportunities for development. More specifically, Lee and Ki (2017) consider the technological trajectory of incremental innovation as a feature of self-independence, and it is impossible to achieve technological change or structural change in technological systems through cumulative incremental innovation. Only when the original technological system enters the period of diminishing returns, and thus the existing economic driving force loses its potential, will a comprehensive adjustment of the economic structure be emerging. In other words, in order to ease market collapse or promote renewed rapid economic growth, the recession in the longwave of the business cycle will not only create new opportunities for changes in the technological track but will also be able to promote the readjustment of the global economic structure. Such significant discontinuities in technological evolution provide the "opportunity window" for developing countries to achieve technological catch-up during the depression period of long economic cycles (Clark et al., 1981).

Clark et al. (1981) argue that although economic depressions deteriorate social and economic conditions in the long-term, they offer great opportunities for developing countries to achieve technological catch-up. Under the combined effect of bounded rationality, irreversibility, and path dependence, each country is only a starter in the evolution of the emerging technological system. Developing countries, without the experience and constraints of the mature technological trajectory, will not face the fierce resistance of the vested interest groups in the original paradigm, and will, therefore, be more easily able to provide a sound supporting environment to develop emerging technologies through extensive social changes, and will replace the technological leaders easily. In the meantime, in order to overcome the limitation of market growth, developed countries usually expand the space for mature technologies through international technology transfer. This actually provides an excellent opportunity for developing countries to achieve technological progress in leaps and bounds. It is not easy for them to obtain these sophisticated technological systems, but developing countries can also modernize and update proven technologies by taking advantage of the emerging generic technologies, thus achieving technological catch-up (Perez, 2009).

2.2 Some reflections on catch-up history

Yu et al. (2015), to some extent, restore the tradition of economic history that focuses on technology and industrialization, focusing on the technological leadership switch among countries. Looking at the evolution of the global economy, the replacement of technological leadership among countries is rare but does exist. The British in the eighteenth century were the first in modern history to substantially widen the technological gap with all other countries in the world. However, at the end of the nineteenth century, the United States and Germany successfully managed to catch up to the United Kingdom, achieving global technological leadership. In the mid-to-late twentieth century, Japan began to catch up with the United States, eventually narrowing the technological gap and gaining a leading position in some technological areas. At the end of the twentieth century, "the miracle of East Asia" showed that technological catch-up at the national level was continuing.

Viotti (1997) argues that the changes in technological trajectories in the long economic wave may generate new leaders and followers. The United Kingdom's global technological leadership, rooted in the radical innovation in the emerging industries (industrial fields) in the mid-eighteenth century as a series of breakthroughs in emerging textile technologies, also benefited from the comprehensive reconstruction of traditional family handicraft industry by emerging technologies. The United States and Germany's catch-up was mainly achieved through radical innovation in emerging industries rather than incremental change in traditional industries (cotton textile industry). Higher labor prices, abundant natural resources, and a huge domestic market in North America have induced the replacement of labor by capital and natural resources, stimulated and formed technological trajectories for labor saving, capital intensive, and standardized production. In the mid-to-late twentieth century, Japan's catch-up not only made breakthroughs in such emerging areas as microelectronics, but the recovery of traditional industries (automotive industry) with emerging technologies was also a critical path (Perez, 2001). The tangible capital, scale-dependent technology track was gradually declining; technological changes favoring intangible productive assets began to emerge. That is, the new technological system placed particular emphasis on the labor force that promoted higher education through the enhancement of demand effects, research and development innovation, and investment in intangible productive assets such as the promotion of new technologies among the public (Engerman and Gallman, 2000). Japan seized this opportunity and successfully reached the high end of the industry. It has fiercely competed with the United States in such traditional areas as the electronics industry, mechatronics and other emerging fields with semiconductors and integrated circuits as its core, and the automobile industry.

To sum up, the history of technological catching-up shows to a certain extent that the changing of technological trajectories has indeed provided an excellent catching-up window for latecomers. The United States, Germany, and Japan have seized the timing opportunity created by technological innovation and successfully achieved technological catching-up. The current digital age is an era of technological trajectories changing. To grasp the essence and opportunity window of innovation in the digital age, China can significantly increase the possibility of catching up.

2.3 Policy implications for technological catch-up

Technological catch-up in developing countries is neither self-development linked with backwardness nor a convergence induced by market forces in a free economy, but a manifestation and result of the political will of the state (Narula, 2003). In this process, social and economic institutions provide the basic rules for the interaction of economic agents and shape the nature, extent, and speed of their technological catch-up (Narula, 2003). To take full advantage of the "opportunity window" for technological catch-up and actively activate the production potential for technological change, the developing countries may completely reconstruct the innovation policies. The crucial issue to establish innovation policies is to adjust various factors, e.g., in the fields of technology, the organizational system, instead of simply formulating a large and lagging central plan and entering a large-scale government investment, which is the exact practice of developing a relatively mature industry. Moreover, the industrial structure also may promptly react to the technology trajectory changes. This interaction process may require governmental efforts, i.e., innovation policies, to coordinate those structural changes to guide and rapidly build an optimal behavioral model that adapts to emerging technologies and makes the best use of these emerging technologies (Dosi, 1982). This pattern of behavior not only effectively addresses the challenges posed by changes in markets, public institutions, and the business environment, but also significantly improves the functioning of national innovation systems and enhances national capacity to respond to and utilize catch-up opportunities (Metcalfe, 1998). Limited by bounded rationality and path dependence, in an economic and social environment that completely adapts to the requirements of the previous technical paradigms, there is no optimal behavioral model to start a new emerging technology by itself and without any price. Despite the fact that developing countries are not bound by the successful experience and are opposed by stakes, since all economic systems have some degree of inertia and economic subjects are not completely rational, the overall adjustment of technology, economy, system, organization, and thinking within developing countries is a slow and challenging process.

Therefore, developing countries need to emphasize consensus within the entire socio-economic system. That is, during the strategic catch-up period, what matters more is not only the rapid economic growth but also the construction of a sustainable growth foundation that requires cultivating the capacity of developing a technological system and emerging industries. At the same time, in this process, an effective promotion and extensive penetration for such radical innovation is the key to being successful in catching up, which means that the construction of the optimal behavioral model that serves the technological evolution has at least a role as crucial as the radical innovation. In addition, intensive innovation policies encompass all government actions aimed at promoting and accelerating technological progress and creating and disseminating new knowledge, new technologies, and new skills through public and private R&D activities, and making effective use of achievements in economic and social fields to increase social wealth (Schmoch et al., 2006). Developing countries may develop their national ability by reshaping educational and training systems, science and technology policies, and other economic actors (Louca and Freeman, 2002). Innovation policies should induce and support collective action by technology-based start-ups and innovative small and medium enterprises in striking the technological frontier. These policies should also encourage enterprises to gradually eradicate the management level within the organization and promote enterprises to build a flexible network. Meanwhile, a presupposition of enabling technological catch-up is that the government extensively protects civil society, providing a broad platform for citizens to communicate with each other. Innovation policies should emphasize citizens' policy participation and participation capabilities, activating the flexibility of all participants through the protection of citizens' property rights and other classical liberal rights.

3 Opportunity windows for China in the digitalization era

Despite the rapid advances in information and communication technology (ICT) that began in the 1990s that have driven the complete integration of the ICT revolution with the last industrial revolution (Rifkin, 2011), technological change and the global economic structure have not stopped. Judging from the *status quo* in the global economy, the impact of the 2008 financial crisis still challenges many of the largest economies. Economic recessions may force economic actors to seek out technological changes (Clark et al., 1981; Perez, 2010). After the financial crisis, both industrialized countries and emerging countries devoted efforts to increase technological innovation and to develop emerging industries as a breakthrough for revitalizing the domestic economy and gaining advantages in the increasingly fierce international competition, and all of them are accelerating the strategic layout of emerging technologies and industries (Rifkin, 2011).

ICT breakthroughs can improve production efficiency, optimize operational practices, and create new business opportunities, which can extend the life cycle of traditional industrial modes to some extent, but does not restructure economic structure. On the contrary, the persistence of the 2008 financial crisis implies that the world is facing an entirely new opportunity to change its technological trajectory and adjust its economic structure. Rifkin (2011) even thinks that the global economic system is on the eve of a new round of industrial revolution. There is no doubt that China is actually in a transformative period that may reshape the global economic pattern. The "opportunity window" for developing countries to achieve technological catch-up is open.

Entering the current historical digital stage of innovation and technological progress, China is rapidly evolving. The new round of an industrial revolution with emerging technologies such as the Internet and AI is accelerating. In this context, in order to implement innovation-driven development and achieve technological catch-up, China may accurately grasp the characteristics of the production mode in the digital era. To sum up, the transformation of the production mode in the digital era is based on ICT and big data technology. The information revolution and the Internet industry will fundamentally change the global economy, reshape the people's economic activities and behavioral patterns, and create a new industrial ecosystem. Regarding China's intensive investment in ICT fields and human capital accumulation in the last two decades, and its aggressive industrial policies, we may propose that the ongoing industrial revolution will be an excellent opportunity for China to realize technological catch-up in these fields.

3.1 Invisible assets in production resources

In the era of the digital economy, invisible information and data have become the most precious resources. The pursuit of intelligence, ecology, and humanity makes the collection, storage, processing, and analysis of data crucial. Since the reform and opening-up, China's economy has been growing at the fastest speed in the world. With its huge economy, high activity level, and increasing level of information development, the new economy represented by the digital economy is booming. China has become one of the countries that produces and accumulates not only the most data, but also the most abundant data types. Data shows that the total number of Internet users worldwide reached 4.02 billion as of 2017 – 772 million of who are Chinese Internet users. Figure 9.1 shows the increasing trend of China's network population over time. Moreover,

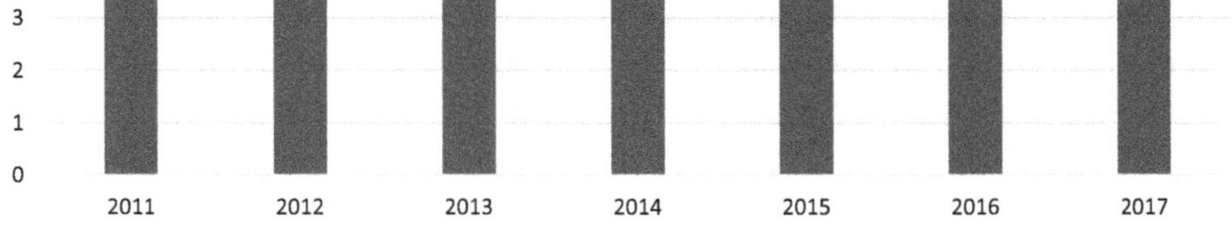

Figure 9.1 Internet population in China (billion)

Source: China Internet Network Information Center (CNNIC)

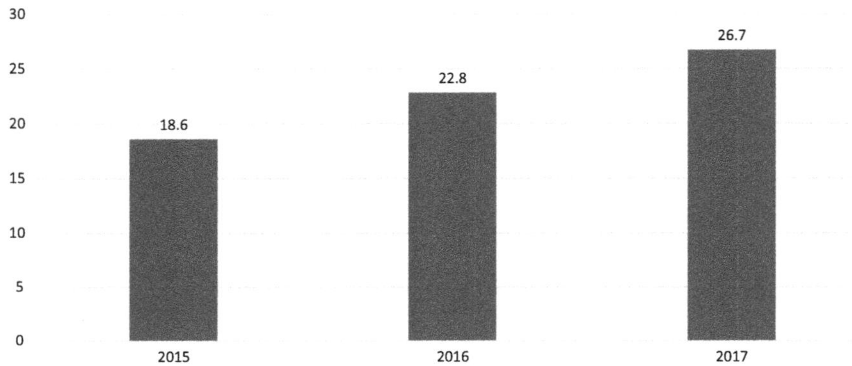

Figure 9.2 The scale of China's digital economy (RMB trillion)

Source: Tencent Research Institute

the development of the digital economy has become the common choice of major countries and regions in the world to reshape global competitiveness. At present, 22% of the global GDP is closely tied to the digital economy, covering skills and capital. In 2017, China's total digital economy reached 26.7 trillion RMB, ranking second in the world and accounting for 32.28% of GDP (Tencent Research Institute, 2018). China's government departments, Internet companies, and large conglomerates have accumulated a large amount of data resources. China has become a country with veritable big data and resources, providing excellent opportunities for technological catch-up in China (Ministry of Industry and Information Technology of the People's Republic of China (MIIT-China), 2017). Figure 9.2 shows the scale (RMB Trillion) of China's digital economy is increasing.

3.2 "Platform" instead of "company" in production organization method

The factory, as a method of production organization, emerged in the first industrial revolution, transforming the model of self-sufficiency and decentralization of agricultural society into a model of separation of workers and peasants, concentrating labor, and greatly liberating and developing productive forces. The "company" appeared in the second industrial revolution, and the limited liability system realized the separation of ownership and management rights, promoting the development of the capital market while greatly liberating and developing productive forces. Nowadays, the global industry is under the impetus of the information revolution, especially Internet technology. The production organization mode is undergoing new changes. The "platform" mode of production organization will gradually become the mainstream mode, and the boundary of enterprises will be blurred increasingly (Hagiu and Wright, 2015). Platform mode is a business model of the multilateral market, which creates value by helping two or more different types of traders to achieve direct transactions. Google, Alibaba, Tencent, Uber, and other companies are very characteristic platforms. However, it has been challenging to figure out the employment attributes. In China, the platform model of production organization has gradually become more popular. The development of an e-commerce platform and the gradual improvement of the service level have become the most dynamic and exemplified areas of the platform model. At present, China's e-commerce service industry has basically formed an ecosystem of e-commerce services with transaction services as the core and support services as the auxiliary and a large number of derivative services coexisting (People's Republic of China Ministry of Commerce, 2017). Statistics show that over 300,000 enterprises of e-commerce service in China support the scale of 26.1 trillion RMB transactions, accounting for 39.2% of the global e-commerce retail market and directly or indirectly boosting the employment of 37 million people (People's Republic of China Ministry of Commerce, 2017). These statistics also show that the revenue scale of China's e-commerce service industry reaches 2.45 trillion RMB (People's Republic of China Ministry of Commerce, 2017). According to an eMarketer report, China was the largest retail e-commerce market in the world in 2016, with sales of more than $899 billion – close to half (47%) of global retail e-commerce. China will remain the world's largest retail e-commerce market leader in the next few years, and the retail e-commerce market will be up to 2.416 trillion US dollars by 2020 (E-Marketer, 2016). Figure 9.3 shows retail e-commerce sales share in China, the US, and worldwide (shown at the

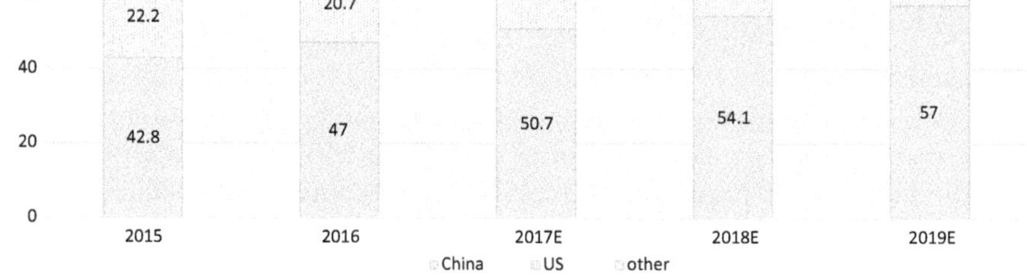

Figure 9.3 Retail e-commerce sales share in China, the US, and worldwide, 2015–2020 (% of total)

Source: eMarketer, Aug 2016.

Note: Includes products or services ordered using the internet via any device, regardless of the method of payment or fulfillment; excludes travel and event tickets; the number may not add up to 100% due to rounding; excludes Hong Kong*; forecast from May 2016.

vertical axis) of the year from 2015 to 2020 (with the horizontal axis representing time).

The rapid growth of e-commerce platforms has become the preferred area for "mass entrepreneurship and innovation" and has stimulated new investment in e-commerce infrastructure, broadband networks, data centers, Internet of Things (IoT), traceability systems, express outlets, distribution centers, and cold chain logistics, and the new industrial chain around e-commerce is rapidly improving. E-commerce has become a vital driving force for China's economic restructuring and upgrading as well as an essential part of the digital economy. It is also a leading industry in China's technological catch-up in terms of promoting consumption, boosting investment and exports, driving employment, and promoting innovation.

3.3 "Short cycle" instead of "long cycle" in product operation

Due to the limitation of technical conditions, it took a long time for the products in the industrial civilization period to change from design, research, and development to product realization, testing, and scale production, and subsequently to marketing and commercialization. Similarly, it takes a long time for a product to reach growth, maturity, and finally, decline. In the information technology and Internet environment, the time spent on research and development, production, and sales is saved; the conversion time between the three links is significantly reduced (Aytac and Wu, 2013); the entire product life cycle is shortened; and the life cycle of many products is only three to five years, or in some cases, as little as six months. In particular, the life cycle of many micro-innovative products may be a few months. The micro-innovations that rely on the open platform is a gradual and innovative way of continuously gaining market acceptance by facing the market demand, focusing on the customer experience, taking the spontaneous innovation of individual or organization as the leading factor, and regarding local continuous improvements in technology, products, services, and business models as the means. For example, Xiaomi mobile phone applied the micro-innovation approach driven by user experience to their operating system, which makes the company a great success in the market.

In the logic of micro-innovation, user experience becomes a more critical factor than technology alone. A typical example is Motorola. Motorola is the first producer of the pager, analog mobile phone, commercial cellular mobile phone, and the smallest and lightest personal mobile phone in the world. Nevertheless, Apple and Samsung under the impact of user experience have gradually overtaken the technology-oriented Motorola.

A considerable number of the middle class population has provided a ground for China's micro-innovation in people's livelihood products and services. The Chinese government has been mobilizing the enthusiasm of the entire economy by guiding and providing basic conditions and facilities, vigorously promoting and setting off a wave of micro-innovation (Kshetri, 2017).

3.4 "Wave curve" instead of "smile curve" in industrial layout

During the first industrial revolution, the colonies provided the raw materials for the sovereign countries that produced and consumed the products. In the early period of the second industrial revolution, the industrialized European countries produced but expanded the market at a global level. Medium-term production began to separate horizontally, and chemical industries were transferred to the United States, Japan, and other emerging capitalist powers (Rifkin, 2011). Later on, with the promotion of multinational corporations, production fields began to be vertically separated, forming a "smile curve" labor division mode. Developed countries were responsible for design, development, and marketing while the developing countries engaged in production or assembly. However, driven by the fourth industrial revolution, which is now ascending under the information technology and internet environment, the global labor division continues to deepen. All areas of R&D, production, and sales can become the ports of integrating the WIC, and all links in the industrial chain will jointly create, pass, and share values. As a result, "Internet + Industry" will reshape the "smile curve" value chain in the manufacturing industry. Personalized customization puts the R&D and design to the users, who place orders to the enterprises directly. It weakens the back-end sales and forms a relatively complete and advantageous industry in each country (region) in the world. Various industries utilize Internet platforms to integrate and transmit the gradual "wavy" layout. Therefore, the "smile curve" of the industrial layout has gradually been leveled off and evolved into a "wave curve." Figure 9.4 shows the difference between the smile curve and the wave curve. In the smile curve of the global value chain, the two ends of the value chain – R&D and marketing – command higher values added to the product than the middle part of the value chain – manufacturing. In comparison, the added-value distribution in each region of the wave curve is relatively even.

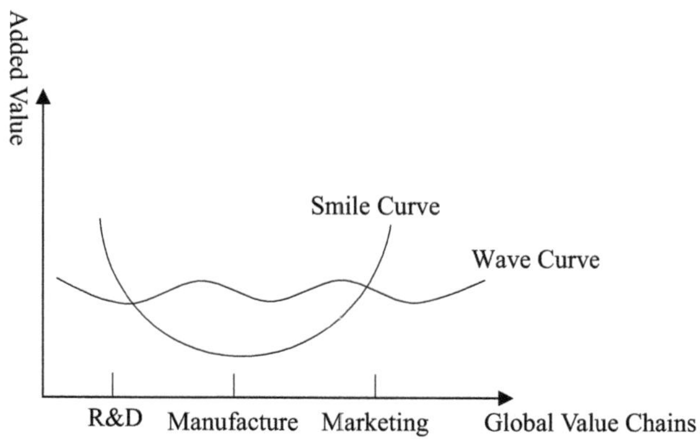

Figure 9.4 The smile and wave curves

Under this background, especially since the 2008 financial crisis, China's industrial structure is undergoing new adjustments and changes, focusing on improving production efficiency and developing new industrial fields. The critical point is to increase capital efficiency and technical capacity, to enhance traditional industries, and to foster strategic emerging industries. China, as the second largest domestic demand market, possesses world-class infrastructure as well as a relatively high quality of university education and low labor costs, which provide a solid foundation for industrial upgrading and a good catch-up opportunity in the global "wavy" industrial layout.

4 China's comprehensive competitive advantage to achieve technological catch-up

Compared with many developed and emerging economies, China has a comprehensive competitive advantage of catching up with technology. Here, comprehensive competitive advantage is different from Ricardo's comparative advantage and Heckscher-Ohlin's factor endowment advantage, which takes institutional innovation as the core, independent technological innovation as the main line, national interests as the guide, human resources cultivation and factor endowment as the support, effective macroeconomic control policies as the guarantee, and gives full playing to the basic role of the market in resource allocation. To detail it, first, China's huge population and rapid urbanization have provided a huge market, which will be a key factor in catching up. Second, China has the most comprehensive industrial system in the world and a good industrial foundation to adapt to the development trend of the new industrial revolution. Third, the Chinese government is a mission-oriented developmental government that can give full play to the advantages of a nationwide system in the process of technological catch-up. Fourth, the current talent system in China is quite attractive and competitive in the world. Finally, the increasingly mature national innovation system promotes China's innovation capability and development level.

4.1 China's market size for the digital industry

From a historical point of view, huge domestic market demand is a key factor in the leading position of "starting countries" in all industrial revolutions (Thurow, 1993). Market uncertainty and consumer acceptance are much higher than that in technological progress. The evolution of technological innovation needs to satisfy the survival of the fittest market selection (Kshetri, 2017). Technological innovations can characterize national indigenous markets in different ways; factors as specific consumer groups, certain market sizes, and their growth rates shape the choice of emerging technologies. Also, there is a "demand-pull hypothesis" in technological innovation (Schmookler, 1966). Following this logic, the domestic market with scale effect not only affects the increase of scale returns of domestic enterprises, but also endogenously induces labor division in the domestic market and the development of enterprises' technological capabilities.

China's vast population base and rapid urbanization have provided a huge market and have shown obvious multilevel and diversified features. China's GDP per capita reached 8,836 US dollars in 2017 with an annual increase of 6.9%. China's consumption structure has already been at the stage of "high-end luxury consumption" from the basic needs of food and clothing, and upgrading consumption will become the biggest driving force of economic growth. At the same time, it also produced the world's largest high-end wealth group. As of 2016, China already has over 4 million millionaires and 150,000 billionaires. More than 70 million people in the middle class own net assets of more than 1 million RMB, with a total wealth of about 30 trillion US dollars, surpassing the United States and Japan, ranking first in the world (Fortune Quality Institute, 2017). The customized production and demand in the digital era further highlight the comprehensive competitive advantage of diversified market size and demand in China. The huge scale and diversified demand will push enterprises to adapt to digital, network, and intelligent manufacturing, speed up the improvement of labor productivity, and promote the transformation and upgrading of traditional industries. The "emerging needs" of rapidly expanding scale will provide vast space for new technologies and products as well as promoting the innovation in the digital era to catch up with the global competitors (Kshetri, 2017).

4.2 Mission-oriented governance

In the digital era, micro-innovation has become a mainstream innovation approach. Although the flat structure and decentralized cooperative business models are more prevalent, some of the scale and integrated innovations that are leading the way for innovation still require the government's dedication to make faster progress. Especially for the industries that have an important leading role in economic growth, it is necessary to establish a government-led technological innovation mechanism. The most convincing examples are the major technological innovations in the United States that were largely derived from government-led basic research in the twentieth century, especially for research related to military technology and military industry. The basic research behind the inventions and breakthroughs of radar, laser, night vision, satellite, communications, computing, superconductivity, nuclear energy, aviation, aerospace, digital imaging, nanotechnology, and other technological fields are all directly or indirectly supported by the United States government (United States Department of Defense, US Department of Energy, US Naval Research Office, NASA, etc.). This example is consistent with the mission-oriented innovation model demonstrated by Mazzucato (2017). In comparison, the Chinese government is a "mission-oriented" developing government with strong autonomy and overall efficiency. It can concentrate its efforts and tackle key problems to speed up breakthroughs in major core technologies, develop major strategic products, and take the lead in national strategic priority areas (The Central Committee of the Communist Party of China, 2016). China's technological progress in the past can provide strong evidence for this conclusion. In the early stage of communist China's history, when it did not have inadequate food and clothing, China developed the "Two Bombs, One Satellite" project at a very fast pace to catch up with the United States, the Soviet Union, and the other developed countries. In fact, the brilliant achievements made in the industrial fields, defense, and agriculture in the first three decades of PRC government were nourished by a nationwide system that "can concentrate on the major events" (Deng, 1993). After the reform and opening-up, the nationwide system even brought human and material resources into contact with the world market to activate China's huge production potential. Then industrial and capital accumulation accelerated the investment cycle, and thus developed industries, science, and technology more intensively. This accumulated wealth, science, and technology activated China's market of over one billion people and formed a broad market supporting sustainable development. At present, China, benefiting from a mission-oriented system, has led the world in new-generation industrial technologies such as information and communications, aerospace, high-speed train, and internet applications.

4.3 China's comprehensive industrial system

China has formed a comprehensive industrial system, a solid agricultural infrastructure system, an independent national defense industrial system (Field, 1992), and has maintained the industrial base to adapt to the trend of the new industrial revolution. On the one hand, China's sound industrial layout provides ample room for enterprises to create a unique industrial chain model. It has strong profitability and risk-resistance capability. Strategic cooperation between different sectors of the industry chain and between different products has been deepened (Qi, 2015). Enterprises can quickly respond to consumer information, which in turn promotes innovation and the improvement of upstream links; this makes the response of the entire industry to the market more sensitive and timely. More importantly, the WIC production model has a scale effect and cost advantage in international competition. On the other hand, with the industrial base to adapt to the trend of the third industrial revolution, industries such as electronic information, the Internet and new energy industries closely linked to innovation in the digital age are the highest in the world. Significant progress has been made in the application of 3D printing in the fields of aerospace and biomedicine. The accelerated development of industrial robots, network size, and the number of Internet users rank first in the world. Basic research and development of the IoT and standards are basically synchronized with international standards while new materials and biotechnology are developing rapidly.

4.4 China's internationally competitive talent introduction and cultivation mechanism

Talent is the core of innovation. In recent years, the Chinese government has formulated a system of using talents with strong international competitiveness, especially the national high level special talent support program (also known as the "Ten Thousand Talents Program"[1]) and the "Thousand Talents Program" that introduces overseas high level talents. The national major talent project and the scope of high level talents and high-tech personnel have been continuously expanding, and the "bonus of science and technology talents" has gradually emerged.

In addition to talent introduction, China has also formed a talent cultivation mechanism with international competitiveness. China's higher education began to shift from elitist to popular. In 2015, China's higher education learning scale was 36.47 million, ranking first in the world. There are 2,852 institutions of higher education, ranking second in the world. The gross enrollment rate is 40%, higher than the global average of middle- and high-income countries (Ministry of Education of the People's Republic of China (MOE of PRC, 2016).

Due to the internationally competitive talent introduction and cultivation mechanism, China has become the first science and technology human resource nation. The data show that the total amount of science and technology human resources in China reached 86.4 million in 2015. The total number of R&D personnel has been growing rapidly. In 2015, the total number of R&D personnel in China was 3.759 million, surpassing that of the United States in absolute terms and ranking first in the world (China Academy of Strategy, 2018).

4.5 The construction of a national innovation system to enhance innovation capabilities

The framework of the national innovation system (NIS), proposed and put forward by Freeman (1987), has become the theoretical foundation for policy practice in many international economic organizations and countries. Major international economic organizations (OECD, UNCTAD, etc.) and major economic powers (US, China, etc.) will build and perfect NIS as the main means to promote technological innovation. As history has consistently shown, achievements do not necessarily belong to those countries that have had the earliest radical innovation but must belong to those countries that are willing to introduce a wide range of changes in the social organization of the country. China is such a country. It has long been aware of the importance of innovation; it clearly proposed to become an innovative country and implemented an innovation-driven strategy of economic growth. China has established a national innovation system, with the government, enterprises, research institutes, and universities. This system plays a decisive role in promoting China's innovation capacity. With the help of the national innovation system, China has significantly enhanced national scientific and technological progress and innovation capability. The overall level has been improved from quantitative increase toward a stage of qualitative improvement. Scientific and technological support led to remarkable achievements in economic and social development and laid the foundation for China to achieve its catch-up. China's total R&D investment amounted to 1.57 trillion RMB in 2016, making it the second largest

R&D investment country in the world after the United States. The number of domestic patents reached 1.013 million, becoming the third country in the world to own more than one million patents after the United States and Japan (Qianzhan Network, 2017). In 2017, China ranked the 22nd in the world in the global innovation index, making it the only middle-income economy to enter the top 25 (Dutta et al., 2017).

5 Conclusion

Technological catch-up in developing countries is not a monotonous linear process. There is no catch-up opportunity in mature technological track, and it is possible to achieve catch-up only when entering the emerging technological track in the period of an "opportunity window." The occurrence and persistence of the financial crisis in 2008 mean that the world is facing a completely new opportunity to change its technological trajectory and adjust its economic structure. Also, we are in a rapidly evolving digital era. A new round of industrial revolution with the Internet, big data, and intelligent manufacturing as the core technologies is taking shape and developing. Therefore, the "opportunity window" for technological catch-up in developing countries has been opened.

This "opportunity window" for technological catch-up has also provided China with a once-in-a-lifetime catch-up opportunity. In the digital age, intangible information data has become the most precious resource, and China is one of the countries that generates and accumulates the most data and the most abundant data types, so it is a country with veritable data and resources. The mode of production organization replaces companies with the platform. In China, the platform model of production organization has been popular gradually and has gradually become the mainstream. The development of an e-commerce platform has become the bright spot and the most dynamic field of China's new economic development. Product operation replaces the "long cycle" with "short cycle." With the development of China's market economy, especially the rise of the middle class, it provides a good opportunity for the micro-innovation of livelihood products and services in China. The industrial layout replaces the "wave curve" with "smile curve." China's industrial structure is undergoing new adjustments and changes, focusing on the improvement of production efficiency and the cultivation of new industries.

In the face of the "opportunity window" that has already been opened up, China also possesses a comprehensive competitive advantage in technological catch-up. The huge population base and rapid urbanization in China have provided and will continually provide a huge market demand and are the critical factors in catching up. China has the most comprehensive industrial system in the world and a good industrial foundation to adapt to the development trend of the new round of industrial revolution. The Chinese government is a mission-oriented developmental government that can give full attention to the advantages of a nationwide system in the process of technological catch-up. The current method of using and introducing talents in China is quite competitive in the world. The increasingly sophisticated national innovation system has comprehensively upgraded the innovation capability.

Note

1 China's national high-level special support program (also known as the "Ten Thousand Talents Program" is located in the domestic high-level personnel training support project, under the unified leadership of the Central Personnel Coordination Team. In 2013, two batches of candidates of "Ten Thousand Talents Program" were announced.

References

Aytac, B. and D. Wu (2013) "Characterization of Demand for Short Life-Cycle Technology Products." *Annals of Operations Research* 203: 255–277.

Bowles, S. (2004) *Microeconomics: Behavior, Institutions and Evolution*, Princeton, NJ: Princeton University Press.

The Central Committee of the Communist Party of China (2016) "National Innovation-Driven Development Strategy Outline." Available at www.most.gov.cn/yw/201605/t20160520_125675.htm (in Chinese).

China Academy of Strategy (2018) *China Science Technology and Engineering Indicators*, Beijing: Tsinghua University Press (in Chinese).

Clark, J., C. Freeman and L. Soete (1981) "Long Waves, Inventions, and Innovations." *Futures* 13: 208–322.

Cooper, R. G. and A. F. Sommer (2016) "From Experience: The Agile-Stage-Gate Hybrid Model: A Promising New Approach and a New Research Opportunity." *Journal of Product Innovation Management* 33: 513–526.

Deng, X. (1993) *Selected Works of Deng Xiaoping*, Beijing: People's Publishing House (in Chinese).

Dosi, G. (1982) "Technological Paradigms and Technological Trajectories – A Suggested Interpretation of the Determinants and Directions of Technical Change." *Research Policy* 11: 147–162.

Dutta, S., B. Lanvin and S. Wunsch-Vincent (2017) "The Global Innovation Index 2017." Available at www.globalinnovationindex.org/gii-2017-report.

E-Marketer (2016) "Retail Ecommerce Sales Share of Worldwide, China vs. US, 2015–2020." Available at www.emarketer.com/Chart/Retail-Ecommerce-Sales-Share-of-Worldwide-China-vs-US-2015-2020-of-total/194512.

Engerman, S. L. and R. E. Gallman (2000) *The Cambridge Economic History of the United States, Volume 3: The Twentieth Century*, Cambridge: Cambridge University Press.

Fan, G. (1998) "On Competitiveness -Reflection on the Relationship between Scientific and Technological Progress and Economic Benefits." *Management World* 3: 10–15 (in Chinese).

Field, R. M. (1992) "China's Industrial Performance Since 1978." *China Quarterly* 100: 577–607.

Fortune Quality Institute (2017) "VVIP Overseas Development Report." Available at www.199it.com/archives/572676.html (in Chinese).

Freeman, C. (1987) *Technology Policy and Economic Performance: Lessons from Japan*, London: Pinter Publishers.

Gerchenkron, A. (1962) *Economic Backwardness in Historical Perspective*, Cambridge MA: Harvard University Press.

Hagiu, A. and J. Wright (2015) "Multi-sided Platforms." *International Journal of Industrial Organization* 43: 162–174.

Hobday, M. (1995) "East Asian Latecomer Firms: Learning the Technology of Electronics." *World Development* 23: 1171–1193.

Klinenberg, E. (2016) "Convergence: News Production in a Digital Age." *The ANNALS of the American Academy of Political and Social Science* 597: 48–64.

Kshetri, N. (2017) "The Evolution of the Internet of Things Industry and Market in China: An Interplay of Institutions, Demands and Supply." *Telecommunications Policy* 41: 49–67.

Lee, K. and J.-H. Ki (2017) "Rise of Latecomers and Catch-Up Cycles in the World Steel Industry." *Research Policy* 46: 365–375.

Lee, K. and C. Lim (2001) "Technological Regimes, Catching-Up and Leapfrogging: Findings from the Korean Industries." *Research Policy* 30: 459–483.

Lin, J.Y., F. Cai and L. Zhou (1996) "The Lessons of China's Transition to a Market Economy." *Cato Journal* 16: 201–231.

Louca, F. and C. Freeman (2002) *As Time Goes by: From the Industrial Revolutions to the Information Revolution*, Oxford: Oxford University Press.

Mathews, John A. (2002) "Competitive Advantages of the Latecomer Firm: A Resource-Based Account of Industrial Catch-Up Strategies." *Asia Pacific Journal of Management* 19: 467–488.

Mazzucato, M. (2017) "Mission-Oriented Innovation Policy: Challenges and Opportunities." Available at https://marianamazzucato.com/wp-content/uploads/2018/03/mission-oriented_ri_in_the_eu_mazzucato_2018.pdf.

Metcalfe, J. S. (1998) *Evolutionary Economics and Creative Destruction*, Abingdon: Routledge.

Ministry of Education of the Peoples Republic of China (MOE of PRC) (2016) "China Higher Education Quality Report (2016)." *China Education Daily* (in Chinese).

Ministry of Industry and Information Technology of the People's Republic of China (Miit-China) (2017) "An Interpretation of the Big Data of Guidebook for the Development of Information Industry." *China Hi-tech* 7: 8–9 (in Chinese).

Narula, R. (2003) *Globalization and Technology: Interdependence, Innovation Systems and Industrial Policy*, Cambridge: Polity Press.

Nolan, P. D. and G. Lenski (1985) "Techno-Economic Heritage, Patterns of Development, and the Advantage of Backwardness." *Social Forces* 64: 341–358.

People's Republic of China Ministry of Commerce (2017) "E-COMMERCE IN CHINA." Available at www.199it.com/archives/60 6896.html (accessed June 29, 2017) (in Chinese).

Perez, C. (2001) "Technological Change and Opportunities for Development as a Moving Target." *Cepal Review* 75: 113–117.

Perez, C. (2009) "Technological Revolutions and Techno-Economic Paradigms." *Cambridge Journal of Economics* 34: 185–202.

Perez, C. (2010) "The Financial Crisis and the Future of Innovation: A View of Technical Change with the Aid of History." *The Other Canon Foundation and Tallinn University of Technology Working Papers in Technology Governance and Economic Dynamics 28*, TUT Ragnar Nurkse Department of Innovation and Governance.

Perez, C. and L. Soete (1988) "Catching-up in Technology: Entry Barriers and Windows of Opportunity." G. Dosi, C. Freeman, R. Nelson, G. Silverberg and L. Soete (eds.), *Technical Change and Economic Theory*, London: Pinter Publishers.

Qi, X. (2015) *Research on the Construction of China's Modern Industrial System*, Bei Jing: China Economic Publishing House (in Chinese).

Qianzhan Network (2017) "Data Sink." Available at https://d.qianzhan.com/xnews/detail/54U170728-532dd7d7.html (in Chinese).

Rifkin, J. (2011) *The Third Industrial Revolution: How Lateral Power Is Transforming Energy, the Economy, and the World*, New York: St. Martin's Press.

Rigby, D. K., J. Sutherland and H. Takeuchi (2016) "Embracing Agile." *Harvard Business Review*: 40–48.

Sawhney, M., G. Verona and E. Prandelli (2005) "Collaborating to Create: The Internet as a Platform for Customer Engagement in Product Innovation." *Journal of Interactive Marketing* 19: 4–17.

Schmoch, U., C. Rammer and H. Legler (2006) *National Systems of Innovation in Comparison: Structure and Performance Indicators for Knowledge Societies*, Dordrecht: Springer.

Schmookler, J. (1966) *Invention and Economic Growth*, Cambridge: Harvard University Press.

Shih, S. (1996) *Me-Too Is Not My Style: Challenge Difficulties Break through Bottlenecks, Create Values*, Taipei: The Acer Foundation.

Shin, J.-S. (2017) "Dynamic Catch-Up Strategy, Capability Expansion and Changing Windows of Opportunity in the Memory Industry." *Research Policy* 46: 404–416.

Steil, B., D. G. Victor and R. R. Nelson (2002) *Technological Innovation and Economic Performance*, Princeton, NJ: Princeton University Press.

Tencent Research Institute (2018) "China Internet Plus Index Report (2018)." Available at www.tisi.org/5025 (in Chinese).

Thurow, L. C. (1993) *Head to Head: The Coming Economic Battle among Japan, Europe, and America*, New York: William Morrow & Co.

Viotti, E. B. (1997) *Passive and Active National Learning Systems*, dissertation, University of Brasília.

Yu, X., G. Dosi, J. Lei and A. Nuvolari (2015) "Institutional Change and Productivity Growth in China's Manufacturing: The Microeconomics of Knowledge Accumulation and 'creative restructuring.'" *Industrial and Corporate Change* 24: 565–602.

10 Realizing stretch goals via exploratory bricolage

The case of Chinese entrepreneurial firms

Shihao Zhou, Peter Ping Li, and Monsol Zhengyin Yang

A fundamental paradox of entrepreneurship is the tension between a passionate entrepreneur's *stretch goal*, i.e., goals that are seemingly impossible given his or her current resources or capabilities, and the serious lack of access to required resources or capabilities. On one hand, a firm's performance is argued to be largely shaped by the valuable, rare, inimitable, and non-substitutable (VRIN) resources it holds (Barney, 1991), and some organizational learning scholars posit that conducting explorative learning for a stretch goal is likely to be harmful for firms facing severe resource constraints (Sitkin et al., 2011). It is self-evident that pursuing stretch goals entails enormous challenges and expenses for firms, especially vulnerable ones with limited resources. On the other hand, in the business world, many well-known entrepreneurs set a stretch goal when their firms are in a severe resource deficiency, and later many of them come up with radical innovations and achieve extraordinary performance far above market expectations. The preceding two views constitute one of the most salient and challenging paradoxes for both scholars and practitioners. We need to go beyond the extant literature so as to effectively explain this specific paradox, especially about how an entrepreneurial firm confronting severe resource constraints can achieve its stretch goal with extraordinary performance.

In particular, the emergence of almost all successful firms in China (e.g., Huawei, Haier, Alibaba, and Tencent, among others) at the initial stages and even the later stages of firm growth, all occurred under similar conditions of serious competitive disadvantages due to the severe lack of VRIN resources. Those firms all started nearly from nothing with no original technology and technical accumulation, no venture capital, no power background, and even no capable talents. For instance, Ren Zhengfei, the CEO and founder of Huawei once advocated that Huawei would ultimately be one of the third top companies in the information and communication industry all over the world in an early stage. Tencent was nearly sold to Sohu in 2000 at a price of 1 million RMB when the founder of Tencent Pony Ma thought he could not sustain the company any longer; the current market value of his company surpasses US$ 500 billion. Their great stretch goals and the absence of VRIN resources are in stark contrast. We can focus on the specific cases of Chinese firms to explain how such a paradox can be effectively managed or balanced.

Specifically, we argue that the notion of bricolage can be evoked to resolve the tension between having a stretch goal and lacking required resources. In terms of "making do by applying combinations of the resources at hand to new problems and opportunities" (Baker and Nelson, 2005, p. 333), *bricolage* is perhaps the most relevant perspective to explain the special entrepreneurial behaviors in resource-scarce contexts (Senyard et al., 2014; Garud and Karnøe, 2003; Guo et al., 2016; Welter et al., 2016). This perspective posits that, in order to resolve the problem of resource constraints, a firm needs to engage in bricolage by challenging the extant institutional assumptions as well as reusing existing resources in new ways (Baker and Nelson, 2005). In particular, bricolage can provide a viable venue for firms in emerging markets such as China to grow under resource constraints (Gurca and Ravishankar, 2016; Wu et al., 2017). From the perspective of bricolage, innovation is explicitly and directly viewed as a solution to the problem of resource constraints. However, the extant research on bricolage is limited in framing it as leading to frugal innovations to the extent that, with substandard resources at hand, some entrepreneurs can only create substandard products that serve customers who cannot afford standard prices (Senyard et al., 2014). Further, bricolage is commonly identified as a pure exploitative search with an emphasis on only short-term or near-term and path-dependent goals (Baker and Nelson, 2005) due to its emphasis on "make-do," which means to employ whatever resources are available. Finally, there is almost a complete blank in terms of literature on the process of bricolage by the firms in the emerging economies (Senyard et al., 2009; Salunke et al., 2013).

Hence, the extant perspective of bricolage seems to imply that bricoleurs can only gain a competitive parity or develop temporary advantages (Baker and Nelson, 2005; Fisher, 2012; Senyard et al., 2014), so it fails to explain why and how some bricoleurs could deliver an extraordinary performance under resource constraints. To fill this gap in the literature, we seek to effectively explain the specific paradox about stretch goal and resource constraints in terms of how an entrepreneurial firm with severe resource constraints can achieve its stretch goal for extraordinary performance.

Specifically, we argue that the extant research on bricolage focuses too narrowly on what we call *exploitative bricolage* as one of multiple mechanisms (i.e., making-do with whatever resources are at hand, similar to the approach of *effectuation* in terms of pursuing only any goal achievable with available resources, Sarasvathy, 2001, 2008), so we intend to develop a novel view by identifying the other mechanism of what we call *exploratory bricolage* (i.e., creating radical innovations or other extraordinary outcomes out of not only ordinary resources, but also even seemingly valueless "*non-resources*"). In particular, we posit that the key antecedent to exploratory bricolage is stretch goal with its unique role in driving entrepreneurs to engage in exploratory bricolage as necessary and salient (cf. Sitkin et al., 2011). We argue that exploratory bricolage can better explain the perspective about "creating something from nothing." We propose an integrative framework of entrepreneurial bricolage with exploratory bricolage as the primary mechanism to explore novel solutions of converting or transforming ordinary resources and/or seemingly valueless non-resources *at hand* into radical outcomes to match the stretch goal.

We analyze three cases to illustrate and enrich the notion of explorative bricolage and discuss the achievement of stretch goals by entrepreneurial firms using substandard resource at hand. In particular, we choose cases from China, where we see several entrepreneurial firms facing severe resource constraints at the beginning that have become global power players through a series of bricolage-driven innovations. Specifically, we discuss the three cases of *Yuanjia Village*, *ZBOM Cabinets Co.*, and *Huawei*.

This chapter aims to explore and explain why those Chinese firms with unprivileged resources have managed to obtain great success via theoretical argument and case analysis. Particularly, we focus on the *how* question, i.e., how have they done that? And what are the core mechanisms and processes? We identify the bricolage pattern with both theoretical and practical implications for both scholars and practitioners. Our research contributes to the organization (Terjesen and Patel, 2017) and entrepreneurship (Fisher, 2012; Welter et al., 2016) literatures by explaining how entrepreneurs can achieve seemingly impossible success via rather radical innovation based on local search.

1 Theoretical background

1.1 Stretch goal

We argue that to better understand the unique pattern of innovation by late-coming firms in China, it is salient to study the role or effect of firm-specific stretch goal. *Stretch goal* is defined as a goal that is extremely difficult and seemingly impossible to achieve given the available resources and capabilities (Gary et al., 2017; Locke and Latham, 2013; Sitkin et al., 2011). Having a stretch goal is critical because it encourages organizations to push the envelope of available resources so as to stimulate innovations within each firm. However, Sitkin et al. (2011) argue that stretch goals can only be achieved by firms with sufficient resources; therefore, pursuing stretch goals under the condition of resource constraints may impede the satisfactory performance of most, if not all, firms, and accordingly create discomfort, stress, and rigidity at both individual and collective levels. Similarly, Gary et al. (2017) find that having stretch goals does not help most individuals or organizations achieve a better performance.

Achieving competitive advantages in terms of innovativeness for late-coming firms in emerging economies can be regarded as a typical stretch goal (Lee and Lim, 2001; Miao et al., 2018). For example, for a Chinese late-coming software company, it will be extremely difficult for the company to challenge the dominant position of Microsoft in operating systems. According to Sitkin et al. (2011), pursuing a stretch goal under resource constraints will impede the typical growth of late-coming firms. However, as known to many, Jack Ma had set the ideal goal for Alibaba to be the greatest IT company on earth since its early days, but this was seemingly impossible for a new firm given its desperate need of resources. This stretch goal has made Alibaba a business leader in the world, which forces us to reconsider the hidden links between available resources, stretch goal, and innovative outcome. Hence, we need to think more deeply about the unique role or effect of bricolage, especially its more creative or exploratory version in contrast to its less creative or exploitative version, as the most relevant means or mechanism to convert or transform available resources into innovative outcomes via the facilitating effect of stretch goals.

Prior literature also indicates that although having a stretch goal may not improve performance generally, the stretch goal can potentially stimulate creativity and innovation (Katila and Shane, 2005; Miron-Spektor and Beenen, 2015). In an individual-level study, Miron-Spektor and Beenen (2015) find that when people who have a specific goal in learning are more likely to explore new knowledge domains, making these people come up with novel ideas. Katila and Shane (2005) examine the relationship between lack of resources and firm innovation. They find that lacking resources may encourage the firm to innovate. These studies imply that exploration and innovation could be an effective way of achieving stretch goals.

1.2 Explorative bricolage

Bricolage has been brought into entrepreneurship and innovation research since the early 2000s (Baker et al., 2003; Baker and Nelson, 2005). Based on this concept, when entrepreneurs are facing resource constraints, they could "make do by applying combinations of the resources at hand to new problems and opportunities" (Baker and Nelson, 2005, p. 333). The insight provided by the notion of bricolage is that entrepreneurs may successfully achieve goals under the condition of resource constraints, and the way to achieve that is to test and challenge existing institutional assumptions (e.g., institutional logics, formal rules, informal norms, dominant logics, prevailing business models, etc.) so as to use ordinary or even seemingly valueless non-resources in novel ways (Baker and Nelson, 2005; Garud and Karnøe, 2003).

The concept of bricolage provides many useful pieces of advice for entrepreneurs to survive under resource constraints while the problem of resource constraints is one of the impeding factors for late-coming start-ups, especially in the emerging economies (Miao et al., 2018). This idea has shaken the position of two theories that hold the view that early-moving firms have better or more advanced capabilities for innovation. First, bricolage challenges the research-based view that the firm-specific competitive advantages are rooted in the ownership ofVRIN resources (Barney, 1991, 2001). In terms of innovation, the resource-based view indicates that innovation must be based on the possession of corresponding resources such as advanced technologies, R&D stock, and R&D experiences (Terziovski, 2010). However, the concept of bricolage indicates that organizations can turn subnormal resources, or even seemingly valueless non-resources, into VRIN resources for competitive advantages so that there is no absolute need for the prior possession of extraordinary resources as a required precondition.

Second, the concept of bricolage also challenges the view of organizational search for innovation and entrepreneurship. Based upon the view of organizational search, innovation, and entrepreneurial opportunities can be detected through knowledge search (Kaish and Gilad, 1991; Levinthal and March, 1993). Scholars of organizational search differentiate local search from nonlocal search, with the former involving the search for knowledge near their current knowledge domains, and the latter involving the search for knowledge in distant domains (Rosenkopf and Almeida, 2003; Rosenkopf and Nerkar, 2001). In the traditional view of organizational search, organizations focus on familiar and easily accessible resources in local search, which often generates incremental and exploitative innovations; in contrast, organizations focus on long-term variables, venture into new fields, and discover novel solutions in nonlocal search, which often generates radical and explorative innovations (Rosenkopf and Nerkar, 2001). However, the concept of bricolage indicates that some radical innovations can derive from local, yet explorative, search. In fact, recent innovation studies show that because local search brings a deep understanding of the relevant institutions, innovators are more likely to modify the underlying institutional logics so as to achieve truly radical innovations via engaging in local, rather than nonlocal, search (Jung and Lee, 2016; Kaplan and Vakili, 2015; Mastrogiorgio and Gilsing, 2016).

However, the extant research on bricolage is limited in framing it as leading to frugal innovations to the extent that, with substandard resources at hand, some entrepreneurs can only create substandard products that serve customers who cannot afford standard prices (Senyard et al., 2014). Furthermore, because bricolage emphasizes "make-do" with resources at hand, it is often viewed as a pure exploitative search with an emphasis on only short-term, or near-term and path-dependent, goals (Baker and Nelson, 2005). Last, little is known about the process of bricolage by the firms in the context of emerging economies (Senyard et al., 2014; Salunke et al., 2013). In other words, the extant perspective of bricolage seems to imply that bricoleurs can only gain a competitive parity or develop temporary advantages (Baker and Nelson, 2005; Fisher, 2012; Senyard et al., 2014), so it fails to explain why and how some bricoleurs could deliver an extraordinary performance under resource constraints. To differentiate our approach to bricolage as radically creative in contrast to the extant notion of bricolage as a simple "make-do with resources at hand," we frame the radical creative type as exploratory bricolage, while the typical type is exploitative bricolage. Figure 10.1 demonstrates the overall pattern of exploratory bricolage.

1.3 The interplay between stretch goal and exploratory bricolage

Combining the interplay between exploratory bricolage and stretch goal for innovation, we argue that firms could achieve a stretch goal by engaging

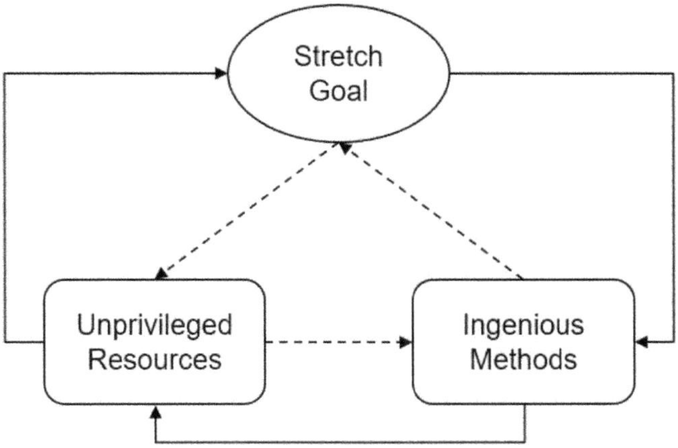

Figure 10.1 The overall pattern of exploratory bricolage

bricolage in a radically creative manner. This type of bricolage is the key to radical innovation for late-coming firms in such emerging economies as China. However, while the extant research on bricolage regards stretch goals for late-coming firms as seemingly impossible (Baker and Nelson, 2005; Senyard et al., 2014), the extant research on stretch goals fails to pay attention to the potential effect of bricolage (Sitkin et al., 2011). In this sense, integrating the two would provide us with more salient insights, especially concerning the interplay between the two factors.

The impossibility of stretch goals derives from the old norms within mature firms, so only by challenging the domain technologies, business models, and operating processes can it achieve radical or disruptive innovations (Wu et al., 2010). In contrast, given the resource constraints of late-coming firms, they must focus on improving the effectiveness of applying currently available or easily accessible resources, which renders stretch goals primarily distractive and harmful. Finally, the traditional theories imply that radical or disruptive innovations cannot be achieved via local research and local resources (Laursen and Salter, 2006; Laursen, 2012; Rosenkopf and Nerkar, 2001). However, bricolage-related activities, such as challenging the current institutional assumptions, can facilitate the creation of radical or disruptive innovations if the current resources are applied in some novel patterns (Baker and Nelson, 2005).

In addition, the notion of exploratory bricolage suggests the way of using local resources in novel way. This is based on the fact that radical or disruptive innovations can be achieved only by breaking and transforming the formal rules and informal norms that are built upon the previous institutional assumptions. The insight of exploratory bricolage is that innovators can conduct radical or disruptive innovations by reexamining the taken-for-granted assumptions (Kaplan and Vakili, 2015).

In particular, stretch goals can serve as salient enablers for bricolage. Even though exploratory bricolage and radical innovation are always hard to achieve, and even harder for late-coming firms from the emerging economies, unexpected outcomes could be achieved in the light of stretch goal, which may guide such firms to the final realization of bricolage. Due to the path-dependence nature of technological trajectory, economists find that it is difficult for the late-coming firms to challenge the early-moving firms in terms of technological innovations (Liebowitz and Margolis, 1995; Nelson, 1990). Because technology development is restrained by path dependence (Mahoney, 2000), the late-coming firms could be locked for a long time in a lower and less competitive position. Advancement in information technology also makes it harder to achieve radical innovations by following the same path of the first movers. Given this situation, radical innovation is the only way for the latecomers to surpass the first movers. Due to the difficulties involved in the innovation process, perhaps only those latecomers with strong stretch goals can push themselves hard enough to adopt radically different patterns for their disruptive innovations.

Radical or disruptive innovation tends to be highly difficult to achieve, especially for the latecomers, even though some latecomers may have potential competitive advantages; so it would be misguided if the latecomers adopt the well-known paths of successful first movers. In this sense, we argue that stretch goal may function as a driving force for radical innovation. From the perspective of behavioral theory of the firm (Cyert and March, 1963), organizational search is always triggered by existing problems. When the traditional solutions to such problems fail, managers can be forced to engage in some innovative activities so as to achieve radical or disruptive innovations as novel solutions to such problems. Hence, pursuing a stretch goal can serve as a salient trigger for exploratory bricolage.

1.4 Composition-based view

The Chinese style or pattern of innovation is argued to be unique in several aspects, and one of them is highlighted as a compositional approach. The compositional approach, coined as "*composition-based view*" (CBV), is proposed to explain how firms with insufficient resources and competencies can create competitive advantages (Luo and Child, 2015). CBV provides some interesting insights into the question about how some firms with ordinary resources can generate extraordinary results by applying their unique integrating capabilities to their own ordinary resources and even others' ordinary resources to develop products with good price-value ratios to better meet the special needs of the mass-market consumers in emerging economies (Luo and Child, 2015). However, we can go one step further by positing that entrepreneurial bricolage can serve as not only the core mechanism for CBV, but also something new beyond CBV by differentiating between three sub-patterns: (1) turning normal or ordinary resources (i.e., regular resources available via market exchange at fair prices) into extraordinary resources (i.e., VRIN resources or core competences for competitive advantages), (2) turning subnormal resources (i.e., irregular resources with controversial values or services, even though available via market exchange at distorted prices) into ordinary and/or extraordinary resources, and (3) turning even seemingly valueless non-resources (i.e., conventionally assumed valueless as measured by functional service or market value due to its public-good nature) into various types of valuable resources (i.e., subnormal, ordinary, and extraordinary or VRIN resources). In general terms, the first sub-pattern is consistent with CBV, but the second and third sub-patterns extend beyond CBV toward our notion of exploratory bricolage.

2 Research methodology

We employ a case study approach to investigate how companies with severe resource constraints achieve stretch goals via ingenious methods. Case study is a useful method for theory building (Eisenhardt and Graebner, 2007). Adopting the case study approach is appropriate for us because the aim of this study is to develop a new concept of explorative bricolage. We choose three cases for data analysis. The multiple-case approach provides a stronger base for theory building than the single-case approach (Yin, 1994), since it enables us to verify our arguments in different contexts and increases the robustness of our findings. Following the suggestions of Eisenhardt and Graebner (2007), we sampled three companies in different industries to enhance our research design.

We analyze three cases to explore the specific mechanisms at different stages of entrepreneurial bricolage, especially the creative type of entrepreneurial bricolage. The three cases are: Yuanjia Village, a rural community that has developed a booming tourist operation with little or no conventional resources available for tourism; ZBOM, a kitchen-furniture manufacturer that has achieved its ambitious goal of super-fast growth; and Huawei, a telecommunication equipment supplier that has transformed from a small local player into a world-class global player within a short period of three decades.

The first and third cases primarily rely on secondary data. It is possible to collect key information from public sources because these two cases, especially Huawei, were widely publicized in media. The published secondary data are more objective than interview data and enable us to conduct cross-checks using multiple sources. The information of Yuanjia Village was collected from the major news outlets and video records of the interviews of the village's leaders and managers. The information of Huawei was collected from the company's news articles, annual reports, and books that were written by the company's senior consultant with the authorization from the company (Tian and Wu, 2015). For the case of ZBOM, although the company is a listed firm, its process of bricolage was not discussed intensively in the public media. Since we had direct access, we interviewed the founder and top executives of the company. All the data were collected from Chinese sources.

3 Case studies

Case study 1: Yuanjia Village

Yuanjia Village, a tourist attraction without literally any tourism resources, is an ordinary village on the Guanzhong plain in Shaanxi Province. Before launching the tourism business, Yuanjia Village had only 62 households and 286 villagers. It is a small, poorly endowed village that has few natural resources, much less those resources required for tourism.

In the 1980s, taking advantage of the flourishing development of township and village enterprises, Yuanjia Village temporarily had a grand occasion under the leadership of the old village chief Guo Yulu. However, in the new century, the village-run enterprises are in a dilemma with the adjustment of national industrial policies. At that time, there was not much difference between Yuanjia Village and China's tens of millions of common rural areas. Most young villagers went out of the village to make a living, and the village became a veritable hollow village. To revive the countryside, Guo Zhanwu, son of the old village chief, returned to be the village head. However, it is undoubtedly difficult to start a secondary startup, and similar to most startups, Yuanjia (refers to the company of Yuanjia, hereinafter) was facing a serious shortage of resources.

Guo Zhanwu later recalls that what he wanted at that time was to help the villagers get rich again through tourism and establish a Century Village of Yuanjia. This idea seemed insipid, and challenging as well. As mentioned before, Yuanjia Village possessed no natural tourism resources on its own. Although only four kilometers away from Zhaoling, the mausoleum of Emperor Li Shimin of the Tang Dynasty, Yuanjia Village cannot be regarded as a particularly attractive attraction in the Guanzhong area where cultural relics and historic sites are all over the country. Moreover, Zhaoling is not in the village, and it is hard to directly rely on Zhaoling tourism to increase the incomes of Yuanjia villagers. Therefore, despite such a vision, the villagers, including the village leaders, did not know how to achieve it. Even more than 20 outside planning experts concluded that Yuanjia Village could not sustain itself on tourism. In a speech in 2016, Guo Zhanwu said frankly that even the planning experts invited at that time thought that Yuanjia Village should cheat the government for subsidies.

In the face of a conflict between a sharp ambitious vision and the lack of resources, Guo Zhanwu led Yuanjia Village to a surprising counterattack. After 2007, Yuanjia Village chose to develop folklore tourism as a starting point, breaking through the paradox of grand vision and the scarcity of resources. In order to achieve the goal of getting rich by developing tourism, the managers of Yuanjia Village exploited two apparent opportunities: fully tapping the local conditions and bold innovating.

In terms of utilizing local conditions, Yuanjia Village focused on old and rustic (original) ecology. The village management team believed that to succeed in rural areas, it was necessary to understand the rural areas and understand peasants, and this is the greatest advantage of Yuanjia's management team. Therefore, in the course of development, Yuanjia Village did not recklessly over-pursue the integration of new resources to set up new scenic spots. Instead, it showed itself the most primitive life of peasants in Guanzhong Plain and opened up a unique tourism model of an ancient town plus food and snacks for visitors. In order to exert the so-called "old-fashioned advantage," Yuanjia Village took the villagers as the main body and mobilized the villagers in an all-round way. All the villagers' clothing, language, and housing were integrated into the scenic spots so as to make tourism more accessible.

In turn, Yuanjia Village firmly grasped new and advanced (fashionable) with regard to bold innovation. The concept of folk-custom tourism developed by the village management team is fundamentally different from the traditional tourism industry based on scenic spots. It can be said that they created a blue ocean market and the demand of experiencing the rural areas of the specific urban consumer groups has been seized. During the development of folk-custom tourism, the village management team flexibly applied novel Internet thinking, such as free entrance tickets, free rental of shops, and the continuous introduction of faddish products or services so as to rapidly attract large numbers of passengers and thus to compete in the highly competitive tourist market. They quickly stood firmly as a latecomer. At the same time, the village management team paid close attention to the management of old and rustic folk activities with the management mode of new and advanced. For example, Yuanjia Village made a unified and reasonable plan for the snacks in the scenic area. While ensuring the variety and quality of snack varieties, it maintained the reasonableness of the competition among the snacks in the village and posted promises of quality assurance and various supporting activities everywhere, all reflecting the managers' unique understanding of new and advanced management thinking.

From 2007 to today, 10 years past, Yuanjia Village has successfully stepped out of the first step of Century Yuanjia Village. Today, Yuanjia Village has become a well-known tourist brand in Shaanxi Province and even the whole country. It has 586 merchants with an annual tourist arrival of 5 million and an annual output value of 280 million yuan. In the Golden Week of 2015, this hollow village, which does not have any natural tourism resources, received a daily average of 180,000 tourists, much higher than the 69,400 visitors of Terracotta Warriors and Horses, ranking the first place in the Golden Week in Shaanxi Province. Competing with more and more imitators, Yuanjia Village is undergoing a new transformation. Its Hanzhong Impression Experience Store has entered the center of Xi'an City, channeling new passenger flow for village enterprises.

Case study 2: ZBOM

ZBOM is a kitchen supplies manufacturer. Before 2008, ZBOM looked like a small and affluent local company specializing in the kitchen cabinet business. From its founding in 1998 until 2008, ZBOM dwelled on its headquarters in Anhui Province without any ambition of expanding to other places. Before it started its entry into the Nanjing market in 2003, ZBOM had never been to any other regions or cities in the past 10 years. However, in the wake of the financial turmoil in 2008 and the downturn in the real estate market, the growth of the cabinet industry had been restrained. Consumers had become cautious about spending on home improvement and were in a wait-and-see attitude. The bleak environment made ZBOM feel the crisis. Surprisingly, the winter was not too cold, as the company doubled its growth that year with sales exceeding RMB 1 billion. This result greatly increased the morale of the team and even led the company to sense the opportunity of the industry: many companies stand by and wait to see the changes in the industry. But ZBOM thought it was a good time to overtake the industry.

At the end of 2009, the company's regular strategic seminar held as scheduled. Fifty executives sat around and routinely planned a second year of development. During the team discussion, the managing vice president held the view that what is now considered impossible will be possible 10 years from now, positing: why should we limit ourselves to the immediate situation? ZBOM could, therefore, enlarge resources, make optimistic and imaginative ideas, and find ways to create such an environment and conditions. "We do not know what happened," all the executives we interviewed recalled, "the annual goal planning quickly evolved into a daring dream for the next decade." The discussion got more exciting, and the final outcome was a co-developed stretch goal: one billion in three years, ten billion in ten years.

Once the goal had been set, related strategic path needed to be determined. Because of their choosing of a stretch goal, in the absence of ample resources, their basic strategic path also had to go beyond the conventional but find a unique strategic path. This is also the need for bricolage, that is, giving full play to the undiscovered potential of existing resources or making full use of the resources of others. This is exactly what ZBOM chose to do. Specifically, the main feature of their ingenious strategy is to separate the existing self-service sales companies and completely release the potential that they have not previously achieved, thus to make them become the vanguard of the massive expansion of ZBOM. In addition, ZBOM was almost desperate to recruit dealers across the country to make use of other resources to fulfill rapid expansion. For example, one billion in three years means that ZBOM would have to build 1,000 dealership stores in 2010 to 2012. The goal was successfully completed in the first two years, simply because it started from a small base. In 2011, ZBOM recruited 210 dealerships. In 2012, according to the plan of one thousand stores in three years, they had to complete the task of recruiting 400 companies. However, at that time, the industry's highest record of recruitment was just about 200! At the time, being driven into a corner, the person in charge of recruitment inadvertently got inspiration from colleagues and proposed the 520-attracting-dealer-strategy: open 25 attracting investment conferences and break down the target of attracting 400 dealership stores; five large investment conferences were expected to draw 40 investment stores for each, which is 200 in total; the remaining 20 small investment conferences would each sign 10 stores, which is 200 in total. Therefore, the stretch goal of 400 stores was achieved. However, at that time, the investment attraction team could only make one investment promotion meeting a month, only 12 meetings throughout the year. How to make 25 promotion activities in a year? They again split the investment department team into two major groups: one was responsible for the areas in the North and the other in the South. The two small teams strived for the aim simultaneously. In 2012, organizational adjustment plus 520-strategy to lay out the national market in only three years, ZBOM signed more than 1,000 dealers across the country, quickly occupying the national market. It is noteworthy that the development of ZBOM slowed down after 2012 and it seems difficult to maintain the momentum of the previous crazy expansion due to the need for stable results after the expansion. It appears that it is difficult for ZBOM to achieve its stretch goal of 10 billion in 2019 unless the top management team can find new ways to realize the stretch goal of bricolage.

ZBOM is praised as a "black horse" in the industry thanks to its outstanding performance during the past few years. Inside ZBOM, they have their own self-deprecating explanation of a "black horse": a horse that is running during both day and night. No one is compelled to behave like this, but it is simply because they have a stretch goal. Since they agree with this goal, they must achieve it. ZBOM has a saying that "one is a hero if he or she succeeds, otherwise he or she is a loser." In fact, it is still inexact to say "success" because, according to staff from ZBOM, "the goal is not to be accomplished but to be surpassed." In other words, both the wolf spirit of a company and its bricolage approach are driven by stretch goals.

Case study 3: Huawei

The success of Huawei in the international market is triggered by its stretch goal, and Huawei's bricolage approach is in turn driven by that stretch goal. This is particularly evident in the early and mid-term development history of Huawei. Huawei wanted to occupy one-third of the market share in the global telecommunication industry: this is a dream goal of Zhengfei Ren, the founder of Huawei. This dream was so ambitious that in the early days of Huawei, Ren was called a crazy man. The stretch goal of Huawei is derived from, on the one hand, the real persecution of long-term survival of the company, which is more obvious in the early and mid-term development of Huawei; and on the other hand, from Zhengfei Ren's grand ideal, which has been proved numerous times throughout the process of Huawei's growth.

Under the guidance of this grand dream, Huawei successfully adopted ingenious strategies of market competition, many of which have obvious features that break the common competition paradigm. There are two specific examples that can illustrate how Huawei adopted explorative bricolage in pursuing its stretch goals. First, normally telecommunication companies need to focus on urban markets where there is stable demand. Such markets are dominated by big companies, which have good relationships with municipal telecommunications bureaus. Hence, the entry barrier of the telecommunication industry is very high, making survival itself a stretch goal for many small companies, such as Huawei in early 1990s. To overcome this challenge, Huawei developed user exchanges that have little to do with the telecommunications bureau and conducted a marketing strategy of rural areas encircling cities. A second case of explorative bricolage is the product of Single-RAN, which is a radio access network (RAN) technology that allows mobile telecommunication operators to support multiple mobile communication standards and wireless telephone services on a single unit. Traditionally, telecommunication companies only provided network technologies to support a single mobile communication standard. However, in 2008, Huawei observed that many customers, especially customers who come from developing countries with restrained financial resources, often operate in multiple mobile communications standards but cannot afford multiple networks. The market leaders at that time, such as Cisco, ignored this market opportunity because their innovation departments were not close enough to the customers, especially those customers from developing countries. Huawei realized this opportunity and launched Single-RAN. The product helped the company to create a competitive advantage in these markets quickly, playing a very important role in Huawei's catch up of the western leading companies. In fact, Single-RAN did not employ very advanced technology. Huawei's success can be largely explained by its bricolage mindset – a mindset that enables the company to challenge the institutional assumptions.

These ingenious ways of competition helped Huawei stand out in the competitive landscape. Obviously, the ingenious mechanisms of Huawei are specific strategic actions for its central dream of occupying one-third of the world market share.

Case study summary

The three cases we discussed illustrate how firms facing resource constraints can achieve extraordinary performance by setting and chasing a stretch goal. To achieve their stretch goals, these three firms not only worked very hard, but also adopted a shared approach: they all stayed in their existing business domains rather than rushing into new domains, and at the same time, they explored and figured out radically novel approaches to reuse their limited resources at hand. As a result, their successes were often unexpected. Our theory of exploratory bricolage provides a good explanation of such success stories concerning the unexpected or reverse entrepreneurship against the odds in the context of emerging economies. We summarize the three cases in Table 10.1.

Table 10.1 Summary of three cases

Case Study	*Time period for bricolage*	*Resource status before bricolage*	*Stretch goal*	*Explorative bricolage*	*Results of bricolage*
Case 1 **The company of Yuanjia Village** (A small-scale collective enterprise)	Transition period (around 2007)	Lack of natural tourism resources Lack of financial resources	Wish to develop tourism with no tourism resources Labeled as "fraud" of national subsidy by tourism experts	Develop "peasant-household tourism" and create a new tourism mode of "Folklore Tourism"; (challenge the assumption that natural tourism resources are necessary for developing a tourism industry; reuse peasant-households as resources for tourism)	Became the most popular destination for tourists Became the most attractive tourist attraction in Shanxi province during the National Holiday
Case 2 **ZBOM** (a small-scale kitchen supplies manufacturer)	2009/12–2012/12	Sales exceed 100 million RMB	Sales reach 1 billion in three years Ranked No. 3 in the field (No. 1 has the sales of up to 300 million in 2008)	520-attracting-dealer-strategy: open 25 attracting investment conferences, breakdown the target of attracting 400 dealership stores (challenge the institutional assumption that a kitchen supplies business is operated in a self-operated business model)	Entered the top three domestic companies in the industry Achieved the goal of 1 billion sales that increased by 10 times in 3 years
Case 3 **Huawei** (a small- to medium-sized telecommunication company which does not have a competitive advantage in the international market)	The 1990s to the mid-2000s	Being a latecomer in the technological race with international competitors such as Cisco	Top three in the world	Marketing strategy of rural areas encircling cities (challenge the assumption that major customer of the industry is in the city) single-RAN (challenge the assumption that a single network can only use a single mobile communication standard)	Caught up the western leading companies

4 Discussion and conclusion

In sum, we believe that the concept of exploratory bricolage provides important insights into the process where resource-constrained latecomers from the emerging economies, such as Huawei, ZBOM, and Yuanjia Village, can convert or transform stretch goals into radical innovations so as to catch up with and even surpass the first movers from the advanced economies. We also note that implementing exploratory bricolage must be supported by a variety of managerial measures. Exploratory bricolage is essentially about using local resources to explore radically novel (thus nonlocal) solutions in the focal organization's current business domain. Given the fact that exploration and exploitation constitute one of the most salient organizational paradoxes (Smith and Lewis, 2011), balancing explorative searches for nonlocal solutions and exploitative searches for local resources is highly challenging because these two search behaviors require incompatible routines, organizational processes, and cognitive frames (Andriopoulos and Lewis, 2009; Smith and Lewis, 2011). Hence, one of the most important antecedents to exploratory bricolage is the managers' paradoxical mindset, which enables them to embrace the opposite elements as a holistic and dynamic balancing so as to engage in explorative and exploitative actions simultaneously (Li, 2012a, 2016).

Our study makes important theoretical contributions to the organizational learning and search literature (March, 1991; Laursen, 2012; Terjesen and Patel, 2017). Different from the traditional view of innovation, which emphasizes the importance of being creative by nonlocal search (Ahuja and Lampert, 2001; Rosenkopf and Nerkar, 2001), but in line with the recent finding of Kaplan and Vakili (2015) and Mastrogiorgio and Gilsing (2016), our theory highlights the importance of local search for nonlocal innovation. Obviously, conducting innovation through nonlocal search is much easier than conducting innovation via local search, because local search often relies more on redundant knowledge elements, but nonlocal search introduces new knowledge elements to the focal organization.

However, nonlocal search has two important limitations. First, in nonlocal search, because the focal organization must enter into an unfamiliar domain, it is difficult to develop in-depth, domain-specific knowledge. Second, search into distant knowledge domains tends to be costly (Ahuja and Lampert, 2001), and small and young organizations with constrained resources may not be able to afford such costs. Local search, on the other hand, requires fewer supporting resources, but deeper domain-specific understanding, so it requires the focal organization to come up with more creative or novel approaches to recombining redundant and familiar resources. Thus, the balance between local search and nonlocal search is an important puzzle in the innovation and organizational learning literature (Gupta et al., 2006; Lavie et al., 2010). We propose a new way of balancing these two search strategies and argue that firms can use local resources to explore nonlocal solutions. By looking at these three cases, we illustrate the usefulness of our approach in analyzing cases of latecomers with a stretch goal and severe resource constraints.

The core component of exploratory bricolage is creativity. We believe that exploratory bricolage, which is based on local search for nonlocal innovation, requires a higher level of creativity than traditional breakthrough innovation based on nonlocal search. Following studies may make a connection between explorative bricolage and the creativity literature (Anderson et al., 2014). Specifically, in the Chinese context, radical creativity is closely related to the concept of "*Wu*," which refers to intuitive imagination for insight via metaphor (Li, 2012b, 2014). The research on "*Wu*" and our concept of exploratory bricolage can be integrated in the future.

Future research can also investigate the organizational enablers of exploratory bricolage. Conducting exploratory bricolage needs to be supported by organizational flexibility and agility. In order to break its path-dependence, the focal organization needs to be agile so as to respond to the changing environment by updating assumptions, routines, and organizational processes (Sambamurthy et al., 2003). Consequently, organizations must have strong dynamic capabilities (Teece, 2007; Teece et al., 1997) to effectively engage in exploratory bricolage. Accordingly, organizational structure, governance structure, reward systems, and employee training programs need to be carefully designed to facilitate the development of dynamic capability and organizational learning.

In addition, exploratory bricolage requires strong leadership, like in our three cases. How to motivate human talents and coordinate their activities is one of the most critical issues of implementing exploratory bricolage. Leaders play a central role in motivating and guiding employees of the whole organization for the pursuit of a stretch goal and also exploratory bricolage. As we can see in the three cases discussed in this chapter, all of them faced frustrations when proposed plans failed to deliver expected performance. If such stress and frustrations cannot be managed well, such organizations would fall into a vicious, downward spiral, and the negative effects of having a stretch goal would occur (Sitkin et al., 2011). A strong leader can serve as a motivator, a role model, and a coordinator, so such a leader helps an organization to commit itself to a stretch goal and maintain a strong motivation during challenging times. In this sense, only a strong leader, who often has features such as transformational leadership and anti-fragility, can manage exploratory bricolage in an effective pattern.

Last but not the least, our study provides important practical implications to the entrepreneurs and managers of late-coming companies. Although more and more recent studies attempt to understand how these firms can catch up in the technological race and compete with first movers and incumbents (Luo and Child, 2015; Miao et al., 2018), we still need more theories to explain this important puzzle. By incorporating the literature of stretch goal, bricolage, and organizational search, our study offers a unique explanation of this puzzle and a useful guideline to practitioners.

References

Ahuja, G. and C. Morris Lampert (2001) "Entrepreneurship in the Large Corporation: A Longitudinal Study of How Established Firms Create Breakthrough Inventions." *Strategic Management Journal* 22(6–7): 521–543.

Anderson, N., K. Potočnik and J. Zhou (2014) "Innovation and Creativity in Organizations: A State-of-the-Science Review, Prospective Commentary, and Guiding Framework." *Journal of Management* 40(5): 1297–1333.

Andriopoulos, C. and M.W. Lewis (2009) "Exploitation – Exploration Tensions and Organizational Ambidexterity: Managing Paradoxes of Innovation." *Organization Science* 20(4): 696–717.

Baker, T. and R. E. Nelson (2005) "Creating Something from Nothing: Resource Construction through Entrepreneurial Bricolage." *Administrative Science Quarterly* 50(3): 329–366.

Baker, T., A. Miner and D. Eesley (2003) "Improvising Firms: Bricolage, Account Giving and Improvisational Competency in the Founding Process." *Research Policy* 32(2): 255–276.

Barney, J. (1991) "Firm Resources and Sustained Competitive Advantage." *Journal of Management* 17(1): 99–120.

Barney, J. B. (2001) "Is the Resource-Based 'view' a Useful Perspective for Strategic Management Research? Yes." *Academy of Management Review* 26(1): 41–56.

Cyert, R. M. and J. G. March (1963) *A Behavioral Theory of the Firm*, Englewood Cliffs, NJ: Prentice Hall.

Eisenhardt, E. and G. Graebner (2007) "Theory Building from Cases: Opportunities and Challenges." *Academy of Management Journal* 50(1): 25–32.

Fisher, G. (2012) "Effectuation, Causation, and Bricolage: A Behavioral Comparison of Emerging Theories in Entrepreneurship Research." *Entrepreneurship Theory and Practice* 36(5): 1019–1051.

Garud, R. and P. Karnøe (2003) "Bricolage versus Breakthrough: Distributed and Embedded Agency in Technology Entrepreneurship." *Research Policy* 32(2): 277–300.

Gary, S., M. Yang, P. Yetton and J. Sterman (2017) "Stretch Goals and the Distribution of Organizational Performance." *Organization Science* 28(3): 395–410.

Guo, H., Z. Su and D. Ahlstrom (2016) "Business Model Innovation: The Effects of Exploratory Orientation, Opportunity Recognition, and Entrepreneurial Bricolage in an Emerging Economy." *Asia Pacific Journal of Management* 33(2): 533–549.

Gupta, A. K., K. Smith and C. E. Shalley (2006) "The Interplay between Exploration and Exploitation." *Academy of Management Journal* 49(4): 693–706.

Gurca, A. and M. Ravishankar (2016) "A Bricolage Perspective on Technological Innovation in Emerging Markets." *IEEE Transactions on Engineering Management* 63(1): 53–66.

Jung, H. and J. Lee (2016) "The Quest for Originality: A New Typology of Knowledge Search and Breakthrough Inventions." *Academy of Management Journal* 59(5): 1725–1753.

Kaish, S. and B. Gilad (1991) "Characteristics of Opportunities Search of Entrepreneurs versus Executives: Sources, Interests, General Alertness." *Journal of Business Venturing* 6(1): 45–61.

Kaplan, S. and K. Vakili (2015) "The Double-Edged Sword of Recombination in Breakthrough Innovation." *Strategic Management Journal* 36(10): 1435–1457.

Katila, R. and S. Shane (2005) "When Are New Firms More Innovative than Established Firms?" *Academy of Management Journal* 48(5): 814–829.

Laursen, K. (2012) "Keep Searching and you'll Find: What Do We Know about Variety Creation through Firms' Search Activities for Innovation?" *Industrial and Corporate Change* 21: 1181–1220.

Laursen, K. and A. J. Salter (2006) "Open for Innovation: The Role of Openness in Explaining Innovative Performance among UK Manufacturing Firms." *Strategic Management Journal* 27: 131–150.

Lavie, D., U. Stettner and M. Tushman (2010) "Exploration and Exploitation within and Across Organizations." *The Academy of Management Annals* 4(1): 109–155.

Lee, K. and C. Lim (2001) "Technological Regimes, Catching-Up and Leapfrogging: Findings from the Korean Industries." *Research Policy* 30(3): 459–483.

Levinthal, D. A. and J. G. March (1993) "The Myopia of Learning." *Strategic Management Journal* 14(S2): 95–112.

Li, P. P. (2012a) "Toward an Integrative Framework of Indigenous Research: The Geocentric Implications of Yin-Yang Balance." *Asia Pacific Journal of Management* 29(4): 849–872.

Li, P. P. (2012b) "Exploring the Unique Roles of Trust and Play in Private Creativity: From the Complexity-Ambiguity-Metaphor Link to the Trust-Play-Creativity Link." *Journal of Trust Research* 2: 71–97.

Li, P. P. (2014) "Toward the Geocentric Framework of Intuition: The Yin-Yang Balancing between the Eastern and Western Perspectives on Intuition." M. Sinclair (ed.), *Handbook of Intuition Research Methodology*, Northampton, MA: Edward Elgar Publishers, Chapter 3, 28–41.

Li, P. P. (2016) "Global Implications of the Indigenous Epistemological System from the East: How to Apply Yin-Yang Balancing to Paradox Management." *Cross Cultural & Strategic Management* 23(1): 42–77.

Liebowitz, S. J. and S. E. Margolis (1995) "Path Dependence, Lock-in, and History." *Journal of Law, Economics, & Organization* 11(1): 205–226.

Locke, E. A. and G. P. Latham (2013) *New Developments in Goal Setting and Task Performance*, London: Routledge.

Luo, Y. and J. Child (2015) "A Composition-Based View of Firm Growth." *Management and Organization Review* 11(3): 379–411.

Mahoney, J. (2000) "Path Dependence in Historical Sociology." *Theory and Society* 29(4): 507–548.

March, J. G. (1991) "Exploration and Exploitation in Organizational Learning." *Organization Science* 2(1): 71–87.

Mastrogiorgio, M. and V. Gilsing (2016) "Innovation through Exaptation and Its Determinants: The Role of Technological Complexity, Analogy Making & Patent Scope." *Research Policy* 45: 1419–1435.

Miao, Y., J. Song, K. Lee and C. Jin (2018) "Technological Catch-Up by East Asian Firms: Trends, Issues, and Future Research Agenda." *Asia Pacific Journal of Management* 35(3): 639–669.

Miron-Spektor, E. and G. Beenen (2015) "Motivating Creativity: The Effects of Sequential and Simultaneous Learning and Performance Achievement Goals on Product Novelty and Usefulness." *Organizational Behavior and Human Decision Processes* 127(2015): 53–65.

Nelson, R. (1990) "US Technological Leadership: Where Did it Come from and Where Did it Go?" *Research Policy* 19(2): 117–132.

Rosenkopf, L. and P. Almeida (2003) "Overcoming Local Search through Alliances and Mobility." *Management Science* 49(6): 751–766.

Rosenkopf, L. and A. Nerkar (2001) "Beyond Local Search: Boundary-Spanning, Exploration, and Impact in the Optical Disk Industry." *Strategic Management Journal* 22(4): 287–306.

Salunke, S., J. Weerawardena and J. R. McColl-Kennedy (2013) "Competing through Service Innovation: The Role of Bricolage and Entrepreneurship in Project-Oriented Firms." *Journal of Business Research* 66(8): 1085–1097.

Sambamurthy, V., A. Bharadwaj and V. Grover (2003) "Shaping Agility through Digital Options: Reconceptualizing the Role of Information Technology in Contemporary Firms." *MIS Quarterly* 27(2): 237–263.

Sarasvathy, S. (2001) "Causation and Effectuation: Toward a Theoretical Shift from Economic Inevitability to Entrepreneurial Contingency." *Academy of Management Review* 26(2): 243–263.

Sarasvathy, S. (2008) *Effectuation – Elements of Entrepreneurial Expertise*, Cheltenham, UK: Edward Elgar.

Senyard, J. M., T. Baker and P. Davidsson (2009) "Entrepreneurial Bricolage: Towards Systematic Empirical Testing." *Thin-Walled Structures* 49(4): 502–512.

Senyard, J., T. Baker, P. Steffens and P. Davidsson (2014) "Bricolage as a Path to Innovativeness for Resource-Constrained New Firms." *Journal of Product Innovation Management* 31(2): 211–230.

Sitkin, S. B., K. E. See, C. C. Miller, M. W. Lawless and A. M. Carton (2011) "The Paradox of Stretch Goals: Organizations in Pursuit of the Seemingly Impossible." *Academy of Management Review* 36(3): 544–566.

Smith, W. K. and M. W. Lewis (2011) "Toward a Theory of Paradox: A Dynamic Equilibrium Model of Organizing." *Academy of Management Review* 36(2): 381–403.

Teece, D. J. (2007) "Explicating Dynamic Capabilities: The Nature and Microfoundations of (Sustainable) Enterprise Performance." *Strategic Management Journal* 28(13): 1319–1350.

Teece, D. J., G. Pisano and A. Shuen (1997) "Dynamic Capabilities and Strategic Management." *Strategic Management Journal* 18(7): 509–533.

Terjesen, S. and P. Patel (2017) "In Search of Process Innovations: The Role of Search Depth, Search Breadth, and the Industry Environment." *Journal of Management* 43(5): 1421–1446.

Terziovski, M. (2010) "Innovation Practice and Its Performance Implications in Small and Medium Enterprises (SMEs) in the Manufacturing Sector: A Resource-based View." *Strategic Management Journal* 31(8): 892–902.

Tian, T. and X. Wu (2015) *Will Huawei Be the Next One to Collapse?* Beijing, China: China Citic Press (in Chinese).

Welter, C., R. Mauer and R. J. Wuebker (2016) "Bridging Behavioral Models and Theoretical Concepts: Effectuation and Bricolage in the Opportunity Creation Framework." *Strategic Entrepreneurship Journal* 10(1): 5–20.

Wu, L., H. Liu and J. Zhang (2017) "Bricolage Effects on New-Product Development Speed and Creativity: The Moderating Role of Technological Turbulence." *Journal of Business Research* 70: 127–135.

Wu, X., R. Ma and Y. Shi (2010) "How do Latecomer Firms Capture Value from Disruptive Technologies? A Secondary Business-Model Innovation Perspective." *IEEE Transactions on Engineering Management* 57(1): 51–62.

Yin, R. K. (1994) *Case Study Research: Design and Methods* (2nd ed.), Newbury Park, CA: Sage.

11 Open innovation ecosystem and traditional industrial cluster upgrading

A case study on the special cable industry cluster in Gaogou Town, Anhui Province

Gang Liu and Jie Liu

1 Introduction

Since the Reform and Opening-up period, China's successful industrialization has enabled it to grow rapidly into the "*Factory of the World*" with a solid cornerstone of manufacturing industrial clusters across the country. In this new stage of development, transforming to be a scientific and technological innovation center and an innovative economy with global impacts has become the primary mission of China's economic upgrading; among which the transformation and upgrading from production clusters to innovative ones are a fundamental prerequisite. The current focus of industrial upgrading is to establish an industrial innovation ecosystem for the purpose of achieving the production of high-end products and to enhance international competitiveness through the introduction and integration of innovative resources.

For simplicity, we may classify China's existing industrial clusters into two types in terms of technology resources: exogenous and endogenous industrial clusters. The exogenous industrial clusters (ExICs) attach to the global value chain (GVC) which is dominated by multinational corporations thanks to China's globalization transition. Because these types of clusters acquire external technologies, multinational corporations are the dominant players in ExICs through transferring technology and management experience, while local enterprises mainly utilize mature and standardized production technologies introduced from developed countries to process and manufacture. The dependence on foreign standardized production technologies has placed ExICs at the low end of the GVC for a long time.

The endogenous industrial clusters (EnICs) are closely associated with agricultural industrialization in China's early stage of industrialization during which technologies mainly came from domestic state-owned enterprises (SOEs), universities, and research institutes. In contrast to ExICs, EnICs refer to clusters that have developed from local technological capacity, industrial foundation, and innovation resources since the Reform and Opening-up period. In terms of technology and knowledge density, we may divide EnICs into high-tech industrial clusters and traditional industrial clusters. The high-tech industrial clusters' development began with a foundation on local innovation resources, emerging technologies, and industrialization. This type of cluster is usually located in large- and medium-size cities where scientific and technological innovation resources are abundant. Traditional industrial clusters refer to those that rely on the original local industrial capacities and existing technologies, and upgrade via self-enhancement. The latter type of EnICs are numerous in China, and widely located in counties and towns where scientific and technological innovation resources are scarce. Although self-enhancement upgrades face many challenges, they still function well in several sectors and regions, which lack the capacity to absorb external resources and technologies. In fact, such mechanisms may interpret China's innovation transformation beyond orthodox frameworks. In the early stages of development, the technologies of traditional industries mainly came from technology transfer and diffusion of SOEs during the planned economy period, then gradually developed and expanded through the continuous absorption and introduction of advanced manufacturing technologies from developed countries. The approach was similar to ExICs. However, as market conditions were changing through the rise of factor costs and the strengthening of environmental protection policies, traditional industrial clusters have been under tremendous pressure to transform and upgrade their core capacity due to their lack of innovative resources and independent innovation capabilities.

This chapter takes the wire and cable industry's transformation and upgrades around Gaogou, Anhui (Gaogou cluster, hereinafter) as a case to reveal a unique upgrading approach and to specify innovation strategies utilized when the enterprises were under unfavorable conditions. In particular, it investigates and analyzes how the special cable industry cluster, dominated by innovative small- and medium-size enterprises, has achieved high-end product manufacturing and import substitution through the collaborative innovation of government, industry, universities, and research institutes. As a typical endogenous traditional industry, wire and cable products are applied in a wide range of industries and therefore are analogized as the "artery" of national economic development. Along with China's industrialization process, the wire and cable industry has rapidly grown to be a leading manufacturing sector in terms of total output, behind the automotive and component manufacturing industries. After a fast growth period, there has been a product-centric structural imbalance problem, i.e., the overcapacity of low-end products and the shortage of high-end products in the wire and cable industry. The overcapacity problem emerged mainly due to unsophisticated technical levels, plain production processes, and low entry barriers. Special wire and cable products that meet the regulatory requirements in environmental protection and flame retardancy require more complex manufacturing techniques and have higher entry barriers. However, before domestic enterprises upgrade their products, major Chinese national projects and strategic emerging industries demand the high-end wire and cable products depend highly on the supply of multinational corporations.

In order to achieve import substitution for high-end products, domestic enterprises have been motivated to upgrade their industrial technology without governmental industrial policy favors. Several wire and cable clusters, including Guanlin Town (Yixing City, Jiangsu Province), Gaogou Town (Wuwei County, Anhui Province), Ningjin County (Hebei Province), Wujiang City (Jiangsu Province), Humen Town (Dongguan City, Guangdong Province), Fuyang City (Zhejiang Province), and Lin'an County (Zhejiang Province), have been developed maturely. The upgrading has developed along two paths: first, relying on large enterprises to create high-end products in large-scale production, to accumulate research and development (R&D) capability, and to strengthen brand presence; second, relying on industrial clusters of SOEs to develop multi-variety and small-scale production of high value-added products through cooperation mechanisms among industries, in addition to relying on universities and research institutes. Yixing and Wujiang City (Jiangsu Province) are typical cases of the first path, whereas Gaogou Town and Ningjin County are examples of the latter case. As a typical EnICs upgrading model, Gaogou Town has gradually developed from an industry cluster that produces ordinary low-end cables to a high-end special wire producing cluster by connecting, introducing, and integrating innovative resources. Around Gaogou, there are 268 cable and related enterprises with 36 billion RMB in total assets and more than 30,000 working positions in Wuwei County. Enterprises there can produce special cables used in, for example, computer, telecommunication, marine, military, and aerospace fields. They have had customers in the whole of China and other Asian countries, as well as African and European countries. Gaogou's cluster has been the largest special cable industrial base, and the second largest cable industrial base in China. China's Ministry of Science and Technology (MoST) has awarded and supported the cluster with the "China Torch Program" and the "National New Industrialization Demonstration Base."

2 Industrial upgrading and innovation system

From the perspective of industrial development, industrial upgrading can be considered an adjustment of industrial structure, which is not just limited to the three industries, but includes the development of strategic emerging industries. As China's economy is approaching a "new normal," scholars have been more concerned with industrial upgrading from the perspective of producer services and strategic emerging industries. Especially in the context of the fourth industrial revolution, most efforts on current industrial structure adjustments focus on how to promote the development of strategic emerging industries through innovation-driven strategies (Gu et al., 2009; Gu et al., 2016; Tian and Pan, 2017). The GVC analysis focuses on the upgrading of ExICs and explores how to promote the industrial chain from low-end production to high-end value-added production by actively introducing multinational R&D institutions and improving innovation capabilities (Nathan et al., 2019; Gereffi, 2014; Humphrey and Schmitz, 2002). From the perspective of cluster development, meeting the demand of the high-end domestic market and improving independent R&D capabilities are the basic driving forces for the upgrading of endogenous traditional industrial clusters. Factors such as cluster network structure (Glückler, 2013), cluster environment (Delgado et al., 2014), and integration degree (He and Rayman-Bacchus, 2013) will affect the innovation performance of industrial clusters.

The development of products from low-end to high-end seems to be the same concept as industrial upgrading, but in essence, reflects the improvement of innovation capabilities of enterprises and industries regardless of exogenous or endogenous traditional industrial clusters. Upgrading innovation capability involves not only raw materials, intermediate products and improvement of manufacturing equipment, but also R&D services and human capital accumulation, which reflect the process of cultivating and perfecting the industrial innovation ecosystem (Adner, 2006; Adner and Kapoor, 2010; Kruss and Gastrow, 2012).

Building up an innovative ecosystem to enhance technology and knowledge supply capability is the essential connotation of industrial upgrading. Before the consideration of an ecosystem perspective, there is a long list of institutions that may be favorable in the upgrading process, i.e., the systemic perspective of innovation. Advocates of the national innovation system (NIS) and the Regional Innovation System (RIS) have been attractive to academics and policymakers for a long time. The NIS discusses the system of institutions supporting innovation (Nelson and Rosenberg, 1993). Compared with developed countries, innovation systems in developing countries and regions should be studied from a development framework (Gu, 1999). Dahlman and Frischtak (1993) found that Brazilian enterprises have distanced from the frontier because domestic enterprises involved in technological development did so inadequately, and the government did not create a long-sighted consideration from a developmental perspective. Instead, East Asian countries, in particular Japan and South Korea, effectively utilized industrial policies to build industrial capabilities (Kim, 1993). Edquist (2001) moved forward with the concept of "development and innovation system" and found four key differences in the development and innovation systems of developing countries compared with those in developed countries. First, product innovation was more important than technical innovation for developing countries; second, incremental innovation was more likely to succeed than radical innovation; third, absorption of technologies in diffusion was more important than original innovation; and lastly, innovation in low to medium technology was more likely to achieve breakthrough than that in high-tech fields.

The Regional Innovation System (RIS) was proposed by Philip Nicholas Cooke and supported among others. RIS emphasizes the functionality of connecting innovation resources within a geographical space. For example, if enterprises within a region can network and integrate an innovation process through information sharing and technology transfer, it may create multiple positive benefits for all (Cooke, 1992). As Doloreux et al. (2003) argue, the core of RIS is that the innovation performance of an economy depends on its innovation capabilities of enterprises and research institutions and their interactions among each other. Facilitating the network among innovation actors is the core mechanism, but it may face many challenges from the institutional and organizational coordination in, for example, the financial and cultural arenas (Cooke et al., 1997). Ronde and Hussler (2005) identified the determinant factors of manufacturing industries in France from a RIS perspective. They found that establishing a mechanism for communication and interaction with external organizations was more important than focusing solely on the development of internal innovation resources, and the focus of regional innovation policy was to support an interactive network among innovation subjects both intra- and inter-regionally. Especially in the absence of local innovation resources, the ability to establish technology and knowledge exchange, and interaction mechanisms with external innovation entities was even more important for the transformation and upgrading of traditional industries.

If we place this discussion in developing economies, challenges will be much more significant. Viotti (2002) argues that the development of innovation systems in developing countries and regions should focus on the diffusion, absorption, and learning of technologies, because developing economies or regions lack the capacity to utilize technological progress as developed economies can. Both system perspectives at a national and regional level fail to examine the complex dynamics of the innovation system carefully. An ecosystem view, which relates to biological or social ecosystems, attempts to fill this gap by applying complexity approaches by, for example, using the complex adaptive systems framework. An innovation ecosystem, in which the major subjects are enterprises, is "the collaborative arrangements through which enterprises combine their individual offerings into a coherent, customer-facing solution" (Adner, 2006, p. 99). The concept of innovation ecosystems emphasizes the diversification and self-organizing process of the innovation actors, which may better reflect developing features. Innovation ecosystems are concerned with how interrelated actors or players make innovation happen (Fransman, 2018), and even how innovators perceive innovation policies (Dai, 2016). The main actors include business enterprises, consumer-users, universities, other institutions, etc. How these actors interact may determine the performance of the system in which the actors are embedded. From a systemic view, there is no standard answer to evaluate the efficiency or optimal level of an ecosystem, but we can identify the relevant parameters (Fransman, 2018). Gawer and Cusumano (2014) suggest an "internal-external" dichotomy to classify industrial platforms. Enterprises may either integrate with other enterprises that share a common structure in developing products or work for further complementary innovation on the open foundation other enterprises provide. However, a more in-depth understanding on how to construct an industrial innovation ecosystem and what kind of industrial innovation ecosystem will promote industrial upgrading still lacks theoretical analysis. China's traditional industrial clusters are confronted with two particular situations: first, the innovation resources within the industrial clusters are extremely scarce due to the influence of national and regional innovation distributions; and second, high-end products are more represented by import substitution, that is, the imitation of high-end products from developed countries. We, therefore, try to investigate the transformation and upgrading of traditional industrial clusters with a focus on how to cultivate an industrial innovation ecosystem. Based on this, we then consider the interactions and collaborations of multiple innovation subjects to determine how to learn, absorb, and imitate the R&D and production technologies of similar high-end products in developed countries to enhance R&D and industrial innovation capability.

3 Research method and design

3.1 Research method

For different types of industrial clusters, there are different industrial upgrading paths in various contexts of markets, technologies, and resources. This chapter takes the endogenous traditional industrial cluster perspective and examines how to connect and introduce external innovation resources under the conditions of insufficient innovation resources within the clusters. Then, it builds an innovation network and industrial innovation ecosystem based on the existing production network, achieving a dynamic evolution process from low- to mid-end products and eventually to high-end ones.

Since the mid-1990s, with the collective entrepreneurial efforts of migrant workers, a wire and cable industrial cluster with 268 enterprises gradually formed around Gaogou Town. Similar to other regions, the wire and cable industrial cluster in Wuwei County was mainly producing low-end cable products. With the intensification of competition in the low-end product market and the emergence of domestic demands for high-end products in around 2008, the wire and cable enterprises in Wuwei County began to explore industrial upgrading. In order to meet market demands, they eventually targeted a high-end product-oriented special wire and cable section through linking with external innovation resources and introducing an open industrial innovation ecosystem. In order to analyze the motivation and upgrading mechanism from production network to innovation network of the wire and cable industrial cluster in Wuwei County, we conducted fieldwork in a select 14 enterprises and one testing institute engaged in new product development.[1] The sample enterprises develop and produce high-end special wire and cable products for high-end equipment manufacturing, including military, vessel, rail transit, industrial robots, and new energy vehicles. In contrast with general production enterprises, all enterprises in this study have provincial enterprise technology centers, engineering technology centers, multiple technology patents, and professional R&D teams. Among these enterprises, some were involved in the ordinary wire and cable sector and have successfully transformed and upgraded; the rest are newly created enterprises in recent years. Also, the research sample also includes National Special Wire and Cable Product Quality Supervision and Inspection Center (Anhui) (hereinafter, "Special Cable Center (Anhui)") established in 2014. Table 11.1 lists the basic information of the survey samples.

Table 11.1 Basic information of survey samples of the Gaogou cluster

Category	*Name*	*Founding Year*	*Main product application areas*	*Technical qualification*
Wire and cable enterprises	Huayuan	1976	Rail transit, military and warship	National High Technology Enterprise Provincial Enterprise Technology Center
	Huaneng	1986	Rail transit	Provincial Postdoctoral Research Station Provincial Enterprise Technology Center
	Jianghuai	1986	Rail transit, military, aerospace	National Key Projects and Military Supporting Production Enterprise Provincial Enterprise Technology Center
	Hualing	1989	Rail transit	Provincial Enterprise Technology Center Provincial Engineering Technology Center
	Lingyu	1989	Mining	Provincial Enterprise Technology Center
	Sunway	1999	Rail transit	Provincial Enterprise Technology Center
	Siait	1992	Rail transit, nuclear, military, aerospace	National High Technology Enterprise Provincial Enterprise Technology Center Provincial Engineering Technology Center
	Hong Yuan	1993	Aerospace	Provincial Enterprise Technology Center Provincial Engineering Technology Center
	Rui Zhi Xing	1993	Rail transit, military	Provincial Enterprise Technology Center
	Xin Ke	1994	Rail transit	National High Technology Enterprise Provincial Technology Center First Institute of Electrical Insulation
	Hua Xing	1995	Electrical equipment	Provincial Enterprise Technology Center Provincial Engineering Technology Center
	Zhongheng Hi-tech	1998	High-speed rail, new energy automobile	Provincial Technology Center
	Hua Yu	2004	Warship	Provincial Enterprise Technology Center Provincial Engineering Technology Center
	Guo Dian	2006	Computer and control equipment	Provincial Enterprise Technology Center
Testing Institute	Special Cable Center (Anhui)	2014	R&D and testing services for the special wire and cable industry	One of the largest and most influential wire and cable testing institutions in China

Source: Websites of enterprises and institutes, 2018.

3.2 Data collection and analysis

We applied the value network analysis method to portray the connections of the 14 enterprises and one institute as sample nodes and to present the connecting nodes that were cooperating with the 15 sample nodes in product development. The connecting nodes and data collection include three types: (1) market information sources of the sample enterprises; (2) sample enterprises' cooperation on R&D in new products and testing services; and (3) human capital training for new product development and production process innovation. Besides the connection data, we also collected detailed information on how they managed these relationships. To simplify the statistical analysis, the value equals one when there are the preceding three relationships between nodes; otherwise, the value will be zero.

The connection data collected in this study was collected from two sources: first, the field survey data of the sample enterprises and institutions; and second, literature and public reports. The connection data of the 15 sample nodes were mainly from field surveys, and the data of the relational connections were from public reports and literature. Based on the collected connection data, we analyzed how the sample nodes and connecting nodes developed new product R&D and cooperation through mutual connections and interactions in order to reveal the motivation and mechanism to promote high-end products and industrial upgrading.

4 Motivation and mechanism to upgrade in the Gaogou cluster

We used Gephi to analyze the network data. On the graph, there are 49 nodes, 15 of which were sample nodes, 34 relational nodes, and 142 edges that represent a connection. First, through the statistical analysis on the value network data in the Gaogou cluster; this section will determine the vital nodes affecting the industrial upgrading process. Thus, based on the connection data and information, we will analyze how the value network between the sample nodes and the relational nodes developed new products and promoted R&D innovation through mutual connections and interactions, and we will establish the motivation and mechanisms to promote high-end products.

4.1 The innovation network structure in the Gaogou cluster

Figure 11.1 shows the topological structure of the innovation network of the Gaogou cluster. The main nodes in the innovation network diagram include: (1) special cable sample enterprises in Wuwei County, which are marked as A1–A14; (2) relational nodes related to obtaining R&D information for new products, including electric power design institutes and industry alliances, marked as BB1–BB8; (3) the special cable center (Anhui), marked as BC; (4) the universities and research institutes related to the R&D of new products, wherein domestic universities are marked as BD1–BD14 and research institutes are marked as BE1–BE4; and (5) the enterprises, among which domestic enterprises are marked as BF1–BF4 whereas foreign enterprises are marked as

BG1–BG6. We list the classification of the nodes and the marks for the corresponding key nodes in Appendix 11-A.

Figure 11.2 shows the distribution of centrality of innovation network nodes which was divided into three groups. The first group includes Special Cable Center (Anhui) (BC), Shanghai Electric Cable Research Institute (BE1),

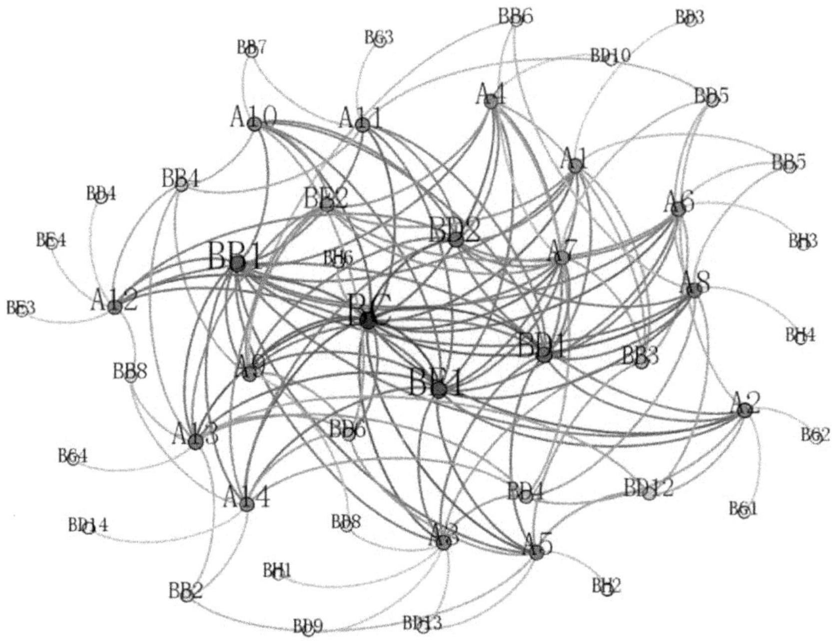

Figure 11.1 Innovation network diagram of the Gaogou cluster

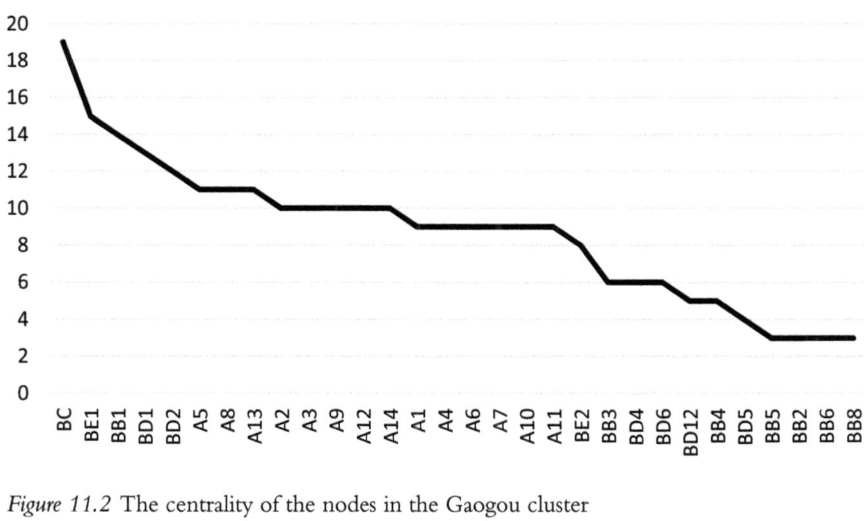

Figure 11.2 The centrality of the nodes in the Gaogou cluster

Table 11.2 The structural indicators of the innovation network of the Gaogou cluster

Indicator	*Graph Distance*	*Graph Density*	*Average Clustering Coefficient*	*Average Distance*
Value	4	0.121	0.062	2.664

Electric Power Design Institute (BB1), Harbin Institute of Technology (BD1), and Xi'an Jiaotong University (BD2). They are the most central nodes in the network, with the exception of the local node BC. The others are relational nodes located outside the industrial cluster; they provide R&D and technology support. Through connections and interactions with the sample enterprises, these central nodes obtain knowledge and technologies required for new product development and information on market demands. The second group consists of the 14 sample enterprises; the third group refers to other relational nodes including domestic and foreign enterprise customers, universities, research institutes, and industry alliances.

Table 11.2 lists the structural indicators of the innovation network of the Gaogou cluster. From both the perspective of the individual sample enterprises and the overall network, the openness was high. This was indicated by the high linkage between the network and external innovation resources indicates that the innovation network of the cluster in Wuwei County.

4.2 Analysis of cooperative relationships for new product R&D

4.2.1 Market information for new product development

As shown in Figure 11.3, we find that the local enterprises obtain market demand information mainly through the following ways: R&D institutes represented by the Shanghai Electric Cable Research Institute, engineering design institutes represented by the Electric Power Design Institute, strategic emerging industry alliances, and client enterprises.

In Wuwei County, the Shanghai Electric Cable Research Institute and the Electric Power Design Institute were the major sources of information for new product development and market demand in the upgrade process of special wire and cable industry, accounting for 24.19% and 22.58% respectively. As the most important R&D and testing organization in the domestic cable industry, the Shanghai Electric Cable Research Institute has abundant resources for scientific and technological innovation, and extensive contacts with domestic and foreign enterprises as well, thus it collects a large amount of market demand information for new wire and cable products. Meanwhile, market demands for high-end cables mainly come from large-scale national engineering projects such as the military industry. The referenced engineering design and R&D departments, such as Electric Power Design Institute, Nuclear Power Institution, and

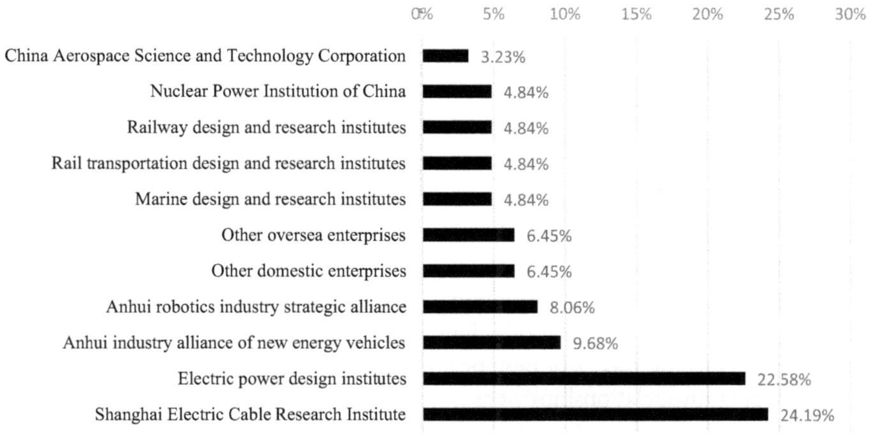

Figure 11.3 Information sources of market demand in the Gaogou cluster

China Academy of Space, involve the use of cables in their overall engineering design and hence unintentionally provide market demand information for high-end new product development as well.

The special wire and cable enterprises in Wuwei County have aimed to be suppliers of key raw materials and components for high-end facilities through participating in the innovation alliance of strategic emerging industries. Recent developments of strategic emerging industries, for instance, new energy vehicles and robotics, have generated a strong market demand for new high-end wire and cable products. The industry is still in the early stage of R&D and marketization, thus enterprises both upstream and downstream have established industrial alliances to jointly promote the product and industrial development. For example, the newly emerged robotics industry has special requirements for the flexibility of wires and cables. By joining in the new energy vehicles and robotics industry alliance, cable enterprises in Wuwei County have actively participated in the development of strategic emerging industries. At the same time, the strategic emerging industries of new energy vehicles and robotics are the main focuses for development in Wuhu City. Market proximity has remained an important factor for the acquisition of market information for new product R&D. As shown in Figure 11.3, the industry alliances engaged in new energy vehicles and robotics have become one of the most important sources of market demand information for new product developments, accounting for 9.68% and 8.06% respectively. For example, as a prioritized strategic emerging industry, the industry alliance of new energy vehicles has been supported by Anhui Province for strategic innovation, covering multiple innovation subjects such as universities, administrative corporates, customers, and raw materials. The Anhui Robotics Industry Strategic Alliance has brought together 14 universities and enterprises including the Harbin Institute of Technology, Hefei University of

Technology, Anhui Ruixiang Industrial Co., Ltd., and Wuhu Binjiang Intelligent Equipment Industry Development Co., Ltd.

4.2.2 Cooperation in product development

Figure 11.4 presents the distribution of cooperative relationships for new product development in the cluster. The Special Cable Center (Anhui) has the closest R&D relationship with the sample enterprises, accounting for 20.21%, followed by the Shanghai Electric Cable Research Institute, Harbin Institute of Technology, and Xi'an Jiaotong University, with 15.96%, 13.83%, and 12.77% respectively. However, the Wuhan High Voltage Research Institute, Hefei University of Technology, and University of Science and Technology of China are also the main partners in the R&D of new products for the wire and cable industry.

The cooperative relationships were categorized based on the organizational type of new product development technology. One category is the testing institutes represented by the Special Cable Center (Anhui) and the Shanghai Electric Cable Research Institute, and the other group includes universities and research institutes represented by the Harbin Institute of Technology, and Xi'an Jiaotong University. As a principal testing institute, the Special Cable Center (Anhui), and the Shanghai Electric Cable Research Institute have a mastery of information and technologies on qualities and raw materials of new products. For example, the Shanghai Electric Cable Research Institute is the only research institute in China that integrates wire and cable R&D, engineering design, test and inspection, and information services. Hence it possesses extensive external links. It cooperates not only with domestic universities, large SOEs and with other units but also with foreign enterprises such

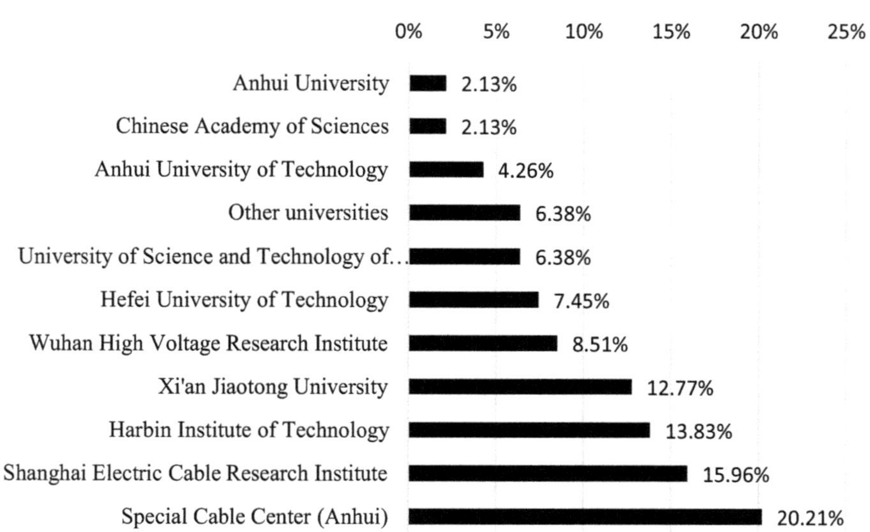

Figure 11.4 Cooperative relationships for new product development in the Gaogou cluster

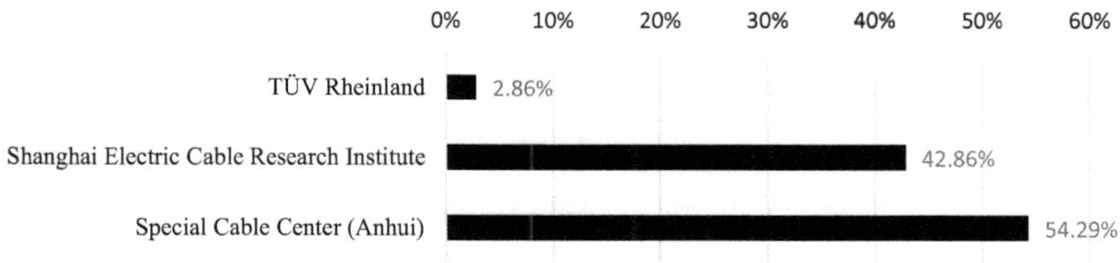

Figure 11.5 Testing institutes in innovation network in the Gaogou cluster

as TÜV Rheinland; this keeps the Shanghai Electric Cable Research Institute at the frontier of domestic cable industry development and playing an important role in the process of new product development and industrial upgrading. Universities and research institutes take their advantages of scientific research and talents to provide high level support for the R&D of high-end products in traditional industries, technology upgrading, and human capital training.

Testing and inspection are important parts of the development and production of new products (shown in Figure 11.5). Before the establishment of the Special Cable Center (Anhui) in 2014 in Wuwei County, main testing and inspections relied on the Shanghai Electric Cable Research Institute. With the upgrade of the special wire and cable industry, the Special Cable Center (Anhui) was established due to the demand for frequent testing and accumulation of related knowledge. After three years of improvement, the Special Cable Center (Anhui) has achieved a leading position in the industry in terms of testing and inspection capability. At the international level, laboratories can carry out wire and cable inspections on 262 products and 228 parameters covering five major cable categories including bare wires, wires, and cables for electrical equipment, electric power cables, telecommunication cables, and optical cables.

As the most authoritative testing institute in China, the Shanghai Electric Cable Research Institute has a national wire and cable quality supervision and inspection center, which is a third-party product-testing laboratory independent of the development, manufacturing, and trade of wire and cable products. However, even after the establishment of the Special Cable Center (Anhui), the Shanghai Electric Cable Research Institute still plays a vital role in the cutting-edge new product testing for wires and cables. In the export process, TÜV Rheinland conducts testing and authentication of exported products for wire and cable enterprises in Wuwei County. The TÜV logo represents a safety certification specifically designed for component products, which is widely accepted in Germany and Europe. Therefore, the certification of TÜV is an important qualification in export.

4.2.3 Cooperative relationships for human capital training

In terms of human capital training in innovation networks in Wuwei County, the Harbin Institute of Technology and Xi'an Jiaotong University, focusing on

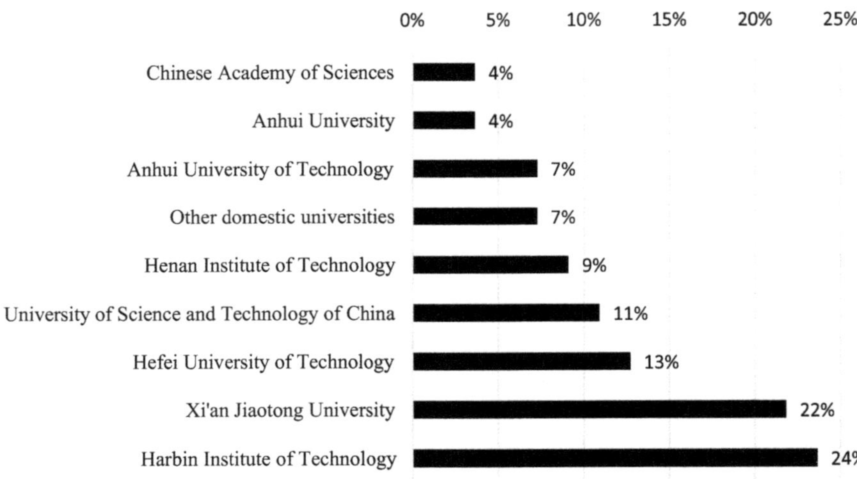

Figure 11.6 Cooperative relationships for human capital training in the Gaogou cluster

the domestic wire and cable industry, have mastered frontier technologies of wires and cables. Through the cultivation of human capital, a large number of talents have been transferred to the special wire and cable industry in Gaogou Town. As shown in Figure 11.6, the cooperative relationships between the Harbin Institute of Technology, Xi'an Jiaotong University, and sample enterprises of special wire and cable industry in Wuwei County account for nearly 45%. Meanwhile, the Hefei University of Technology and China University of Science and Technology, with their geographical proximity and related disciplines, have also become important institutions for human capital training in the cluster. The Henan Institute of Technology (formerly Henan Mechanical and Electrical College), a vocational and technical college, has sent a mass of skilled workers to the wire and cable industry in Wuwei as well.

4.3 An open industry innovation ecosystem

We have learned a few critical messages from the cooperation relationship in the development and production processes. First, the local wire and cable enterprises have been active and dominating in creating the cooperative system in the innovative transformation process. Second, the industrial innovation ecosystem has been highly open and thus has been an important way to develop high-end products and to connect with external innovation resources. Third, public research and testing platforms have been constructive in R&D organizations. For instance, as a public service platform, Special Cable Center (Anhui) has served to accumulate and share new product development, knowledge, and technologies, and has been the core node of the industrial innovation ecosystem. Fourth, the active participation in the strategic emerging industry alliances has been a valuable channel for R&D and production.

The principal motivation behind the upgrade in the wire and cable industry originated from the high saturation of low-end domestic products, the competition among homogenized products and the continuous increase of raw material prices. In contrast to the overcapacity of low-end products, the mid- to high-end product market, especially the special wire and cable market, was encountered with a serious supply shortage. Due to special safety and environmental requirements, the development and production of the high-end cable products were constrained by complicated technical barriers, which were basically monopolized by the US, Japan, and European companies.

Substituting foreign high-end imported products has become the basic strategy of upgrading the wire and cable industry cluster in Wuwei County. In order to develop and produce substitute-worthy high-end cable products, the special wire and cable enterprises in Wuwei began the upgrading with the establishment of new technology centers for production-oriented enterprises and R&D activities under the support of government policies. Among 268 production enterprises, 27 have established provincial-level enterprise technology centers, nine have established provincial-level engineering technology centers, and one has set up an academician workstation while five have set up postdoctoral workstations. By setting up internal technology centers, some production-oriented enterprises have transformed into innovative enterprises, and with further steps into the leading groups in the industry.

Due to the lack of local science and technology innovation resources, the special wire and cable enterprises in the cluster had to rely on the internally established technology centers and introduce external innovation resources to develop and produce new products. The development of new products was on a contract basis, which refers to the cooperation with scientific research institutions and their professionals through formal and informal contracts.

In the process of industrial upgrading, those new products needed in the domestic market are often those high-end products that have already been mass-produced in developed countries. Hence, the analysis and imitation of the high-end foreign products as well as technological improvement have become key to the development of new products. Domestic universities and research institutes that have extensive contacts with foreign enterprises and research institutions have actually been learning the information on foreign high-end product technical parameters and qualities. The research and testing capabilities of universities and research institutes represented by the Shanghai Electric Cable Research Institute have been the source of access to innovative resources. At the same time, domestic market demand has been mainly for large-scale or special national projects; hence state-owned engineering design institutes have better knowledge about domestic product market demands, technologies, and qualities. Therefore, cooperating with state-owned engineering design institutes would help to comprehend the technical parameters and demand information about the new products.

When new product development reaches the mass production stage, enterprises will cooperate with universities and research institutes such as the Harbin Institute of Technology to improve the production process and human capital training. For example, Harbin Institute of Technology, known as the "*Whampoa Academy*" in the wire and cable industry, boasts cutting-edge technology on cables. The wire and cable enterprises in Wuwei County can improve their knowledge of and technology for new productions through cooperation with the Harbin Institute of Technology.

Since 2008, the wire and cable enterprises in Wuwei County have continuously upgraded their R&D capabilities based on the self-constructed technology centers through extensive cooperation with universities and research institutes. As of 2017, more than 70 private special cable enterprises and 300 related enterprises in upstream and downstream industries have aggregated in Gaogou's Industrial Park, forming a new special cable industry innovation cluster in Wuwei County and an enterprise-oriented open innovation ecosystem focusing on high-end product development and production, including service systems such as: R&D, testing, intellectual property, technology transfer and consulting.

In the industrial innovation ecosystem in the cluster, the Special Cable Center (Anhui), established by the government in 2014, has been the most noteworthy. The special wire and cable industry has a wide variety of different product standards due to unique environmental requirements of product use. Every type of new product is frequently tested during the development and production processes; testing institutes are therefore an important carrier for local industrial knowledge accumulation. The establishment of the Special Cable Center (Anhui) has enabled the local special wire and cable enterprises to set up its own innovation platform. As a public service platform, the Special Cable Center (Anhui) has played a role in the aggregation and diffusion of technology, knowledge, and experience in the process of product testing for enterprises within the cluster; further, the enterprises can access information of the tested parameters from each other. On the one hand, the establishment of a public testing platform enables the enterprises within the cluster to better learn from external innovation resources and knowledge, and on the other hand, it promotes learning and imitation between enterprises within the cluster through the accumulation of specific knowledge and technology. For example, in order to be visible in the network and promote knowledge sharing, one enterprise in Gaogou will make public its knowledge one year after the development of a new product, thus enabling other enterprises to follow suit on production.

In addition to participating in key national projects, the special wire and cable industry in Gaogou has also become an important supplier in the high-end equipment manufacturing sector with the rise of strategic emerging industries such as new energy vehicles and robotics. The Emerging Industrial Innovation Alliance has been an essential source for special wire and cable enterprises in Gaogou to absorb market information on new product development and technologies. The exchange of knowledge and technology between enterprises within the industrial alliance has become a vital driving force for industrial upgrading.

Since 2005, with continuous effort during the decade, the wire and cable industry cluster has grown from an industrial cluster mainly producing ordinary products to a high-end special cable-producing cluster. Also, it has not only participated in a series of key national projects on hydropower, nuclear power, military, and high-speed rail, but also been the supplier of necessary spare parts for those strategic emerging industries such as new energy vehicles and robotics. High-end production is just a facade of the industrial upgrading, while its substance lies in the construction of an enterprise-oriented open innovation ecosystem and the improvement of enterprise innovation capability.

5 A further theoretical explanation

Does the case we studied generalize a path of industrial upgrading for an endogenous traditional industrial cluster? Conventionally, the primary goal of industrial upgrading toward high-end products is import substitution of foreign products (Baer, 1972; Baer and Kerstenetzky, 1964; Epshtein, 2017). Similar products are produced abroad, hence the basic strategy of upgrading traditional industrial clusters is to master the R&D, design, and production technologies of the foreign high-end products. The traditional industrial cluster is a production network composed of small- and medium-size enterprises, and the independent innovation capabilities of these enterprises are insufficient. Most of them in China were developed in the rural industrialization stage away from main cities, while most of the scientific and technological innovation resources are distributed mainly in provincial capital cities, regional main cities, and municipalities. Therefore, the spatial distribution of innovative resources related to industrial upgrading has led to the fact that to achieve high-end production, endogenous traditional industrial clusters far from main cities must enhance their innovation capabilities by accessing external innovation resources.

We exhibit the upgrade dynamics and mechanisms of China's domestic traditional industrial clusters in Figure 11.7. In the initial state, the basis of industrial cluster upgrading was based on the production network for the domestic low-end product market. As main parts of the production network, production-oriented enterprises carry out scale production by imitating and introducing mature domestic products and standardized production technologies.

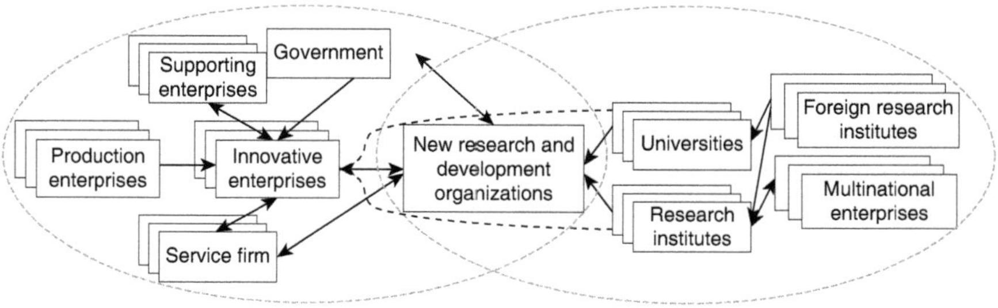

Figure 11.7 Motivation and upgrade mechanism of endogenous traditional industry clusters

In the past, when the market competition of low-end products became intensive, enterprises switched to high-end products for higher marginal profits. However, when foreign high-end product manufacturers restrict technology transfer, the only solution for the enterprises is to break through technological barriers with independent innovation to develop and produce high-end products with high margins. Within this context, latecomers should actively apply the open innovation model to alleviate barriers (Wang and Zhou, 2012).

Regarding the adaptation to the changing market, some production-oriented enterprises and start-ups have gradually developed into innovative enterprises by establishing technological R&D departments to carry out innovation activities. Due to the lack of innovative resources within the cluster, innovative enterprises had to rely on their own technological departments to access innovative resources outside the cluster and cultivate independent innovation capabilities through the construction of an open innovation network. Universities, research institutes, and testing institutes with relevant technologies have become primary targets for those innovative enterprises as sources of technology introduction and connection.

When pursuing high-end products and implementing independent innovation strategies become collective actions within the cluster, the shared demand lies in how to internalize external innovation resources. Once the demand for services related to R&D and technological innovation have reached a certain scale, governments should introduce and create new R&D organizations to meet the collective innovation requirements of the enterprises and meanwhile promote the industrial upgrading of the entire cluster. The new R&D organizations play the following roles: first, representations of the government's initiatives to promote industrial transformation and upgrading; second, carriers of key technologies, common technologies, and knowledge accumulation; and third, links between the innovation needs of enterprises within the cluster and external innovation resources. Therefore, the new R&D organizations are combinations of collaboration amongst the government, industry, universities, and research institutes, etc.

The new R&D organizations serve the common and large-scale needs for enterprise innovation and integrate functions such as government policies, technology, and knowledge carriers, and innovative resource connection; the latter most being the core node of the open industrial innovation ecosystem. The emergence of new R&D organizations cannot completely substitute for external innovation resources, including universities and research institutes that have extensive contact with innovative enterprises at home and abroad. In particular, the connection with R&D institutions and multinational corporations in developed countries are essential channels to acquire information on new product developments, technologies, and qualities, and are an essential part of the open innovation ecosystem required for cluster upgrading.

The industrial innovation ecosystem set up by EnICs is highly open. On the one hand, it is the connection between innovative enterprises within the cluster and external innovation institutions; on the other hand, it is the connection between external institutions and other foreign innovation institutions and multinational corporations. Local innovation institutions are important components of national and regional innovation systems, while international innovation institutions are essential parts of the global industrial innovation system. With economic globalization, an important mechanism for the upgrading of EnICs is to connect and integrate the industrial innovation ecosystems between clusters on a national and global scale. In addition to universities, research institutes, and testing institutes, the industrial innovation alliance, which was set up for applications of emerging technologies and the development of emerging industries, has also been a crucial external innovation institution. Due to high uncertainties of industrial development, actively participating in emerging industrial innovation alliances helps to detect opportunities for industrial development and effectively master the market and technical information of new product development.

Therefore, the industrial innovation ecosystem that drives the upgrading of EnICs includes three key factors: (1) the emergence of innovative enterprises within the cluster, which refers to the transformed production enterprises and new ventures; (2) the new R&D organizations, collaborated on by the government, industry, universities, and research institutes – the primary functions of the new R&D organizations being to implement innovation policies, to have contact with external innovation resources and to accumulate common technical knowledge; (3) the external innovation institutions and organizations, which exist as important parts of the industrial innovation ecosystem. As a link between the internal and external innovation entities of the cluster, innovation institutions and organizations provide not only technological support for product developments but also offer opportunities to develop cutting-edge new products (Harper, 2018).

Promoting an active mutual connection and interaction among multiple innovation entities is crucial to an open innovation ecosystem for the endogenous traditional industrial clusters. After new product developments of enterprises within the cluster, the knowledge and technology spillovers from external innovation institutions play vital roles. The knowledge and technologies of new products are acquired through the interactions between innovative enterprises and external innovation institutions. Meanwhile, the accumulation and diffusion of common knowledge and technologies are realized through communications between enterprises within the cluster and via external innovation institutions. Therefore, the starting point and fundamental frame of government policies must be to formulate incentives to promote the connections and interactions of multiple innovation entities effectively. Creating such a friendly climate for open innovation may benefit the overall economy as well (Chesbrough et al., 2011).

6 Summary and policy implications

Based on the investigation and value network analysis of an endogenous traditional industrial cluster upgrading, this chapter provides a few conclusions. For developing countries, the transformation from producing low-end products to high-end ones appears to be an industrial upgrade, but in essence, it is a process to enhance the innovation capability of enterprises and industries through the construction of an open industrial innovation ecosystem. Innovative enterprises are the pioneers of industrial upgrading by actively promoting the construction of an open industrial innovation ecosystem, creating R&D departments in enterprises and accessing external innovation resources. The role of the government is to respond to the demand of enterprises within the cluster for key and common technologies and knowledge in the process of innovation capability upgrading, and to further establishment of new R&D organizations. As the core node of an open industrial innovation ecosystem, the new R&D organizations combine government policies, carriers of technologies and knowledge, and external innovation resources to connect the multiple functions. The openness of the industrial innovation ecosystem in the cluster connects extensively not only with domestic innovation institutions but also between domestic and international innovation institutions.

The conclusion of this chapter contains two suggestions to policymaking: First, most endogenous traditional industrial clusters are located far away from innovative and resource-intensive main cities. Therefore, actively developing innovative enterprises within the cluster and establishing new R&D organizations to absorb, introduce, and integrate innovative resources should be an important initiative for local governments to promote industrial upgrading. Second, the cluster industrial innovation ecosystem has been highly open during the industrial upgrading process and has close links with the national and global industrial innovation systems. In the transition from made-in-China to created-in-China, the highly open national and regional innovation system corresponding to industry upgrading is vital for implementing innovation-driven development and an innovative economy.

Notes

1 According to the Wuwei County government and industry associations, there are 27 wire and cable enterprises in Wuwei County with qualifications of provincial technology centers and engineering technology centers. This chapter mainly selected 14 enterprises with those qualifications originating from Gaogou Town as samples for investigation and data collection, accounting for 51.8% of all enterprises with provincial technical centers and engineering technology centers.

References

Adner, R. (2006) "Match your Innovation Strategy to your Innovation Ecosystem." *Harvard Business Review* 84(4): 98.

Adner, R. and R. Kapoor (2010) "Value Creation in Innovation Ecosystems: How the Structure of Technological Interdependence Affects Firm Performance in New Technology Generations." *Strategic Management Journal* 31(3): 306–333.

Baer, W. (1972) "Import Substitution and Industrialization in Latin America: Experiences and Interpretations." *Latin American Research Review* 7(1): 95–122.

Baer, W. and I. Kerstenetzky (1964) "Import Substitution and Industrialization in Brazil." *American Economic Review* 54(3): 411–425.

Chesbrough, H., W. Vanhaverbeke, T. Bakici and H. Lopez-Vega (2011) "Open Innovation and Public Policy in Europe." EASADE Report. Available at http://innovation.esadeblogs.com/files/2012/01/Open-Innovation-and-Public-Policy-ScienceBusiness-Innovation-Board-Report1.pdf (accessed March 13, 2019).

Cooke, P., M. G. Uranga and G. Etxebarria (1997) "Regional Innovation Systems: Institutional and Organisational Dimensions." *Research Policy* 26(4–5): 475–491.

Cooke, P. H. (1992) "Regional Innovation System: Competitive Regulation in the New Europe." *Geoforum* 23(2): 365–382.

Dahlman, C. J. and C. R. Frischtak (1993) "National Systems Supporting Technical Advance in Industry: The Brazilian Experience." R. R. Nelson (ed.), *National Innovation Systems: A Comparative Analysis*, New York: Oxford University Press, 414–450.

Dai, S. (2016) "Innovation and National Systems of Innovation Policies: A Network Approach." Claudius Gräbner, T. Heinrich and H. Schwardt (eds.), *Policy Implications of Recent Advances in Evolutionary and Institutional Economics*, London, UK and New York: Routledge and Taylor & Francis Group, 189–206.

Delgado, M., M. E. Porter and S. Stern (2014) "Clusters, Convergence, and Economic Performance." *Research Policy* 43(10): 1785–1799.

Doloreux, David, Charles Edquist and Leif Hommen (2003) "The Institutional and Functional Underpinnings of the Regional Innovation System of East-Gothia in Sweden." Paper Presented at the DRUED Summer Conference 2003 on Creating, Sharing and Transferring Knowledge: The Role of Geography, Institutions and Organizations. Copenhagen, June 12–14, 34–41.

Edquist, C. (2001) "Systems of Innovation for Development. Background Paper for Chapter1: Competitiveness, Innovation and Learning: Analytical Framework." The UNIDO World Industrial Development Report.

Epshtein, D. (2017) "Import Substitution and Neo-Industrialization: What Must Be Done." *Problems of Economic Transition* 59(1–3): 186–201.

Fransman, Martin (2018) *Innovation Ecosystems: Increasing Competitiveness*, Cambridge, UK: Cambridge University Press.

Gawer, A. and M. A. Cusumano (2014) "Industry Platforms and Ecosystem Innovation." *Journal of Product Innovation Management* 31(3): 417–433.

Gereffi, G. (2014) "Global Value Chains in a Post-Washington Consensus World." *Review of International Political Economy* 21(1): 9–37.

Glückler, J. (2013) "Knowledge, Networks and Space: Connectivity and the Problem of Non-interactive Learning." *Regional Studies* 47: 880–894.

Gu, S. (1999) "Implications of National Innovation Systems for Developing Countries: Managing Change and Complexity in Economic Development." UNV-INTECH Discussion Paper Series 03, United Nations University.

Gu, S., S. S. Serger and B. Å. Lundvall (2016) "China's Innovation System: Ten Years on." *Innovation: Management, Policy and Practice* 18(4): 441–448.

Gu, S. et al. (2009) "China's System and Vision of Innovation: An Analysis in Relation to the Strategic Adjustment and the Medium- to Long-Term S&T Development Plan (2006–20)." *Industry and Innovation* 16(4–5): 369–388.

Harper, D. A. (2018) "Innovation and Institutions from the Bottom Up: An Introduction." *Journal of Institutional Economics* 14(6): 975–1001.

He, Z. and L. Rayman-Bacchus (2013) "Cluster Network and Innovation Under Transitional Economies." *Chinese Management Studies* 4(4): 360–384.

Humphrey, J. and H. Schmitz (2002) "How Does Insertion in Global Value Chains Affect Upgrading in Industrial Clusters?" *Regional Studies* 36(9): 1017–1027.

Kim, L. (1993) "National System of Industrial Innovation: Dynamics of Capability Building in Korea." R. R. Nelson (ed.), *National Innovation Systems: A Comparative Analysis*, New York: Oxford University Press, 357–383.

Kruss, G. and M. Gastrow (2012) "Global Innovation Networks, Human Capital, and Development." *Innovation and Development* 2(2): 205–208.

Nathan, D., M. Tewari and S. Sarkar (eds.) (2019) *Development with Global Value Chains: Upgrading and Innovation in Asia (Development Trajectories in Global Value Chains)*, Cambridge, UK: Cambridge University Press.

Nelson, R. R. and N. Rosenberg (1993) "Technical Innovation and National Systems." R. R. Nelson (ed.), *National Innovation Systems: A Comparative Analysis*, New York: Oxford University Press, 3–21.

Ronde, Patric and Caroline Hussler (2005) "Innovation in Regions: What Does Really Matter." *Research Policy* 34(8): 1150–1172.

Tian, S. and Z. Pan (2017) "'Made in China 2015' and 'Industrie 4.0' Motion Together." U. Sendler (ed.), *The Internet of Things*, Berlin and Heidelberg, Germany: Springer, 87–113.

Viotti, E. B. (2002) "National Learning Systems: A New Approach on Technological Change in Late Industrializing Economies and Evidences from the Cases of Brazil and South Korea." *Technological Forecasting and Social Change* 69(7): 653–680.

Wang, Y. and Z. Zhou (2012) "Can Open Innovation Approach Be Applied by Latecomer Firms in Emerging Countries?" *Journal of Knowledge-based Innovation in China* 4(3): 163–173.

Appendix 11-A

Names and codes of the innovation network nodes in the Gaogou cluster

Category	**1 – Wire and cable enterprises**							
Code	**A1**	**A2**	**A3**	**A4**	**A5**	**A6**	**A7**	**A8**
Node	Guo Dian	Hong Yuan	Hua Ling	Hua Neng	Hua Xing	Hua Yu	Hua Yuan	Jiang Huai
Code	**A9**	**A10**	**A11**	**A12**	**A13**	**A14**		
Node	Ling Yu	Sunway	Rui Zhi Xing	Xin Ke	Siait	Zong Heng Hi-Tech		
Category	**2 – Source of information**							
Code	**BB1**	**BB2**	**BB3**	**BB4**	**BB5**	**BB6**	**BB7**	**BB8**
Node	Electric Power Design Institutes	Railway Design and Research Institutes	Industrial Alliance of New Energy Vehicle industry	Industrial Alliance of Robotics industry	Nuclear Power Institution of China	Marine Design and Research Institute	China Aerospace Science & Technology Corporation	Rail Transportation Design and Research Institute
Category	**3 – Testing Institute**							
Code	**BC**							
Node	Special Cable Center (Anhui)							
Category	**4 – Universities**							
Code	**BD1**	**BD2**	**BD3**	**BD4**	**BD5**	**BD6**	**BD7**	**BD8**
Node	Harbin Institute of Technology	Xi'an Jiaotong University	Wuhan University	Hefei University of Technology	Anhui University of Technology	University of Science and Technology of China	Hefei University	Chinese Academy of Sciences
Code	**BD9**		**BD10**		**BD11**		**BD12**	
Node	Beihang University		Jiangnan University		Anhui University		Henan Institute of Technology	

(Continued)

(Continued)

Category	**5 – Research institutes**				
Code	**BE1**	**BE2**	**BE3**	**BE4**	
Node	Shanghai Electric Cable Research Institute	Wuhan High Voltage Research Institute	The Fifth Research Institute of Telecommunications Technology	The 23rd Research Institute for Electronics of Ministry of Industry and Information Technology	
Category	**6 – Domestic enterprises**				
Code	**BF1**	**BF2**		**BF3**	**BF4**
Node	China Aerospace Science and Technology Corporation	China National Nuclear Corporation		China Best Group Holding Limited	China National Machinery Imp. & Exp. Corporation
Category	**7 – Foreign enterprises**				
Code	**BG1**	**BG2**	**BG3**	**BG4**	**BG5**
Node	NKT GmbH & Co. KG, Cologne (Germany)	Adani Group (India)	Yazdan Kalaye Talesh (Iran)	PMS Trading (France)	TÜV Rheinland (Germany)

12 An "Iron Triangle" in Northeastern China

Revisit the new Northeast phenomenon and its innovation ecosystem

Donglin Song, Changcheng Yao and Xin Fan

1 Introduction

Since the reform and opening-up period, scientific and technological breakthroughs have been made in various undertakings in China. Efforts in building an innovative nation have achieved fruitful results such as the Five-hundred-meter Aperture Spherical radio Telescope (FAST), the Dark Matter Particle Explorer (DAMPE), the Quantum Experiments at Space Scale (QUESS), and many other major scientific and technological infrastructures which consolidate the basis of China's innovation and sustainable development (Yang, 2016). At the 19th Congress, The Communist Party of China (CPC) claimed that China would continue to devote efforts toward catching up with the leading countries and becoming an innovative country by 2035. However, at present, China still faces challenges such as insufficient innovation ability and inadequate innovation dynamics. Building an innovation-driven economy requires strengthening basic research, deepening reforms in the science and technology system, training a large number of world-leading scientists and engineers, polishing industrial policymaking, and improving the innovation ecosystem (Lundvall, 1992; Fransman, 2018). The United States, as the most innovative and dynamic country, not only benefits from its advanced national innovation system, but from its market's institutional setup (Berger, 2013; Locke and Wellhausen, 2015). China, however, has a vast territory and population, which may provide vast diversification in shaping its innovation environment. This advantage allows us to make use of the current capacity and build an indigenous innovation ecosystem in various regions.

The three northeastern provinces we will focus on – Liaoning, Jilin, and Heilongjiang – have outstanding science and education resources, and in terms of knowledge competitiveness and technological facilities rank among the highest in China (Song, 2015). For example, at the end of 2016, there were 258 research institutes, colleges, and universities in the three northeastern provinces, whereas there were 2,596 total in China; i.e., around 10% of scientific resources were in the Northeast (NBS, 2017). According to the Academic Ranking of World Universities (ARWU) released by Shanghai Jiaotong University in 2018, three universities in the northeastern provinces rank in the top 300 in the world, whereas only another 20 Chinese universities reach such a ranking level. Meanwhile, Northeast China has a comprehensive industrial system and well-developed infrastructure for large-scale manufacturing production (Zhang, 2008). Regarding the transportation infrastructure alone, the total railway mileage in the three northeastern provinces reached 17,100 km in 2015, accounting for 14.13% of the national railway mileage. We might conclude that these favorable conditions have made the Northeast economy innovative; however, if we look at their innovation performance, these three provinces are not active in many aspects. Innovation capacity for Liaoning province, Jilin province and Heilongjiang province reported yearly in *The Report of China Regional Innovation Capability Evaluation* show dropping trends in recent years. Liaoning ranked at 8th place in 2011, but at 18th place in 2016. Jilin dropped from 16th place in 2011 to 27th place in 2016. Heilongjiang fell from the 17th place in 2009 to the 22th in 2016 (see Figure 12.1). Therefore, a paradox may have emerged: Why can favorable knowledge resources and industrial foundation not be transferred into knowledge competitiveness, generate the driving force of innovation, and create wealth? This is the so-called "*New Northeast Phenomenon*," which should be further investigated.

The argument of the "New Northeast Phenomenon" evolves from the "Northeast Phenomenon" concept which captures the paradox between Northeast China's slow market transformation and comprehensive industrial foundation since the 1980s. For example, in the 1990s, many state-owned enterprises (SOEs) of the old industrial bases in Northeast China had gone bankrupt during the process of institutional transition and marketization (Chen and Liu, 2017). Since 2013, the economic situation in Northeast China became even worse, despite existing under strong governmental stimulation initiated at the beginning of the 2000s. In 2016, the GDP growth rates of Liaoning, Jilin, and Heilongjiang ranked as some of the lowest, the seventh lowest, and the third lowest respectively among the 31 provinces and municipalities of China. This chapter is trying to uncover this phenomenon from the innovation ecosystem perspective.

Although these two types of "Northeast Phenomenon" are different, they may also have some similarities and correlation when we look further inside the reasons of the "New Northeast Phenomenon." Song (2015) argues that, besides slowing economic growth that is claimed by others (e.g., Chen and Liu, 2017), because of factors like systemic problems and industry structure, low innovation capacity in manufacturing enterprises which are highly embedded in the "Northeast Phenomenon" is still at the heart of the unsolved problems. Hence, the old industrial bases in Northeast China have simultaneously dealt with the slowdown in economic growth while making difficult structural adjustments and absorbing the effects of previous economic stimulus policies, which further highlighted the historical problems caused by the traditional industrial structure and the planned economic system and resulted in a significant slowdown of economic growth. However, Zhao (2015) also emphasizes that the phenomenon is not totally caused by or related to overall slowing growth; it

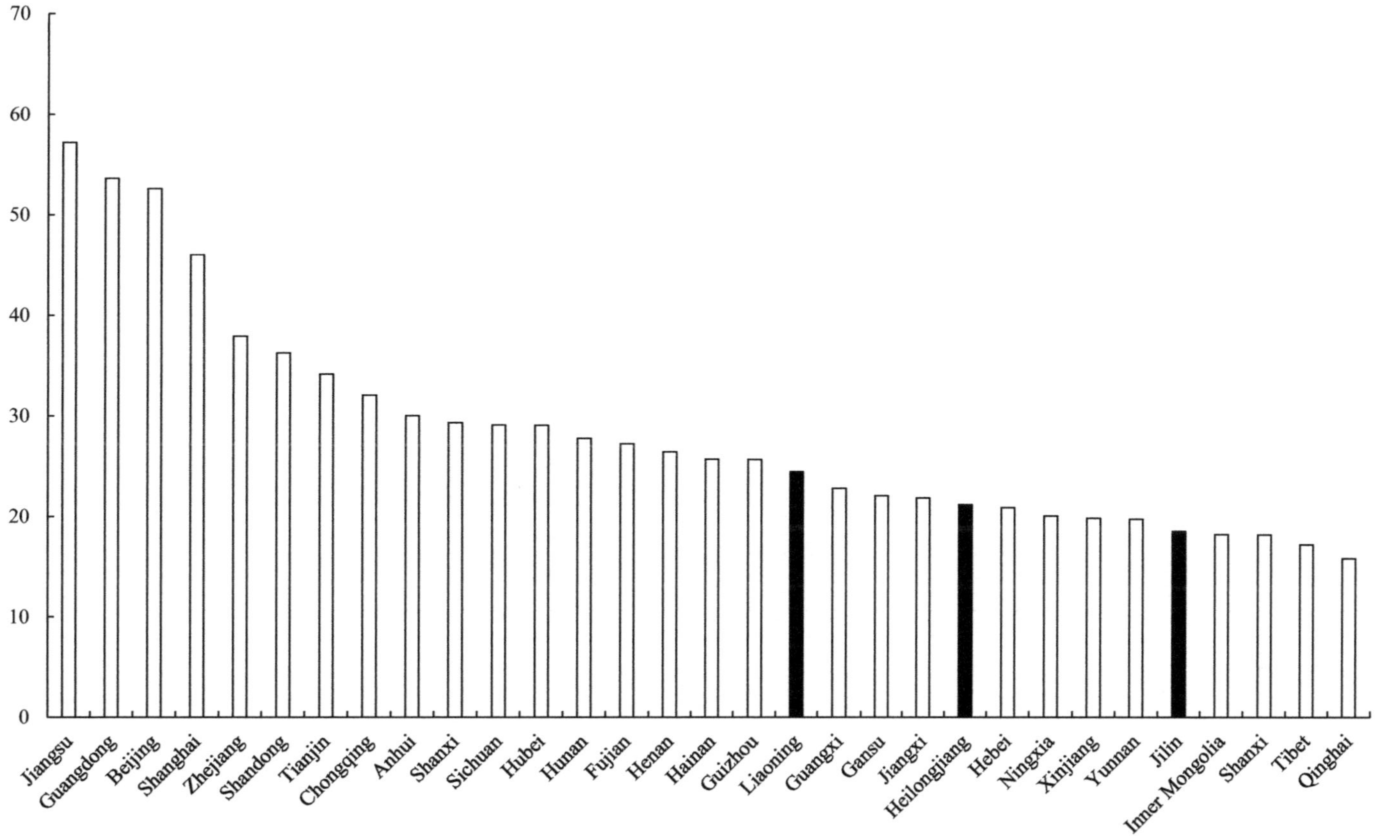

Figure 12.1 China regional innovation capacity evaluation (2016)

Source: China Science and Technology Development Strategy Research group (2016). The Report of China Regional Innovation Capability Evaluation. Beijing. Scientific and Technical Documentation Press. P. 8.

has other causes. To be more specific, it is due to problems coming from the manufacturing industry. As the Chinese economy is under a structural transformation, the Northeast region's downward economic pressure is relatively large. Although the government has implemented a number of reform measures, the development of the manufacturing industry, which is the pillar industry of the Northeast economic growth, is still relatively slow. This is especially true for the traditional manufacturing industry, whose development faces enormous challenges (Zhao, 2015). More specifically, the difficulties in the manufacturing industry in Northeast China lead to poor innovation capability of manufacturing enterprises, and an innovation-driven transition will be instrumental in transforming the economic development mode and upgrading the manufacturing sectors (Song et al., 2016).

Low marketization level is another reason. SOEs currently have the majority share of the whole economy, and the private economy is spiritless. There are also many problems in the fields of economic ideology, management and governance system, industrial development, policymaking, regulations, and even legal barriers in Northeast China (Song, 2015). This leads to the "New Northeast Phenomenon" in terms of innovation capacity problems, and therefore economic performance issues. Thus, Zhao (2015) suggests the fundamental way for the Northeast to improve its situation is to deepen reform and promote transformation. With such respects, measures focused on should include promoting the marketization of the allocation of public resources, developing a factor market, accelerating the reform of SOEs and the improvement of SOEs in general, restructuring industrial structure, reshaping local government behavioral patterns, and improving government governance capabilities.

Overall, under the contexts of the "New Normal" and an "Innovation-Driven" China, establishing innovation capacity has become an essential step for economic structural transformation and industrial upgrading. Reinvigorating the economy in the northeast region is far from simply taking one or two measures or policies on improving innovation capability (Wei, 2017), but rather it is a systematical venture that is supposed to be comprehensive, sustainable, and long-term (Zeng, 2013).

The rest of this chapter is organized as follows: the second section gives an overview of the *status quo* and problems of innovation development in Northeast China. Northeast China is equipped with a relatively comprehensive industrial system and infrastructure and benefits from abundant science and education resources, but its innovation capacity still needs to be improved and its innovation ecosystem should be reformed. The third section analyzes the main obstacles of innovation in Northeast China. It also proposes the "iron triangle" model that is comprised of a rigid system mechanism, the single industrial structure and the spiritless micro market economies. Under this model, the upgrade trend of innovation in Northeast China is thus locked. The model helps us to fully understand the dynamic development of the market economy and the innovation ecosystem in Northeast China. Because the innovation ecosystem in Northeast China has not yet been established, this chapter also suggests a dynamic innovation ecosystem that is mutually beneficial, open, and competitive. The last section concludes the chapter.

2 The present situation and problems of innovation development in Northeast China

Since the implementation of the strategy for rejuvenating the Northeast's old industrial base by the national government in October 2003, Northeast China has enjoyed a golden decade with fast economic growth. However, the resource-policy-driven model is unsustainable, and all three provinces have experienced a "growth collapse" since 2013. If we have a closer look at their innovation capacity, their performance signifies such collapse in a more depressive way, as we discussed using Figure 12.1.

A transition to being innovation driven has become the primary strategic choice for revitalizing the Northeastern economy, and such an argument has been widely acknowledged among governmental practices, academia, and even local residence. Yet, according to the 2016 assessment report on China's regional innovation capability released by China's Ministry of Science and Technology (MoST), the ranking of innovation capabilities in the three northeastern provinces continues to fall. In addition, the report shows that the overall level of scientific and technological progress in the three provinces is also relatively low. In all of China, Liaoning province, Heilongjiang province, and Jilin province fall in the second category group for scientific and technological progress (where the overall index of science and technology progress is below the national average of 67.57%, but higher than 50%) (see Figure 12.2).

2.1 Lack of innovation in high-tech industries

The Northeast was an important region for exploitation and processing of natural resources in China, especially during the planned economy period before 1978. These favorable conditions have laid an admirable material-based foundation for industrial development. Most leading industries in the Northeast, therefore, are natural resource-based and in traditional manufacturing sectors. However, emerging high-tech industries only survive in the cracks, and their potential for further development is insufficient. Due to the depletion of resource exploitation, resource-based industries have been gradually declining and traditional manufacturing sectors with technological obsolescence have lost their competitiveness in the market. Although the high-tech industry has been improved to some extent in the recent decade, its innovative ability is still weak.

From the perspective of innovation input of high-tech industries, the internal expenditures of R&D funds and R&D per capita in the Northeast are below the national average (see Figure 12.3 and Figure 12.4). However, Liaoning province invested more than the other two provinces and has surpassed the national average level since 2011.

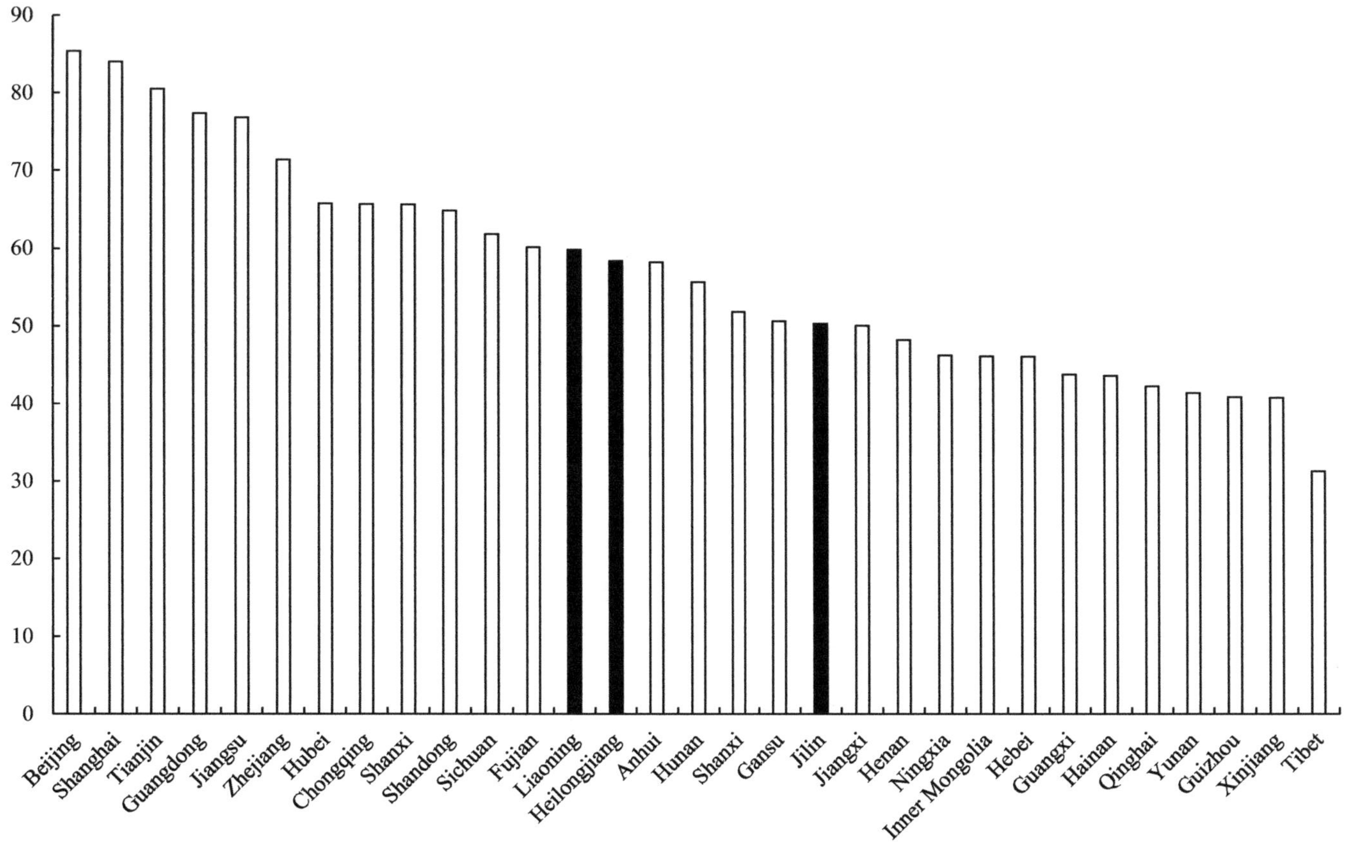

Figure 12.2 Evaluation of comprehensive scientific and technological progress in China (2016)

Source: China Academy of Science and Technology Development strategy (2016–2017). The Report of China Regional Science and Technology Innovation Evaluation. Beijing. Scientific and Technical Documentation Press. P. 7.

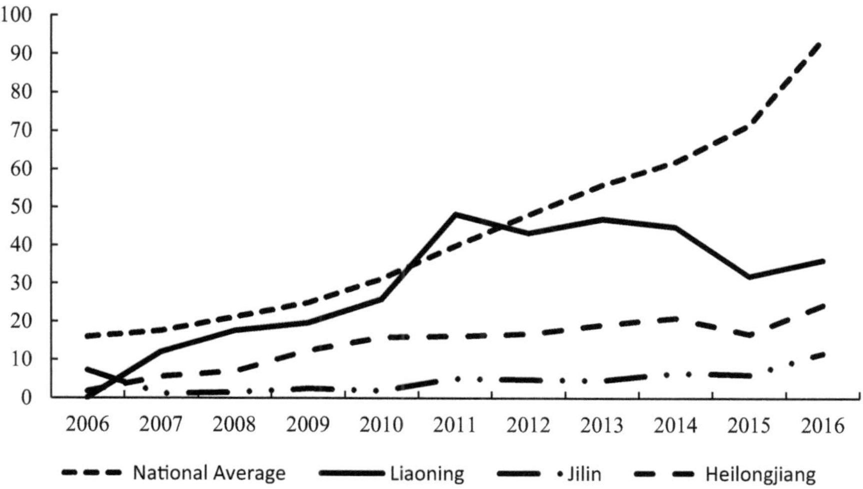

Figure 12.3 High-tech industries full-time equivalent of R&D per capita in the Northeast (man-year) (2006–2016)

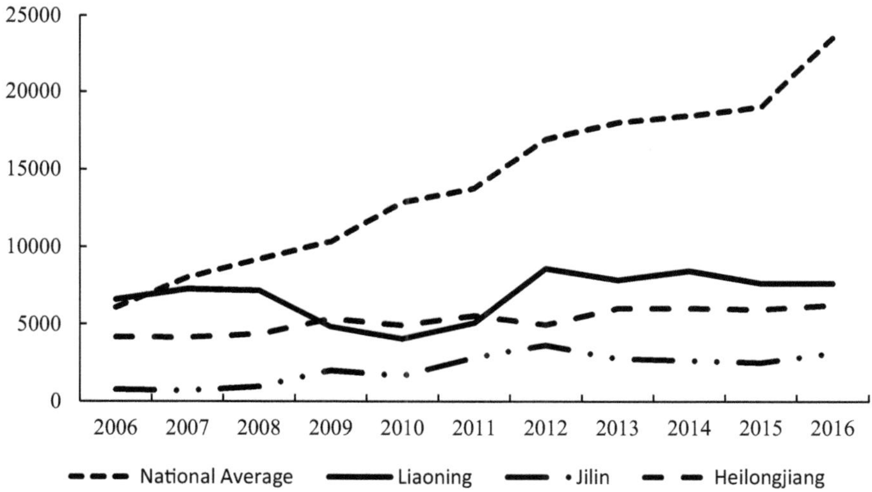

Figure. 12.4 High-tech industries R&D internal expenditure in the Northeast (hundred million Yuan) (2006–2016)

Regarding innovation output of high-tech industries, both the sales revenue of new products and effective invention patents in the three northeastern provinces are far below the national average (see Figure 12.5 and 12.6). Although the number of patents has shown a certain upward trend, the revenue of their

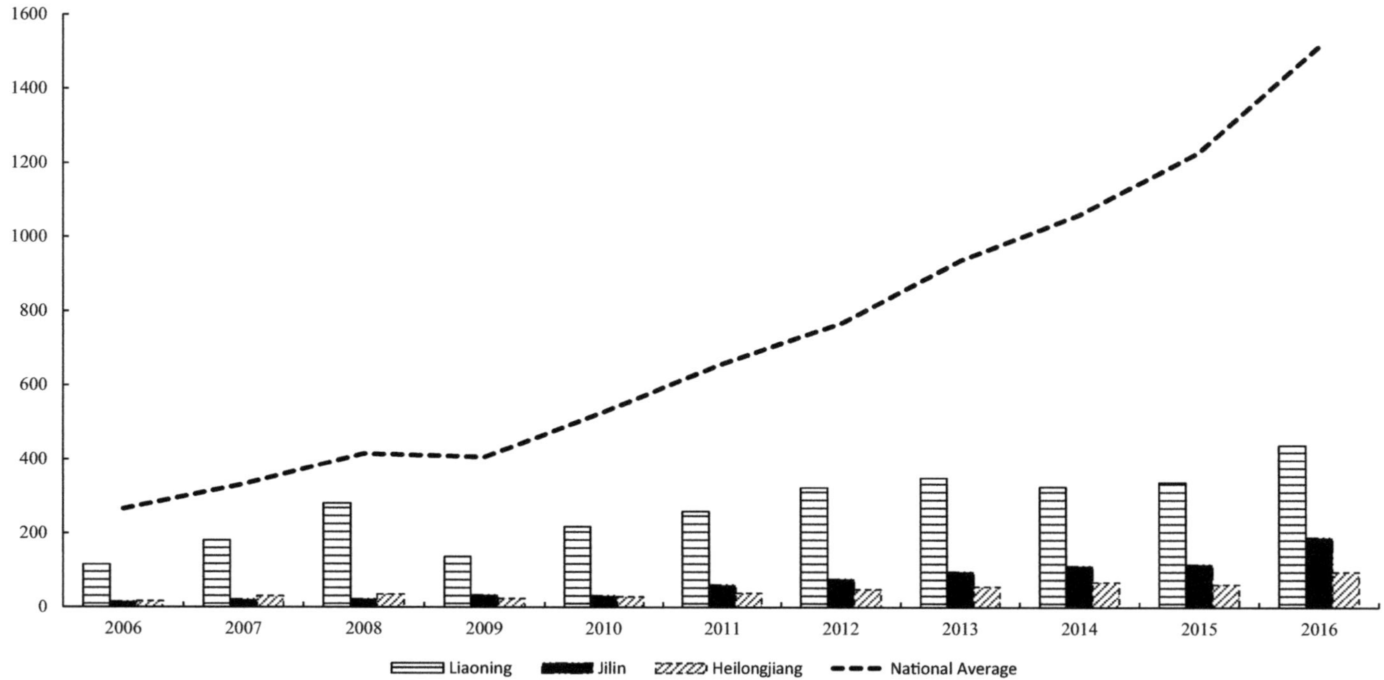

Figure 12.5 High-tech industries new product sales in the Northeast (hundred million Yuan) (2006–2016)

Source: China Statistical Yearbook on Science and Technology (2007–2017)

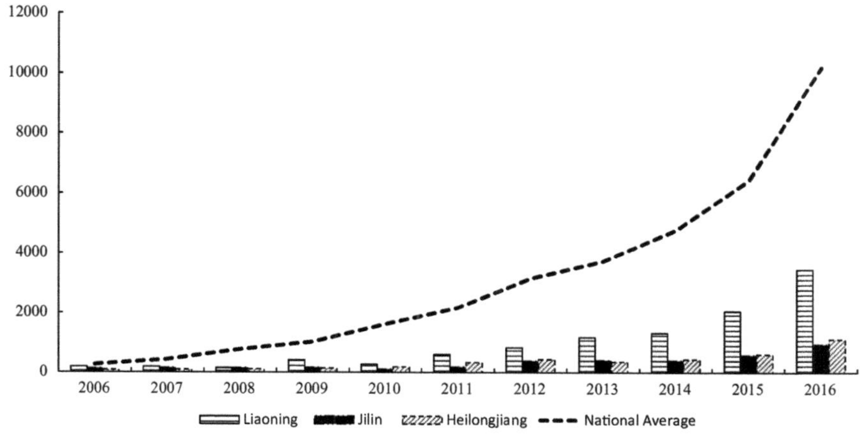

Figure 12.6 High-tech industries effective patents in the Northeast (piece) (2006–2016)

Source: China Statistical Yearbook on Science and Technology (2007–2017)

new products has stagnated, which reflects that the provinces' high-tech industries have lost their competitiveness in the new product market. In terms of internal comparison among the three northeastern provinces, the innovation output of high-tech industries in Liaoning province is slightly higher than that of the other two provinces.

2.2 Lack of innovation motivation for industrial enterprises

In the planned economy era, governments and state-owned sectors dominated the economy, and the driving force for innovation mainly came from governmental efforts. However, since the socialist market economic system is in a transitional period, the subjects of innovation have gradually shifted from the government to firms. In the Northeast, heavy industry development has trapped the economy in the planned economy stage, and now is blocking the transition. The state-owned economy is still dominant and the private economy is underdeveloped. The innovation capacities of SOEs are obviously insufficient, as the pressure of competition is absent.

With respect to the input and output of innovation in industries, the innovation efficiency gap between the Northeast and other regions in China is large (See Figures 12.7 to 12.10). Only the internal expenditure on R&D and new product sales revenue in Liaoning province come close to surpassing the national average or do surpass it. However, Liaoning province's numbers started to fall after 2013 and it gradually lost its advantage of competition compared with other provinces. Although the investment in R&D personnel, internal expenditure on R&D, sales of new products and effective invention patents in Jilin province have increased year by year, it still lags far behind the national

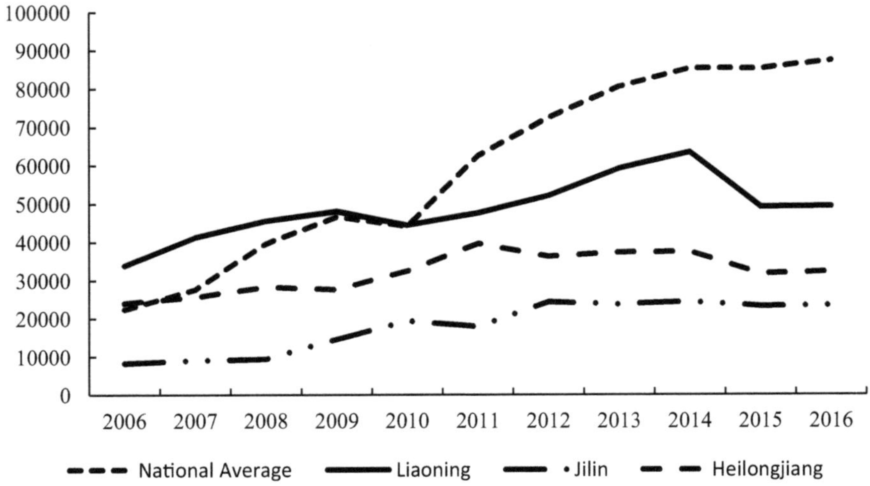

Figure 12.7 Industrial full-time equivalent of R&D personnel in the Northeast (man-year) (2006–2016)

Source: China Statistical Yearbook on Science and Technology (2007–2017)

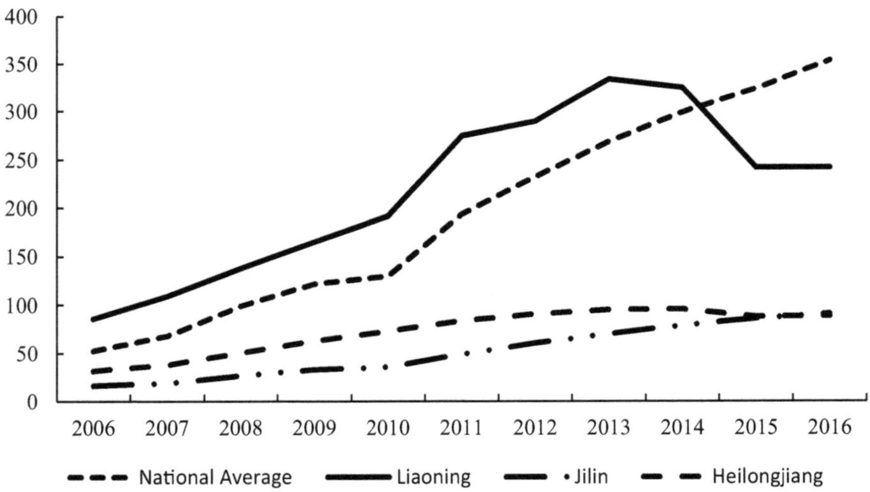

Figure 12.8 Industrial R&D internal expenditure in the Northeast (hundred million Yuan) (2006–2016)

Source: China Statistical Yearbook on Science and Technology (2007–2017)

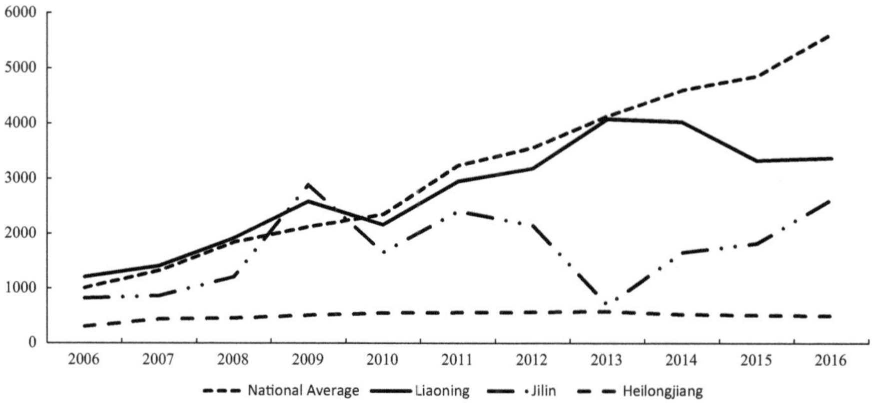

Figure 12.9 Industrial new product sales in the Northeast (hundred million Yuan) (2006–2016)
Source: China Statistical Yearbook on Science and Technology (2007–2017)

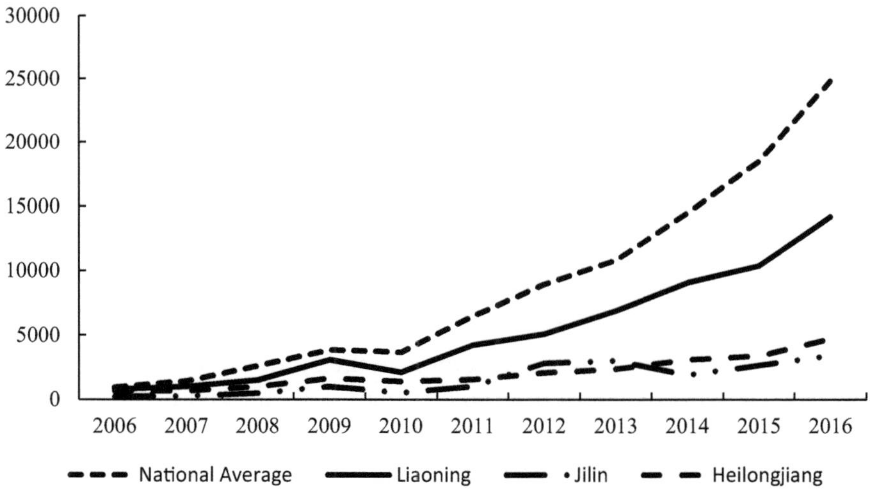

Figure 12.10 Industrial effective patents in the Northeast (piece) (2006–2016)
Source: China Statistical Yearbook on Science and Technology (2007–2017)

average after 2013. Moreover, Heilongjiang province performs poorly in new product sales compared with other two provinces investigated.

2.3 The governmental debt and its weak financial support

In November 2008, the central government issued a "four trillion stimulus package" as a response to the global financial crisis aimed at further expanding domestic demand and promoting stable and rapid economic growth. Thus, local governments at all levels increased their investment in transportation infrastructure, and consequently the average national fiscal deficit rose rapidly (see Figure 12.11). Northeast China's fiscal deficit appears worse when compared to the national average level. Besides the fact that the scale of fiscal deficit in Jilin province has been controlled at below the national average after 2009, the gap between Heilongjiang province and the national average is gradually widening and the scale of fiscal deficit in Liaoning province is consistently above or at the national average level.

Judging from the government's debt ratio by the end of 2016, the debt ratios of Liaoning, Heilongjiang, and Jilin provinces reached 204%, 152%, and 138% respectively. Except for Jilin province, the debt ratios of the provinces have exceeded the 90% to 150% range of the security cordon set by the International Monetary Fund (IMF). Due to the huge fiscal deficit, the Northeast has much lower support for science and technology than the national average both in terms of absolute expenditure and relative expenditure. According to the latest data released by the National Bureau of Statistics of China, the total national expenditure on science and technology in 2016 amounted to 65.64 billion yuan, accounting for 3.50% of the total fiscal expenditure. However, the total expenditure on science and technology in Liaoning province was only 6.16 billion yuan, accounting for 1.34% of the total expenditure. The total expenditure on science and technology in Heilongjiang province was only 4.49 billion yuan, accounting for 1.06% of the total expenditure. The total expenditure on science and technology in Jilin province was also only 4.10 billion yuan, accounting for 1.14% of the total expenditure. Hence, intervention from the government's side in industrial adjustment has been highly limited.

2.4 *Strong scientific research strength of higher education institutions*

As we stressed before, the scientific profile in the Northeast is actually impressive, and has much potential that can be explored. By the end of 2016, among the 2,596 higher education and research institutions in China, the three Northeastern provinces accounted for 258, of which 116 were in Liaoning province, 60 in Jilin province, and 82 in Heilongjiang Province. They also respectively ranked as the 9th, the 23rd, and the 16th best universities in China. In terms of academic professionals, in Liaoning province, with a rank of the 8th most in China, there are 9,048 teachers with a senior professional title. For the other two provinces those indicators are: 6,352 teachers with a senior professional title in Jilin province, ranking 15th; and 7538 teachers with senior professional titles in Heilongjiang province, ranking 13th. Overall, no matter the number of universities or the number of qualified teachers in the Northeast, academia takes a pivotal position in the country and provides indispensable intellectual support for innovation and development in the region.

In terms of R&D investment in research institutions (see Figures 12.12–12.13), the internal expenditures of R&D funds and R&D personnel in the

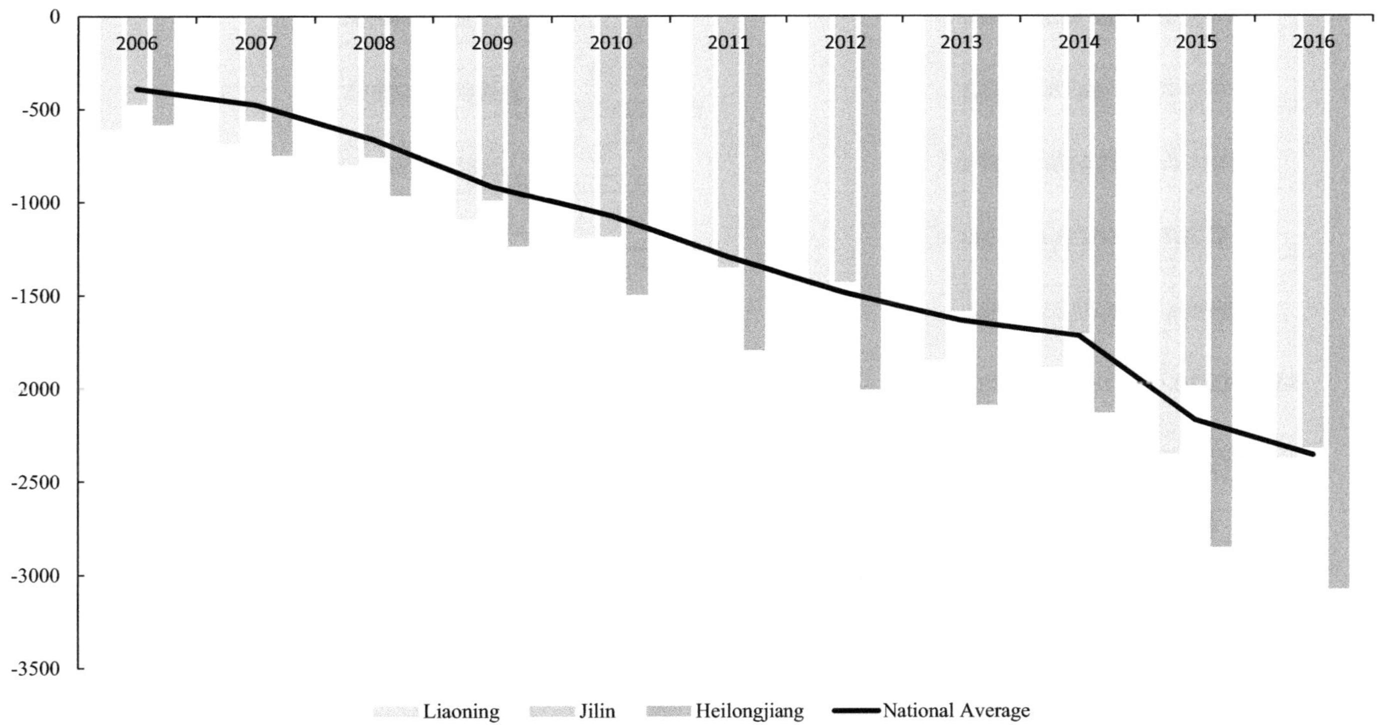

Figure 12.11 Government deficit changes in the Northeast China (hundred million Yuan) (2006–2016)

Source: China Statistical Yearbook (2007–2017)

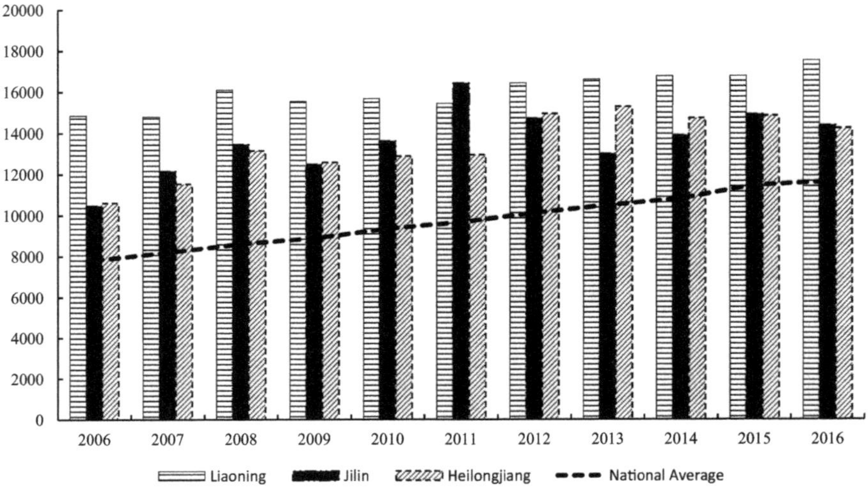

Figure 12.12 Higher research institutes of the Northeast full-time equivalent of R&D Personnel (man-year) (2006–2016)

Source: China Statistical Yearbook on Science and Technology (2007–2017)

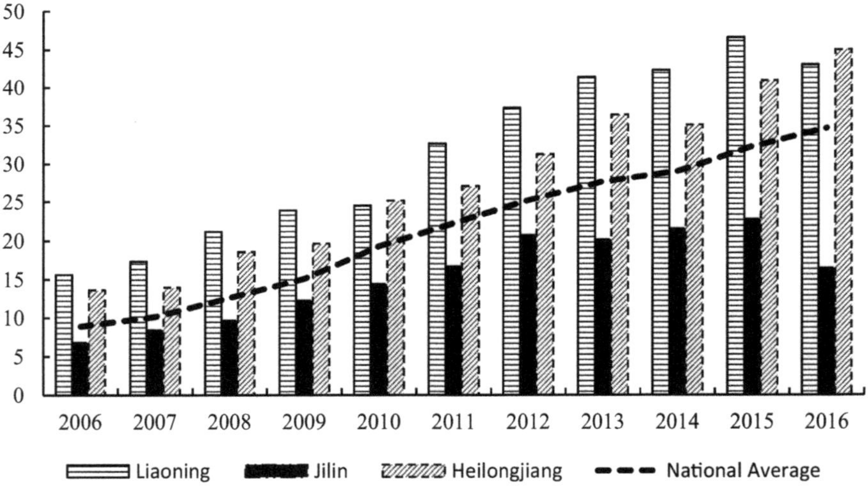

Figure 12.13 Higher research institutes of the Northeast R&D internal expenditure (hundred million Yuan) (2006–2016)

Source: China Statistical Yearbook on Science and Technology (2007–2017)

Northeast are significantly higher than the national average, and meanwhile the three provinces have shown an increasing annual investment in innovation.

In terms of innovative output (see Table 12.1), Heilongjiang province is in the leading position both in the number of patent applications and effective

Table 12.1 Patent of colleges and universities in China (2016) Unit: 10,000 pieces

Province	*Patent Applications*	*Province*	*Patent Applications*	*Province*	*Effective Patents*	*Province*	*Effective Patents*
Jiangsu	3.55	Guangxi	0.57	Beijing	3.90	Chongqing	0.53
Zhajiang	1.81	Fujian	0.57	Jiangsu	3.14	Anhui	0.48
Guangdong	1.57	Chongqing	0.51	Zhajiang	2.11	Hebei	0.35
Beijing	1.50	Jiangxi	0.50	Shanghai	2.03	**Jilin**	0.32
Hubei	1.43	Hebei	0.48	Shaanxi	1.47	Guangxi	0.31
Shaanxi	1.38	**Jilin**	0.42	Guangdong	1.14	Yunnan	0.26
Shandong	1.24	Yunnan	0.30	Hubei	1.08	Shanxi	0.26
Shanghai	1.08	Shanxi	0.19	**Heilongjiang**	1.07	Jiangxi	0.22
Anhui	1.05	Guizhou	0.18	Shandong	1.07	Gansu	0.15
Sichuan	1.00	Gansu	0.17	**Liaoning**	0.94	Guizhou	0.09
Hunan	0.95	Xinjiang	0.12	Sichuan	0.93	Inner Mongolia	0.06
Liaoning	0.80	Inner Mongolia	0.07	Hunan	0.71	Xinjiang	0.06
Henan	0.79	Hainan	0.05	Tianjin	0.70	Hainan	0.02
Heilongjiang	0.77	Ningxia	0.02	Fujian	0.57	Ningxia	0.01
Tianjin	0.60	Qinghai	0.01	Henan	0.55	Qinhai	0.01

Source: China Statistical Yearbook on Science and Technology (2017)

patents, while Liaoning province follows. Although the input level of innovation in Jilin province is above the national average, its innovation output lags 50% behind that of the whole country, which shows that the transformation of innovation achievements in Jilin province needs to be further improved.

However, universities are still the main forces of innovation in Northeast China, while enterprises are expected to be activated and become the new important innovation forces. Government participation in innovation cooperation is lower. Regardless, the Government-Industry-University cooperation has effectively reduced the uncertainty of the scientific research system (Han et al., 2018).

3 An "Iron Triangle" model

The Northeast has a relatively comprehensive industrial system and infrastructure, and abundant resources in science and education, but its innovation outcome remains relatively low. This "New Northeast Phenomenon" may be affixed with the adjective "new," but essentially it is still an old problem (Song, 2015). The reasons are mainly manifested in the following three areas: institutional mechanisms, industrial structure, and microeconomic subjects. These three featured aspects are interconnected but at the same time block each other like an "Iron Triangle" (see Figure 12.14).

History is the basis of reality. The institutional mechanism issues of the Northeast's old industrial base have a long tradition in the combination of a strong government and a weak market, and the government has played a decisive role in the allocation of market resources for a while. Neither before nor after the Reform and Opening-up policy, nor even today, has there been a fundamental change. Accordingly, the foundations of the market economy, including the price system, labor market institutions, regulation system, etc., are far behind the reform schedule.

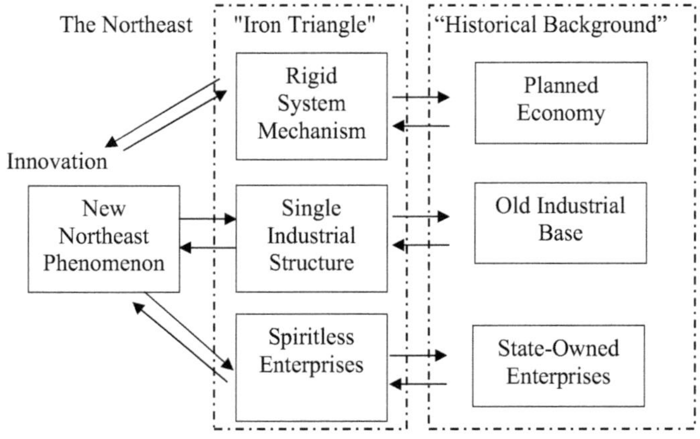

Figure 12.14 The Iron Triangle Model

Second, with the existing industrial layout and structure in the Northeast, a market economy could not be established spontaneously, although such a market economic pattern was a common strategy adopted by the socialist transition in the rest of the nation. Following the process of Reform and Opening-up, especially with the changes in mode of coordination (from plan to market), in scope (from domestic to global), and in resource allocation, the advantage of the traditional heavy industry customized by the traditional planned economy no longer exists. The new industrialization driven by the competition of the market economy calls for reforming institutional setups; however, an institutional mechanism that is favorable for the market often depends on industrial structure and adjustments. The industrial structure in Northeast China is so hegemonic that it is difficult to break the loop and complete such a transformation, which is a special feature in the Northeast compared to other regions in China (Song, 2017).

Considering the microeconomic subjects, the large SOEs have fallen habit to the traditional institutional mechanisms and the heavy industrial structure. The SOEs in Northeast China can be divided into two categories: central enterprises and local SOEs. The former has a strong degree of competitiveness, relying on its original foundation and monopoly position. In the latter, only a few enterprises have been competitive after the reform. At the beginning of the revitalization of the Northeast in 2003, the proportion of the state-owned economy in Heilongjiang province, Jilin province, and Liaoning province once reached up to between 80% and 85%. After the reform, it dropped to about 50%; however, it is still higher than the national average level. Objectively speaking, SOEs are neither instinctive inefficiencies, nor a natural shortage of innovation impulse. The key point is to have institutional mechanisms and environments that stimulate vitality and introduce competition (Song, 2017), but the SOEs in the Northeast are just trapped by the traditional institutional mechanisms and the traditional industrial structure. The question is why most SOEs fail to be innovative; we try to explain it from four aspects.

First, monopoly restrains the competition that brings about innovation. Second, these regions lack a market-driven industrial division link between enterprises. Third, these regions lack a synergistic mechanism between central enterprises that are directly operated under the control of the central government and the local economy. Finally, the division of labor in the central enterprises has not formed a spillover effect yet, and thus fails to promote the extension of the industrial value chain and the segmentation of the market, which benefits the development of the local economy. However, most small- and medium-sized enterprises, which represent the private economy in the Northeast, also failed to be innovative. The reason behind this phenomenon mainly comes from the composition of the area's industrial structure. Most of them are in the industry of resource exploration, real estate, life service, and complementary industries to the large enterprises, which all have a strong government-leading pattern. The innovation of private enterprises in such an SOE-dominated context is also trapped in traditional institutional mechanisms and industrial structure.

An iron triangle structure, supported by institutional mechanisms, industrial structure, and microeconomic subjects that curb and bind the vitality of the market, leads to the serious shortage of innovation in Northeast China. Low transformation rate is a sign of a failure to convert knowledge competitiveness into productivity. We suggest that the reasons for this low transformation rate are due to not only the inappropriate incentive mechanism of local universities and scientific research institutes, but also the shortage of demand for innovation in the local market, from which innovation originates. The Northeast fails to establish a fully competitive environment since the vitality of the market is weak. The market subjects lack a motivation and passion for being innovative; they are satisfied with the existing situation and are reluctant to take risks, so they prefer to spend money on rent seeking rather than increasing R&D investment, which reflects that they pay more attention to short-term benefits rather than long-term projects. The problems existing with the market subjects inevitably lead to a lack of demand for innovation. What's more, the poor implementation of property rights regulations; the incomplete service platforms with weak interconnections and support functions; the incompatible, incoherent, and unsystematic supporting policies; and rigid commercial culture are also crucial reasons for the shortage of demands for innovation.

From the supply perspective, the existing education paradigm in colleges and universities makes cultivating talents with a spirit for innovation difficult. First, some courses in colleges and universities are obsolete and backward, and its design system is not reasonable. Second, the knowledge obtained by the students, which mainly comes from the teachers' classroom instructions, is restricted to textbooks and concepts, and some parts of these textbooks are seriously divorced from reality. Standardized tests are based on a strict answer from a textbook, which is not conducive to the training of students' problem consciousness and critical spirit, and this is contradictory to the idea of innovation. With such an education paradigm, when graduated students are engaging in tasks, the thoughts that come to their minds first are: "the teacher told me how to do it," "what is right?," "what is wrong?," and "what is the answer from the book?" They do not start by considering a problem in practice or working creatively based on the actual needs. Therefore, in order to promote innovation, the reform of the training mode of talents in colleges and universities must be carried out. Third, each course is set up separately and has formed an isolated system of knowledge. The "Internet plus" model has made a very good counterexample of that system. It links unrelated subjects together and forms new knowledge in practice. In the course of future education reform, the situation of isolated subjects system should be broken. Otherwise, new knowledge cannot be created, and new attempts and practices cannot be explored.

4 Improving innovation ecosystem in the Northeast

The rejuvenation of the Northeast's old industrial base has entered crucial stages of consideration: how to break the shackles of obsolete institutional mechanisms, how to improve the dilemma of a single industrial structure, and how to enhance the market competitiveness of microeconomic subjects, etc. Undoubtedly, being innovative in many aspects will be an immediate solution. Innovation, especially technological innovation, has been the core driving force for economic development (Schumpeter, 1942; 1949). Yet, technical barriers inevitably arise which make "technological innovation" an exclusive product of knowledge-intensive industries.

On the issue of innovation, scholars, based on the micro subjects – e.g., enterprises – presently study the improvement of innovation capability within enterprises and the improvement of the innovation environment (Li and Yu, 2015; Jiang, 2016). However, evolution cannot be achieved in a vacuum. Enterprises are a part of the economic system and inevitably have connections with customers, suppliers, investors, governments, trade unions, and society (Moore, 1993). Lundvall's (1985) concept of the "innovation system" creates a new space to understand innovation from a more comprehensive and systematical perspective. Iansiti and Levien (2004) propose that the innovation ecosystem consists of different but related niche firms. Once one of the niches changes, the other niches will change accordingly. Adner (2006), on the other hand, treats the innovation ecosystem as a synergistic mechanism by which lead enterprises as a whole produce values. Innovation diffusion can help firms and individuals surmount technical barriers and leads technology itself to update and evolve (Rogers, 1995).

The innovation ecosystem, at the macro level, comes from the national innovation system (NIS) proposed by Chris Freeman when he studied Japan's technical and economic performance. He defines NIS as the network of institutions in the public and private sectors whose activities and interactions initiate, import, modify, and diffuse new technologies (Freeman, 1987; 1995). While Lundvall (1992) treats it as the elements and relationships which interact in the production, diffusion, and use of new knowledge, and are either located within or rooted inside the borders of a nation state. Nelson (1993) defines it as a set of institutions whose interactions determine the innovative performance of national firms. Lundvall (1992) argues that the core of an NIS is the interactive learning activities among producers and users, while OECD (1997) proposes that the NIS is to emphasize the technical cooperation and interaction between enterprises, universities, research institutes, and other relevant agencies. However, most of these NIS concepts are linear, and they fail to reflect the dynamic evolution of innovation activities. We may move forward with and apply a type of embedded, interactive, and symbiotic innovation system with the form of a four-helix structure, characterized by being dynamic and non-linear, involving the government (public institutions), enterprises (industry), universities, and users (citizens) (Carayannis and Campbell, 2009; Frenkel and Maital, 2014).

At present, the innovation cooperation network of the equipment manufacturing industry in Northeast China is in the initial stage of formation. However, the networking partners can be much closer as the current situation, and innovation spillover effect is relatively deficient, and the efficiency of the use of external resources by innovation entities is not significant (Han et al., 2018). Thus, the four-helix structure involving government, enterprises, universities, and users in Northeast China is hardly cultivated. Questions like how to improve the integration efficiency of innovative resources and how to enhance the ecological efficiency of the entire innovation system in order to achieve rapid growth require specific guidelines for cultivating an innovation ecosystem (Chesbrough et al., 2014). In addition, the implementation strategy lacks systematic design and targeted breakthrough points (Jin et al., 2016). The Northeast has a special social and economic environment which has natural resources, institutional systems, and regional culture heavily embedded in it. These factors make it so that an innovative ecosystem of developed coastal areas or other regions may not necessarily adapt to the situation in the Northeast, and needs to be redesigned for Northeast China according to their own endowments.

The establishment of an innovation ecosystem is a systematic project covering all aspects of society, economy, politics, and environment. Nevertheless, in Northeast China we must emphasize its particularity in the shackles of an iron triangle structure which is formed between the rigid system mechanisms, the single industrial structure, and spiritless microeconomic subjects. Only in this way can the rejuvenation and development of Northeast China be better targeted.

The governments in the Northeast have devoted efforts to push innovative activities forward through extensive industrial policies, even political slogans. However, such a governmental intervention pattern is not sustainable and is misleading. The process of innovation is complex, in which innovation capacity is not spontaneously formed; it needs to be cultivated gradually. We may consider the cultivation of innovation as a dynamic evolutionary process of an innovative ecosystem. In this process, each innovation subject ("government-enterprise-university-citizen") exchanges its material, energy, and information with others (Li and Yu, 2015), and it is because of this exchange that innovation has the characteristics of openness, symbiosis, competition, and dynamism.

Innovation needs people, that is to say, human capital. Everyone needs to favor innovation, but not everyone would be an innovating entrepreneur. Innovating entrepreneurs are scarce resources; they need aptitude, ability, and opportunity for innovating (Song, 2015). Second, innovation also requires the active participation of the government, enterprises, and scientific research institutes (Carayannis and Campbell, 2009). The subjects of innovation are not only the individual entrepreneurs but also the government and scientific research institutes. Especially in the era of the planned economy, the government's contributions were heavily weighted since they were the main force of national scientific and technological innovation. Third, at any time, scientific research institutes are the best incubators for invention and creation, and its R&D strength directly determines the success of national major technological breakthroughs. The Northeast has a certain comparative advantage in the cultivation of the subjects of innovation; meanwhile, there are also many practical barriers to innovation. On the one hand, there are abundant resources for science and education in the Northeast. The innovation ability of Northeast colleges and universities is strong, and the numbers of patent applications and effective patents are in the leading positions of the whole country. On the other hand, governmental financial support in the Northeast is weak, the proportion of government expenditure on science and technology is low, the institutional mechanisms of local SOEs are rigid, and the innovation input and output are insufficient. Moreover, the private economy has a strong attachment to large SOEs, so their competitive consciousness and motivation for innovation are constrained by the monopoly status of SOEs. Based on these reasons, the key point to the cultivation of innovation subjects in Northeast China, including governments, enterprises, universities, and users, is to establish a coordination mechanism among them. This means to combine the innovation output of colleges and universities with the needs of the market enterprises and the public, and meanwhile the government will play the coordinating and supervising role to maintain market operation.

The cultivation of the innovation environment is complicated. Innovation needs a suitable environment and necessary conditions supporting those entrepreneurs who are willing to take risks and are capable of innovation (West and Wood, 2008). These kinds of environments and conditions should not only include a perfect market economy infrastructure, but also an adapted innovative and entrepreneurial culture. The Northeast has a relatively comprehensive industrial system, a suitable base for socialized mass production, an established transportation infrastructure and a relatively perfect public infrastructure; all of these strengths provide a natural fertile soil for the cultivation of the environment for innovation. However, the problems of institutional mechanisms of the Northeast's old industrial base have a long history and are connected to many other institutional obstacles. The combination of a strong government and a weak market means the government played a decisive role in the regulation of market resources for a long time, and it is challenging to break this habit. Neither before nor after the Reform and Opening-up policy, nor even today, has there been a fundamental change. The market system, the price system and the socialized division of labor system have not yet been formed. The drawbacks of these institutional mechanisms also lay obstacles to the creation of a desirable environment for innovation. Current national urbanization efforts may provide an opportunity for Northeast China to break the rigid institutional mechanisms, to rebuild a new microeconomic subject and to upgrade the traditional industrial system. In the process of new town construction, the government can set up a pilot to cultivate the hardware and software environment for innovation, which promotes the realization of an effective innovative ecosystem.

The ecosystem of innovation is a process of continuous evolution which changes according to the external environment, thus it puts forward higher requirements for innovation system design and services (Mercan and Goktas, 2011). With a favorable innovation ecosystem, each innovative entrepreneur and service provider plays their respective roles in the chain of labor division and forms a symbiotic relationship. Furthermore, the government must play a critical role in the creation and evolution of an innovation ecosystem; it should be the designer and maintainer of the system; and there should be an incentivized and compatible system designed which aims at supporting innovation. Policies issued should be practical in order to make innovation subjects know how to progress on each step of execution. What's more, the policies also should be continuously optimized in accordance with the condition of change; to be more specific, the policies should be turned to the corresponding service platforms and concrete measures that are more guidable should be utilized.

5 Conclusion

Northeast China has a special social and economic environment; there is not only the lock-in effect of resources and institutional mechanisms but also the lock-in effect of regional culture. These reasons determine that schemes which could be suitable for the developed coastal areas cannot be suitable for Northeast China. It is necessary to understand the general regularity of innovation and the way to achieve it under specific conditions. In conclusion, in order to study the transformation from factor-driven to innovation-driven, we need to start from the research of regularity by studying, the internal mechanisms of transformation, the pattern and path of transformation and the process and specific stages of transformation. Such as, how does one judge the stage of change in endogenous driving forces of economic growth, what kind of policies are designed, what conditions are created at different stages to promote these changes, and so on.

In August 2014, the state promulgated the *State Council's opinion on recent major policies initiatives to support the revitalization of the Northeast* and put forward 35 policies and measures regarding 11 aspects. Measures included carrying out reform pilots for private economic development, innovating supporting models and relevant policies, strengthening a batch of private enterprise groups, encouraging private enterprises to establish a modern enterprise system and exploring effective ways of accelerating the development of the private economy in the old industrial base. At the micro level, reforms in SOEs happen through vigorously promoting the capitalization and securitization of state-owned assets and gradually allowing employees of mixed ownership in the Northeast. The central enterprises also can play a significant role via cooperating with local SOEs and even private firms. Local governments should devote more passion into establishing industrial parks and investment projects under the market regulations, for instance, the pilot projects of cooperative innovation reform of the university-industry-market relationship may accelerate the transformation and popularization of technical achievements. In particular, in order to lead the transformation and upgrading of the manufacturing industry, a number of major innovation and demonstration projects related to the advantages and potentials of the Northeast would lead to the upgrade of manufacturing capacity in a faster way. For instance, with the technical equipment industry, major strategic products with independent intellectual property rights and strong market competitive advantages around the industrial chain may have more chance to utilize the industrial knowledge and facilities in the Northeast. Industrial policies perspective is another cornerstone. The central government can allow the Northeast to establish regional innovation policies, for example, setting up a National Independent Innovation Demonstration (NIID) Zone in the Northeast and implementing the existing pilot policies of in other NIID Zones, which promotes the enterprises to take technological innovation as the internal demand and stimulating their innovation vitality. Finally, measures also include strengthening the construction of basic conditions for innovation, building a number of research and development platforms, such as national engineering technology research centers and key laboratories, selecting a batch of innovative leading enterprises, and cultivating and introducing a number of innovative talents and teams. Obviously, the policies and measures mentioned here start from invigorating the market, promoting the development of the private economy, deepening the reform of SOEs, and establishing NIID Zones. This will undoubtedly further promote the revitalization of the Northeast's old industrial base and innovation.

In conclusion, the construction of the innovative ecosystem in the Northeast needs to break the old institutional mechanisms first. In order to cultivate an innovation ecological environment, which is conducive to innovation, efforts should be made in areas that are service oriented, such as deepening the transformation of the governmental function, in order to properly handle the relationship between the government and the market. In addition, it is also important to cultivate vigorous innovation subjects. Market competition is the exact source of innovation power, microeconomic subjects need to actively participate in the market competition and further stimulate their consciousness of innovation by strengthening the awareness of competition. Finally, adjusting the single industrial structure, vigorously developing new industries and gradually replacing the traditional resource-based industries are also a crucial strategy to establish an innovative ecosystem.

References

Adner, R. (2006) "Match Your Innovation Strategy to Your Innovation Ecosystem." *Harvard Business Review* 84(4): 98–107.

Berger, Suzanne (2013) *Making in America*, Cambridge, MA: The MIT Press.

Carayannis, Elias G. and David F. J. Campbell (2009) "'Mode 3' and 'Quadruple Helix': Toward a 21st Century Fractal Innovation Ecosystem." *International Journal Technology Management* 46(3–4): 201–234.

Chen, Chunming and Xinhua Liu (2017) "Innovative Development of Manufacturing Industry in Northeast China under the Background of Supply-side Structural Reform." *Social Science Front* 12: 256–260 (in Chinese).

Chesbrough, H., Sohyeong Kim and A. Agogino (2014) "Building an Open Innovation Ecosystem." *California Management Review* 56(4): 144–171.

Fransman, Martin (2018) *Innovation Ecosystems: Increasing Competitiveness*, Cambridge, UK: Cambridge University Press.

Freeman, C. (1987) *Technology Policy and Economic Performance: Lessons from Japan*, London: Printer.

Freeman, C. (1995) "The National System of Innovation in Historical Perspective." *Cambridge Journal of Economics* (19): 5–24.

Frenkel, Amnon and Shlomo Maital (2014) *Mapping National Innovation Ecosystems: Foundations for Policy Consensus*, Cheltenham, UK: Edward Elgar.

Han, Zenglin, Yingying Yuan and Fei Peng (2018) "Research on the Co-Innovation Network of Government-Industry-University of the Equipment Manufacturing Industry in Northeast China." *Economic Geography* 38(1): 103–111 (in Chinese).

Iansiti, M. and R. Levien (2004) "Strategy as Ecology." *Harvard Business Review* 82(3): 68–81.

Jiang, Xuanyu (2016) "Government Decentralization and State-owned Enterprise Innovation – Based on the Pyramid Structure of Local State-owned Enterprises." *Management World* 9: 120–135 (in Chinese).

Jin, Fengjun, Jiaoe Wang, Yu Yang, Li Ma and Yuanjing Qi (2016) "The Paths and Solutions of Innovation Development in Northeast China." *Scientia Geographica Sinica* 36(9): 1285–1292.

Li, Wengui and Minggui Yu (2015) "Ownership Structure and Enterprise Innovation of Privatized Enterprises." *Management World* 4: 112–125 (in Chinese).

Locke, Richard M. and Rachel L. Wellhausen (eds.) (2015) *Production in the Innovation Economy*, Cambridge, MA and London, UK: The MIT Press.

Lundvall, B-A. (1985) "Product Innovation and User-Producer Interaction." Industrial Development Research Series No. 31, Aalborg University Press.

Lundvall, B-A. (1992) *National System of Innovation: Towards a Theory of Innovation and Interactive Learning*, London: Printer.

Mercan, B. and D. Goktas (2011) "Components of Innovation Ecosystems: A Cross-Country Study." *International Research Journal of Finance and Economics* 76: 102–112.

Ministry of Science and Technology (MoST) (2016) *China Academy of Science and Technology Development strategy (2016–2017): The Report of China Regional Science and Technology Innovation Evaluation*, Beijing: Scientific and Technical Documentation Press.

Ministry of Science and Technology (MoST) (2017) *China Statistical Yearbook on Science and Technology*, Beijing: China Statistics Press (in Chinese).

Moore, J. F. (1993) "Predators and Prey: A New Ecology of Competition." *Harvard Business Review* 71(3): 75–86.

National Bureau of Statistics (NBS) (2017) *China Statistical Yearbook*, Beijing: China Statistics Press.

Nelson, R. (ed.) (1993) *National Innovation Systems: A Comparative Analysis*, New York and Oxford: Oxford University Press.

OECD (1997) *National Innovation Systems*, Paris: OECD Publications.

Rogers, E. (1995) *Diffusion of Innovation* (4th ed.), New York: The Free Press.

Schumpeter, J.A. (1942) *Capitalism, Socialism and Democracy*, New York, NY: Harper and Brothers.

Schumpeter, J. A. (1949) *The Theory of Economic Development: An Inquiry into Profits, Capital, Credit, Interest, and the Business Cycle*, Cambridge, MA: Harvard University Press.

Song, Donglin (2015) "Main Factors and Suggestions of Restricting Innovation and Entrepreneurship in Northeast Old Industrial Base." *Economic Review* 7: 11–13 (in Chinese).

Song, Donglin (2017) "Political Economy Reflections on the Revitalization of Old Industrial Bases in Northeast China." *Study & Exploration* 7: 118–122 (in Chinese).

Song, Zhouying, Shuyun Che and Jiaoe Wang (2016) "The Spatio-Temporal Analysis of Regional Innovation Capacity and Its Economic Contribution in Northeast China." *Scientia Geographica Sinica* 36(9): 1388–1396 (in Chinese).

Wei, Houkai (2017) "The New Dilemma of Northeastern Economy and the Strategy of Revitalizing." *Social Science Journal* 1: 26–32 (in Chinese).
West, Joel and David Wood (2008) "Creating and Evolving an Open Innovation Ecosystem: Lessons from Symbian Ltd." Working Paper, July 11. Available at SSRN: https://ssrn.com/abstract=1532926 (accessed January 10, 2019).
Yang, Wei (2016) "Boost Basic Research in China." *Nature* 534: 467–469.
Zeng, Guoping, Youzhao Gou and Lei Liu (2013) "From Innovation System to Innovation Ecosystem." *Studies in Science of Science* 31(1): 4–12 (in Chinese).
Zhang, Pingyu (2008) "Revitalizing Old Industrial Base of Northeast China: Process, Policy and Challenge." *Chinese Geographical Science* 18(2): 109–118.
Zhao, Cangwen (2015) "A Study of the Northeast Phenomenon and the Cultivation of New Growth Engine in Northeast China." *Economic Review* 7: 7–10 (in Chinese).

Index

absorptive capacity 178
Acs, Z. J. 152, 158
Adner, R. 277
advantage of backwardness theory 196–197
adverse self-organization mechanisms 22; behavior-related 29–30; technology-related 28–29
Agarwal, R. N. 77
Ahlstrom, D. 151, 153
Anderson, Philip 129
Antonelli, C. 28
architectural innovation: concept of 129–132; defining 129–135; introduction to 126–129; patterns of, in China's passenger vehicle sector 135–142; strategies of 132–135
architectural innovation in China's passenger vehicle sector 135–142; development and change in 138–142; main trajectory of 135–137
Arrow, K. J. 15
Athey, S. 173
Atuahene-Gima, K. 154
Axelrod, R. 34, 35

Bai, C. E. 154
Beenen, G. 219
behavioral innovation 32–33; futurity and 33–34
behavioral institutionalization 32
Benner, M. 51
black-swan phenomena 19
Boeing, P. 51
Bowles, S. 199
break out, self-organization mechanisms and 29
bricolage *see* exploratory bricolage
Bruton, G. 151, 153
business sector R&D role 76–77
business strategies, technological/economic development in China and 113–119

CAS *see* complex adaptive economic system (economic CAS)
Casper, Steven 131
catching-up economy; *see also* technological catch-up: history of 200–201; policy implications for 201–202; theoretical framework of 196–202; trajectory switches and 196–199
Chen, C. 115, 117
Chen, Y. 154
Chen, Z. 154
Chesbrough, H. 63
China's NIS innovation policy 59–62
China's passenger vehicle sector, architectural innovation in 135–142
"Chinese Citizens' Scientific Competence Action Plan" 59
Christensen, C. 27
Clark, J. 199
Clark, Kim B. 127, 130
Cohen, W. 178
Collaborative Innovation Center 63
Community Innovation Surveys (CIS) 175
competition 27
complex adaptive economic system (economic CAS) 10; self-organization mechanisms in 19, 22; socio-economic 23; theorizing 21–23
Complexity (journal) 28
complexity economics (CE) 12; *see also* economic complexity; innovation as field of 26–28
complexity-innovation literature: examples from 27; quotes from 27–28

complexity policy 35
composition-based view (CBV) 222–223
comprehensive competitive advantage: comprehensive industrial system in China and 210; digital industry market size in China and 208–209; international competitiveness and cultivation mechanism 210–211; mission-oriented governance and 209–210; national innovation system and 211–212; overview of 208; technological catch-up and 208–212
comprehensive industrial system, technological catch-up and 210
comprehensive innovation in China 37–40, 210
concealment, legitimacy building and 150
Cooke, Philip Nicholas 238
Coombs, J. E. 153
co-option, legitimacy building and 150
creative destruction 27
creator 13
Crowther, A. K. 63
Cusumano, M. A. 239

Dahlman, C. J. 238
Dai, S. 51
Dark Matter Particle Explorer (DAMPE) 259
Debreu, G. 15
"Decision on Implementing the Outline of the Scientific and Technological Plan and Enhancing Independent Innovation Capacity" (State Council) 2, 50
Deng Xiaoping 1
deregulation 38–39
design and manufacturing tasks, dimensions of 132–133
digital age innovation: comprehensive competitive advantage in China for 208–212; drivers of 195; introduction to 195–196; opportunity windows for China in 202–208; theoretical framework for developing countries 196–202 (*see also* technological catch-up); whole-industry-chain and 195
digitalization era, opportunity windows for China in 202–208; overview of 202–203; platform *vs.* company organization method and 204–206; production resource assets and 203–204; short cycle *vs.* long cycle product operation and 206; wave curve *vs.* smile curve industrial layout and 207–208
Doloreux, David 238
Dominguez Lacasa, I. 92, 98
Dopfer, K. 111
Dosi, G. 109
dotcom crisis 24
double-interactive policy 35
dynamic specialization 100, 101

economic complexity 17–26; CAS, theorizing 21–23; innovation and 25–26; policy implications 24–25; real-world economic systems 17–21; self-organization mechanisms and 28–31; structural stability and 23–24
economic development: business strategies and industry shifts 113–119; evolutionary theory of 107–112; future research topics for 120–122; introduction to 106–107; R&D expenditure and 119–120; reform policies review 112–113; technological and, in China 112–120
economic environment, technological/economic development in China and 113–119
economic reforms, technological/economic development in China and 112–113
Edquist, C. 238
Eisenhardt, E. 223"Endogenous Growth Theory" (Romer) 17
endogenous industrial clusters (EnICs) 235–236
entrepreneurial society 64
entrepreneurial state 38
Ernst, Dieter 131
escapism, legitimacy building and 150
European Patent Office (EPO) 91
Evolutionary Complexity of Endogenous Innovation (Antonelli) 28
evolutionary-institutional economics (OIE) 30
"Evolutionary Theory of Economic Change, An" (Nelson and Winter) 108
evolutionary theory of economic development 107–112; innovation from 110–111; overview of 107–108; routines and 109–110
"evolution-of-cooperation" approach 31–37; described 31–34; interdependence structures and 34–37
exogenous industrial clusters (ExICs) 235
exploitative bricolage 217

exploratory bricolage: composition-based view and 222–223; concept of, described 219–220; defined 217; future research for 231; Huawei case study 227–229; introduction to 216–218; research conclusions 230–231; research methodology used 223; stretch goals and 216–217, 218–219, 220–222; VRIN resources and 219–220; Yuanjia Village case study 224–225, 228–229; ZBOM Cabinets Co. case study 225–227, 228–229

Fan, S. 120
finance as obstacle blocking innovation 195
financial crisis, 2008 24
financialization 27
first-mover advantages 29
Five-hundred-meter Aperture Spherical radio Telescope (FAST) 259
Fontana, M. 28
Ford, Henry 135, 136
foreign direct investment (FDI) 109, 112, 115–116, 117–118
framework policy approach 35
Freeman, C. 60–61, 277
Frischtak, C. R. 238
Fu, Dahai 80–81
Fujimoto, Takahiro 127, 132, 137
futurity 33–34

Galia, F. 171
Gaogou cluster case study 242–251; critical messages from 248–251; human capital training, cooperative relationships for 247–248; innovation network structure in 242–244; new product development, cooperative relationships for 246–247; new product development, market information for 244–246; overview of 242
Gard, L. 158
Gary, S. 218
Gawer, A. 239
general equilibrium research, exhaustion of 14–15
general equilibrium theory (GET) 13–14
general-trust level 39–40
genes, as routines 109
Gerchenkron, A. 196–197
Gilsing, V. 230
Godfrey, P. C. 152, 153
Go Global policy 82
government R&D support 79–81
Graebner, G. 223
Griffin, J. J. 158
Guan, J. C. 51
guanxi 117
Guanyu, Huang 150
Guideline for the National Medium-and Long-term Science and Technology Development Programs (2006–2020) 79
Guo Yulu 224
Guo Zhanwu 224

habituated behavioral institution 32
Heinrich, T. 22, 23
Hempel, J. 158
Henderson, Rebecca M. 127, 130
Herrmann-Pillath, C. 28
higher education institutions, scientific research strength of 270–274
high technology 78, 138, 154, 241
Himmelberg, C. 178
Hodgson, G. M. 108
Hong, Jin 82–83
Huang, K. 108
Huawei case study 227–229
Hussler, Caroline 239

Iansiti, M. 277
ideal market 13
incentive structures 35–36
indigenous innovation policies 53–59; Policy I 52, 54–55, 56; Policy II 52, 55, 57–58; Policy III 52–53, 58–59
individualist culture 30
industrial cluster upgrading: Gaogou cluster case study 242–251; innovation system and 237–240, 257–258; introduction to 235–237; policy implications for 253–254; research method/design used 240–242; theoretical explanation for 251–253
industry shifts, technological/economic development in China and 113–119
influence as engagement, legitimacy building and 150
information and communication technology (ICT) 202–203
information competition as obstacle blocking innovation 195
information loss *vs.* information retention 22
innovation: comprehensive, in China 37–40, 210; in digital age (*see* digital age innovation; technological catch-up);

disruptive effects and types of 129; economic complexity and 25–26; from evolutionary perspective 110–111; as exogenous and erratic 17; as field of complexity economics 26–28; as idiosyncratic 11; industrial cluster upgrading and 237–240, 257–258; institutional foundations of 1–3; lack of, in high-tech industries 263–267; neoclassical/neoliberal economic orthodoxy and 17; obstacles blocking (*see* obstacles blocking innovation); performance, measures for 175–177; Schumpeter's definition of 110; system of 110–111; technological/economic development in China and 119–120
innovation development in Northeast China 263–274; higher education institutions, scientific research strength of 270–274; lack of, for industrial enterprises 267–269; lack of, in high-tech industries 263–267; overview of 263; weak financial support, governmental debt and 269–270
innovation ecosystem; *see also* industrial cluster upgrading; Northeast China phenomenon: in Northeast China, improving 276–280
innovation motivation, lack of for industrial enterprises 267–269
innovation policies, China's post 2006 68–70; China's NIS 59–62; evolution of 59–65; framework of national system of 52–53; indigenous 53–59; innovative and entrepreneurial society concept 64–65; introduction to 50–51; open and shared concept 62–63; Policy I 52, 54–55, 56; Policy II 52, 55, 57–58; Policy III 52–53, 58–59; questions concerning 65; shared tags for 53
innovation proper: conditions of comprehensive, in China 37–40; economic complexity and 17–26; "evolution-of-cooperation" approach 31–37; future understanding/qualification of 40–41; innovation as field of complexity economics 26–28; interdependence structures and 34–37; introduction to 10–12; neoclassical/neoliberal economic orthodoxy 13–17; self-organization mechanisms 28–31
innovative and entrepreneurial society concept 64–65
Innovator's Dilemma, The (Christensen) 27
institutional lock-in 30
institutional policy 35
intellectual property rights (IPR) 51, 53, 55–59, 61, 81, 84
interdependence structures 34–37
international competitiveness and cultivation mechanism 210–211
international opening, technological/economic development in China and 112–113
International Patent Classification (IPC) system 93
Internet plus 63–64, 276
Investment Climate Survey (ICS) 175
invisible hand 13
"Iron Triangle" model 274–276; *see also* Northeast China phenomenon

Jamali, D. 153

Kaplan, S. 230
Katila, R. 219
Kauffman, S. A. 28
Ki, J.-H. 199
Kroll, H. 61

labor as obstacle blocking innovation 195
Langlois, Richard N. 133
Lee, K. 199
legitimacy building: introduction to 149–151; organizational, moral capital and 151–155, 156–157, 158; political 154–155, 157–158; research findings 158–163; research methodology used 155–158; strategic responses to build 150
Legros, D. 171
Levien, R. 277
Levinthal, D. 178
Li, H. 154
Li Keqiang 63, 64
List, Friedrich 60
Liu, F. 50
lost opportunities 100, 101
Lu, J. 163
Lundvall, B-A. 60, 187, 277
Luo, Y. 154
Lyons, Thomas P. 138

Ma, D. 153
Ma, Jack 218–219
MacDuffie, John Paul 137

"Made in China 2025" 63
Mahon, J. F. 158
Mahoney, Joseph T. 130
manufacturing innovation 127
market economy 13, 14; in China 37–38; as network 17; self-organization mechanisms in 28–31
market equilibrium, neoclassical/neoliberal economic orthodoxy and 13–14
market size, technological catch-up and 208–209
Marshall, A. 19
Marukawa, Tomoo 140, 141
"Mass Entrepreneurship and Innovation" (MEI) 64
Mastrogiorgio, M. 230
Mazzucato, M. 209
middle-income trap 1
Milgrom, P. 171
Ministry of Science and Technology (MoST) 50, 51, 79, 237, 263
Miron-Spektor, E. 219
mirroring hypothesis 130
Mirshak, R. 153
mission-oriented governance, technological catch-up and 209–210
mobility, social capital and 36
Mohnen, P. 171
monopolized firms 27
moral capital: defined 152; organizational legitimacy building and 151–155, 158
moral legitimacy 151
Mulgan, G. 28

Nahm, Jonas 131
National Bureau of Statistics (NBS) 84
"National Guidelines for the Medium-and Long-Term Plan for Science and Technology Development (2006–2020)" (State Council) 2, 50
National Independent Innovation Demonstration (NIID) Zone 281
national innovation system (NIS): definitions of 277; technological catch-up and 211–212
Naughton, Barry 131
negative complementarity 171, 172
Nelson, R. 108, 109–110, 113, 187, 277
neoclassical/neoliberal economic orthodoxy 13–17; general equilibrium research, exhaustion of 14–15; innovation and 17; market equilibrium 13–14; "T-i-n-a-There is no alternative" policy 16
network structures 37
"New Northeast Phenomenon" 260; *see also* Northeast China phenomenon
Niehm, L. S. 155
NIS innovation policy 59–62
Nobeoka, Kentaro 132
Northeast China phenomenon: governmental debt and 269–270; higher education institutions, scientific research strength of 270–274; high-tech industries, lack of innovation in 263–267; industrial enterprises, lack of innovation motivation for 267–269; innovation development 263–274; innovation ecosystem in, improving 276–280; introduction to 259–263; "Iron Triangle" model 274–276

obstacles blocking innovation: complementarity between 171–173; data/descriptive statistics of 175–181; defined 170; identification of top four 193–194; innovation output impact of 170–171; introduction to 169–170; model used for research of 171–175; nature of 170–171; patterns of 178–180; performance 173–174; policy suggestions for 187–188; research findings 181–187
OECD 53, 277
offshore investment and innovation effect, research and development 81–83
open and shared innovation system 62–63, 127
optimal forgetting 22
organizational legitimacy 149, 156–157; lack of 152–153; moral capital and 151–155
Orr, G. 117
over-and under-innovation 22

Parish, W. L. 153
patent intensity indicator 92, 96–98
patents: applications for, China 1985–2015 121; defined 91
Pavitt, K. 91
Peng, M. W. 154
Perez, C. 198
Petersen, B. 178
Piatier, A. 179
platform *vs.* company organization method 204–206
Polanyian countermotions 11
Policy I, innovation 52, 54–55, 56

Policy II, innovation 52, 55, 57–58
Policy III, innovation 52–53, 58–59
political capital 157–158
political networking 150, 153–154
political participation 150, 154–155
Porter, Michael E. 130
positive complementarity 171, 172
Potts, J. 111
preferential attachment mechanism 23
priority filings (PF) 92

Quantum Experiments at Space Scale (QUESS) 259

R&D *see* research and development (R&D)
real-world economic systems 17–21
Regional Innovation System (RIS) 238–239
relative technological specialization 93
Ren, Zhengfei 227
research and development (R&D): business sector role in 76–77; components of embodied 73–74; expenditure, in China 1996–2015 118–120; future research topics for economic development 120–122; general equilibrium research, exhaustion of 14–15; government support 79–81; higher education institutions 270–274; high technology 78, 138, 154, 241; industrial cluster upgrading 240–242; industrial subsectors, assessment of 77–79; industry shifts 113–119; intellectual property rights (IPR) 51, 53, 55–59, 61, 81, 84; intersectoral technology diffusion 74–76; legitimacy building 155–163; new product development, in Gaogou cluster case study 244–247; Northeast China phenomenon 263–274; obstacles blocking innovation 171–175, 181–187; offshore investment and innovation effect 81–83; outlook and challenges in 83–86; overview of 71; spending, by industrial sectors 77–79; spending, by ownership 76–77; strength of, in higher education institutions 270–274; technological capabilities, evolution of 91–96, 103–104; trends in, activities 71–76; university-industry collaboration 79–81
retreat sectors 100, 101
Revealed Technological Advantage Index (RTA) 93, 96; shifting sectors 98–99; specialization rates 100–101; technological sectors, dynamism of 99–100
Rifkin, J. 202
Roberts, J. 171
Röller, L.-H. 171
Romer, P. 17
Ronde, Patric 239
Roth, E. 117
routines 109–110
rule-based behavior 32

Saiia, D. H. 152
Sanchez, Ron 130
Santangelo, G. D. 107
Savignac, F. 178
scale-free network 20
Schmoch, U. 93
Schneider, F. 178
Schumpeter, J. 110, 129, 197, 199
search processes 109–110
self-organization mechanisms 12, 19, 22, 28–31; adverse behavior-related 29–30; adverse technology-related 28–29; and break out 29
Shane, S. 219
Shi, Xing 73–74, 75–76, 80–81
short cycle *vs.* long cycle product operation 206
Siddharthan, N. S. 77
Silva, S.T. 111
Sitkin, S. B. 218
small-world network structures 35, 37
Smith, Adam 14, 34, 37
social capital, mobility and 36
social legitimacy 151–152
Solow, R. M. 106
Song, Donglin 260
Soskice, David 130–131
"Special Economic Zones" (SEZ) 112
state-owned enterprises (SOEs) 150
State Steering Committee of Science and Technology (S&T) and Education 79
static specialization 100, 101
Steinfeld, Edward S. 131
Stern, S. 173
Stockdale, B. 178
strategic philanthropy, defined 152
stretch goals: defined 218; exploratory bricolage and 216–217, 220–222; late-coming firms and 218–219
structural stability 23–24
structures of initial interaction arenas 36–37
Sull, D. N. 115, 117

Sun, Y. 50
Swan, T. W. 106

tail risks 19
tax as obstacle blocking innovation 195
technological capabilities: Chinese vertical/horizontal improvements in 90–91; defined 90; development of 96–98
technological capabilities, evolution of: further research outlooks 103–104; introduction to 90–91; with relevance to developed/emerging economies 96–98; research methodology, data and indicators 91–96; specialization and dynamism indicators 98–103
technological catch-up; *see also* digital age innovation: comprehensive industrial system and 210; defined 196; history of 200–201; international competitiveness and cultivation mechanism 210–211; market size in China and 208–209; mission-oriented governance and 209–210; national innovation system and 211–212; policy implications for 201–202; theoretical framework of 196–202; trajectory switches and 196–199
technological dynamics indicator 93
technological/economic development, in China 112–120; economic environment, business strategies, and industry shifts 113–119; economic reforms and 112–113; innovation and 119–120; international opening and 112–113
technological inventive activities 93
technological specialization *vs.* other emerging economies 98–103
Technosphere Science 28
Teixeira, A. A. C. 111
Tencent (company) 216–217
Ten Thousand Talents Program 210–211
"Theory of Economic Development" (Schumpeter) 110
Theory of Moral Sentiments (Smith) 14
theory of the second-best (Lipsey and Lancaster) 16
Thousand Talents Program 211
"T-i-n-a- There is no alternative" policy 16
"too-big-to-fails" 19
top-down politics 2
Touve, D. 154
trajectory switches, technological catch-up and 196–199
transnational patent applications (TN) 91–92
Tsang, E. W. K. 150, 151
Tushman, Michael L. 129

uniformism 13–14
university-industry research and development collaboration 79–81

Vakili, K. 230
valuable, rare, inimitable, and non-substitutable (VRIN) resources 216, 219–220
Veblen, Thorstein 30
Vietor, R. H. K. 113
Viotti, E. B. 200, 239
VRIN *see* valuable, rare, inimitable, and non-substitutable (VRIN) resources

Wang, Hua 140
Wang, K. 157
Wang, Y. 115, 117
wave curve *vs.* smile curve industrial layout 207–208
Wealth of Nations (Smith) 14
whole-industry-chain (WIC) 195
Wilson, D. S. 24
Winter, S. G. 108, 109–110, 113
Winter, Sidney 108
World Trade Organization (WTO) 50, 113, 156
Worldwide Patent Statistical Database (PATSTAT) 91
Wu, J. 120
Wu, Yanrui 73–74, 75–76, 77, 78, 80–81
Wu concept 231

Yam, R. C. M. 51
Ye, K. 155
Yu, X. 200
Yuanjia Village case study 224–225, 228–229

ZBOM Cabinets Co. case study 225–227, 228–229
Zeitz, G. J. 151
Zhang, R. 155
Zhao, Cangwen 260, 262
Zhao, H. 163
Zhengfei, Ren 216
Zhou, Chongyang 82
Zimmerman, M. A. 151

For Product Safety Concerns and Information please contact our EU
representative GPSR@taylorandfrancis.com
Taylor & Francis Verlag GmbH, Kaufingerstraße 24, 80331 München, Germany

www.ingramcontent.com/pod-product-compliance
Ingram Content Group UK Ltd.
Pitfield, Milton Keynes, MK11 3LW, UK
UKHW022013180926
475701UK00003B/340
* 9 7 8 1 0 3 2 0 8 6 1 9 4 *